Uniform Building Code Compliance Manual

Uniform Building Code Compliance Manual

1997 Uniform Building Code™

Scott Parish

McGraw-Hill

New York   San Francisco   Washington, D.C.   Auckland   Bogotá
Caracas   Lisbon   London   Madrid   Mexico City   Milan
Montreal   New Delhi   San Juan   Singapore
Sydney   Tokyo   Toronto

Library of Congress Cataloging-in-Publication Data

Parish, Scott.
   Uniform building code compliance manual : 1997 uniform building
code / Scott Parish.
    p. cm.
   ISBN 0-07-048611-5
   1. Building laws—United States. I. Title.
  KF5701.P373   1998
  343.73'07869—dc21   98-20269
                                      CIP

McGraw-Hill

A Division of The McGraw-Hill Companies

   3 4 5 6 7 8 9 0 DOC/DOC   0 3 2 1 0

P/N 048629-8
Part of
ISBN 0-07-048611-5

*The sponsoring editor for this book was Wendy Lochner, the editing supervisor was Paul R. Sobel,
and the production supervisor was Modestine Cameron.*

Printed and bound by R. R. Donnelley & Sons Company.

This book is printed on recycled, acid-free paper containing a minimum of 50%
recycled, de-inked fiber.

Table of Contents

Part 1 CODE INFORMATION

Part 2 DESIGN REQUIREMENTS

Part 3   *DETAILED CONSTRUCTION REQUIREMENTS*

Part 4 STRUCTURAL DOCUMENTATION REQUIREMENTS

Part 5 SPECIFICATION REQUIREMENTS

Acknowledgments

It is only proper to acknowledge those who have contributed to this book either directly through their review and input, or indirectly through their encouragement and efforts in training and mentoring me over the years. My thanks to Norm Pfaff, Rick Mangini, George Blecha, Ron Thurber, Michael Tellian, Dennis Hutsell, and Rohn Price.

It is also necessary to thank family and friends who have supported and encouraged this endeavor, especially my wife Sandy and our four children.

Introduction

Purpose

Achieving compliance with the laws, regulations, and codes affecting a project will always be a monumental task for design professionals. Not only do these requirements change periodically, but over the years they have expanded in size, ballooning to gigantic proportions. These requirements are just one aspect of the many that the design professional must take into account in bringing a project to a successful completion.

The building design profession is recognizing that successful projects are the result of purposeful methods of developing projects from beginning to end; a recognition that quality service, quality design methods, and quality construction documents translate into profitability and continuing viability for the firm.

Quality assurance is a popular theme today, encompassing the entire operations and activities of the design firm. Quality assurance programs, whether formal or informal, include methods of quality control, such as checklists for reviews of work in progress and completed work. These checklists and reviews recognize the huge task of making all the right decisions and documenting those decisions consistently. They follow behind the design team to assure quality in the end product: the drawings and specifications.

The Uniform Building Code is a sizable publication, governing everything from building size to nail size. The sheer volume of information presented requires careful study and review to understand how the requirements of the Code

apply to the project. *The Uniform Building Code Compliance Manual* was conceived as a tool to assist in the assurance of one very important aspect of quality building design, building code compliance.

Special Features

Building codes define the minimum standard of quality necessary to protect persons and property. Design professionals are required to design buildings and structures to the minimum standards set by local or state building codes. In fact, it is the very least they must do. Failure to design to the requirements of the Code often means expensive change orders during construction and delays. More serious consequences include the loss of a client's trust, future business, time-consuming claims, and sometimes full-blown litigation.

The use of quality assurance checklists to reduce the occurrence of such errors and omissions in construction documents is nothing new, but a checklist based on the building code is a new concept. Using the 1997 Uniform Building Code as its basis, *The Uniform Building Code Compliance Manual* provides the following unique features:

- It places the condensed code requirements into a checklist format, allowing easy scanning for code review and document checking.
- It reformats the code requirements to align with the normal progression of professional services and allows the design professional to focus on those requirements that apply to the project at

the particular time of the review.

- It provides the checklists in electronic format allowing viewing of the lists on a PC and reproduction of selected files for use in code compliance reviews.
- As part of the project file, it provides tangible evidence that a code compliance review was performed.

Limitations

The design professional is encouraged to view building code requirements as the minimum standard of care required for the design of any construction project. Local practice and conditions, owner requirements, and project specific requirements may be more stringent than the requirements of the building code. The governing code jurisdiction should be consulted to verify amendments adopted by local and state code jurisdictions.

Code compliance is also subject to the varying interpretations of design professionals and building officials. Due to this fact, this book cannot claim to provide a warranty of complete code compliance. It is intended to organize the review process, reduce errors and omissions related to code compliance, and assist in identifying problem areas that can be resolved with the governing code officials.

Use of the Uniform Building Code

A copy of the Uniform Building Code is required to use this book. This book is not intended to provide legal wording for code interpretations. Referring to the Uniform Building Code itself will be necessary for word definitions, tables and figures, and detailed descriptions of construction assemblies and building systems.

Quality Construction Documents

Construction Documents

Construction documents are a vital ingredient of today's construction process. Modern construction documents, consisting of drawings and project manual, communicate building design and construction requirements to many entities and individuals. These include the building owner, the code official, regulatory agencies, the general contractor, subcontractors, material suppliers, manufacturers and fabricators, and construction workers. The quality and accuracy of the documents have a direct effect on the success of the project, both in tangible and intangible terms.

The building code defines the minimum standard of construction necessary to protect persons and property. The design professional's task is to identify the code requirements that apply to the project, incorporate them into the design in a manner acceptable to the governing code jurisdiction, and document those requirements in written and graphic form in the construction documents to communicate them to the building contractor.

The contractor relies on this communication to construct a code-complying building for the owner. The accuracy and completeness of this communication plays an important part in the success or failure of the project.

Construction documents are legal documents, forming the contract between the owner and the contractor. The contractor is bound to provide the construction described by the construction documents. When the documents fail to describe code-complying construction, modifications must be made to change the contract to include the necessary corrections.

Document Organization

Construction documents can be broken down into two main components: *the drawings* and *the project manual.*

The drawings consist of plans, elevations, sections, details, and schedules to describe the location, size, quantity, and configuration of the construction, graphically describing how the materials and equipment are assembled to provide a completed building.

The project manual commonly consists of several components: the bidding requirements, the contract and conditions of the contract, the general requirements, and the technical specifications. The bidding requirements are often not legally considered contract documents but are necessary to provide guidance to bidders in presenting a bid proposal to the building owner.

The project manual is normally organized using the CSI 16-Division format, which provides a consistent location for information within the project manual and internally organizes the way information is presented.

The basis for code compliance is laid from the very beginning as building size and configuration are developed and solidified, being dictated by the area and height limitations of the code. Fire-rated separations and egress provisions further define the shape and configuration of the project. As the project design moves toward completion, drawings are developed to document detailed construction, weathertightness, fasteners, fire-rated assemblies, and building system requirements. Specifications are developed to describe quality and execution, testing, and administrative requirements. Therefore, the construction documents are the vehicles of communicating the requirements of the code and provide part of the legal basis for code enforcement.

Design Services

Design services are normally broken down into several distinct phases. Smaller projects combine phases and may not provide distinct milestones at the end of each phase, but successful projects of any size follow a similar organized methodology. This methodology begins as a broad brush approach, goes on to develop major components and systems, and finishes with the details. The basic phases of design services can be described as follows:

The Schematic Design Phase develops the general scope, scale, and relationship of the project components.

The Design Development Phase fixes and further expands the schematic design to establish the final scope, relationships, forms, size, and appearance.

The Construction Documents Phase builds upon previous phases to set forth in detail the requirements for construction of the project.

Different requirements of the code apply to each phase. One unique aspect of this book is that it provides a review tool focused on the requirements relating to the different phases.

The Need for Review

Most projects fall somewhere between success and failure. The reasons for this can usually be traced back to acts, errors, or omissions on the part of the owner, the building contractor, or the design professional. The results of these acts or failure to act are delays, extra costs, claims and counter-claims, and sometimes full-blown litigation. The direct result is monetary loss on the part of one or more of the parties. Other negative results are the loss of trust and respect that can mean the loss of valuable business relationships.

The construction documents prepared by the design professional are a major source of conflicts. While it is acknowledged that perfection is impossible, a good set of documents forms a good foundation for the success of the building construction.

Many factors contribute to errors and omissions in construction documents. Each project is unique, a one-time invention. The design professional has no opportunity to test the construction, to try the fit. Thousands of pieces must fit together, allowing for construction tolerances and working space. Electrical conduits, air ducts, fire sprinkler lines, plumbing pipes, and structural members often clog hidden spaces, forcing changes and compromises as the building is constructed. In reality, the design process continues through the construction process.

The design process is a continuous investigation of solutions. Adjustments are made as the process develops toward greater detail to accommodate the realities of materials and construction methods. This often means going back to change previous work. Last minute changes to the documents are difficult to coordinate fully and often contribute to errors. The sheer number of decisions to make and coordinate among the various disciplines is staggering.

Design teams are made up of human individuals. Each brings a different level of experience and expertise. Each is subject to the emotions of the working day. Continuity is often broken as management responds to changing priorities and the local economy. Individuals change jobs.

All this means that errors and omissions occur regularly in construction documents. Unless a conscious effort is made to identify and correct them, they remain hidden in the documents until the contractor finds them and begins the change order process.

Reviews Make a Difference

A good set of documents is no accident. It is the result of a purposeful effort by the design professional, combining experience, methodology, attention to detail, and good management. A quality control review, following up this effort, is a vital part of tying up the loose ends, coordinating the different disciplines, and identifying potential problems.

Pressure is being exerted on design professionals, primarily from the public sector, to perform formal quality control reviews; sometimes it is made a provision of the design agreement. Professional liability insurers are promoting quality control reviews as a loss prevention tool and offer premium discounts for their clients who make them a part of their design process.

Many design firms are recognizing that time spent in identifying and correcting errors and omissions prior to construction is less expensive than dealing with them during construction. A review at the end of each design phase is necessary to keep the project on track and reduce time and profit-consuming changes in the documents as the project develops.

A review at the end of the schematic design phase focuses on meeting the owner's program and basic code requirements which limit area, height, and construction.

A review at the end of the design development phase revisits basic code requirements to make sure design changes have not invalidated previous code decisions. It also focuses heavily on fire-resistive construction and related separations.

A review at the end of the construction documents phase focuses on the details of fire-resistive assemblies, weathertightness, life-safety systems, and construction details.

The Importance of Review Tools

Experience is the primary tool necessary to produce quality construction documents. Experience is also a key factor in reviewing drawings to identify errors and omissions because experience knows where to look. However, the sheer volume of code requirements and the change of the codes over time makes relying on memory a dangerous practice. Most design professionals refer to the code often to make sure their understanding of the requirements is correct, or to refresh their memory.

The Uniform Building Code Compliance Manual's checklists bring organization to the review process and form a vital part of a thorough and complete review.

Instructions

Book Overview

Reviewing drawings for code compliance is no easy task, and many firms have developed checklists of some type to facilitate the job. This book provides a comprehensive checklist for code compliance, broken down according to the phases of a design professional's services. This groups information into categories that begin with general broad brush requirements dictating overall area and height, and progresses into more detailed requirements needed later in the project development.

This book provides a means of documenting preliminary code information and design decisions, of facilitating a review of preliminary and final design and construction documents and specifications, and provides a means of documenting compliance or noncompliance identified by the review.

Documentation of design decisions, whether related to the building code or not, is important to provide a record of the project. This not only helps the project team develop a "project memory" to refer to; it also is useful when explaining why certain decisions were made to owners, code officials, contractors, and attorneys. The project record is often vital in defending against claims of negligence and provides the basis for establishing that the standard of care was met.

Summary of Contents

This book provides checklists of code requirements aimed at five different aspects of the design professional's services, as follows:

Code Information Form: The Schematic Design Phase develops the general scope, scale, and relationship of the project components. Early in this phase, as the building's basic size, shape, and location on the property are being determined, the code parameters affecting the basic design need to be reviewed and documented for future reference. The Code Information Form facilitates review and documentation of occupancy classification, type of construction, location on property, allowable floor area, height and number of stories, egress, and construction requirements, all of which are basic to the project design.

Design Requirements: The Design Development Phase fixes and further expands the schematic design to establish the final scope, relationships, forms, size, and appearance. Code requirements related to this phase set the building configuration, layout, fire-resistive properties, and systems (smoke, fire alarm, stair pressurization). The Design Requirements checklists are used to determine if the requirements of the code have been met in terms of area, shape, height, fire-resistive construction, structural systems, and critical dimensional clearances.

Detailed Construction Requirements: The Construction Documents Phase builds upon previous phases to set forth in detail the requirements for construction of the project. The Detailed Construction Requirements checklists are used to determine if the requirements of the code have been met in terms of detailed architectural construction, finishes, attachments, materials and thicknesses, assemblies, weathertightness, and life safety systems.

Structural Requirements: The Structural Requirements checklists are used to determine if the requirements of the code have been met in terms of detailed structural construction and supports, attachments, materials and thicknesses.

Specifications Requirements: The Specifications Requirements checklists are used in the preparation of the specifications and to determine if the requirements of the code have been met in terms of the quality of materials, systems and equipment, standards of workmanship, submittals, performance criteria, and testing requirements.

These five groupings of information allow the reviewer to concentrate on the specific needs of the review process and on the information needed at that particular point in the phase of the design services that the review occurs.

Correlation with the Uniform Building Code

This book is design to be used in conjunction with the 1997 edition of the Uniform Building Code. The user will need to refer to the NBC for information found in tables and figures, for word definitions, for detailed descriptions of equipment functions and construction assemblies, and for actual code wording for legal purposes. These checklists will not include code requirements describing or regulating engineering calculations and structural design, or code administrative requirements. The focus of the checklists will be on general building planning and on information that will appear on construction contract documents.

Code Information Form Format

The Code Information Form format is different from the remainder of the book. Because it is used to facilitate and document the preliminary code investigation, it provides space to insert statistical information and provides boxes to check for each particular code requirement that applies to the project. Specific instructions for the use of the Code Information Form are provided in the body of the form.

Checklist Format

The format of Parts 2, 3, 4, and 5 is designed to document compliance or noncompliance by checking the appropriate box.

Each checklist provides the code section number and code requirement text.

Columns are provided after the text to document the compliance status of each item. If compliance is satisfactory, check or fill in the "OK" column. If the item is not applicable to the project, check or fill in the "NA" column. If compliance has not been achieved, the "ID" column provides space to begin numbering the noncomplying items or the box can simply be checked.

Numbered noncomplying items can be documented in the Deficiency Worksheet. Suggested corrective measures can be written for the use of those making changes in the documents. A "checkoff" column is provided in the worksheet for use in following up deficient items.

Text Format

The text used in the checklists is intended to provide a "process-based" list that tells the user what to do as opposed to a "memory-jogger" list that presents a list of items to be considered but does not tell the user what to look for or what to do when the item is found.

For the most part, the text is not a direct quotation of the code language. Each requirement is condensed as much as possible, using the imperative mood. This places the verb that defines the action required as the first word of the sentence.

The streamlined format normally found in specifications is also used to reduce verbiage and yet retain the meaning. This technique places the subject as a heading, separated from the rest of the sentence by a colon, and therefore provides key words for quick reference.

Bold Titles

Bold titles are used for each major compliance item to enable the user to quickly scan the text for applicable requirements.

Indentation and Text Grouping

Related requirements are grouped by the code section number reference column. This column spans the entire length of the requirements falling under that section. Major subjects within each section are denoted by bold titles. Indented text denotes subordination to the text above.

Measurement Abbreviations

The Uniform Building Code uses both English units and metric units. Metric measurement abbreviations are the same as listed in the code. English units have been abbreviated using obvious abbreviations, as follows:

cf	cubic foot (feet)
cfm	cubic feet per minute
fc	footcandles
ft	feet
fps	feet per second
gal	gallon(s)
gpm	gallons per minute
in	inch, inches
lbs	pounds
lf	linear foot (feet)
oz/sf	ounces per square foot
oz/si	ounces per square inch
pcf	pound(s) per cubic foot (feet)
ppm	parts per million
psy	pounds per square yard
sf	square foot (feet)
si	square inch(es)
sy	square yard(s)

Wording

To reduce volume and redundant wording, some words have been purposely omitted. For example, the words, "floor area" or "wall area" have been omitted where the context of the wording is obvious.

Materials allowed by the code are all subject to the approval of the governing code jurisdiction. Therefore, it should be understood that approval is required without having to repeat it again.

Listed or tested assemblies mean tested by an independent testing agency approved by the governing code jurisdiction.

The word "occupied" means used for human occupancy.

The word "rated" means fire-resistance rated in terms of hours or fractions of hours as determined by fire tests in accordance with Chapter 7 of the UBC. *All rating shall be understood to be a minimum requirement and other requirements may dictate a greater rating.*

The word "sprinkled" shall mean *automatic sprinkler system* designed and constructed in accordance with UBC Section 904. Similarly, the words "suppression system" shall also mean *automatic suppression system* designed and constructed in accordance with NBC Section 904.

The words "use group" have been shortened to "group."

Word Definitions

Definitions of words are an important part of interpreting the Code. No attempt has been made to include definitions in this book. The user will need to refer to the Code where any question exists as to the meaning of any word.

The Review Process

The code review process must be approached in a logical and orderly manner. *The Uniform Building Code Compliance Manual* has been formatted to assist in bringing order and direction to the review process.

Reproducing Checklists

A CD-ROM has been provided with the book as the means of reproducing the checklists. Use the table of contents to determine the checklists needed for each project. The chapter number in the Table of Contents corresponds to the file number of each chapter.

Schematic Design

Use the Code Information Form at the beginning of the Schematic Design Phase to review and document basic code requirements governing building design. At the end of the phase, review the status of code compliance with the completed Code Information Form. Any changes in design concept that affected the information recorded on the form should be reviewed and the form modified to match the final design.

A copy of the final schematic plans should be noted with the code information relating to the Schematic Design Phase. This records the code review process and provides a foundation upon which to build the next phases. At a minimum, information documented on these plans should identify the following items:

* Actual building area, number of stories, and height.
* Allowable building area, number of stories, and height and allowable modifications and increases.
* Use group classifications and type of construction.
* Occupancy specific requirements and limitations.
* Fire rated exterior walls, fire walls, fire separation assemblies, and other rated separations.
* Occupant load of each space, exit widths, and length of exit access travel.

This set of noted plans forms the basis for code compliance and reference during the design process.

Design Development

Use the applicable checklists from Part 2 of this book to review code compliance at the end of the Design Development Phase. Always review the "Building Planning" list to make sure design changes during this phase meet the requirements determined on the Code Information Form or have not invalidated past code decisions. The design development drawings should document all applicable code requirements in some manner. At the end of the phase, note opening protectives and other detailed rated separations and construction on a copy of the drawings as the basis for code compliance during development of the construction documents.

Construction Documents

Use the applicable checklists from Parts 2, 3, 4, and five of this book to review the drawings and specifications at the end of the Construction Documents Phase. It is recommended that the final drawings graphically show code compliance or that "life safety plans" specifically showing code requirements be developed to clearly show compliance to interested parties. This clarifies code compliance when plans are drawn at smaller scales and are filled with other information.

Deficiency Worksheet

This worksheet can be used by the reviewer to document noncompliance items identified by the review. A numbering system on the checklists in the "ID" column provides a numbered identification of these items making reporting and follow-up smoother.

Project Files

The checklists and deficiency worksheets should be filed in the project record. This records the fact that a review was performed, and records the results of that review. It is vital to the success of the project that deficiencies are corrected in each phase.

A thorough review of all projects will reduce errors and omissions. The result is greater profitability for all parties.

Deficiency Worksheet

Project Name: _____ **Reviewer:** _____

Design Firm: _____ **Project No.:** _____

Construction Type: _____ **Occupancy Group:** _____ **Date:** _____

ID	Code Ref.	Sheet	Corrective Measure	✓

ID	Code Ref.	Sheet	Corrective Measure	✓

UBC Compliance Manual

Deficiency Worksheet
___ **of** ___

Uniform Building Code Compliance Manual

Part 1:
Code Information

Uniform Building Code Compliance Manual
1997 Uniform Building Code

Building Code Information Form

Project Name: _____

Project Number: _____ Date: _____

Owner: _____

Project Location: _____

_____

Project Description: _____

_____

Code Jurisdiction: _____

Reviewer: _____

Appendix Chapters Applicable to the Project

- ☐ **A3 Division I:** Detention and Correctional Facilities
- ☐ **A3 Division II:** Agricultural Buildings
- ☐ **A3 Division IV:** Group R-4 Occupancies
- ☐ **A4 Division I:** Barriers for Pools, Spas, and Hot Tubs
- ☐ **A4 Division II:** Aviation Control Towers
- ☐ **A9:** Basement Pipe Inlets
- ☐ **A11 Division I:** Site Accessibility
- ☐ **A11, Division II:** Accessibility for Existing Buildings
- ☐ **A12:** Interior Environment
- ☐ **A15:** Reroofing
- ☐ **A18:** Waterproofing and Dampproofing

- ☐ **A21:** Prescriptive Masonry Construction in High-wind Areas
- ☐ **A23:** Conventional Light-frame Construction in High-wind Areas
- ☐ **A29:** Minimum Plumbing Fixtures
- ☐ **A30:** Elevators, Dumbwaiters, Escalators, and Moving Walks
- ☐ **A31 Division I:** Flood Resistant Construction
- ☐ **A31 Division II:** Membrane Structures
- ☐ **A31 Division III:** Patio Covers
- ☐ **A33:** Excavation and Grading
- ☐ **A34 Division I:** Life Safety Requirements for Existing Buildings
- ☐ **A34 Division II:** Life Safety Requirements for Existing High-rise Buildings

Instructions for Use

The Code Information Form facilitates the investigation and documentation of basic code requirements which dictate building size and construction, fire resistive construction, egress, fire protection systems, and structural forces. It leads the user through the process of documenting how the building code applies to the project.

Some users will choose to only use parts of the Code Information Form. Accordingly, the form is broken down into five parts. The first part is designed to facilitate review of the code at the beginning of the Schematic Design Phase, dealing primarily with basic statistical information. The remaining parts provide additional detail as the schematic design process develops the project. The entire form should be reviewed and completed by the end of the Schematic Design Phase. The five parts are described as follows:

- **Part 1 - Building Classification:** Tables 1.1 through 1.18.
- **Part 2 - Fire Resistive Construction:** Tables 2.1 through 2.10.
- **Part 3 - Means of Egress:** Tables 3.1 through 3.18.
- **Part 4 - Fire Protection Systems:** Tables 4.1 through 4.8.
- **Part 5 - Structural Forces:** Tables 5.1 through 5.5.

Use the Code Information Form as follows:

- Using the table of contents below, determine the parts and individual tables which will be used, based on the use groups anticipated for the project. Assemble the necessary tables for the investigation process.

- Enter the required statistical information in the blanks provided and document the requirements which apply to the project by checking or marking in the appropriate box.

- Document the area of each occupancy group in the building, total building area, and total building height from the lowest level of fire department access in Table 1.1. Document the type of construction and the related allowable area, height, and stories for each occupancy group in Table 1.2. Determine any allowable area and height modifications based on Tables 1.3 through 1.18, referring to the UBC sections and tables referenced for the required statistical information.

- Document the fire resistive construction requirements which apply to the project based on Tables 2.1 through 2.10, referring to the UBC sections and tables referenced for the required information.

- Document the egress requirements for the project based on Tables 3.1 through 3.18, referring to the UBC sections and tables referenced for the required information.

- Document the fire protection system requirements for the project based on Tables 4.1 through 4.8, referring to the UBC sections and tables referenced for the required information.

- Document the structural forces applying to the project based on Tables 5.1 through 5.5, referring to the UBC sections and tables referenced for the required information.

- Graphically document the applicable code requirements on a copy of the Schematic Phase documents, delineating occupancies, fire separation distance, occupancy separation ratings, fire wall ratings, exterior wall ratings, occupant loads, exits, exit widths, travel distance, and structural forces. This provides a graphic reference for the basis of code compliance during the next phases of the design process.

Table of Contents

Part 1 - Building Classification

Table 1.1: Actual Area and Height

Story/ Bldg.	Occupant Group	Area

	Height	Total Area:
	Stories	

Table 1.2: Allowable Floor Area and Height
UBC Table 5-B and Sections 504 and 506

Construction Type	Occupant Group	Allowable		
		Height	Stories	Area
Allowable Area Increase See Tables 1.3 and 1.4				
Area Increase by Occupancy See Tables 1.8 through 1.18				
Total Allowable Area				
Mixed Occupancy Floor Area Ratios See Table 1.5				
Allowable Height Increase See Table 1.6				
Height Increase by Occupancy See Tables 1.8 through 1.18				
Total Allowable Height				
Total Allowable Height in Stories				

☐ **Area Separation Walls - Section 504.6:** When actual building area is more than basic allowable area plus any allowed area increases, provide area separation walls.

☐ **Mixed Types of Construction - Section 601.2:** When building contains more than 1 type of construction, area of entire building shall not exceed the least area permitted for types of construction involved.

   ☐ **Exception:** Consider each portion of building as a separate building when separated by area separation wall of the most restrictive requirement for such walls based on types of construction.

Table 1.3: Allowable Area Increases
Section 505

Type of Increase		Allowable Area Increase

Separation - Section 505.1: Where public ways or yards over 20'-0" (6096 mm) wide adjoin building:
❑ **Separation on 2 Sides:** Increase area by 1.25% for every foot (305 mm) over 20'-0" (6096 mm); 50% maximum increase.
❑ **Separation on 3 Sides:** Increase area by 2.25% for every foot (305 mm) over 20'-0" (6096 mm); 100% maximum increase.
❑ **Separation on All Sides:** Increase area by 5% for every foot (305 mm) over 20'-0" (6096 mm); 100% maximum increase except greater increases permitted in:
  ❑ **Group S-1:** 1 story aircraft storage hangars.
  ❑ **Group S-2 or F-2:** 1 or 2 stories.
  ❑ **Group H-5:** 1 story aircraft repair hangars. Do not exceed 500% increase except in unlimited area buildings.
	Calculation: (For each occupancy)	

Automatic Sprinklers - Section 505.3: In fully sprinklered buildings: ❑ **Triple** area in 1-story buildings. ❑ **Double** area in multi-story buildings. ❑ **Increase Does Not Apply:** When sprinklers are used to increase stories (Section 506), substitute for 1-hour construction (Section 508), for atria (Section 402), or Groups H-1 and H-2 (Section 904.2.6).		

Total Area Increase For Each Occupancy		

Table 1.4: Unlimited Area Buildings
Section 505.2

❑ **1 or 2 Story Buildings, Groups B, F-1, F-2, M, S-1, S-2, S-3, S-4, S-5, H-5:** Area may be unlimited when fully sprinklered and when public ways or yards 60'-0" (18 288 mm) minimum width on all sides.

❑ **Groups S-2 or F-2:** Area may be unlimited in 1-story Type II, III -hour, or IV buildings where public ways or yards are 60'-0" (18 288 mm) minimum width on all sides.

Table 1.5: Floor Area for Mixed Occupancies
Section 504.3

❑ **Basic Mixed Occupancy:** Sum of the ratios of the actual area of each separate occupancy (See Table 1.1) divided by total allowable area for each occupancy (See Table 1.2) shall not exceed 1.

Calculations:

❑ **Exceptions:**

❑ **90% Rule:** Use major occupancy to determine allowable area when such occupancy is 90% or more of area of any floor, minor accessory uses do not exceed basic area permitted by UBC Table 5-B, and occupancies are separated as required by Section 302.4. *See Table 2.9 below.*

❑ **Unlimited Area, Buildings of Groups B and H-5 - 10% Rule:** May contain other occupancies not exceeding more than 10% of area of any floor nor more than basic area permitted by UBC Table 5-B when such occupancies are separated as required by UBC Table 3-B.

Table 1.6: Allowable Height and Height Increases
Section 506

☐ **Height:** Compute from lowest level of fire department access.

☐ **Mixed Occupancy Height - Section 302.1:** Do not locate occupancies above story or height permitted by UBC Table 5-B.

☐ **Automatic Sprinklers:**
  ☐ May increase height by 1 story.
  ☐ Does not apply when sprinklers are used for:
    ☐ Area increases per Section 505.3;
    ☐ Substitution of 1-hour construction per Section 508;
    ☐ Atria per Section 402;
    ☐ Groups H-1, H-2, H-3, H-6, and H-7 per Section 904.2.5; or
    ☐ Groups I-1.1 and I-1.2 used as hospitals, nursing homes, or health-care centers in Types II 1-hour, III 1-hour, IV, or V 1-hour construction per Section 904.2.6.

☐ **Towers, Spires, or Steeples:** Where not used for habitation or storage:
  ☐ **Noncombustible Construction:** May be unlimited height.
  ☐ **Combustible Construction:** May not exceed 20'-0" (6096 mm) above height in UBC Table 5-B.

☐ **1-story Aircraft Hangars and Airplane Manufacturing Buildings:** May be of unlimited height where fully sprinklered and separated on all sides with public ways or yards not less than 1-1/2 times building height.

Table 1.7: Basements and Mezzanines
Sections 504 and 507

☐ **Basements - Section 504.5:** Need not be included in allowable area if basement does not exceed area permitted for 1-story building.

☐ **Mezzanines - Sections 504.4 and 507:** Unless considered a second story, include mezzanine area in allowable floor area of story in which it is located.
  ☐ Need not be counted as story when:
    ☐ Construct as required by construction type of building, but only 1-hour required in unenclosed mezzanines. Provide 7'-0" (2134 mm) minimum clear height above and below mezzanine floor construction.
    ☐ No more than 2 levels of mezzanine in a room; no limit on number of mezzanines in a room.
    ☐ Aggregate area of mezzanines in a room does not exceed 1/3 of area of room.
    ☐ All portions of mezzanine are open to room, except for columns and protective walls or railings 44" (1118 mm) high minimum.
    Exceptions:
    ☐ Partitioning is allowed if aggregate area of enclosed space does not exceed 10% of mezzanine area, or if occupant load of enclosed area does not exceed 10.
    ☐ Mezzanines with 2 or more means of egress need not be open to room if at least 1 means of egress gives direct access to protected corridor, exit court, or exit.
    ☐ Mezzanines for control equipment in industrial facilities may be glazed on all sides.

Table 1.8: Group A
Section 303

- ❏ **Group A, 1,000 or more Occupants - Section 303.2.1:** Do not locate in basements except in Type I or II-FR construction.
- ❏ **Group A-2.1, 1,000 or more Occupants - Section 303.2.2.1:** Type I, II-FR, II 1-hour, or IV construction.

- ❏ **Group A, Location on Property - Section 303.3:**
  - ❏ Front buildings on or discharge to public street 20'-0" (6096 mm) minimum width.
  - ❏ 20'-0" (6096 mm) minimum width exit discharge, unobstructed to public street.
  - ❏ Locate main entrance on public street or on exit discharge.

- ❏ **Group A-4 Grandstands, Bleachers, or Reviewing Stands - Section 303.2.2.3:**
  - ❏ **Maximum Height:**
    - ❏ **40'-0"** (12 192 mm) to highest seat board level in Type III 1-hour, IV, or V 1-hour construction.
    - ❏ **20'-0"** (6096 mm) to highest seat board level in Type II-N or V-N construction.
    - ❏ **12'-0"** (3658 mm) to highest seat board level where enclosed and combustible structural members are used.
  - ❏ **Area:** May be unlimited where of open skeleton structure without roof, cover, or enclosed useable space except in Type III-N and V-N construction.

Table 1.9: Group E
Section 305

- ❏ **Allowable Area - Section 305.2.1:** May be increased 50% when maximum travel distance is reduced by 50%. *See Table 3.8 below.*

- ❏ **Room Location, Groups E-1 or E-2 Kindergarten, First, or Second Grade Rooms and Group E-3 - Section 305.2.3:** Locate such rooms only on first story.
  - ❏ **Exceptions:**
    - ❏ When basements or stories are within 4'-0" (1219 mm) vertically from ground level at level of exit discharge where exterior exit doors are provided at that level.
    - ❏ May be on second story when buildings are fully sprinklered and have at least 2 exterior exit doors for exclusive use of day care, kindergarten, first, or second grade.
    - ❏ **Group E-3** may be located above first story in Types I, II-FR, II 1-hour, and III 1-hour construction when all of following apply:
      - ❏ Rooms with children under age 7 or containing more than 12 children per story are not located above fourth floor;
      - ❏ Entire story is provided with manual fire alarm and smoke detection system;
      - ❏ Day-care facilities more than 1,000 sf (92.9 m²) are divided into at least 2 compartments of equal size by smoke barrier of at least 1-hour rating,
      - ❏ At least 2 exits or exit access doors are provided from each smoke barrier compartment, of which 1 may pass through adjoining compartment;
      - ❏ At least 1 exit or exit access doors from E-3 is into separate means of egress;
      - ❏ Building is fully sprinklered.

- ❏ **Location on Property - Section 305.3:**
  - ❏ Front all buildings directly on public street or exit discharge at least 20'-0" (6096 mm) wide.
  - ❏ 20'-0" (6096 mm) minimum exit discharge width, unobstructed access way to public street.
  - ❏ Locate at least 1 exit on public street or exit discharge.

Table 1.10: Group H
Section 307

☐ **Control Areas - Section 307.1:**
- ☐ **Control Area Definition:** The maximum area of building or portion of building in which amounts of hazardous materials exempted by UBC Table 3-D and 3-E may be stored, dispensed, handled, or used.
- ☐ **Separation:** Provide 1-hour occupancy separation from other control areas.
- ☐ **Maximum Number of Control Areas Permitted:**
  - ☐ 2 in buildings used for retail or wholesale sales.
  - ☐ 4 in buildings with other uses.

☐ **Mixed Occupancies with Group H-6 - Section 302.1:** Do not exceed 3 stories and 55'-0" (16 764 mm) for portion containing Group H-6.

☐ **Location on Property - Section 503.4.5:** Regardless of any other requirements, provide minimum distances to property line, measured to all property lines, as follows:
- ☐ **Group H-1:** 75'-0" (22 860 mm) and not less than required by UBC Table 3-F.
- ☐ **Group H-2:** 30'-0" (9144 mm) when more than 1,000 sf (93 m^2) and not required to be in detached building.
- ☐ **Groups H-2 and H-3:** 50'-0" (15 240 mm) when detached building is required by UBC Table 3-F.
- ☐ **Groups H-2 and H-3:** As required by UBC Table 3-F when containing explosive materials.

☐ **Group H-1 - Section 307.2.8:**
- ☐ No other use allowed in building.
- ☐ Basements, crawl spaces, or other under-floor spaces not permitted.
- ☐ When building contains materials which are both physical and health hazards exceeding UBC Table 3-E, comply with Groups H-1 and H-7 requirements.

☐ **Group H-2 and H-3 - Section 307.2.9:** When hazardous materials exceed UBC Table 3-G:
- ☐ No other use allowed in building.
- ☐ Only 1 story permitted.
- ☐ Basements, crawl spaces, or other under-floor spaces not permitted.

☐ **Group H-4 - Section 307.2.10:** When not more than 2,500 sf (232 m^2), exterior walls may be at least 2-hour construction when less than 5'-0" (1524 mm) from property line, and at least 1-hour when over 5'-0" (1524 mm) but less than 20'-0" (6096 mm) from property line.

☐ **Location on Property - Section 307.3:**
- ☐ **Group H - General:** Comply with UBC Table 3-F.
- ☐ **Groups H-2 and H-3 - Room Location:** Not less than 25% of perimeter wall shall be an exterior wall.
  - ☐ **Exceptions:**
    - ☐ **Liquid Use, Dispensing, and Mixing Rooms:** Need not be on exterior wall when 500 sf (93 m^2) maximum and when complying with Section 307.1.3.
    - ☐ **Liquid Storage Rooms:** Need not be on exterior wall when 1000 sf (46.5 m^2) maximum and when complying with Section 307.1.4.
    - ☐ **Spray Paint Booths:** Need not be on exterior wall when complying with Fire Code.

☐ **Location of HPM Room in Building - Section 307.11.5.2:** Provide at least 1 exterior wall 30'-0" (9144 mm) minimum from property lines, including property lines adjacent to public ways.

Table 1.11: Group I
Section 308

☐ **Area and Height Exceptions to Table 5-B and Sections 504, 505, and 506 - Section 308.2.1:**
- ☐ **1 story height maximum** in fully sprinklered buildings of Types III 1-hour, IV, and V 1-hour construction for Group I-1.1 hospitals and nursing homes and Group I-1.2 health-care centers for ambulatory patients.
- ☐ **5 story height maximum** in Type II FR construction and **3 story maximum height** in Type II 1-hour construction in fully sprinklered buildings for Group I-1.1 hospitals and nursing homes and Group I-1.2 health-care centers for ambulatory patients with sprinklers throughout.
    - ☐ Area increase for sprinkler systems applies only when number of stories is 1 less than permitted above.
- ☐ **1 story height maximum** in fully sprinklered buildings of Type II-N construction for Group I-1.1 hospitals and nursing homes and Group I-1.2 health-care centers for ambulatory patients.
    - ☐ 13,500 sf (1254 m^2) maximum plus any allowable area increase for separation of public space or yards.
☐ **Group I-3 - Section 308.2.2.2:** Provide Type I or II FR construction.
- ☐ **Exception:** Type II 1-hour, III 1-hour, or V 1-hour construction permitted when area does not exceed 3,900 sf (362 m^2) between 2-hour separation walls with 1-1/2 hour opening protection.

Table 1.12: Group S-3
Section 311

☐ **Group S-3 with A-3, B, M, or R-1 Above - Section 311.2.2.1:** Basement or first story may be considered separate building for area and story limitations, and construction type when:
- ☐ Basement or first story is Type I construction and separated from building above with 3-hour occupancy separation;
- ☐ Building above 3-hour occupancy separation contains only Groups A-3, B, M, or R-1;
- ☐ Building below is Group S-3 is only for parking and storage of private or pleasure motor vehicles, except:
    - ☐ **Exceptions:**
        - ☐ Entry lobbies, mechanical rooms, and similar uses incidental to operation of buildings.
        - ☐ Group A-3 and B office, drinking, and dining establishments, and Group M retail occupancies in addition to uses incidental to operation of building (including storage areas), if entire structure below 3-hour occupancy separation is fully sprinklered; and
        - ☐ Maximum building height does not exceed UBC Table 5-B for least type of construction involved.

☐ **Group S-3 with S-4 Above - Section 311.2.2.2:** Basement or first story may be considered separate building for determining construction type when:
- ☐ Allowable area is the sum of ratios of actual area divided by allowable area for each occupancy where ratio is 1 or less.
- ☐ Group S-3 is Type I or II construction and is of fire resistance equal to Group S-4 occupancy;
- ☐ Limit height and number of tiers above basement to UBC Table 3-H and Section 311.9.5;
- ☐ Protect floor-ceiling separating Groups S-3 and S-4 as required for Group S-3; openings need no protection except for exit openings; and
- ☐ Group S-3 is only used for parking or storage of private or pleasure-type motor vehicles, but may contain mechanical equipment rooms incidental to operation of building, and office, waiting, and toilet rooms not exceeding 1,000 sf (93 m^2) total.

Table 1.13: Group S-4 Open Parking Garage
Section 311

- ❑ **Floor Area Calculation - Section 311.9.4:** In structures having spiral or sloping floor, the horizontal projection of structure at any cross section shall not exceed allowable area per parking tier, UBC Table 3-H. In cases of continuous spiral floors, consider each 9'-6" (2896 mm) height, or portion thereof a tier.

- ❑ **Area and Height Increases for Open Area - Section 311.9.5:** Areas and height of structures with cross ventilation throughout may be increased. Consider sides open when total area of openings along side is not less than 50% of interior area of side at each tier and openings are uniformly distributed along length.
  - ❑ **Sides open on 75% of building perimeter:** 25% allowable area increase, 1 tier height increase.
  - ❑ **Sides open on 100% of building perimeter:** 50% allowable area increase, 1 tier height increase.

- ❑ **Area Increases - Section 311.9.5:**
  - ❑ Where height is less than maximum in UBC Table 3-H, individual tiers may exceed area limits provided total building area does not exceed that permitted.
  - ❑ Provide continuous horizontal openings on at least 3 sides not less than 30" (762 mm) high extending at least 80% of length of sides, and no part of such larger tier may be more than 200'-0" (60 960 mm) horizontally from such openings.
    - ❑ Face each such opening to street or yard accessible to street with a 30'-0" (9144 mm) minimum width for full length of opening.
    - ❑ Provide standpipes in each such tier.
  - ❑ Area may be unlimited in Types II-FR, II 1-hour, or II-N construction with all sides open, when height does not exceed 75'-0" (22 860 mm).
  - ❑ Consider sides open when area of openings along side is 50% or more of interior area of side at each tier, uniformly distributed along length.
  - ❑ No part of such tier may be more than 200'-0" (60 960 mm) horizontally from such openings.

- ❑ **Prohibited Uses - Section 311.9.12:** Automobile repair work, parking of buses, trucks, and similar vehicles, partial or complete closing of required openings in exterior walls by tarpaulins or other means, dispensing of fuel.

- ❑ **Accessory Uses - Section 311.9.2.1:** Grade level tier may contain office, waiting, and toilet rooms 1,000 sf (93 m^2) maximum total area.
  - ❑ Such area need not be separated from open parking garage.

Table 1.14: Group U
Section 312

- ❑ **Height - Section 312.2.1:** May not exceed 1,000 sf (99 m^2) or 1 story in height.

- ❑ **Special Area Provisions - Section 312.2.2:**
  - ❑ Private garages used only for private or pleasure-type motor vehicles where no repair work is done or fuel dispensed may be 3,000 sf (279 m^2) provided requirements of items below are met.
    - ❑ Provide exterior wall and opening protection as required for major occupancy in mixed occupancy buildings. Floor area shall be as permitted for the major occupancy.
    - ❑ Use Group R-1 requirements for exterior wall and opening protection for buildings containing only Group U.
  - ❑ More than one 3,000 sf (279 m^2) Group U occupancy may be within the same building provided they are separated by area separation walls.

Table 1.15: Atria
Section 402

☐ **General Requirements:**
   ☐ Fully sprinkle buildings with atria.
   ☐ No atria permitted in Group H buildings.

☐ **Atria Minimum Opening Area and Dimensions:**

Height in Stories	Minimum Clear Opening	Minimum Area
3-4	20'-0" (6096 mm)	400 sf (37.2 m^2)
5-7	30'-0" (9144 mm)	900 sf (83.6 m^2)
8 or more	40'-0" (12 192 mm)	1,600 sf (148.6 m^2)

Table 1.16: Group B Office and Group R-1 High Rise Buildings
Section 403

☐ **Scope - Section 403.1:** Section applies when occupied floors are more than 75'-0" (22 860 mm) above lowest level of fire department vehicle access.

☐ **Construction - Section 403.1:**
   ☐ Type I or Type II-FR construction.
   ☐ Fully sprinkle buildings.

☐ **Code Requirement Modifications - Section 403.2.2:** The following are permitted:
   ☐ **Type I Construction:** Fire ratings in UBC Table 6-A for interior bearing walls, exterior bearing and nonbearing walls, roofs, and supporting beams that do not frame into columns may be reduced by 1 hour.
   ☐ **Type II Construction:** Fire ratings in UBC Table 6-A for interior bearing walls, and exterior bearing and nonbearing walls may be reduced by 1 hour.
   ☐ **Sprinklers in Vertical Shafts:** In other than stairway enclosures and elevator shafts, fire rating for vertical shafts may be reduced to 1 hour if sprinklers are installed in shafts at alternate floors.
   ☐ **Interior Nonbearing Walls:** May be non-rated when of noncombustible construction except for corridors and partitions separating dwelling units or guest rooms.

Table 1.17: Covered Mall Buildings
Section 404

- ☐ **Purpose - Section 404.1.1:** Applies to covered mall buildings not over 3 stories.

- ☐ **Scope - Section 404.1.2:** Section 404 supersedes other similar code requirements except for:
  - ☐ Covered mall buildings conforming to all other applicable provisions of the code.
  - ☐ Transportation facility terminals and lobbies of hotels, apartments, and office buildings.

- ☐ **Occupancy - Section 404.5.1:**
  - ☐ Classify covered mall buildings as Group B or M.
  - ☐ May contain accessory uses consisting of Groups A, E, or R-1.
    - ☐ Area of individual accessory uses may not exceed 3 times basic area permitted by UBC Table 5-B.
    - ☐ Aggregate area of all accessory uses within covered mall buildings shall not exceed 25% of gross leasable area.
  - ☐ Attached garages for parking or storing private or pleasure motor vehicles having capacity of 9 persons maximum and open parking garages may be considered separate buildings when separated from covered mall building by at least 2-hour occupancy separation.

- ☐ **Mixed Occupancy - Section 404.5.2:** Separate individual tenant spaces comprising a distinct occupancy from other occupancies; see UBC Table 3-B.
  - ☐ **Exceptions:**
    - ☐ Main entrances which open onto a mall not required to be separated.
    - ☐ Occupancy separation not required between food court and adjacent tenant spaces or mall.

- ☐ **Anchor Buildings and Parking Garages - Section 404.2.1:** Height and area limitations per Sections 504, 505, and 506.

- ☐ **Type of Construction - Section 404.2.1:**
  - ☐ **1 and 2 level malls:** Any type.
  - ☐ **3 level malls:** Type II 1-hour minimum.

- ☐ **Required Yards for Unlimited Area - Section 404.2.2:** Unlimited area permitted when covered mall building, attached anchor buildings, and parking garages are adjoined by public ways, streets, or yards not less than 60'-0" (18 288 mm) wide along exterior walls.

Table 1.18: Amusement Buildings
Section 408

- ☐ **Classification - Section 408.1:**
  - ☐ **Occupant load of 50 or more:** Comply with appropriate Group A.
  - ☐ **Occupant load of less than 50:** Comply with appropriate Group B.
  - ☐ **Exception:** Amusement buildings or portions thereof with no walls or roof and constructed to prevent the accumulation of smoke in assembly areas.

Part 2 - Fire-Resistive Construction

Table 2.1: Fire-Resistive Requirements for Building Elements
UBC Table 6-A

Building Element	Required Rating	Rated Assembly Identification	
Bearing Walls - Exterior			**Fire Rating Exceptions - Section 601.5:**
Bearing Walls - Interior			❐ Fixed interior nonbearing partitions in stores and offices.
Nonbearing Walls - Exterior			❐ Fixed interior nonbearing partitions in hotels and apartments
Structural Frame			❐ Folding, portable, or moveable partitions.
Partitions - Permanent			❐ Certain elements of walls fronting on streets or yards.
Shaft Enclosures			❐ Exterior loading platforms.
Floors and Floor-Ceilings			
Roofs and Roof-Ceilings			**Structural Frame - Section 601.4:**
Exterior Doors and Windows			Defined as the columns, and the girders, beams, trusses, and spandrels directly connecting to the columns and bracing members designed to carry gravity loads.
Stairway Construction			

❐ **Fire Resistive Substitution:** Automatic sprinklers may be substituted for rated construction in Types II 1-hour, III 1-hour, and V 1-hour construction. *See Table 2.3 below.*

Table 2.2: Fire Resistive Requirements By Occupancy

❐ **Group A Roof Framing - Section 303.2.1:** May be unprotected when without concealed spaces and open to assembly area in 1-story portions of Types II 1-hour, III 1-hour, and V construction.

❐ **Group A-3 - Section 303.2.2.2:** Provide at least 1-hour construction when located in basement or above first story.
   ❐ When located over usable space and containing 50 or more occupants, provide 1-hour separation from such space.

❐ **Group F-2 Roof Framing - Section 306.2.2:** May be unprotected construction.

❐ **Group H-4 - Section 307.2.11:** Exterior walls may be 2-hour when H-4 is not more than 2,500 sf (232 m^2) and less than 5'-0" (1524 mm) from property line, and at least 1-hour when 5'-0" (1524 mm) or more but less than 20'-0" (6096 mm) from property line.

❐ **Group R-1 Construction - Section 310.2.2:** Where more than 2 stories in height or having more than 3,000 sf (279 m^2) above the first story, provide 1-hour construction throughout.

❐ **Group S Marine or Motor Vehicle Fuel-Dispensing Stations - Section 311.2.3.2:** Provide noncombustible construction, fire-retardant treated wood, or 1-hour construction, including canopies and supports over pumps.
   ❐ **Exceptions:**
      ❐ Roofs of 1 story fuel-dispensing stations may be heavy timber.
      ❐ Canopies with plastic panels complying with Section 2603.13.

❐ **Group S-2 Roof Framing - Section 311.2.3.4:** May be unprotected.

Table 2.3: Fire Resistive Substitution
Section 508

☐ **Automatic Sprinklers:** May substitute for rated construction in Type II 1-hour, III 1-hour, and V 1-hour construction.

☐ **Substitution does not waive or reduce:**
   ☐ Occupancy separations (Section 302.3).
   ☐ Exterior wall protection due to proximity of property lines (Section 503.2).
   ☐ Area separations (Section 504.6).
   ☐ Dwelling unit separations (Section 310.2.2).
   ☐ Shaft enclosures (Section 711).
   ☐ Corridors (Sections 1004.3.4.3.1 and 1004.3.4.3.2).
   ☐ Stair enclosures (Section 1005.3.3).
   ☐ Exit passageways (Section 1005.3.4).
   ☐ Type of construction separation (Section 601.1).
   ☐ Boiler, central heating plant, or hot-water supply boiler room enclosures (Section 302.5).

Table 2.4: Location on Property
Section 503

☐ **General - Section 503.1:** Provide public way or yard on at least 1 side, or provide access to a public way or yard.
   ☐ Consider centerline of adjoining public way an adjacent property line.

☐ **Exterior Wall Projections - Section 503.2.1:**
   ☐ Shall not extend beyond a point 1/3 the distance to property line from an assumed vertical plane located where opening protection is first required due to location on property.
   ☐ Shall not extend more than 12" (305 mm) into areas where openings are prohibited.

☐ **Buildings on Same Property - Section 503.3:** Assume a property line between buildings on the same property to determine wall and opening protection and roof covering requirements.
   ☐ **Exceptions:**
      ☐ 2 or more buildings on 1 site may be considered 1 building when aggregate area is within allowable area limitations.
      ☐ When such buildings contain 2 or more occupancies, use most restrictive requirements of construction type or occupancy to determine basic allowable area.
      ☐ Locate property lines between new structures and existing buildings for exterior wall and opening protection required by the type of construction and UBC Table 5-A.

☐ **Buildings with Courts - Section 503.3:** Assume property line between court walls of buildings over 1 story.
   ☐ **Exception:** Opening protection may be omitted if only 2 levels open onto court; aggregate area of building, including court, is within allowable area; and building is not Group I occupancy.

Table 2.5: Fire Resistance of Exterior Walls
Section 503.2 and UBC Table 5-A

Side	Occupancy Group	Construction Type	Distance to Property Line	Bearing Wall Rating	Nonbearing Wall Rating	Opening Protection

- **Measurements to Property Line - Section 503.2.1:**
  - Measure distance at right angles to property lines.
  - Measure from building wall to property line or center of public way.
  - Ratings do not apply to walls at right angles to property lines.

- **Maximum Area of Protected Openings - Section 503.2.2:** When required to be protected due to distance to property line, sum of area of openings shall not exceed 50% of total area of wall in each story.

- **Minimum Exterior Opening Protection - UBC Table 5-A, Note 5:** 3/4-hour.

Table 2.6: Exceptions to UBC Table 5-A
Section 503.4

- **1-story, Groups B, F, M and S:** Rating not required for exterior walls of 1-story Type II-N buildings not more than 1,000 sf (93 m²) and when such wall is at least 5'-0" (1524 mm) from property line.

- **Fire-Retardant Wood Framing:** May be used in exterior walls of Types III and IV construction when Table 5-A allows 2-hour rating or less, if rating is maintained and exposed outer and inner faces of walls are noncombustible.

- **Wood Columns and Arches:** In Types III and IV construction, such members conforming to heavy-timber sizes may be used externally when exterior walls may be unprotected, noncombustible construction or when 1-hour noncombustible exterior walls are permitted.

- **Groups H-1, H-2, and H-3 - Detached Buildings:** When detached building is required by UBC Table 3-G, there are no requirements for wall and opening protection based on location on property.

- **Group H-4 Buildings not more than 2,500 sf (232 m²):** Exterior bearing walls may be 2-hour when not less than 5'-0" (1524 mm) from property line, and 1-hour when not less than 20'-0" (6096 mm).

Table 2.7: Occupancy Separations
UBC Table 3-B

Occupancy Group	Occupancy Group	Separation Fire Rating	Fire Separation Design
	/		
	/		
	/		
	/		
	/		
	/		
	/		
	/		
	/		

☐ **Occupancy Separation Exceptions - Section 302.1:**
- ☐ Spray booths complying with Fire Code within Groups B, F, H, M, or S.
- ☐ Assembly rooms not over 750 sf (69 m^2) accessory to other occupancies.
- ☐ Administrative and clerical offices accessory to other occupancies and not exceeding 25% of area of major use, except in Groups H-2 and H-3.
- ☐ Gift shops and administrative offices accessory to Group R-1, not exceeding 10% of area of major use.
- ☐ Kitchens serving dining areas to which they are accessory.
- ☐ Customer waiting rooms accessory to other occupancies, not over 450 sf (41.8 m^2), and having an exit directly to exterior, except in Group H.
- ☐ No separation required between Group R-3 and carports having no enclosed uses above, when carport is entirely open on 2 or more sides.
- ☐ No separation required between Group S-4 open parking garage and Group S-3 parking garages with no repair or refueling.

Table 2.8: Occupancy Separation Fire Rating Exceptions
Section 302.4 and UBC Table 3-B

- ☐ Separation may be 3-hour between Group A-1 and Group S-3 parking garages with no repair or refueling.
- ☐ Separation may be 2-hour between Groups A-2, A-2.1, A-3, A-4, E, or I and Group S-3 parking garages with no repair or refueling.
- ☐ Unless a 3-hour separation is required by Section 311.2.2, separation may be 2-hour between Group R-1 and Group S-3 parking garages with no repair or refueling, and may be 1-hour where Group S-3 is 3,000 sf (279 m^2) or less.
- ☐ Minimum 1-hour construction on garage side between Group R-3 and Group U.
- ☐ No separation required between Groups H-7 and H-2 or H-3 when all occupancies comply with Group H-7 requirements.

Table 2.9: Area Separation Walls
Section 504.6

❐ **Area Separation Walls Required - Section 504.6.1:** When actual building area is more than basic allowable area plus any allowed area increases, provide area separation walls.

❐ **Construction - Section 504.6.2:**
- ❐ **Construction Type I, II-FR, III, and IV:** 4-hour; 3-hour opening protection.
- ❐ **Construction Type II 1-hour, II-N, and V:** 2-hour; 1-1/2 hour opening protection.

Table 2.10: Construction Type Requirements
Chapter 6

Construction Type:
- ❐ Type I FR
- ❐ Type II FR
- ❐ Type II 1-Hr
- ❐ Type II N
- ❐ Type III 1-Hr
- ❐ Type III N
- ❐ Type IV
- ❐ Type V 1-Hr
- ❐ Type V N

Structural Framework:

❐ **Type I:**	❐ **Type II:**	❐ **Type III:**	❐ **Type IV:**	❐ **Type V:**
❐ Steel	❐ Steel	❐ Steel	❐ Steel	❐ Steel
❐ Concrete	❐ Concrete	❐ Concrete	❐ Concrete	❐ Concrete
❐ Masonry	❐ Masonry	❐ Masonry	❐ Masonry	❐ Masonry
		❐ Wood	❐ Wood	❐ Wood
			❐ Heavy Timber	

Minimum Roof Class - Table 15-A:
- ❐ Class A
- ❐ Class B
- ❐ Class C

Part 3 - Means of Egress

Table 3.1: Occupant Load Calculations and Exits Required
Section 1003, and UBC Table 10-A

Story	Occupancy or Use	Area	Occupant Load Factor	Occupant Load	Exits Required
			÷	=	
			÷	=	
			÷	=	
			÷	=	
			÷	=	
			÷	=	
			÷	=	
			÷	=	
			÷	=	
			÷	=	
			÷	=	
			÷	=	
			÷	=	
			÷	=	
			÷	=	
			÷	=	
			÷	=	
			÷	=	
			÷	=	
			÷	=	
			÷	=	
			÷	=	
			÷	=	
			÷	=	
			÷	=	
See Table 3.2 below for further occupant load requirements.			**Total Occupants**		

Table 3.2: Occupant Load
Section 1003.2.2

☐ **Occupant Load - Section 1003.2.2.2.1:** Assume all portions of building are occupied at once.
   ☐ **Accessory spaces:** Accessory spaces used by occupants of main areas need not be included in occupant load computation of building.

☐ **Areas Without Fixed Seats - Section 1003.2.2.2.2:**
   ☐ Determine occupants by dividing area by occupant load factor assigned by UBC Table 10-A.
   ☐ Determine occupant load of buildings or areas containing 2 or more occupancies by adding loads of various uses as computed.
   ☐ Where spaces have more than 1 use, determine occupant load by use yeilding most occupants.

☐ **Areas With Fixed Seating - Section 1003.2.2.2.3:**
   ☐ **Fixed Seating:** Determine occupants by number of fixed seats. Do not use required width of aisles for any other purpose.
   ☐ **Fixed Pews or Benches:** 1 occupant for every 18" (457 mm) of bench or pew length.
   ☐ **Dining Booths:** 1 occupant for every 24" (610 mm) of length.

☐ **Outdoor Areas - Section 1003.2.2.2.4:**
   ☐ Assign occupant load to yards, patios, courts and similar spaces for anticipated use.
   ☐ Provide means of egress required by occupant load and use.
   ☐ Where outdoor areas exit through buildings, consider occupant load of outdoor area in design of means of egress.

☐ **Mezzanines - Section 507:**
   ☐ Add mezzanine occupants to occupant load of room below mezzanine when a required means of egress enters the room below.
   ☐ Provide 2 exits when required by UBC Table 10-A.

Table 3.3: Separation of Exits or Exit-Access Doorways
Section 1004.2.4

☐ **2 Exits or Exit-Access Doorways Required:** Place a distance apart not less than 1/2 length of maximum diagonal dimension of building or area served, measured in a straight line between exits or exit-access doorways.

☐ **Exit Separation - 3 or more Exits Required:** Where 3 or more exits are required, arrange at least 2 exits as required above, with additional exits placed a reasonable distance apart.

☐ **Exception:** Separation distance may be measured along line of travel within corridor. Walls of such exit enclosure shall be not less than 30'-0" (9144 mm), measured in straight line, from walls of another exit enclosure.

Table 3.4: Egress Width Calculations
Section 1003.2.3 and UBC Table 10-B

Means of Egress Component	Story	Occupant Load	Egress Factor	Minimum Width
			X	=
			X	=
			X	=
			X	=
			X	=
			X	=
			X	=
			X	=
			X	=
			X	=
			X	=
			X	=
			X	=
			X	=
			X	=
			X	=
			X	=
			X	=
			X	=
			X	=
			X	=
			X	=
			X	=
			X	=
			X	=
			X	=
			X	=
			X	=
			X	=

See Table 3.5 below for additional requirements.

Table 3.5: Egress Width Requirements
Section 1003.3

☐ **Minimum Egress Width - Section 1003.2.3.2:** Where more than 1 exit or exit-access doorway serves building or space, width may be divided approximately equally between exits or exit-access doorways.

☐ **Maintaining Width - Section 1003.2.3.3:**
- ☐ Maintain width required from any story until egress from building is provided.
- ☐ Increase width where cumulative occupant load served increases.
- ☐ **Exception:** Except in Groups H-1, H-2, H-3, and H-7, width of exterior exit doors from exit enclosure may be based on largest occupant load of all levels served by such exit enclosure multiplied by factor of 0.2 (5.08).

☐ **Exiting From Adjacent Levels - Section 1003.2.3.4:**
- ☐ No cumulative or contributing occupant loads from adjacent building levels need be considered when determining required width of means of egress components from a given level.
- ☐ Where an exit from an upper floor and a lower floor converge at an intermediate floor, base width of exit from intermediate floor on sum of occupant loads of such upper and lower floors.

☐ **2-Way Exits - Section 1003.2.3.5:**
- ☐ Where exit or exit-access doorways serve paths of exit travel from opposite directions, base their width on largest occupant load served.
- ☐ Where such exit or exit-access doorways are required to swing in direction of exit travel, base exit width for each path of exit travel on occupant load of area served.

☐ **Group I Minimum Clear Width - Section 1007.5.1:**
- ☐ **44"** (1118 mm) minimum where serving areas occupied or used by bed/litter patients, allow for passage of beds, gurneys, and equipment.
- ☐ **32"** (813 mm) for other aisles.

Table 3.6: Access to Exits
Section 1004.2.3

☐ **General - Section 1004.2.3.1:**
  ☐ Provide exits for each level and occupied area.
  ☐ Provide access to exits from occupied areas.
  ☐ Maintain maximum number of exits required from each story, basement, or individual space until arrival at grade or public way.

☐ **Access to Exits from Individual Floors - Section 1004.2.3.2:**
  ☐ **First Story:** Provide access to at least 1 exit from first story, or 2 or more exits where required by UBC Table 10-A.
  ☐ **Occupied Basements and Stories above the First Story:** Provide access to at least 2 separate exits.
    ☐ Second stories with less than 10 occupants may have only 1 exit.
    ☐ 2 or more dwelling units on second story or in basement may access 1 exit when occupant load served by exit does not exceed 10.
    ☐ Only 1 exit needed from second floor or basement in dwelling unit or Group R-3 congregate residence, except as required by UBC Table 10-A.
    ☐ Only 1 exit needed from third floor in dwelling unit or Group R-3 congregate residence when 500 sf (46.45 m^2) or less.
    ☐ Occupied Group R-3 roofs may have only 1 exit if less than 500 sf (46.45 m^2) and if no higher than immediately above second story.
    ☐ Floors or basements used exclusively for service of building may have only 1 exit. Do not consider storage rooms, laundry rooms, and maintenance offices as providing service.

☐ **Access to Exits from Individual Spaces - Section 1004.2.3.3:**
  ☐ Provide access to at least 1 exit or exit-access doorway.
  ☐ Provide access to at least 2 or more exits or exit access-doorways, or combination thereof, where required by UBC Table 10-A.
  ☐ **Exceptions:**
    ☐ Elevator lobbies may have access to only 1 exit or exit-access doorway provided keys, special tools, special knowledge or effort is not required.
    ☐ Storage, laundry, and maintenance offices 300 sf (27.87 m^2) or less may have access to only 1 exit or exit-access doorway.

☐ **Additional Access to Exits Required by Occupant Load - Section 1004.2.3.4:**
  ☐ **501 to 1,000 Occupants:** Provide access to at least 3 exits or exit-access doorways.
  ☐ **1,001 or more Occupants:** Provide access to at least 4 exits or exit-access doorways.

☐ **Dead Ends - Section 1004.2.6:** 20'-0" (6096 mm) maximum when more than 1 exit or exit-access doorway is required.

☐ **Group H Access to Exits - Section 1007.4.1:** Provide access to at least 2 exits or exit-access doorways from each area 200 sf (18.58 m^2) or more.
  ☐ **Exception:** Group H-4 with less than 1,000 sf (92.9 m^2) may have 1 exit.

☐ **Group S-4 Parking Garages, Stairs and Means of Egress - Section 311.9.7:**
  ☐ When persons other than parking attendants are permitted, provide means of egress based on occupant load of 200 sf (18.6 m^2) per occupant.
  ☐ Where only attendants are permitted, provide at least two 3'-0" (914 mm) wide stairs.
  ☐ Lifts may be provided for attendant use only when completely enclosed by noncombustible materials.

Table 3.7: Travel Through Intervening Rooms

- ❑ **Exit Access - Section 1004.2.2:**
  - ❑ Provide required access to exits from any portion of building directly from the space to an exit or to a corridor providing direct access to an exit.
  - ❑ Do not interrupt exit access by intervening space.
  - ❑ **Exceptions:**
    - ❑ Access to exits may occur through foyers, lobbies, and reception rooms.
    - ❑ Where only 1 exit is required from space, exit access may occur through an adjoining or intervening room, which in turn provides direct access to an exit or corridor that provides direct access to an exit.
    - ❑ Rooms with occupant load of 10 or less may exit through more than 1 intervening room.
    - ❑ Where more than 1 exit is required from space, such space may access 1 required exit through an adjoining or intervening room, which in turn provides direct access to an exit or corridor that provides direct access to an exit. All other required access to exits shall be directly from space to an exit or corridor that provides direct access to an exit.
    - ❑ 1- or 2-story Group F, S, or H-5 offices or similar administrative areas may have access to 2 required exits through an adjoining or intervening room, which in turn provides direct access to an exit or corridor that provides direct access to an exit, if building is fully sprinkled and provided with smoke and heat ventilation per Section 906. Such area shall not exceed 25% of floor area of major use.
    - ❑ Rooms in dwelling units may exit through more than 1 intervening room.
  - ❑ Consider hallways as an intervening room.
  - ❑ Consider interior courts enclosed on all sides as an intervening room.
    - ❑ **Exception:** Courts not less than 10'-0" (3048 mm) wide or less than minimum width required and providing direct access to an exit need not be considered intervening rooms.
  - ❑ **Group H:** Means of egress serving Group H shall not pass through rooms containing Group H.

- ❑ **Exits - Section 1005.2.1:** Do not interrupt by intervening rooms.
  - ❑ **Exceptions:**
    - ❑ **Horizontal Exits:** May lead to exit-access element.
    - ❑ **Office Buildings and Group I-1.1 Hospitals and Nursing Homes:** 50% of exits may pass through street floor lobby if street floor is fully sprinkled.

- ❑ **Exit Passageways - Section 1005.3.4.5:** Do not interrupt by intervening rooms.
  - ❑ **Office Buildings and Group I-1.1 Hospitals and Nursing Homes:** 50% of exits may pass through street floor lobby if street floor is fully sprinkled.

Table 3.8: Maximum Travel Distance
Section 1004.2.5

- ☐ **Travel Distance Definition - Section 1004.2.5.1:**
  - ☐ Distance occupant must travel from any point in occupied portions of exit access to door of nearest exit.
  - ☐ Measure in straight line along path of exit travel from most remote point through center of exit-access doorways to center of exit door.
  - ☐ Unless prohibited elsewhere, travel may occur on multiple levels in unenclosed stairs or ramps.
  - ☐ Where path of travel includes unenclosed stairs or ramps within exit access, include distance of travel on such stairs or ramps in travel distance measurement. Measure along plane parallel and tangent to stair tread nosings in center of stairway.

- ☐ **Basic Maximum Distance - Section 1004.2.5.2:**
  - ☐ **Nonsprinkled Buildings:**
    - ☐ 200'-0" (60 960 mm), or
    - ☐ 300'-0" (91 440 mm) where last 100'-0" (30 480 mm) occurs entirely in 1-hour corridor.
  - ☐ **Fully Sprinklered Buildings:**
    - ☐ 250'-0" (76 200 mm) maximum, or
    - ☐ 350'-0" (106 680 mm) where last 100'-0" (30 480 mm) occurs entirely in 1-hour corridor.

- ☐ **Open Parking Garages - Section 1004.2.5.2.4:**
  - ☐ 300'-0" (91 440 mm) in unsprinkled buildings,
  - ☐ 400'-0" (121 920 mm) in sprinklered buildings; may be measured to unenclosed open stairways.

- ☐ **1-Story Group H-5 Aircraft Repair Hangar, Group F or S - Section 1004.2.5.2.5:**
  - ☐ 300'-0" (91 440 mm) in unsprinkled buildings.
  - ☐ 400'-0" (121 920 mm) in sprinklered buildings with smoke and heat ventilation.

- ☐ **Travel Distance within Exits - Section 1005.2.2:** Not limited within exit enclosure or exit passageway.

- ☐ **Atria - Section 402.5.1:** 100'-0" (30 480 mm) maximum on open exit-access balcony within atrium.

- ☐ **Group E - Section 1007.3.3:**
  - ☐ **Within Rooms:** 75'-0" (22 860 mm) from any point in room to corridor or exit.
    - ☐ 90'-0" (27 432 mm) where building is 1 or 2 stories with smoke detectors throughout.
    - ☐ 110'-0" (33 528 mm) in fully sprinkled buildings.
  - ☐ **From any Location:** 150'-0" (45 720 mm) in unsprinkled buildings.
    - ☐ 175'-0" (53 340 mm) in 1 or 2 story buildings protected throughout with smoke detectors.
    - ☐ 225'-0" (68 580 mm) in fully sprinklered buildings.
  - ☐ **Increase:** Distance may be increased by 100'-0" (30 480 mm) where last portion of travel occurs entirely in 1-hour corridor.

- ☐ **Group H:**
  - ☐ **Groups H-1, H-2, and H-3 - Section 1007.4.2:** 75'-0" (22 860 mm).
  - ☐ **Group H-7 and Group H-6 Fabrication Areas - Section 1007.4.2:** 100'-0" (30 480 mm).
  - ☐ **Increase:** Distance may be increased by 100'-0" (30 480 mm) where last portion of travel occurs entirely in 1-hour corridor.
  - ☐ **Group H-6 Service Corridor - Section 307.11.4:** 75'-0" (22 860 mm) from any point in service corridor to exit or door into fabrication area.

- ☐ **Group I-1.1 or I-3 - Section 1007.5.2:** 200'-0" (76 200 mm) to an exit.

Table 3.9: Exit Discharge
Section 1006

❑ **General - Section 1006.1:**
- ❑ **Definition:** Means of egress from exit to public way; includes exterior exit balconies, exterior exit stairways, exterior exit ramps, exit courts and yards, and other means of egress components.
- ❑ **Safe Dispersal Area:** Exit discharge may lead to safe dispersal area on same property, located at least 50'-0" (15 240 mm) from building.

❑ **Location - Section 1006.2.1:**
- ❑ At grade or provide direct access to grade.
- ❑ Do not reenter building.
- ❑ Do not locate exterior exit balconies, exterior exit stairways, exterior exit ramps where exterior openings not permitted or protected per UBC Table 5-A.

❑ **Access to Grade - Section 1006.2.2:**
- ❑ Where exits discharge at other than grade level, provide at least 2 separate paths of travel to grade.
- ❑ No dead ends more than 20'-0" (6096 mm).
- ❑ **Exceptions:**
  - ❑ Only 1 path of travel to grade required where occupant load served is less than 10.
  - ❑ Where exits discharge to exterior exit stairway, stairway may serve as a single path of exit travel to grade.

❑ **Travel Distance - Section 1006.2.3:**
- ❑ **At Grade Level:** Not limited.
- ❑ **Other than at Grade Level:**
  - ❑ **Nonsprinkled Buildings:** 200'-0" (60960 mm) maximum.
  - ❑ **Fully Sprinkled Buildings:** 250'-0" (76 200 mm) maximum.
- ❑ Where path of travel includes unenclosed stairways or ramps within exit discharge, include travel distance on such components in measurement.

❑ **Exterior Exit Balconies - Section 1006.3.2:**
- ❑ **Minimum Width:**
  - ❑ Width required by occupant load, but not less than **44"** (1118 mm). *See Table 3.4 above.*
  - ❑ **36"** (914 mm) where serving occupant loads less than 50.
- ❑ **Openness:** 50% open on long side, openings distributed to prevent accumulation of smoke.

❑ **Exterior Exit Stairways - Section 1006.3.3:**
- ❑ Open on at least 2 sides, except for required structural columns and open handrails and guardrails.
- ❑ Open to yards, exit courts, or public ways; remaining sides enclosed by exterior walls.

❑ **Exterior Exit Ramps - Section 1006.3.4:**
- ❑ Open on at least 2 sides, except for required structural columns and open handrails and guardrails.
- ❑ Open to yards, exit courts, or public ways; remaining sides enclosed by exterior walls.

❑ **Exit Courts - Section 1006.3.5:** Court or yard providing access to public way for 1 or more required exits.
- ❑ **Minimum Width:**
  - ❑ Width required by occupant load, but not less than **44"** (1118 mm). *See Table 3.4 above.*
  - ❑ **36"** (914 mm) where serving Group R-3 or U.

Table 3.10: Means of Egress - Group A
Section 1007.2

- ❑ **Groups A-1, A-2, and A-2.1:**
  - ❑ **Main Exit - Section 1007.2.1:** Provide main exit sufficient width to accommodate 1/2 of total occupant load, but not less than total required width of aisles, exit passageways, and stairways leading to it.
  - ❑ **Auditorium and Theater Side Exits - Section 1007.2.2:**
    - ❑ Provide exits on each side of sufficient width to accommodate 1/3 of total occupant load served;
    - ❑ Open side exits directly to a public way, or into exit or exit discharge leading to public way.
    - ❑ Make side exits accessible from a cross aisle.

- ❑ **Balcony and Mezzanine Exits - Section 1007.2.3:**
  - ❑ Provide at least 2 exits for balconies with 10 or more occupants, opening directly to exterior stairway, interior stairway, or ramp.
  - ❑ Where there are 2 or more balconies, provide access directly into exit enclosure or exterior stairway, or ramp.
  - ❑ Make balcony exits accessible from cross aisle.

- ❑ **Multitheater Complex - Main Exit - Section 1007.2.5:** Sufficient width to accommodate 1/2 of aggregate occupant load of complex.

Table 3.11: Means of Egress - Group E
Section 1004.2.3

- ❑ **Separate Exit Systems - Section 1007.3.2:** Atmospheric separation of means of egress systems.
  - ❑ Provide at least 1 separate means of egress system for rooms with occupant load of 300 or more.

  - ❑ No more than 2 required exits or exit-access doorways shall enter into same means of egress system.

- ❑ **Exit Travel Through Intervening Rooms - Section 1007.3.4:** Do not pass through laboratories using hazardous materials, industrial shops, or similar spaces.

- ❑ **Stairs - Section 1007.3.6:** Stairs serving 100 or more occupants require clear width of at least 5'-0" (1524 mm).

- ❑ **Group E-1 - Exits serving Auditoriums - Section 1007.3.7:** In determining means of egress design, auditorium may be considered as accessory use area if auditorium is not used simultaneously with the other rooms.

- ❑ **Laboratories - Section 1007.3.8:**
  - ❑ Provide 2 exits or exit-access doorways when over 200 sf (18.6 m^2);
  - ❑ All portions of room within 75'-0" (22 860 mm) of exit.

- ❑ **Basement Room Exit Stairs - Section 1007.3.9:** Open directly to exterior without entering first floor.

Table 3.12: Means of Egress - Group I
Section 1007.5

☐ **Basement Exits - Section 1007.5.6:** Make 1 exit lead directly to exterior from every basement room.

☐ **Suites - Section 1007.5.9:**
   ☐ **General:** Group of rooms in Groups I-1.1, I-1.2, and I-2 may be considered as a suite when complying with following:
      ☐ **Suite or Room Area:** 10,000 sf (929 m^2) maximum.
      ☐ **Area of Suites with Patient Sleeping Rooms:** 5,000 sf (464.5 m^2) maximum.
      ☐ **Occupancy Separation:** Separate suite from building by at least 1-hour occupancy separation.
      ☐ **Visual Supervision:** Locate each room to permit direct and constant visual supervision by staff.
      ☐ **Other Exits:** Exits for portions of building outside suite may not pass through suite.
   ☐ **Corridors:** Rated construction not required within suite.
   ☐ **Travel through Adjoining Rooms:**
      ☐ Rooms within suites may have access to exits through 1 adjoining room where travel distance inside suite is maximum of 100'-0" (30 480 mm) to exit or to a corridor providing direct access to an exit.
      ☐ Rooms other than patient sleeping rooms may access exits through 2 adjoining rooms where travel distance inside suite is maximum of 50'-0" (15 240 mm) to exit or to a corridor providing direct access to an exit.

Table 3.13: Horizontal Exits
Section 1005.3.5

☐ **General - Section 1005.3.5.1:**
   ☐ **Definition:** Wall that completely divides a floor of a building into 2 or more separate exit-access areas to afford safety from fire and smoke in exit-access area of incident origin.
   ☐ **Permitted Use as an Exit:**
      ☐ May serve as an exit for each adjacent exit-access area (e.g., a two-way exit), providing that exit-access requirements for each exit-access area are independently satisfied.
      ☐ May not serve as only exit from exit access.
      ☐ Where 2 or more exits are required from exit-access, not more than 1/2 of total exits or total exit width may be provided by horizontal exits.

☐ **Refuge Area - Section 1005.3.5.4:**
   ☐ **Floor Area:** Accommodate 100% of occupant load of exit access from which refuge is sought, plus 100% of normal occupant load of exit access serving as refuge area.
   ☐ **Capacity of Refuge Floor Area - General:**
      ☐ 3 sf (0.28 m^2) net clear floor of aisles, hallways, and corridors per occupant.
      ☐ Do not use stairs, elevators, or other shafts.
   ☐ **Capacity of Refuge Floor Area - Group I-1.1:** 15 sf (1.4 m^2) per ambulatory occupant and 30 sf (2.8 m^2) per nonambulatory occupant.
   ☐ **Exit-Access Design:** Base exit access serving as refuge area on normal occupant load.

Table 3.14: Exit Enclosures
Section 1005.3.3

- ❒ **Exit Components to be Enclosed - Section 1005.1:** Portion of means of egress components between exit access and exit discharge or public way, including exterior exit doors, exit enclosures, exit passageways, and horizontal exits.

- ❒ **Stair, Ramp, and Escalator Enclosure - Section 1005.3.3.1:** Enclose interior stairs and ramps where serving as means of egress.
  - ❒ **Enclosure Exceptions:** Enclosure not required for:
    - ❒ Stairways and ramps serving only 1 adjacent floor except in Groups H and I. Such interconnected floors shall not be open to other floors.
    - ❒ Stairs within individual dwelling units in Group R-1.
    - ❒ Stairs in Group R-3.
    - ❒ Stairs in open parking garages.

- ❒ **Enclosure Construction - Section 1005.3.3.2:**
  - ❒ **Type I and II-FR Construction:** 2-hour minimum.
  - ❒ **Buildings 3-stories or Less:** 1-hour minimum.
  - ❒ **Buildings 4-stories or More:** 2-hour minimum.

- ❒ **Extent of Exit Enclosure - Section 1005.3.3.3:** Include landings and parts of floors connecting stairway flights in enclosure.
  - ❒ Exit enclosure shall exit directly to exterior of building or shall include an exit passageway on ground floor leading from exit enclosure directly to exterior of building.
  - ❒ **Exceptions:**
    - ❒ Exit passageways not required from unenclosed stairways or ramps.
    - ❒ 50% of exits may pass through street floor lobby in office buildings provided exit width is maintained unobstructed and street floor is fully sprinkled.

Table 3.15: Stairs and Ramps
Sections 1003.3.3 and 1003.3.4

- ❒ **Minimum Stair Width - Section 1003.3.3.2:**
  - ❒ Width required by occupant load, but not less than **44"** (1118 mm). *See Table 3.4 above.*
  - ❒ **36"** (914 mm) where serving less than 50 occupants.

- ❒ **Stairway to Roof - Building 4 Stories or More - Section 1003.3.3.11:** Extend at least 1 stair to roof unless roof slope is greater than 4:12.

- ❒ **Minimum Ramp Width - Section 1003.3.4.2:**
  - ❒ Width required by occupant load, but not less than **44"** (1118 mm). *See Table 3.4 above.*
  - ❒ **36"** (914 mm) where serving less than 50 occupants.

Table 3.16: Hallways, Corridors, and Exit Passageways
Section 1004.3.3 and 1004.3.4

- ❏ **Hallways - Section 1004.3.3:** May be used as exit-access unless prohibited.
  - ❏ Consider hallways as intervening rooms.
  - ❏ **Minimum Width:**
    - ❏ Width required by occupant load, but not less than **44"** (1118 mm). *See Table 3.4 above.*
    - ❏ **36"** (914 mm) where serving occupant loads less than 50.

- ❏ **Corridors - Section 1004.3.4:** Applies to required corridors serving as portion of exit access.
  - ❏ **Minimum Width for All Corridors - Section 1004.3.4.2:**
    - ❏ Width required by occupant load, but not less than **44"** (1118 mm). *See Table 3.4 above.*
    - ❏ **36"** (914 mm) where serving occupant loads less than 50.

- ❏ **Group E Hallways and Corridors - Section 1007.3.5:**
  - ❏ Width required by occupant load plus 2'-0" (610 mm), **6'-0"** (1829 mm) minimum. *See Table 3.4 above.*
  - ❏ **44"** (1118 mm) minimum where serving less than 100 occupants.

- ❏ **Group I Minimum Hallway and Corridor Width - Section 1007.5.3 and 1007.5.4:**
  - ❏ **8'-0"** (2432 mm) where serving nonambulatory persons.
  - ❏ **6'-0"** (1829 mm) where serving Group I-1.2 surgical areas.
  - ❏ Width required by occupant load, but not less than **44"** (1118 mm) in other corridors. *See Table 3.4 above.*

- ❏ **Exit Passageways - Section 1005.3.4:**
  - ❏ **Minimum Width - Section 1005.3.4.2:**
    - ❏ Width required by occupant load, but not less than **44"** (1118 mm). *See Table 3.4 above.*
    - ❏ **36"** (914 mm) where serving occupant loads less than 50.

Table 3.17: Elevator Lobbies
Sections 403.7 and 1004.3.4.5

- ❏ **High Rise Buildings:**
  - ❏ **Elevator Lobbies Required - Section 403.7:** Provide elevator lobby on all floors.
    - ❏ **Exceptions:**
      - ❏ Main entrance elevator lobbies in office buildings.
      - ❏ Elevator lobbies located within atrium.
      - ❏ Corridors may lead through enclosed elevator lobbies if all areas of building have access to at least 1 required means of egress without passing through such lobby.
- ❏ **Other Buildings:**
  - ❏ **Elevator Lobbies Required - Section 1004.3.4.5:** Provide elevator lobby at each floor where elevator opens into corridor.
    - ❏ **Elevator Lobbies Not Required:**
      - ❏ At street floor lobbies of office buildings if entire street floor is fully sprinklered.
      - ❏ At elevators not required to meet shaft enclosure requirements of Section 711.
      - ❏ **Section 1004.3.3.5:** Where elevator opens into hallway unless smoke- and draft-control assemblies are required for protection of elevator door openings.

Table 3.18: Occupant Load and Exits for Covered Mall Buildings
Section 404.4

❒ **General:** Provide mall building and each tenant space with means of egress.

❒ **Occupant Load - Section 404.4.2:** Assume all portions, including individual tenant spaces, as occupied at same time; provide means of egress for occupant load determined as follows:
  ❒ Divide gross leasable area by 30 for buildings up to 150,000 sf (13 935 m^2).
  ❒ Divide gross leasable area by 40 for buildings up to 350,000 sf (32 516 m^2).
  ❒ Divide gross leasable area by 50 for buildings more than 350,000 sf (32 516 m^2).
  ❒ Do not add occupant load of anchor buildings to mall building.

  ❒ **Food Court Occupant Load:** Compute per UBC Table 10-A. Add to occupant load of mall building.
  ❒ **Anchor Buildings:** Do not include occupant load of anchor buildings in determining means of egress requirements for mall.

❒ **Number of Means of Egress in Tenant Spaces - Section 404.4.3:** Provide at least 2 exits when travel distance to mall exceeds 75'-0" (22 860 mm) within public area of tenant space, or when occupant load of area served by means of egress to mall exceeds 50.
  ❒ **Occupant Load - Public Sales Area:** Compute at 30 sf (2.8 m^2) per occupant.
  ❒ **Occupant Load - Other Areas:** Compute per UBC Table 10-A.

❒ **Means of Egress Arrangement - Section 404.4.4:** Locate Groups A-1, A-2, and A-2.1, except for drinking and dining establishments, so that their entrance is immediately adjacent to a principal entrance to mall. Open not less than half of their required means of egress directly to building exterior.
  ❒ Do not egress malls through anchor buildings.
  ❒ Malls terminating at anchor building with no other means of egress are dead-end malls.
  ❒ **Anchor Buildings:** Provide means of egress independent of mall exit system.

❒ **Maximum Travel Distance - Section 404.5:**
  ❒ **200'-0"** (60 960 mm) from within each individual tenant space.
  ❒ **200'-0"** (60 960 mm) from any point within mall.

❒ **Exit Access - Section 404.4.6:** Arrange means of egress so it is possible to go either direction from any point to separate exit, except for dead ends not exceeding a length 2 times the width of mall at narrowest point within dead-end portion.
  ❒ **Means of Egress Minimum Width:** 66" (1676 mm).

❒ **Malls As Corridors - Section 404.4.7:** Malls may be considered corridors for providing egress but need not be of rated construction or have protected openings when width of mall is as required below:
  ❒ **Minimum Aggregate Clear Width:** 20'-0" (6096 mm).
  ❒ **Minimum Clear Width at Obstructions:** 10'-0" (3048 mm) to a height of 8'-0" (2438 mm) on each side of mall between any projection from tenant space bordering mall and nearest kiosk, vending machine, bench, display, food court, or other egress obstruction.
  ❒ **Kiosks, vending machines and similar uses:** Space at least 20'-0" (6096 mm) apart; 300 sf (28 m^2) maximum area.

Part 4 - Fire Protection Systems

Table 4.1: Sprinkler Systems - General
Section 904.2

☐ **Sprinkler system not required.** (Review all other provisions below prior to checking "Not Required.")
☐ **Sprinkler system required:**
    ☐ Required for construction, area, or height. *See Tables 1.8 through 1.18 above*.
    ☐ Used for Area Increase per Section 505.3. *See Table 1.3 above.*
    ☐ Used for Height or Story Increase per Section 506. *See Table 1.6 above.*
    ☐ Used for Fire Resistive Substitution per Section 508. *See Tables 2.3 above.*
☐ **Sprinkler system required in all Occupancies except R-3 and U - Section 904.2:**
    ☐ **Exterior Openings:**
        ☐ In every story or basement exceeding 1,500 sf (139.4 m^2) without a minimum of 20 sf (1.86 m^2) of opening entirely above ground in each 50 lf (15 240 mm) of exterior wall or fraction thereof, on at least 1 side; 30" (762 mm) minimum opening dimension.
        ☐ When such openings in story or basement are provided on only 1 side and opposite wall of story is more than 75'-0" (22 860 mm) from such openings, unless openings are on 2 sides of story.
        ☐ If any portion of basement is more than 75'-0" (22 860 mm) from such openings, fully sprinkle basement.
    ☐ At top of rubbish and linen chutes and in their terminal rooms.
    ☐ In rooms where nitrate film is stored or handled.
    ☐ In protected combustible fiber storage vaults.
    ☐ Throughout buildings where story with 30 or more occupants is 55"-0" (16 764 mm) above lowest level of fire department access.
    ☐ **Exceptions:**
        ☐ Airport control towers.
        ☐ Open parking structures.
        ☐ Group F-2.
    ☐ In medical gas cylinder storage rooms in Groups B and I where room is not on exterior wall.

Table 4.2: Sprinkler Systems - Group A
Section 904.2

☐ **Group A - Section 904.2.3:** Sprinkler systems required:
    ☐ In assembly rooms where alcoholic beverages are consumed and in unseparated accessory spaces where total area of such accessory spaces and assembly rooms exceeds 5,000 sf (465 m^2). Fully sprinkle other use areas unless separated by 1-hour occupancy separation.
    ☐ In Group A occupancy basements exceeding 1,500 sf (139 m^2).
    ☐ In exhibition and display rooms exceeding 12,000 sf (1114.8 m^2).
    ☐ In enclosed useable space above or below a stairway in Group A.
    ☐ In buildings with multitheater complexes.
    ☐ In amusement buildings except for temporary buildings under 1,000 sf (92.9 m^2) where exit travel distance from any point is less than 50'-0" (15 240 mm).
    ☐ In stages and accessory spaces such as dressing rooms, workshops, and storerooms.
    ☐ In all areas enclosed with walls or ceilings in buildings containing smoke-protected assembly seating.
        ☐ **Exception:** Press boxes and storage facilities less than 1,000 sf (92.9 m^2) in conjunction with outdoor seating where all means of egress in seating area are essentially open to outside.

Table 4.3: Sprinkler Systems - Groups E, F, H, I, M, and R-1
Section 904.2

☐ **Group E - Section 904.2.4:** Sprinkler systems required:
  ☐ In all buildings housing Group E-1 occupancies except:
    ☐ When instruction rooms with at least 1 exterior exit door directly to exterior at ground level and assembly rooms have at least half of required exits directly to exterior at ground level.
    ☐ When area separation or occupancy separation walls of at least 2-hour rating subdivide building into separate compartments, each 20,000 sf (1858 m^2) maximum.
  ☐ In Group E-1 occupancy basements.
  ☐ In enclosed useable space above or below a stairway in Group E-1.

☐ **Group F - Section 904.2.5:** Sprinkler systems required in woodworking occupancies exceeding 2,500 sf (232.3 m^2) containing equipment, machinery, or appliances which generate finely divided combustible waste or which use finely divided combustible material.

☐ **Group H - Section 904.2.6:** Sprinkler systems required:
  ☐ In all Group H-1, H-2, H-3, and H-7 occupancies.
  ☐ In Group H-4 occupancies over 3,000 sf (279 m^2).
  ☐ In buildings with Group H-6 occupancies.

☐ **Group I - Section 904.2.7:** Sprinkler systems required in all Group I occupancies.

☐ **Group M - Section 905.2.8:** Sprinkler systems required:
  ☐ In Group M occupancy rooms exceeding 12,000 sf (1114.8 m^2) on any floor, or 24,000 sf (1858 m^2) on all floors, including area of mezzanines.
  ☐ In Group M occupancies more than 3 stories.

☐ **Group R-1 - Section 905.2.9:** Sprinkler systems required:
  ☐ In apartment houses over 2 stories or containing 16 or more dwelling units.
  ☐ In congregate residences over 2 stories or having more than 19 occupants.
  ☐ In hotels over 2 stories or having more than 19 guest rooms.

Table 4.4: Sprinkler Systems - Special Uses
Chapter 4

☐ **Atria - Section 402.1:** Sprinkler systems throughout buildings with atria.

☐ **Group B Office and Group R-1 High Rise - Section 403.1:** Sprinkler systems required throughout building; may be combined with standpipe system riser.

☐ **Covered Mall Buildings - Section 404.3.1:** Sprinkler systems required throughout building.

Table 4.5: Permissible Sprinkler Omissions
Section 904.4

Sprinklers may be omitted in rooms or areas when permitted by governing jurisdictions as follows:

- ❐ When sprinklers are considered undesirable due to room contents or in noncombustible rooms of wholly noncombustible contents not exposed to other areas.
- ❐ When application of water or flame and water to contents may constitute serious life or fire hazard as in the manufacture or storage of aluminum powder, calcium carbide, calcium phosphide, metallic sodium and potassium, quicklime, magnesium powder, and sodium peroxide.
- ❐ In safe deposit or other vaults of rated construction when used for storage of records, files, or documents are stored in metal cabinets.
- ❐ In communication equipment areas under exclusive control of public communication utility agency provided:
    - ❐ Equipment areas are separated from remainder of building by 1-hour occupancy separation; and
    - ❐ Such areas are used exclusively for such equipment; and
    - ❐ Automatic smoke detection system is installed in such areas and is under central, proprietary, or remote station service or a local alarm giving audible signal at a constantly attended location; and
    - ❐ Other fire-protection equipment such as portable fire extinguishers or Class II standpipes are provided in such areas.
- ❐ Other automatic fire-extinguishing systems may be provided to protect special hazards or occupancies in lieu of automatic sprinklers.

Table 4.6: Standpipes
Table 9-A

- ❐ **Standpipes required:**

❐ **Nonsprinklered building:**	❐ **Sprinklered building:**	❐ **Standpipe system combined with sprinkler system.**
❐ **Standpipe Class:**	❐ **Standpipe Class:**	
❐ Class I	❐ Class I	❐ **Standpipe system required in covered mall buildings.**
❐ Class II	❐ Class II	
❐ Class III	❐ Class III	
❐ **Hose Requirement:**	❐ **Hose Requirement:**	
❐ Not required.	❐ Not required.	
❐ Required.	❐ Required.	

Table 4.7: Smoke Control Systems
Section 905

- ❐ **Smoke Control Systems Required:**

    - ❐ In atrium and areas open to atrium.
    - ❐ In Group B and R-1 high rise buildings.
    - ❐ In stairways serving normally occupied floors more than 75'-0" (22 860 mm) above lowest level of fire department access.
    - ❐ In stages over 1,000 sf (93 m^2).
    - ❐ In stages over 50'-0" (15 240 mm) high.
    - ❐ In covered malls except where mall is only 1 story or where gross leasable area is 24,000 sf (2230 m^2) maximum.

Table 4.8: Fire Alarm and Detection Systems
Section 905

☐ **Group A - Section 303.9:** Provide fire alarm system in A-1, A-2, and A-3.
   ☐ **Amusement Buildings:** Provide smoke detection system and alarm system.

☐ **Group E - Section 305.9:** Provide fire alarm system when occupant load is 50 or more.

☐ **Group H - Section 307.9:** Provide automatic fire alarm system in organic coating manufacturing plants and in aerosol storage warehouses.

☐ **Group H - Section 307.9:** Provide automatic smoke detection system in rooms used for storage, dispensing, use, and handling of hazardous materials when required by Fire Code.

☐ **Group H-6 Storage of Hazardous Materials - Section 307.11.5.5:** Provide manual fire alarm system.

☐ **Group I - Section 308.9:** Provide manual and automatic fire alarm system.

☐ **Group R-1 - Section 310.10:** Provide manual and automatic fire alarm system in:
   ☐ Apartment houses 3 or more stories high or containing more than 15 dwelling units.
   ☐ Hotels more than 2 stories or containing more than 19 guest rooms.
   ☐ Congregate residences more than 2 stories or with more than 19 occupants.
   ☐ **Exceptions:**
      ☐ Manual fire alarm not required in 1 or 2 story buildings when dwelling units and contiguous attic and crawl spaces are separated from each other and public or common areas by 1-hour occupancy separation and each dwelling unit or guest room has exit directly to a public way, exit court, or yard.
      ☐ Separate fire alarm system not required in buildings with supervised sprinkler system throughout and local alarm to notify occupants.

☐ **Group R-1 High Rise - Section 310.10:** Provide fire alarm and communication system.

Part 5 - Structural Forces

Table 5.1: Foundations

Foundation Investigation: _____
Section 1804

_____

Soil Classification: _____
UBC Table 18-I-A

Foundation Pressure: _____
UBC Table 18-I-A

Lateral Pressure:
UBC Table 18-I-A

Expansive Soils: ☐ Yes   ☐ No
Section 1803.2, UBC Tables 18-I-B and 18-I-C

Retaining Wall Pressures: _____
Section 1611.6

Hydrostatic Uplift: _____
Section 1611.8

Liquefaction/Strength Loss Evaluation:
Sections 1804.2 ☐ Required ☐ Not Required
and 1804.5

Frost Line Depth: _____
Section 1806.1

Foundation Type: _____

Table 5.2: Floor Loads
UBC Table 16-A

Floor Area or Use	Uniform Load	Concentrated Load
_____	_____	_____
_____	_____	_____
_____	_____	_____

Impact Loads:

Special Loads:
UBC Table 16-B

Partition Loads:
Section 1606.2

Live Load Reduction:
Sections 1607.5 and 1607.6

Table 5.3: Roof Loads
UBC Table 16-C

Minimum Roof Live Load: _____
UBC Table 16-C

Roof Snow Load: _____
Per Building Official

Live Load Reduction: _____
Section 1607.6

Snow Load Reduction: _____
Section 1614

Table 5.4: Wind Loads

Wind Speed:
UBC Figure 16-1

Exposure:
Section 1616

Equation:
Section 1620

$P = C_e\, C_q\, q_s\, I_w$
$P = Design\ Wind\ Pressure$

**Combined Height, Exposure,
and Gust Factor (C_e):** _____
UBC Table 16-G

Importance Factor (I_w): _____
UBC Table 16-K

Wind Stagnation Pressure (q_s):_____
UBC Table 16-F

Pressure Coefficient (C_q): _____
UBC Table 16-H

Computed Wind Loads:

Wall Field:_____

Wall Areas of Discontinuity: _____

Roof Field: _____

Roof Areas of Discontinuity: _____

Roof Overhangs: _____

Other Elements: _____

Table 5.5: Seismic Loads

Seismic Zone: _____
UBC Figure 16-2

Zone Factor (Z): _____
UBC Table 16-I

Soil Profile Type (S): _____
UBC Table 16-J

Occupancy Category: (I) _____ **(I_p)** _____
Table 16-K

Vertical Structural Irregularities: _____
UBC Table 16-L

Structural System: (R)_____ **(Ω_0)** _____
UBC Table 16-N

Height Limitations: _____
UBC Table 16-N

Horizontal Force Factor: (a_p) _____ **(R_p)** _____
UBC Table 16-O

Nonbuilding Structure Factor: (R)_____ **(Ω_0)** _____
UBC Table 16-P

Plan Structural Irregularities: _____
UBC Table 16-M

Part 2:
Design Requirements

Uniform Building Code Compliance Manual

1997 Uniform Building Code

Building Planning

Code Information Form Review

CIF Table	Code Compliance Item	OK	NA	ID
1.1 - 1.7	**Building Classification:** **Area:** Verify that actual building area is still within limits determined by basic allowable area and area increases.			
	Height: Verify that building height is still within limits determined by basic allowable height and any height increases.			
1.5	**Mixed Occupancy Ratio:** Verify that ratio remains at 1 or less.			
1.8 - 1.18	**Occupancy Requirements:** Verify that specific occupancy requirements have been addressed.			
2.1 - 2.2	**Fire Resistive Construction:** **Fire Resistive Requirements for Building Elements:** Verify that building elements are protected as required by UBC Table 6-A; identify rated assembly designs.			
2.3	**Fire Resistive Substitution:** Verify that fire resistive substitution requirements have been addressed.			
2.4	**Location on Property:** Verify that property line and assumed property lines between buildings on the same lot are identified.			
2.5 - 2.6	**Fire Resistance of Exterior Walls:** Verify that exterior walls and exterior wall openings are protected as required.			
2.7 - 2.8	**Occupancy Separations:** Verify that occupancy groups have been separated as required by UBC Table 3-B.			
2.9	**Area Separation Walls:** Verify that area separation walls divide building areas as required and area separation wall and openings are protected as required.			
2.10	**Construction Type Requirements:** Verify that construction type requirements are documented.			

CIF Table	Code Compliance Item	OK	NA	ID
3.1 - 3.2	**Means of Egress:** **Occupant Load Calculations and Exits Required:** Verify that occupant load and number of exits from individual spaces and from building meet minimum requirements.			
3.3	**Separation of Exits or Exit-Access Doorways:** Verify that exits and exit-access doorways have been separated as required.			
3.4 - 3.5	**Egress Width:** Verify that minimum required egress width has been provided from each means of egress component and from building.			
3.6	**Access to Exits:** Verify that required access to exits from floors and spaces has been provided.			
3.7	**Travel Through Intervening Rooms:** Verify that access to exits is not interrupted by intervening rooms.			
3.8	**Maximum Travel Distance:** Verify that exit travel distance is within maximum allowable distance.			
3.9	**Exit Discharge:** Verify that exits discharge from building according to minimum requirements.			
3.10 - 3.12	**Occupancy Specific Means of Egress Requirements:** Verify that means of egress requirements specific to occupancies have been addressed.			
3.13	**Horizontal Exits:** Verify that horizontal exits meet minimum requirements.			
3.14	**Exit Enclosures:** Verify that means of egress components between exit access and exit discharge are enclosed as required.			
3.15	**Stairs and Ramps:** Verify that width meets minimum requirements.			
3.16	**Hallways, Corridors, and Exit Passageways:** Verify that width meets minimum requirements.			
3.17	**Elevators Lobbies:** Verify that lobbies have been provided where required.			
3.18	**Occupant Load and Exits for Covered Mall Buildings:** Verify that exits, travel distance, exit configuration, and mall width meet minimum requirements.			
4.1 - 4.5	**Fire Protection Systems:** **Sprinkler Systems:** Verify that required systems have been provided.			
4.6	**Standpipes:** Verify that standpipes have been provided where required.			
4.7	**Smoke Control Systems:** Verify that smoke control systems have been provided for where required.			
4.8	**Fire Alarm and Detection Systems:** Verify that fire alarm and detection systems have been provided where required.			
5.1 - 5.5	**Structural Forces:** Verify that the correct structural forces have been used for structural design and for structural support of nonstructural building elements.			

Mixed Use or Occupancy

UBC Section 302

Code Ref.	Code Compliance Item	OK	NA	ID
302.2	**Forms of Occupancy Separations:** Provide complete separation between occupancies using vertical, horizontal, or other separations. See UBC Table 3-A.			
	Horizontal Separations: Protect supporting structural members by equivalent rated construction.			
302.3.1	**4-Hour Occupancy Separations - Walls and Floors:** 4-hour construction; no openings.			
302.3.2	**3-Hour Occupancy Separations - Walls:** 3-hour construction; 3-hour opening protection, total width of all openings not to exceed 25% of wall length in that story, no single opening greater than 120 sf (11 m^2).			
	3-Hour Occupancy Separations - Floors: 3-hour construction; 2-hour opening protection by shaft, stairway, ramp, or escalator enclosures extending above and below openings; 1-1/2 hour enclosure opening protection.			
	Exception: Vertical enclosures above floor opening may be 1-hour if 3-hour vertical enclosures extend below floor opening to foundation with openings protected by 3-hour assemblies provided that:			
	Occupancy above is not required to be Type I FR or Type II FR construction; and			
	Enclosure walls do not enclose an exit stairway, ramp, or escalator required to have 2-hour enclosure.			
302.3.3	**2-Hour Occupancy Separations - Walls and Floors:** 2-hour construction; 1-1/2 hour opening protection.			
302.3.4	**1-Hour Occupancy Separations - Walls and Floors:** 1-hour construction; 1-hour opening protection.			

Group A Occupancies

UBC Section 303

Code Ref.	Code Compliance Item	OK	NA	ID
302.5	**Heating Equipment Room Separation:** 1-hour occupancy separation between rooms containing boilers, central heating plants or hot-water supply boilers, and other spaces when largest piece of fuel equipment exceeds 400,000 Btu per hour (117.2 kW) input.			
	Exterior Wall Openings in Heating Equipment Rooms: 3/4-hour assembly; fixed, self-closing, or automatic closing by smoke detector, when heating room separation is required and when such rooms are located below openings in another story or less than 10'-0" (3048 mm) from other doors or windows of the same building.			
303.2.2 1003.3.4	**Assembly Room Main Floor, Maximum Slope:** **Ramped Aisles:** 1:8 (12.5%).			
	Accessible Ramps: 1:12 (8%).			
	Other Ramps: 1:8 (12.5%).			
303.2.2.2	**Group A-3 Provisions:** Separate Group A-3 spaces with 50 or more occupants from useable space below by 1-hour construction.			
	Group A-3/S-3 Separation: Separate Group A-3 spaces from Group S-3 parking garages in basement or first story by 3-hour construction when S-3 parking garage is considered a separate building for area, story, and construction type.			
303.8	**Special Hazard:** Do not use or store Class I, II, or III liquids in Group A.			

Group B Occupancies

UBC Section 304

Code Ref.	Code Compliance Item	OK	NA	ID
302.5	**Heating Equipment Room Separation:** 1-hour occupancy separation between rooms containing boilers, central heating plants or hot-water supply boilers, and other spaces when largest piece of fuel equipment exceeds 400,000 Btu per hour (117.2 kW) input.			
304.2.2.1	**Laboratories and Vocational Shops - Separation:** Provide 1-hour occupancy separation between spaces containing hazardous materials from each other and other spaces.			
	Laboratories and Vocational Shops - Hazardous Materials: Store and use flammable and combustible liquids as required by Fire Code when quantities do not exceed UBC Tables 3-D or 3-E.			
	Class use as appropriate Group H when hazardous materials exceed UBC Tables 3-D or 3-E.			
	Waste Collection and Removal System: Provide for machinery and equipment which generate finely divided combustible waste or use finely divided combustible material.			
	Exits or Exit-Access Doors: Provide at least 2 in laboratories exceeding 200 sf (18.6 m²).			
	Travel Distance within Laboratories: 75'-0" (22 860 mm) from any point to an exit or exit-access door.			
304.6	**Escalator Enclosure:** Not required in fully sprinkled buildings where 12" (305 mm) draft curtain is provided at the ceiling around perimeter of floor opening.			
304.8	**Special Hazard:** Comply with Fire Code for storage or use of flammable or combustible liquids.			

Group E Occupancies

UBC Section 305

Code Ref.	Code Compliance Item	OK	NA	ID
302.5 305.8	**Heating Equipment Room Separation:** 1-hour occupancy separation between rooms containing boilers, central heating plants or hot-water supply boilers, and other spaces when largest piece of fuel equipment exceeds 400,000 Btu per hour (117.2 kW) input.			
	Exterior Wall Openings in Heating Equipment Rooms: 3/4-hour assembly, fixed, self-closing, or automatic closing by smoke detector, when heating room separation is required and when such rooms are located below openings in another story or less than 10'-0" (3048 mm) from other doors or windows of the same building.			
305.2.4	**Laboratories and Vocational Shops - Separation:** Provide 1-hour occupancy separation between spaces containing hazardous materials from each other and other spaces.			
	Laboratories and Vocational Shops - Hazardous Materials: Store and use flammable and combustible liquids as required by Fire Code when quantities do not exceed UBC Tables 3-D or 3-E; class use as appropriate Group H when quantities exceed UBC Tables 3-D or 3-E.			
	Laboratories and Vocational Shops - Dust Collection and Exhaust System: Provide for machinery and equipment which generate or emit explosive dust or fibers; comply with Mechanical Code.			
	Explosion Venting or Containment System: Provide for systems or equipment used to collect, process, or convey combustible dust or fibers.			
307.8	**Combustible Fiber Storage Rooms:** Separate storage rooms with capacity less than 500 cf (14.2 m^3) from other spaces by 1-hour separation.			
	Separate storage rooms with capacity 500 cf (14.2 m^3) or more from other spaces by 2-hour separation.			
305.8	**Hazardous Material Storage and Use:** Do not place, store, or use Class I, II, or III-A liquids except as necessary in laboratories and classrooms for operation and maintenance; comply with Fire Code.			

Group F Occupancies

UBC Section 306

Code Ref.	Code Compliance Item	OK	NA	ID
302.5	**Heating Equipment Room Separation:** 1-hour occupancy separation between rooms containing boilers, central heating plants or hot-water supply boilers and other spaces when largest piece of fuel equipment exceeds 400,000 Btu per hour (117.2 kW) input.			
306.6	**Group F-2 Floor Opening Enclosure:** Through-floor openings that are not exit enclosures need not be enclosed.			
	Escalator Enclosure: Not required in fully sprinkled buildings where 12" (305 mm) draft curtain is provided at ceiling around floor opening.			
306.8	**Hazardous Materials:** Store and use flammable and combustible liquids in accordance with Fire Code.			
	High-piled Combustible Stock or Aerosol Storage: Comply with Fire Code.			
	Waste Removal and Collection System: Provide for machinery and equipment which generate or emit finely divided combustible waste or use finely divided combustible material.			

Group H Occupancies

UBC Section 307

Code Ref.	Code Compliance Item	OK	NA	ID
302.5	**Heating Equipment Room Separation:** 2-hour occupancy separation between rooms containing boilers, central heating plants or hot-water supply boilers and other spaces;			
	Groups H-1 and H-2: No openings permitted except for necessary piping and ducts.			
307.1.2	**Multiple Hazards:** Address and control all hazards of multiple hazard chemicals.			
307.1.3	**Liquid Use, Dispensing, and Mixing Rooms for Class I, II, and III-A Flammable or Combustible Liquids:** When open containers are used, construct rooms as required for Group H-2 and as follows:			
	Fire Department Access: Provide at least 1 exterior exit door approved by Fire Department for rooms over 500 sf (46.5 m^2).			
	Occupancy Separation: **Rooms up to 150 sf (13.9 m^2):** At least 1-hour separation from other areas.			
	Rooms over 150 sf (13.9 m^2): At least 2-hour separation from other areas.			
	Separations from other occupancies as required by UBC Table 3-B.			
	Room Location: Do not locate in a basement.			
307.1.4	**Liquid Storage Rooms for Class I, II, and III-A Flammable or Combustible Liquids:** When closed containers are used, construct rooms as required for Group H-3 and as follows:			
	Fire Department Access: Provide at least 1 exterior exit door approved by Fire Department for rooms over 500 sf (46.5 m^2).			
307.1.4	**Occupancy Separation:** **Rooms up to 150 sf (13.9 m^2):** At least 1-hour separation from other areas.			
	Rooms over 150 sf (13.9 m^2): At least 2-hour separation from other areas.			

Code Ref.	Code Compliance Item	OK	NA	ID
307.1.4	**Liquid Storage Rooms for Class I, II, and III-A Flammable or Combustible Liquids:** **Occupancy Separations, Continued:** Separations from other occupancies per Section 302 and UBC Table 3-B.			
	Class I Flammable Liquid Storage Rooms: Do not locate in a basement.			
307.1.5	**Liquid Storage Warehouses for Class I, II, and III-A Flammable or Combustible Liquids:** When stored in closed containers, construct rooms as required for H-3 and as follows:			
	Occupancy Separation: 4-hour separation from all other uses.			
	Class I Flammable Liquid Storage Room Location: Do not locate in basement.			
307.1.6	**Hazard Protection Report:** Contact building official to determine need for hazard protection report. *Special expertise is required.*			
307.8	**Waste Removal and Collection System:** Provide for machinery and equipment which generates or emits explosive dust or fibers; comply with Mechanical Code.			
	Explosion Venting or Containment System: Provide for systems or equipment used to collect, process, or convey combustible dust or fibers.			
	Combustible Fiber Storage Room Separation: Separate storage rooms with capacity of 500 cf (14.2 m^3) or less from other spaces by 1-hour occupancy separation.			
	Separate storage rooms with capacity 500 cf (14.2 m^3) or more from other spaces by 2-hour occupancy separation.			
307.10	**Explosion Control - Deflagration:** Provide explosion control, protective devices or suppression systems, or barricades to minimize structural or mechanical damage by controlling or venting gases as required by Fire Code.			
	Explosion Control - Detonation: Provide protective devices or systems such as fully contained barricades.			
	Explosion venting is permitted to minimize damage from less than 2 grams of TNT.			
	Explosion Venting: Provide in exterior walls or roof only. *Special expertise required to design such systems.*			
	Design: Recognize nature of material and behavior in explosions.			
	Prevent serious structural damage and production of lethal projectiles.			
	Regulate aggregate clear vent relief area by pressure resistance of nonrelieving portion of building.			

Group H-6 Occupancies

UBC Section 307.11

Code Ref.	Code Compliance Item	OK	NA	ID
307.11.1	**General:** Comply with Fire Code.			
307.11.2.1	**Fabrication Area Occupancy Separation:** 1-hour occupancy separation between fabrication areas whose size is limited by quantities of hazardous production materials (HPM) permitted by Fire Code, and from corridors and other parts of building.			
	Locate fabrication areas at or above first story.			
	Doors in Occupancy Separations: 3/4-hour rated, self-closing only.			
	Windows Between Fabrication Areas and Corridors: When in 1-hour walls, limit to 25% of area of room/corridor wall, 3/4-hour rated.			
307.11.2.2	**Fabrication Area Floor Openings:** Unprotected when interconnected levels are used only for mechanical equipment directly related to fabrication area.			
307.11.4	**Service Corridors:** Classify as Group H-6 occupancy.			
	1-hour occupancy separation from corridors.			
	Exits from Service Corridors: At least 2, not more than half of which may open into a fabrication area.			
	Doors from Service Corridors: Swing in direction of exit travel, self-closing.			
	Minimum Clear Width: 5'-0" (1524 mm), or 33" (838 mm) wider than widest cart or truck used, whichever is greater.			
307.11.5.1	**Storage of Hazardous Production Materials:** When quantities exceed UBC Tables 3-D or 3-E, store materials in liquid storage rooms, HPM rooms, or gas rooms per Fire Code.			
	HPM Storage Room Separations: Separated from other areas per UBC Table 3-B and as follows:			
	At least 2-hour occupancy separation when 300 sf (27.9 m^2) or more.			
	At least 1-hour occupancy separation when less than 300 sf (27.9 m^2).			
307.11.5.3	**HPM Storage Room Means of Egress:** When 2 are required, provide 1 directly to exterior.			

Group I Occupancies

UBC Section 308

Code Ref.	Code Compliance Item	OK	NA	ID
302.5 308.8	**Heating Equipment Room Separation:** 1-hour occupancy separation between rooms containing boilers, central heating plants or hot-water supply boilers and other spaces when largest piece of fuel equipment exceeds 400,000 Btu per hour (117.2 kW) input.			
	Exterior Wall Openings in Heating Equipment Rooms: 3/4-hour assembly, fixed, self-closing, or automatic closing by smoke detector, when heating room separation is required and when such rooms are located below openings in another story or less than 10'-0" (3048 mm) from other doors or windows of the same building.			
308.2.2.1	**Group I-1.1 - Smoke Barriers:** Divide floor levels with occupant load of 50 or more used by inpatients for sleeping or treatment into at least 2 compartments by 1-hour smoke barriers complying with Section 905.2.3.			
	Group I-1.1 - Smoke Control Zone Area: Not more than 22,500 sf (2090 m^2), width and length not exceeding 150'-0" (45 720 mm).			
	Accommodate occupants of smoke zone and any adjoining smoke zone with not less than 30 sf (2.8 m^2) net clear area for bed and litter patients and 6 sf (0.6 m^2) net clear area for other occupants.			
	Group I-1.1 - Doors in Smoke Barriers: Minimum 44" (1118 mm) for passage of beds and equipment and 32" (813 mm) for other exits; 20-minute rated.			
	When installed across corridors, provide pair of opposite-swinging doors without center mullion or horizontal sliding doors.			
	Group I-1.1 - Smoke Control Zone Means of Egress: At least 2 means of egress from each zone.			
	Means of egress may pass through adjacent zones provided it does not return through the zone where exiting originated.			
308.8	**Special Hazards:** Provide occupancy separations between specific use areas and Group I-1.1 hospitals or nursing homes in accordance with UBC Table 3-C.			
	Store and handle flammable or combustible liquids per Fire Code.			

Group M Occupancies

UBC Section 309

Code Ref.	Code Compliance Item	OK	NA	ID
302.5	**Heating Equipment Room Occupancy:** 1-hour separation between rooms containing boilers, central heating plants or hot-water supply boilers and other spaces when largest piece of fuel equipment exceeds 400,000 Btu per hour (117.2 kW) input.			
309.3	**Storage Area Provisions:** Separate wholesale or retail sales storage areas from public areas by 1-hour occupancy separation.			
	Exceptions:			
	Storage area is 1,000 sf (93 m^2) or less,			
	Storage area is sprinklered and is 3,000 sf (279 m^2) or less, or			
	. Building is fully sprinklered.			
309.6	**Escalator Enclosure:** Not required in fully sprinkled buildings where 12" (305 mm) draft curtain is provided at ceiling around perimeter of floor opening.			
309.8	**Special Hazards:** Comply with Fire Code for storage and use of flammable and combustible liquids and for housing of high-piled combustible stock or aerosols.			

Group R Occupancies

UBC Section 310

Code Ref.	Code Compliance Item	OK	NA	ID
302.5	**Heating Equipment Room Occupancy Separation:** 1-hour separation between rooms containing boilers, central heating plants or hot-water supply boilers and other spaces when largest piece of fuel equipment exceeds 400,000 Btu per hour (117.2 kW) input.			
	Group R-1: No separation required when equipment serves only 1 dwelling unit.			
310.2.2	**Group R-1 Separation:** Separate dwelling units and hotel guest rooms from each other with 1-hour construction.			
	Group R-1 Storage or Laundry Rooms: When used in common by tenants, provide not less than 1-hour occupancy separation from the rest of building.			
310.4	**Emergency Escapes:** For dwelling unit basements and sleeping rooms below fourth story, provide at least 1 operable window or door for emergency or rescue opening into public street, public alley, yard, or exit court.			
	Exception: Such window or door may open into atrium provided it opens onto exit-access balcony and dwelling or guest room has another exit or exit-access doorway not opening into atrium.			
	Escape and Rescue Windows - Sill Below Finish Grade: Provide window well as follows:			
	Clear horizontal dimensions of window well: Allow the window to fully open, 9 sf (0.84 m²) minimum accessible net clear opening, minimum dimension of 36" (914 mm).			
	Well depth over 44" (1118 mm): Provide permanent fixed ladder or stairs accessible when window is in full open position; 6" (1829 mm) maximum encroachment of stair or ladder into required well dimension.			

Code Ref.	Code Compliance Item	OK	NA	ID
310.6.1	**Minimum Ceiling Heights:** 7'-6" (2286 mm) in habitable spaces.			
	7'-0" (2134 mm) to lowest projection in kitchens, halls, bathrooms, toilet compartments.			
	At exposed beams, measure from bottom of exposed beams where beams are less than 48" (1219 mm) on center or from bottom of deck where beams are more than 48" (1219 mm) on center; 7'-0" (2134 mm) minimum from bottom of beams.			
	Minimum Ceiling Height - Sloped Ceiling: Minimum height required in half of room only. Do not include areas with ceiling less than 5'-0" (1524 mm) in minimum area computations.			
	Minimum Ceiling Height - Furred Ceilings: 7'-0" (2134 mm) in not more than 1/3 of room area.			
310.6.2	**Floor Area - Dwelling Units and Congregate Residences:** Minimum of 1 room not less than 120 sf (11.2 m²).			
	Other Habitable Rooms: 70 sf (6.5 m²) minimum, except kitchens.			
310.6.3	**Room Dimensions - Width:** Except for kitchens, 7'-0" (2134 mm) minimum in any dimension.			
310.7	**Efficiency Dwelling Units - Minimum Requirements:** **Living Rooms:** Minimum 220 sf (20.4 m²) superficial area; add 100 sf (9.3 m²) for each occupant over 2.			
	Separate Closet: Minimum 1 required.			
	Kitchens: Sink, cooking appliance, refrigerator, with 30" (762 mm) minimum clear working space in front of each.			
	Bathroom: Water closet, lavatory, bathtub or shower.			

Group S Occupancies

UBC Section 311

Code Ref.	Code Compliance Item	OK	NA	ID
302.5	**Heating Equipment Room Separation:** 1-hour occupancy separation between rooms containing boilers, central heating plants or hot-water supply boilers and other spaces when largest piece of fuel equipment exceeds 400,000 Btu per hour (117.2 kW) input.			
311.2.3.2	**Canopies over Fuel Dispensers:** 13'-6" (4114 mm) clear, unobstructed height to lowest projection in vehicle drive-through area.			
	Occupancy Separation between Canopy Covered Fuel Dispensers and Group M Retail Store: Not required where canopy is open on at least 3 sides, Group M retail store is less than 2,500 sf (225 m²), and when following conditions exist:			
	Retail store has 2 exits or exit-access doorways, not located on the same exterior wall, separated by a distance equal to half of maximum overall diagonal dimension of building, measured in straight line between exits.			
	Fuel dispenser islands are at least 20'-0" (6096 mm) from retail store.			
311.2.3.3	**Parking Garage - Minimum Headroom:** 7'-0" (2134 mm) to any ceiling, beam, pipe, or similar obstruction, except for wall-mounted shelves, storage surfaces, racks, or cabinets.			
311.6	**Group S-2 Floor Openings:** Need not be enclosed except for exits.			
	Escalator Enclosure: Not required in fully sprinkled buildings where 12" (305 mm) draft curtain is provided around perimeter of floor opening.			
311.9.2.2	**Group S-4 Parking Garages:** **Exterior Ventilation Openings:** Provide uniformly distributed ventilation openings in exterior walls on 2 or more sides.			
	Provide open area of at least 20% of total perimeter wall area of each tier.			
	Provide minimum of 40% of perimeter of tier as aggregate length of ventilation openings.			
	Interior Ventilation Openings: Uniformly distribute ventilation openings in interior walls and column lines.			
	Provide open area of at least 20% of wall area.			
311.9.3	**Group S-4 Parking Garage Construction:** Provide noncombustible materials.			

Code Ref.	Code Compliance Item	OK	NA	ID
311.9.10	**Group S-4 Parking Garages - Vertical Opening Enclosure:** Not required except for lifts provided for attendants only.			
311.10.2	**Helistops - Touchdown or Landing Area Size:** 20'-0" by 20'-0" (6096 mm by 6096 mm) minimum for 3,500 lb (1588 kg) helicopters.			
	Clear Area: Provide average width of 15'-0" (4572 mm) on all sides, 5'-0" (1424 mm) minimum.			
311.10.3	**Helistops - Design:** Noncombustible construction for landing area and supports.			
	Design landing area to confine Class I, II, or II-A liquid spillage to landing area and drain spillage away from exits or stairway serving landing area or from structures housing such exits or stairway.			
311.10.4	**Helistops - Means of Egress:** Provide at least 2 means of egress from landing areas located on buildings or structures.			
	When landing area or roof area is less than 60'-0" (18 288 mm) long or less than 2,000 sf (186 m²), second means of egress may be fire escape or ladder to floor below.			

Group U Occupancies

UBC Section 312

Code Ref.	Code Compliance Item	OK	NA	ID
312.2.3	**Headroom Clearance:** 7'-0" (2134 mm) to any ceiling, beam, pipe, or similar structure in garages connected with Group R-1, except for wall-mounted shelves, storage surfaces, racks, or cabinets.			
312.4	**Special Hazards:** Do not use private garages for sleeping purposes.			
312.4	**Special Hazards:** Do not store or use Class I, II, or III-A liquids unless complying with Fire Code.			
312.5	**Garage Floor Surface:** Noncombustible materials or asphaltic paving where motor vehicles are stored or operated.			
503.4.8	**Exception to Table 5-A - Group U-1:** Exterior walls required to be 1-hour due to location on property may be protected only on exterior side with materials permitted for 1-hour construction.			

Atria

UBC Section 402

Code Ref.	Code Compliance Item	OK	NA	ID
402.3	**Enclosure of Atria:** Separate from adjacent spaces by minimum of 1-hour construction.			
	Exceptions: Separation between atria and tenant spaces which are not guest rooms, congregate residences, or dwelling units may be omitted at 3 floor levels.			
	Open exit balconies are permitted within atrium.			
	Enclosure Doors: 20 minute.			
402.4	**Escalators and Elevators:** May be unenclosed where located entirely in atrium, unless required to be enclosed by Chapter 30.			
402.5.2	**Group I Exits:** Except in jails, prisons, and reformatories, Group I sleeping rooms may not have required means of egress through atriums.			
402.5.3	**Stairs and Ramps:** Enclose stairs and ramps in atrium.			
	Exceptions: Stairs and ramps not required for egress.			
	Stairs and ramps connecting only lowest 2 floors in atrium.			
	Stairs and ramps connecting floor levels within a story.			
402.6	**Occupancy Separation Exceptions:** Vertical portion of separation adjacent to atrium may be omitted between Group B office, Group M sales area, Group A-3, or Group R-1 apartment, congregate residence, or guest room located on another level.			

High Rise Buildings
(Group B Office and Group R-1)

UBC Section 403

Code Ref.	Code Compliance Item	OK	NA	ID
403.2.2	**Group R Emergency Windows:** Not required.			
403.4	**Smoke Control:** Provide system in complying with Chapter 9.			
403.5	**Fire Alarm and Communication System:** Provide fire alarm, emergency voice/alarm signaling system, and fire department communication system complying with Fire Code and this section.			
403.6	**Central Control Station:** Provide central control station room for fire department operations, located and accessible as approved by the fire department.			
	Separation: 1-hour occupancy separation from all other areas.			
	Minimum Dimensions: 96 sf (9 m^2) and 8'-0" (2438 mm) in any direction.			
403.7	**Elevator Lobbies:** Provide on all floors.			
	Elevator Lobby Separation: 1-hour separation from other areas of building, including means of egress.			
	Exceptions: Main entrance elevator lobbies in office buildings.			
	Elevator lobbies located within atrium.			
	Corridors may lead through enclosed elevator lobbies if all areas of building have access to at least 1 required means of egress without passing through such lobby.			
	Elevator Lobby Doors: Minimum 20-minute.			
	Elevator Lobby Fixed Glazing: 3/4-hour rated, not exceeding 25% of area of common wall between atrium and room.			

Covered Mall Buildings

UBC Section 404

Code Ref.	Code Compliance Item	OK	NA	ID
404.1.1	**Scope and Purpose:** Applies to covered mall buildings not more than 3 levels except for covered mall buildings conforming with all other applicable code provisions and terminals for transportation facilities and lobbies of hotels, apartments, and office buildings.			
	Covered Mall Building Definition: Single building enclosing a number of tenants such as retail stores, drinking and eating establishments, entertainment and amusement facilities, offices, and other similar uses wherein 2 or more tenants have main entrance into mall.			
404.3.5	**Tenant Separation:** 1-hour separation from other tenant spaces extending from floor to underside of ceiling above. Ceiling need not be rated unless required elsewhere.			
	No separation required between tenant space and mall except where required for occupancy separation or for smoke control purposes.			
404.3.9	**Anchor Building Openings Into Mall:** Need not be protected in Type I, Type II-FR, Type II 1-hour, or Type II-N except for occupancy separations between Group R-1 sleeping rooms and mall.			

Stages and Platforms

UBC Section 405

Code Ref.	Code Compliance Item	OK	NA	ID
405.3.1	**Stage Construction:** Provide minimum type of construction as required for building. Floor finish may be wood in all types of construction.			
	Stages - Separation: Provide 2-hour occupancy separation from other areas when stage is 50'-0" (15 240 mm) high or more.			
	Accessory Space Separation: Where stage is 50'-0" (15 240 mm) or less, provide 1-hour occupancy separation from other accessory spaces.			
	Exception: Control rooms and follow spot rooms may be open to audience.			
405.3.2	**Accessory Rooms:** Separate dressing rooms, workshops, storerooms, and other accessory spaces contiguous to stages from each other and other building areas by 1-hour occupancy separation.			
	Exception: No separation required for stages 500 sf (46.5 m²) or less.			
405.3.4	**Proscenium Opening:** Where 2-hour proscenium wall protection is required, protect opening by fire curtain or water curtain complying with UBC Standard 4-1.			

Motion Picture Projection Rooms

UBC Section 406

Code Ref.	Code Compliance Item	OK	NA	ID
406.1	**Scope:** Section applies where ribbon-type cellulose acetate or other safety film is used in conjunction with electric arc, xenon, or other light-source projection equipment which develops hazardous gases, dust, or radiation.			
	Comply with Fire Code where cellulose nitrate film is used.			
406.1.2	**Projection Room:** Enclose motion picture machine in a projection room.			
406.2	**Projection Room Construction:** Permanent construction, consistent with building type, opening protection not required.			
	Projection Room Area: 80 sf (7.4 m^2) minimum for single machine and 40 sf (3.7 m^2) minimum for each additional machine.			
	Minimum Working Space: 30" by 30" (762 mm by 762 mm) on each side and rear of each projector, floodlight, spotlight, or similar equipment; only 1 such space required between 2 adjacent projectors.			
406.2	**Ceiling Height - Projection Room and Appurtenant Rooms:** 7'-6" (2287 mm) minimum.			
406.3	**Means of Egress - Safety Film Projection Rooms:** Only 1 exit or exi- access door required.			
406.4	**Projection Ports and Openings:** Maximum aggregate opening of 25% of area of wall between projection room and auditorium.			
	Provide glass or other approved material to completely close all openings.			
406.6	**Miscellaneous Equipment:** Provide rewind and film storage in each projection room.			
	Only 4 containers for flammable liquids permitted in each projection booth; containers not greater than 16 oz (473.2 mL) capacity each.			
406.7	**Sanitary Facilities:** Provide lavatory and water closet where room serves an assembly occupancy.			
	Exception: Where automatic projection equipment does not require projectionist.			

Pedestrian Walkways

UBC Section 409

Code Ref.	Code Compliance Item	OK	NA	ID
409.1	**General:** Consider as a separate building when determining roof covering classification in UBC Table 15-A.			
	When walkway connects separate buildings, need not be considered as separate building, and need not be considered in allowable floor area of connected buildings when walkway complies with the section.			
409.2	**Construction:** Noncombustible materials.			
	Exceptions: May be heavy timber where walkways connect Type III, IV, or V construction.			
	May be of any materials when located on grade, having both sides open by at least 50%, and connecting buildings of Type III, IV, or V construction.			
409.3	**Openings Between Pedestrian Walkways and Buildings:** In addition to other requirements for openings, comply with Section 1005.8 for opening protection or construction walkway with both sides open 50% minimum, openings distributed to prevent accumulation of smoke and gases.			
409.4	**Unobstructed Width:** 44" (1118 mm) minimum, 30'-0" (9144 mm) maximum.			
409.5	**Maximum Length:** **Unsprinkled:** 300'-0" (91.44 m). **Sprinkled:** 400'-0" (121.92 m). **Unenclosed Walkways at Grade:** Unlimited.			
409.6	**Multiple Walkways:** 40'-0" (2 192 mm) minimum distance between walkways on same horizontal plane.			
409.7	**Required Means of Egress:** Do not use pedestrian walkways as required means of egress unless at grade.			
	Where at grade and used as required means of egress, provide unobstructed egress to public way; width in inches not less than occupant load multiplied by 0.3 (7.62).			
	Exception: Pedestrian walkways meeting requirements for horizontal exits may be used as means of egress.			
409.8	**Walkways over Public Streets:** Obtain approval of local jurisdictions.			

General Building Limitations

UBC Chapter 5

Code Ref.	Code Compliance Item	OK	NA	ID
504.6	**Area Separation Walls:** Provide a complete separation where area separation walls are required.			
	Area Separation Walls and Occupancy Separation Walls: Where separation walls serve to separate occupancies and area, apply the most restrictive requirements to walls and openings.			
504.6.2	**Area Separation Wall Fire Resistance:** Not less than 4-hours in Types I, II-FR, III, and IV.			
	Not less than 2-hours in Types II 1-hour, II-N, and V.			
	Wall Openings: Do not exceed 25% of length of wall in each story.			

Types of Construction

UBC Chapter 6

Code Ref.	Code Compliance Item	OK	NA	ID
602.1	**Type I Buildings:** **Walls and Permanent Partitions:** Noncombustible rated construction.			
	Fire-retardant treated wood permitted in 1- or 2-hour rated permanent nonload-bearing partitions.			
602.2	**Structural Framework:** Structural steel, reinforced concrete, or reinforced masonry.			
602.3	**Exterior Walls and Openings:** Per Section 503 and UBC Tables 5-A and 6-A.			
602.4	**Stairway Construction:** Reinforced concrete or steel with treads and risers of concrete or steel.			
	Brick, marble, tile, or other hard noncombustible materials permitted for finish of treads and risers.			
	Exception: Finish may be any material permitted on unenclosed stairs.			
602.5	**Roofs:** Except in Group M or S-1 retail sales and storage areas and Group H, roofs and members, except for structural frame, may be unprotected noncombustible materials when every part of roof framing, including structural frame is 25'-0" (7620 mm) or more above floor, balcony, or gallery immediately below.			
	Heavy-timber members permitted as such unprotected members in 1-story buildings.			
	Where every part of structural framework of roof of Group A or E or an atrium is at least 25'-0" (7620 mm) above any floor, balcony or gallery, protection of roof construction and structural frame may be omitted.			
	Heavy-timber members permitted as such unprotected members in 1-story buildings.			

Code Ref.	Code Compliance Item	OK	NA	ID
602.5	**Type I Buildings:** **Roofs, Continued:** Unprotected noncombustible or heavy-timber construction may be less than 25'-0" (7620 mm) above any floor, balcony, or gallery of Group A2.1 with 10,000 or more occupants under following conditions:			
	Building is 1-story except for multi-level areas under roof and used for locker rooms, exiting, concession stands, mechanical rooms, and other rooms accessory to assembly room.			
	Area where roof clearance is less than 25'-0" (7620 mm) is not more than 35% of area encompassed by exterior walls.			
	Building is fully sprinkled.			
	Where every part of structural steel framework in Group A or E is more than 18'-0" (5486 mm) and less than 25'-0" (7620 mm) above any floor, balcony, or gallery, protect roof construction by 1-hour ceiling.			
603.1	**Type II Buildings:** **Structural Elements - Type II-FR:** Steel, concrete, or masonry.			
	Structural Elements - Type II 1-Hour and Type II-N: Noncombustible.			
	Walls and Partitions - Type II-FR: Noncombustible and rated.			
	Fire-retardant treated wood permitted in assemblies of 1- or 2-hour rated permanent nonload-bearing partitions.			
	Walls and Partitions - Type II-N: Noncombustible construction.			
	Type II 1-Hour Construction: Noncombustible and 1-hour rated throughout.			
	Fire-retardant treated wood permitted permanent nonload-bearing partitions if rating requirements are met.			
603.3	**Exterior Walls and Openings:** Section 503 and UBC Tables 5-A and 6-A.			
603.4	**Stairway Construction - Type II-FR:** Reinforced concrete or steel with treads and risers of concrete or steel.			
	Brick, marble, tile, or other hard noncombustible materials permitted for finish of treads and risers.			
	Stairway Construction - Type II 1-Hour and Type II-N: Noncombustible construction.			
	Exception: Finish may be any material permitted on unenclosed stairs.			
603.5	**Roofs:** Noncombustible construction.			
	Type II-FR and Type II 1-Hour: Construction per Section 602.5 permitted.			
604.2	**Type III Buildings:** **Structural Framework:** Steel, concrete, masonry, or wood.			

Code Ref.	Code Compliance Item	OK	NA	ID
604.3	**Type III Buildings, Continued:** **Exterior Walls and Openings:** Section 503 and UBC Tables 5-A and 6-A.			
604.4	**Interior Stairways:** Any material permitted in buildings 3-stories or less.			
	As required for Type I construction in buildings 4-stories or more.			
	Exterior Stairways: Noncombustible construction.			
	May be of wood in buildings 2-stories or less, at least 2" (51 mm) nominal thickness.			
604.5	**Roofs:** Except in Group M or S-1 retail sales and storage areas and Group H, roofs and members, except for structural frame, may be unprotected noncombustible materials when every part of roof framing, including structural frame is 25'-0" (7620 mm) or more above floor, balcony, or gallery immediately below.			
	Heavy-timber members permitted as such unprotected members in 1-story buildings.			
605.1	**Type IV Buildings:** **Definition:** May be of any material permitted.			
	Conform to 605.6 below except that permanent partitions and members of structural frame may be of other materials provided they are at least 1-hour rated.			
605.2	**Structural Framework:** Steel, concrete, masonry, or wood.			
605.3	**Exterior Walls and Openings:** Section 503 and UBC Tables 5-A and 6-A.			
605.4	**Interior Stairways:** Wood or per Type I construction in buildings 3-stories or less.			
	Constructed per Type I construction in buildings 4-stories or more.			
	Exterior Stairways: Noncombustible construction.			
	May be of wood in buildings 2-stories or less, at least 2" (51 mm) nominal thickness.			
605.6	**Type IV - Heavy-Timber Construction:** **General:** Framed sawn timbers or structural glued-laminated timber. All dimensions below are nominal.			
605.6.2	**Columns:** Minimum 8" (203 mm) in any dimension when supporting roof or floor loads, except for arches in 605.6.4 below.			
605.6.3	**Floor Framing:** Minimum 6" (152 mm) width, 10" (254 mm) depth.			
	Where arches spring from floor line and support floor loads, minimum 8" (203 mm) in any dimension.			
	Trusses supporting floor loads: 8" (203 mm) in any dimension.			

Code Ref.	Code Compliance Item	OK	NA	ID
605.6.4	**Type IV - Heavy-Timber Construction, Continued:** **Roof Framing:** Minimum 6" (152 mm) width and 8" (203 mm) depth for lower half of height and 6" (152 mm) depth for upper half for arches springing from floor line and not supporting floor loads.			
	Minimum 4" (102 mm) width, 6" (152 mm) depth for arches springing from tops of walls or abutments, trusses or other framing not supporting floors.			
	Spaced members may be 2 or more pieces, minimum 3" (76 mm) thick, when solid blocked throughout intervening spaces, or when such spaces are tightly closed by continuous wood cover plate of 2" (51 mm) minimum thickness, secured to underside of members.			
	Splice plates: Minimum 3" (76 mm) thick.			
	Sprinkler System Under Roof Deck: 3" (76 mm) minimum thickness framing members permitted.			
605.6.5	**Floors:** No concealed spaces allowed.			
	Splined or tongue-and-groove planks, minimum 3" (76 mm) thick, covered with 1" (25 mm) thick tongue-and-groove flooring or 15/32" (12 mm) thick wood structural panels.			
	Planks, 4" (102 mm) width, set on edge close together, well spiked, covered with 1" (25 mm) thick tongue-and-groove flooring or 15/32" (12 mm) thick wood structural panels.			
605.6.6	**Roof Decks:** No concealed spaces allowed.			
	Splined or tongue-and-groove planks, minimum 2" (51 mm) thick, 1-1/8" (29 mm) tongue-and-groove structural panels with exterior glue.			
	Double thickness, 1" (25 mm) thick tongue-and-groove boards.			
	Lumber 3" (76 mm) width, set on edge close together, well spiked.			
606.1	**Type V Buildings:** May be of any permitted materials.			
606.2	**Structural Framework:** Steel, concrete, masonry, or wood.			
606.3	**Exterior Walls and Openings:** Section 503 and UBC Tables 5-A and 6-A.			
606.4	**Interior Stairways:** Any permitted material.			
	Exterior Stairways: Wood at least 2" (51 mm) nominal thickness or noncombustible materials.			
606.5	**Roofs:** Except in Group M, S-1 retail sales and storage areas, and Group H, roofs and members, except structural frame, may be unprotected noncombustible materials when roof framing, including structural frame is 25'-0" (7620 mm) or more above floor, balcony, or gallery immediately below.			
	Heavy-timber members permitted as such unprotected members in 1-story buildings.			

Fire-Resistant Materials and Construction

UBC Chapter 7

Code Ref.	Code Compliance Item	OK	NA	ID
709.4.1	**Parapets:** Provide on all exterior walls.			
	Parapets not required where: Wall is not required to be rated.			
	Wall may have unprotected openings due to location on property.			
	Building is not more than 1,000 sf (93 m^2) on any floor.			
	Walls which terminate at roofs of not less than 2-hour construction or roofs constructed of noncombustible materials.			
	1-hour rated exterior walls may terminate at underside of roof sheathing, deck or slab.			
	Where roof-ceiling framing is parallel to wall, framing and elements supporting such framing shall be 1-hour rated for a width of 5'-0" (1524 mm) measured from interior side of wall for Groups M and R and 10'-0" (3048 mm) for other occupancies.			
	Where roof-ceiling framing is perpendicular to wall, entire span of such framing and elements supporting such framing shall be 1-hour rated.			
	Do not locate openings in roof closer than 5'-0" (1524 mm) of 1-hour exterior wall for Groups M and R and 10'-0" (3048 mm) for other occupancies.			
	Entire building has Class B roof assembly.			

Code Ref.	Code Compliance Item	OK	NA	ID
709.4.2	**Parapet Construction - Height:** 30" minimum from point where roof surface and parapet wall intersect.			
	Height at Sloping Roofs - Slopes Greater than 2:12 (16.7%): Extend parapet to same height as any portion of roof within the distance where exterior opening protection is required, 30" minimum.			
711.2	**Shaft Enclosures:** Enclose openings through floors and extend enclosures from lowest floor opening through successive floor openings; enclose top and bottom.			
	Exceptions: Top enclosure not required where shafts extend to underside of roof sheathing, deck, or slab.			
	Bottom enclosure not required when protected by fire dampers at lowest floor level within shaft enclosure.			
711.3	**Shaft Enclosures - Special Provision:** Except in Group I, openings which penetrate only 1 floor and are not connected with openings communicating with other stories or basements and which are not concealed in building construction assemblies need not be enclosed.			
711.5	**Rubbish and Linen Chutes:** Terminate in rooms separated from remainder of building by occupancy separation rated as required for shafts, not less than 1-hour.			
	Do not locate openings in exit corridors or stairways.			

Fire-Protection Systems

UBC Chapter 9

Code Ref.	Code Compliance Item	OK	NA	ID
904.5	**Standpipes:** Verify that sufficient space has been provided to keep standpipes and outlets out of required stairway widths.			
904.5.3	**Class I Standpipes - Location:** Provide outlet connection at every floor-level landing of every required stairway above or below grade.			
	Locate outlets at stairways in exit enclosure.			
	Outlets at pressurized enclosures may be located in vestibule or exterior balcony giving access to stairway.			
	Provide outlet locations on each side of wall adjacent to exit openings of horizontal exits.			
	Enclosure: Protect risers and laterals not in exit enclosure with same rating as required for shaft enclosures.			
	Such enclosure not required in fully sprinklered buildings.			
904.5.4	**Class II Standpipes - Location:** Provide in accessible locations such that all portions of building are within 30'-0" (9144 mm) of nozzle on 100'-0" (30 480 mm) hose.			
	Groups A-1 and A-2.1: Where occupant load exceeds 1,000, locate outlets on each side of stage, on each side of rear of auditorium, and on each side of balcony.			
904.5.5	**Class III Standpipes - Location:** Provide outlet connection at every floor-level landing of every required stairway above or below grade.			
	Locate outlets at stairways in exit enclosure.			
	Outlets at pressurized enclosures may be located in vestibule or exterior balcony giving access to stairway.			
	Provide outlet connections on each side of wall adjacent to exit openings of horizontal exits.			
	Enclosure: Protect risers and laterals not in exit enclosure with same rating required for shaft enclosures; enclosure not required in sprinkled buildings.			
	Laterals for Class II outlets on Class III systems need not be protected.			

Code Ref.	Code Compliance Item	OK	NA	ID
904.5.5	**Standpipes in Groups A-1 and A-2.1:** Provide Class II outlets where occupant load exceeds 1,000, locate outlets on each side of stage, on each side of rear of auditorium, and on each side of balcony.			
905.1	**Smoke Control System:** Provide smoke control systems in locations as follows:			
	In atrium and areas open to atrium.			
	In Group B and R-1 high rise buildings.			
	In covered malls except where mall is only 1 story or where gross leasable area is not over 24,000 sf (2230 m^2).			
	In stages over 1,000 sf (93 m2) or stages over 50'-0" (15 240 mm) high.			
	In stairways serving normally occupied floors more than 75'-0" above lowest level of fire department access.			

Means of Egress

UBC Chapter 10

Code Ref.	Code Compliance Item	OK	NA	ID
1003.2.4	**Means of Egress Height:** Minimum 7'-0" (2134 mm) clear height to lowest projection or overhead structure.			
1003.2.6	**Changes in Elevation:** Provide stairs, steps, or ramps at interior and exterior changes of 12" (305 mm) or more.			
	Provide ramps at interior changes less than 12" (305 mm) along exits serving more than 10 occupants, except in Group R-3 and Group R-1 dwelling units, and along aisles adjoining seating areas.			
1003.2.7	**Elevators and Escalators:** Do not use as required exit.			
1003.3.1.2	**Special Doors:** Do not use revolving, sliding, or overhead doors as required exits where serving 10 or more occupants.			
	Exceptions: **Revolving Doors:** Permitted where:			
	Leaves collapse under opposing pressure.			
	6'-6" (1981 mm) minimum width.			
	1 conforming exit door is adjacent.			
	Revolving door is not considered to provide required means of egress width.			
	Horizontal Sliding Doors: Permitted where complying with UBC Standard 7-8 in elevator lobby separations, in smoke barriers in other than Groups A and H, and when serving less than 50 occupants in other than Group H.			
	Power Operated Doors: May be used as exits when complying with UBC Standard 10-1.			
1003.3.1.3	**Exit Door - Minimum Width and Height:** 3'-0" (914 mm) wide, 6'-8" (2032 mm) height; 32" (813 mm) minimum clear opening.			
1003.3.1.4	**Exit Door - Maximum Leaf Width:** 48" (1219 mm).			

Code Ref.	Code Compliance Item	OK	NA	ID
1003.3.1.5	**Exit Doors - Swing and Opening Force:** Pivoted or side-hinged swinging type.			
	Swing in direction of travel when serving hazardous areas or occupant loads of 50 or more.			
1003.3.1.5	**Double Acting Doors:** Not permitted as exit when:			
	Occupant load served by door is 100 or more.			
	Door is part of fire assembly.			
	Door is part of smoke/draft control assembly.			
	Panic hardware is required or provided on door.			
1003.3.1.6	**Floor Level at Doors:** Provide floor or landing on each side of door.			
	Exceptions: Doors serving building equipment rooms not normally occupied.			
	Groups R-3, U and Individual Dwelling Units of R-1: Door may open at top step of interior flight of stairs, provided door does not swing over top step.			
	Door may open at landing not more than 8" (203 mm) lower than floor level, provided door does not swing over landing.			
	Screen and storm doors may swing over stairs, landings, or steps.			
1003.3.1.7	**Landings at Doors:** Provide landing width not less than width of stairway or door, whichever is greater.			
	Fully open doors shall not reduce required width more than 7" (178 mm).			
	When landing serves 50 or more occupants, doors in any position shall not reduce landing to less than 1/2 of required width.			
	Minimum Landing Dimension: 44" (1118 mm) in direction of travel, 36" (914 mm) in Groups R-3 and U and in individual R-1 dwelling units.			
1004.2.6	**Dead Ends:** Arrange exits to provide 2 directions of egress to separate exit at any point in corridor, except for deadends 20'-0" (6096 mm) maximum length.			
1004.3.3.2	**Hallway Width:** Provide unobstructed width except that handrails, and fully open doors shall not reduce width more than 7" (178 mm).			
	Doors in any position shall not reduce required width by more than 1/2.			
1004.3.4.2	**Corridor Width:** Provide unobstructed width except that handrails, and doors when fully opened, shall not reduce width by more than 7" (178 mm).			
	Doors in any position shall not reduce required width by more than 1/2.			
1004.3.4.3	**Corridor Construction:** Enclose by walls, floor, ceiling, and protected openings.			
	1-hour where serving occupancies with 30 or more occupants.			
	1-hour in Group I or Group R-1 with 10 or more occupants.			

Code Ref.	Code Compliance Item	OK	NA	ID
1004.3.4.3	**Corridor Construction, Continued:** **Nonrated Construction Permitted In:**			
	1-story Group F-2 or S-2 buildings.			
	Corridors over 30'-0" (9144 mm) wide where occupancies served have at least 1 other independent exit.			
	Group I-3 where open-barred cells form corridors.			
	Office spaces with 100 or less occupants where story is fully sprinkled and corridor is provided with automatic smoke detection system.			
	Office spaces with 100 or less occupants in fully sprinkled buildings.			
	Office spaces of a single tenant in Group B office buildings of Type I, Type II-FR, or Type II 1-hour construction where story is fully sprinkled and corridor is provided with automatic smoke detection system.			
1004.3.4.3 .2	**Corridor Openings:** Protect openings except in: Nonrated corridors.			
	Exterior openings on exterior walls where permitted by UBC Table 5-A.			
	Corridors in multitheater complexes where each motion picture auditorium has at least 1/2 of required exits or exit-access doorways opening directly to exterior or into an exit passageway.			
	Corridor Doors: 20-minute, tight-fitting smoke/draft assembly, self-closing or automatic closing by smoke detector, no louvers permitted.			
	Corridor Windows: 3/4-hour rated, limit aggregate area to 25% of area of room/corridor wall of any room.			
	Corridor Duct Openings: Provide smoke and fire dampers.			
1004.3.4.4	**Corridors - Intervening Rooms:** Do not interrupt corridors with intervening rooms.			
	Exceptions: Foyers, lobbies, or reception rooms constructed as corridors.			
	In fully sprinkled office buildings, corridors may lead through enclosed elevator lobbies if all areas of building have access to at least 1 required exit without passing through elevator lobby.			
1004.3.4.5	**Elevator Lobbies:** Construct as required for corridors.			
	Protect openings as required for corridors.			
1005.3	**Exit Components:** Do not reduce rating of exit components until arrival at exit discharge or public way.			
	Exception: Horizontal exits may lead to exit-access element.			
	Doors of Exit Components Opening to Exterior: Not permitted where exterior openings are not permitted by UBC Table 5-A.			

Code Ref.	Code Compliance Item	OK	NA	ID
1005.3.3.2	**Exit Enclosure:** May include 3/4-rated windows in fully sprinkled Group S-3 parking garages with no repair or refuel.			
1005.3.5.2	**Horizontal Exit Construction:** 2-hour occupancy separation.			
	Continuous from exterior wall to exterior wall and from floor to underside of floor or roof above.			
1005.3.5.3	**Horizontal Exit Openings:** 1-1/2 hour fire assemblies, self-closing or automatic closing by smoke detector.			
1006.3.2	**Exit Discharge Components:** Make sufficiently open to exterior to prevent accumulation of smoke and toxic gases.			
1006.3.2.2	**Exterior Exit Balconies - Width:** Provide unobstructed width.			
	Handrails and doors when fully opened may not reduce width by more than 7" (178 mm).			
	Doors in any position shall not reduce required width by more than 1/2.			
1006.3.3	**Exterior Exit Stairways:** No enclosed useable space permitted under stairway.			
	Protection of Exterior Wall Openings: Protect openings below and within 10'-0" (3048 mm) of exterior exit stairway serving building 2 stories or more, or a floor level with openings having such openings in 2 or more floors below.			
	3/4-hour, fixed or self-closing fire assemblies.			
	Exceptions: Group R-3.			
	Openings may be unprotected where 2 separated exterior stairways are served by a common exterior exit balcony.			
	Protection of openings not required for open parking garages.			
1006.3.4	**Exterior Exit Ramps:** No enclosed useable space permitted under stairway.			
	Protection of Exterior Wall Openings: Protect openings below and within 10'-0" (3048 mm) of exterior exit stairway serving building 2 stories or more, or a floor level with openings having such openings in 2 or more floors below.			
	3/4-hour, fixed or self-closing fire assemblies.			
	Exceptions: Group R-3.			
	Openings may be unprotected where 2 separated exterior stairways are served by a common exterior exit balcony.			
	Protection of openings not required for open parking garages.			
1006.3.5	**Exit Courts:** Discharge into public way or exit passageway.			
	Minimum Height: 7'-0" (2134 mm).			

Code Ref.	Code Compliance Item	OK	NA	ID
1006.3.5	**Exit Courts, Continued:** **Width Reduction:** Make reductions gradually by guardrail, minimum 3'-0" (914 mm) high, making angle of not more than 30° with axis of exit court.			
	Number of Exits: Provide exits based on occupant load.			
	Construction and Openings: When serving 10 or more occupants and less than 10'-0" (3048 mm) wide, provide 1-hour construction to 10'-0" (3048 mm) above floor.			
	3/4-hour opening protection.			
1006.3.5.2	**Exit Courts - Width:** Provide unobstructed width except that handrails, and doors when fully opened, shall not reduce width by more than 7" (178 mm).			
	Doors in any position shall not reduce required width by more than 1/2.			
1007.7.1	**Special Hazards - Rooms Containing Fuel-fired Equipment:** Except in Group R-3, provide 2 exits from rooms containing boilers, furnaces, incinerators or other fuel-fired equipment when area exceeds 500 sf (46.45 m^2) and largest fuel-fired equipment exceeds 400,000 Btu per hour (117 228 W) input capacity.			
	When 2 exits are required, 1 may be by fixed ladder.			
	Separate exits by not less than 1/2 the greatest horizontal dimension of room.			
	Interior openings between Group H and incinerator rooms are prohibited.			
1007.7.2	**Special Hazards - Refrigeration Machinery Rooms:** **Access to Exits:** Provide at least 2 exits where over 1,000 sf (92.9 m^2).			
	Maximum Travel Distance: 50'-0" (15 240 mm) from any point in room to exit or exit-access doorway.			
	Door Swing: In direction of exit travel.			
1007.7.3	**Special Hazards - Refrigerated Rooms or Spaces:** **Access to Exits:** Provide 2 exits or exit-access doors when 1,000 sf (92.9 m^2) or more and room contains refrigerant evaporator maintained at below 68° F (20°C).			
	Maximum Travel Distance: 150'-0" (45 720 mm) from any point in room to exit or exit-access doorway where room is not fully sprinkled.			
	Egress is allowed through adjoining refrigerated rooms.			
1007.7.4	**Special Hazards - Cellulose Nitrate Film Handling:** Provide 2 exits from film laboratories, projection rooms, and film processing rooms.			
	Doors self-closing, 1-hour protection.			

Stairs and Ramps

UBC Sections 1003.3.3 and 1003.3.4

Code Ref.	Code Compliance Item	OK	NA	ID
1003.3.3.1	**Stairways - General:** Section applies when stairs have 2 or more risers.			
	Aisles in assembly rooms with steps shall comply with Section 1004.3.2.			
1003.3.3.2	**Stairway Width:** Where part of required means of egress, provide required exit width noted on Code Information Form.			
1003.3.3.3	**Riser Height:** 4" (102 mm) minimum, 7" (178 mm) maximum.			
	Tread Run: 11" (279 mm) minimum.			
	Private steps, stairs serving 10 occupants or less, and stairways to unoccupied roofs may have 8" (203 mm) maximum rise and 9" (229 mm) minimum run.			
	Where top or bottom riser adjoins sloping public way, walk, or driveway serving as landing, bottom or top riser may be reduced along slope to less than 4" (102 mm) with variation in height not to exceed 3" (76 mm) in every 36" (914 mm) of stair width.			
1003.3.3.5	**Stair Landings:** Provide floor or landing at top and bottom of stairs.			
	Landing Length: Provide dimension in direction of travel not less than width of stair; need not exceed 44" (1118 mm) when stair has straight run.			
	36" (914 mm) minimum at straight run stair in Groups R-3, U, and in R-1 individual dwelling units.			
	Stairs serving unoccupied roofs.			
	Landing Height: 12'-0" (3658 mm) maximum vertically between landings.			
	Landings at Doors: Provide landing width not less than width of stairway or door, whichever is greater.			
	Doors in fully open position shall not reduce required dimension more than 7" (178 mm).			
	When landing serves 50 or more occupants, doors in any position shall not reduce landing to less than 1/2 of required width.			

Code Ref.	Code Compliance Item	OK	NA	ID
1003.3.8.1	**Circular Stairways:** May be used as exit provided tread run is 10" (254 mm) minimum and inside radius is not less than twice width of stair.			
1003.3.8.2	**Winding Stairways:** May be used in R-3 and private stairways in R-1 if minimum tread run is provided at maximum of 12" (305 mm) from narrow side; 6" (152 mm) minimum tread at any point.			
1003.3.8.3	**Spiral Stairways:** May be used in R-3 and private stairways in R-1; may be required exit when serving less than 400 sf (37.16 m²).			
	Provide clear walking area on tread of 26" (660 mm) minimum from outer edge of supporting column to inner edge of handrail.			
	Spiral Stairways - Tread Run: 7-1/2" (191 mm) minimum run at 12" (305 mm) out from narrowest point of tread.			
	Provide rise sufficient for 6'-6" (1981 mm) headroom minimum; 9-1/2" (241 mm) maximum riser height.			
1003.3.3.10	**Stairways - Protection of Exterior Wall Openings:** 3/4-hour fixed, self-closing, or automatic-closing assemblies for openings in exterior wall below and within 10'-0" (3048 mm) horizontally of exterior exit stair, or within 10'-0" (3048 mm) horizontally of unprotected openings in an interior exit stair serving 2 stories or floor level having such openings in 2 or more floors below.			
	Protection not required when 2 separated exterior stairways serve an exterior exit balcony.			
	Protection not required in open parking garages.			
1003.3.4.2	**Ramp Width:** Where part of required means of egress, provide required exit width noted on Code Information Form.			
1003.3.4.3	**Ramp Slope:** 1:12 (8%) maximum where on accessible route of travel and 1:8 (12.5%) maximum for other ramps.			
1003.3.4.4	**Ramp Landings:** When ramps are steeper than 1:15 (6.7%), provide top and bottom landings.			
	Provide intermediate landings for each 5'-0" (1524 mm) of rise.			
	Top and Intermediate Landings: Minimum 5'-0" (1524 mm) in direction of ramp run.			
	Bottom Landing: Minimum 6'-0" (1829 mm) in direction of ramp run.			
	Doors at Landings: Do not reduce minimum landing dimension to less than 42" (1067 mm) in any position.			
	Do not reduce required width more than 3-1/2" (89 mm) when fully open.			
	Doors at Accessible Ramp Landings: Where door swings over landing, extend landing 24" (610 mm) beyond latch edge; provide minimum 5'-0" (1524 mm) dimension parallel to direction of travel through door.			

Exit Enclosures and Passageways

UBC Sections 1005.3.3 and 1005.3.4

Code Ref.	Code Compliance Item	OK	NA	ID
1005.3.3.2	**Exit Enclosure Construction:** **Type I or II Construction:** Noncombustible.			
	Type III, IV, or V Construction: Combustible or noncombustible.			
1005.3.3.5	**Enclosure Openings:** Other than permitted exterior openings, limit openings to those necessary for exiting from occupied spaces into enclosure and those exiting from enclosure.			
	Penetrations and communicating openings between adjacent enclosures not permitted.			
	Opening Protection: 1-1/2 hour door at 2-hour enclosure.			
	1-hour door at 1-hour enclosure.			
1005.3.3.6	**Use of Space Under Stair and Ramp:** Do not use or enclose useable space under stairs or ramps that are within enclosures.			
1005.3.3.7	**Pressurized Stair Enclosures:** Required in buildings with occupied floors more than 75'-0" (22 860 mm) above lowest level of fire department access.			
	Provide pressurized entrance vestibules for pressurized enclosures.			
	Pressurized Vestibules: **Minimum Size:** 44" (1118 mm) wide, 72" (1829 mm) in direction of travel.			
	Construction: At least 2-hour floors, walls and ceilings.			
	Doors: 1-1/2 hour door from building into vestibule.			
	20-minute smoke/draft control door from vestibule into stair.			

Code Ref.	Code Compliance Item	OK	NA	ID
1005.3.4.3	**Exit Passageway - Construction:** **Less than 400'-0" (121 920 mm):** 1-hour walls, ceilings, and floors.			
	400'-0" (121 920 mm) or More: 2-hour walls, ceilings, and floors.			
	Type I and II Construction: Noncombustible except where combustible permitted.			
	Type III, IV, and V Construction: Combustible or noncombustible.			
1005.3.4.4	**Exit Passageway - Openings:** Limit to openings necessary for egress into exit passageway and egress from passageway.			
	Elevators shall not open into exit passageways.			
	Interior Doors: 1-hour in 1-hour walls.			
	1-1/2 hour in 2-hour walls.			

Aisles

UBC Section 1004.3.2

Code Ref.	Code Compliance Item	OK	NA	ID
1004.3.2.2	**Minimum Aisle Width - Occupancies Without Fixed Seats:** **24"** (610 mm) where serving employees only; not less than computed per UBC Table 10-B.			
	36" (914 mm) minimum in public areas of Groups B and M, and in assembly occupancies where tables, counters, furnishings, merchandise, or obstructions are placed on 1 side of aisle only, and **44"** (1118 mm) where placed on 2 sides.			
1004.3.2.3	**Minimum Aisle Width - Occupancies with Fixed Seats:** **Without Smoke Protected Assembly Seating:** Use UBC Table 10-C.			
	Smoke Protected Assembly Seating: Use UBC Table 10-D.			

	Clear Width Modifications:
	❐ **Factor *A*:**
	  ❐ For risers more than 7" (178 mm).
	
	    $A = 1 + \dfrac{(\text{riser height} - 7")}{5} = \underline{\hspace{3cm}}$
	
	  For SI: $A = 1 + \dfrac{(\text{riser height} - 178\text{ mm})}{127} = \underline{\hspace{2cm}}$
	  ❐ **1.0** for risers 7" (178 mm) or less.
	
	❐ **Factor *B*:**
	  ❐ **1.25** increase for stairs without a handrail within 30" (760 mm) horizontal distance.
	  ❐ **1.0** for all other stairs.
	
	❐ **Factor *C*:**
	  ❐ **1.10** for ramps steeper than 1:10 slope where used in ascent.
	  ❐ **1.0** for ramps 1:10 slope or less.			

	Aisle Width Calculations:			

Code Ref.	Code Compliance Item	OK	NA	ID
1004.3.2.3	**Fixed Seats in Rows:** Provide minimum clear width of aisles per calculations above or as follows:			
	48" (1219 mm) for stairs with seats both sides.			
	36" (914 mm) for stairs with seats 1 side.			
	23" (584 mm) between a stair handrail and seats when handrail subdivides aisles.			
	42" (1067 mm) for level or ramped aisles with seats 1 side.			
	36" (914 mm) for level or ramped aisles with seats 1 side.			
	23" (584 mm) between stair handrail and seats when aisle serves maximum of 5 rows on 1 side.			
	Where exiting is possible in 2 directions, provide uniform aisle width throughout entire length.			
	Where aisles converge to form a single path of exit travel, provide minimum width based on the combined required width of the converging aisles.			
1004.3.2.3 .2	**Seat Spacing - Clear Width Between Rows:** **Minimum Width: 12"** (305 mm) minimum where rows have 14 seats or less, measured as clear distance from back of row ahead to nearest projection of row behind.			
	Automatic or Self-rising Seats: May measure with seats in raised position.			
	Non-automatic or Non-self-rising Seats: Measure with seats in down position.			
	Required Clear Width Increases: **Rows Served by Aisles or Doorways Both Ends:** No more than 100 seats permitted per row; increase clear width by 0.3" (7.62 mm) for each seat beyond 14; width need not exceed 22" (559 mm).			
	Smoke Protected Seating Exception: Row length limits may be increased per UBC Table 10-E.			
	Rows Served by Aisles or Doorways 1 End Only: Increase clear width by 0.6" (15 mm) for every seat beyond 7; width need not exceed 22" (559 mm).			
	Smoke Protected Seating Exception: Row length limits may be increased per UBC Table 10-E.			
	2 Directions of Travel: Do not exceed 30'-0" (9144 mm) from point where occupant is seated to point where occupant has choice of 2 directions.			
	Smoke Protected Seating Exception: Distance may be increased to 50'-0" (15 240 mm) maximum.			

Code Ref.	Code Compliance Item	OK	NA	ID
1004.3.2.4	**Aisle Termination:** Terminate aisles at cross aisle, foyer, doorway, or vomitory.			
	Dead Ends: No deadends greater than 20'-0" (6096 mm).			
	Dead End Exceptions: Longer dead ends permitted when seats served by dead-end aisle are not more than 24 seats from another aisle measured along row of seats having minimum clear width of 12" (305 mm) plus 0.6" (15 mm) for each additional seat more than 7 in a row.			
	When seats are without backrests, dead ends in vertical aisles may be 16 rows maximum.			
	In smoke-protected seating, dead ends in vertical aisles may be 21 rows maximum.			
	In smoke-protected seating, longer dead ends permitted when seats served by dead-end aisle are not more than 40 seats from another aisle measured along row of seats having minimum clear width of 12" (305 mm) plus 0.3" (7.6 mm) for each additional seat more than 7 in a row.			
	Cross Aisles: Terminate at aisles, foyers, doorways, or vomitories.			
1004.3.2.5	**Aisle Steps Prohibited:** In aisles with slope of 1:8 (12.5%) or less.			
	Aisle Steps Required: In aisles with slope steeper than 1:8 (12.5%). Provide risers and treads extending entire width of aisle.			
	Risers: 7" (178 mm) maximum, 4" (102 mm) minimum, uniform height in each flight.			
	Treads: 11" (279 mm) minimum, uniform length throughout aisle.			
	When slope of aisle steps and adjoining seating area is the same, riser heights may be increased to 9" (229 mm) and may be non-uniform only to extent necessary by changes in slope of adjoining seating area to maintain adequate sight lines.			
1004.3.2.6	**Ramp Slope:** 1:8 (12.5%) maximum; provide slip-resistant surface.			

Means of Egress
Groups E, H, I and R

UBC Section 1007

Code Ref.	Code Compliance Item	OK	NA	ID
1007.3.2	**Group E - Separate Exit Systems:** Provide atmospheric separation between at least 2 paths of exit travel to preclude contamination of both by same fire.			
1007.3.5	**Group E - Hallways, Corridors, and Exit Balconies:** Provide ramps for changes of elevation less than 24" (610 mm).			
1007.4.3	**Group H - Corridor Doors:** 3/4-hour.			
1007.4.4	**Group H - Exit or Exit-Access Door Swing:** Swing in direction of travel where serving hazardous occupancies.			
1007.5.4	**Group I-1.1 Hospitals and Nursing Homes - Corridor Exceptions:** Nurses' stations, including doctors'/nurses' charting and communication spaces, constructed as corridors need no separation from corridors.			
	Waiting areas constructed as corridors need no separation from corridors provided:			
	Where aggregate area of waiting areas in each smoke compartment is 600 sf (55.7 m^2) maximum:			
	Each area is located to permit direct visual supervision by staff;			
	Each area is protected by electrically-supervised automatic smoke detection system; and			
	Each area is arranged not to obstruct access to required exits.			
	Where such spaces may be unlimited in size and open to corridor:			
	Spaces are not used for patient sleeping rooms, treatment rooms, hazardous areas or special use areas per UBC Table 3-C;			
	Each space is located to permit direct visual supervision by staff;			
	Space and corridors that space open onto in same smoke compartment are protected by electrically-supervised automatic smoke detection system; and			
	Space is arranged not to obstruct access to required exits.			

Code Ref.	Code Compliance Item	OK	NA	ID
1007.5.4	**Group I Corridors - Changes in Elevation:** Use ramps where serving nonambulatory persons.			
1007.5.5	**Group I - Required Exterior Exit Doors:** Open in direction of exit travel.			
1007.5.7	**Group I-1.1 and I-1.2 - First Story above Grade Level:** Provide ramp from first story to exterior at ground floor level for nonambulatory patients.			
1007.6.1	**Group R Hallways:** Construct as required for corridors where serving 10 or more occupants.			

Grandstands and Bleachers

UBC Section 1008

Code Ref.	Code Compliance Item	OK	NA	ID
1008.1	**Scope:** Applies to reviewing stands, grandstands, bleachers, and telescoping and folding seating.			
303.2.2.3	**Maximum Height:** **Type III 1-hour, IV, or V 1-hour:** 40'-0" (12 192 mm) **Type III-N, V-N:** 20'-0" (6096 mm). **Indoor, combustible structural members:** 12'-0" (3658 mm).			
	Useable Space (including exits) Beneath Group A-4 Structures: Separate from Group A-4 (including means of egress) with 1-hour walls, floors, and ceilings.			
	Exceptions: Means of egress under temporary grandstands.			
	When the underside of outdoor continuous steel deck grandstands is used for public toilets.			
1008.5.1	**Row Spacing:** 12" (305 mm) minimum clear space measured from back of seat to front of seat behind.			
	Minimum Seat Spacing Within Row: **Seats without backrests:** 22" (559 mm). **Seats with backrests:** 30" (762 mm). **Chair seating:** 33" (838 mm).			
1008.5.2	**Maximum Rise Between Rows:** 16" (406 mm) unless seat spacing back to back is 40" (1016 mm) or more.			
	24" (610 mm) with automatic or self-rising seats with 33" (838 mm) back-to-back spacing.			
1021.5.3	**Bench-type Seating Capacity:** 1 person for each 18" (457 mm) length.			

Code Ref.	Code Compliance Item	OK	NA	ID
1008.5.4.1	**Aisles:** Provide in all facilities, except when all of following are met:			
	Seats are without backrests.			
	Row-to-row rise is 6" (152 mm) maximum per row.			
	Row spacing is 28" (711 mm) maximum unless seatboards and footboards are at same elevation.			
	Number of rows is not more than 16 in height.			
	First seating board is +12" (305) maximum.			
	Seat boards are continuous flat surfaces.			
	Seat boards provide walking surface with 11" (279 mm) minimum width.			
1008.5.4.2	**Obstructions:** Do not obstruct required width of aisles or means of egress.			
1008.5.4.3	**Aisle Width:** Refer to aisle width required by Code Information Form.			
	Seats both sides: 44" (1118 mm) minimum.			
	Seats on 1 side: 36" (914 mm) minimum.			
1008.5.5	**Cross Aisles and Vomitories:** 54" (1372 mm) minimum clear width, extending to exit or exterior perimeter ramp.			
	Refer to aisle width required by Code Information Form.			
1008.5.6	**Stairways and Ramps:** Comply with general requirements for stairs and ramps.			
	8" (203 mm) maximum rise on stairs and ramps within seating facility serving at right angles to rows of seats.			
	Provide stair or ramp full width of aisle where aisle terminates at elevation more than 8" (203 mm) above grade or floor.			
1008.6	**Grandstands and Bleachers Within Buildings:** 9 seats maximum between any seat and aisle when seats are without backrests.			
	Deadend Aisles: 16 row depth maximum, when seats are without backrests.			
1008.7	**Smoke-protected Assembly Seating:** **Minimum Roof Height:** 15'-0" (4572 mm) above highest aisle or aisle accessway.			
	Smoke Control: Provide automatic smoke control per Section 905.			
	Smoke control not required when natural venting system is provided.			
	Maximum Travel Distance: 200'-0" (60 960 mm) from seat to nearest entrance to egress concourse.			
	200'-0" (60 960 mm) from entrance to vomitory portal or egress concourse to egress stair, ramp, or walk at building exterior.			
	Maximum Travel Distance in Outdoor Facilities: 400'-0" (121 920 mm).			
	Type I or II Construction: Unlimited where open to outside.			

Accessibility

UBC Chapter 11

Code Ref.	Code Compliance Item	OK	NA	ID
1101.2	**Design Standard:** CABO/ANSI A117.1-1992.			
	Comply with 1106 below for Type B dwelling units.			
1103.1.1	**Accessibility Required:** In all buildings and portions of buildings except for:			
	Areas not customarily occupied including elevator pits; security observation galleries; elevator penthouses; nonoccupiable spaces accessed by ladders, catwalks, crawl spaces or freight elevators; piping and equipment catwalks; and machinery, mechanical, and electrical equipment rooms.			
	Areas where work cannot reasonably be performed by persons with severe impairments where approved by building official.			
	Temporary structures, sites, and equipment associated with construction, except for walkways and pedestrian protection.			
1103.1.2	**Group A Exception:** Accessibility not required in assembly area of dining and drinking establishments in nonelevator buildings, when the area of mezzanine seating is not more than 25% of total seating, as accessible means of vertical access to the mezzanine is not required, provided the same services are provided in an accessible space.			
1103.1.2.7	**Group I:** Provide accessibility in public-use, common-use, and employee-use areas; and patient rooms, cells, or treatment rooms as follows:			
	Group I-1.1: Patient-care hospital units specializing in treating conditions affecting mobility, all patient rooms including associated toilet/bath rooms.			
	Group I-1.1: Patient-care hospital units not specializing in treating conditions affecting mobility, at least 1 in 10 patient rooms or fraction thereof, including associated toilet rooms and bathrooms.			
	Group I-1.1 and 1.2: Nursing homes /long-term care facilities, at least 1 in 2 patient rooms or fraction thereof, including associated toilet/bath rooms.			
	Group I-3: Mental health occupancies, at least 1 in 10 patient rooms or fraction thereof, including associated toilet rooms and bathrooms.			
	Group I-3: Jails and prisons, at least 1 in 20 rooms or cells or fraction thereof, including associated toilet rooms and bathrooms.			
	Group I: All treatment and exam rooms.			

Code Ref.	Code Compliance Item	OK	NA	ID
1103.1.9.1	**Group R:** Provide accessible public- and common-use areas and facilities for general public and residents of Group R-1 accessible dwelling units.			
	When accessory recreational facilities serve accessible dwelling units, 25%, but not less than 1 of each type in each group of such facilities, need be accessible; consider all facilities of each site to determine number of each type required to be accessible.			
1103.1.9.2	**Hotels, Lodging Houses, and Congregate Residence:** When containing 6 or more guest rooms, multibed rooms or spaces for more than 6 occupants, provide 1 accessible room for first 30, and 1 for each additional 100 guest rooms or fraction thereof.			
	Hotels with more than 50 Sleeping Rooms and Suites: Provide 50% of accessible rooms with roll-in shower, but not less than 1.			
	Guest Rooms for Hearing Impairments: Provide per UBC Table 11-B.			
1103.1.9.3	**Multi-unit Dwellings:** Make all Group R-1 apartments with 4 or more units or Group R-3 with 4 or more dwellings in single structure Type B dwelling units.			
	Group R-1 with more than 20 Dwelling Units: Make 2% accessible, but not less than 1 Type A dwelling units.			
	Exceptions: Where elevators are not provided, Type B units may be only on ground floor.			
	Where elevators are not provided and ground floor has no dwelling units, only Group R-1 or R-3 on first floor need comply.			
	Multistory dwelling not provided with elevator need not comply with Type B unit requirements.			
	Where elevator is provided to only 1 floor, that floor shall comply with Type B unit requirements; provide toilet facility on that floor.			
	Number of Type B units in multiple nonelevator buildings on 1 site may be reduced to percentage of ground floor units equal to percentage of entire site having grades, prior to development, of 10% or less; but no less than 20% of ground floor dwelling units on entire site.			
	Required number Type A and Type B units does not apply to site where lowest floor or lowest structural building members is required to be at or above base flood elevation resulting in:			
	A difference in elevation between minimum required floor elevation at primary entrances and all vehicular and pedestrian arrival points within 50'-0" (15 240 mm) exceeding 30" (762 mm).			
	A slope exceeding 10% between the minimum required floor elevation at primary entrances and all vehicular and pedestrian arrival points within 50'-0" (15 240 mm).			
	Where no such arrival points are within 50'-0" (15 240 mm) of primary entrances, use closest arrival point.			

Code Ref.	Code Compliance Item	OK	NA	ID
1103.1.11	**Group U:** Provide accessible garages and carports when containing accessible parking.			
	Group U-1 Agricultural: Provide accessible access at least to paved work areas and areas open to public.			
1103.2.2	**Accessible Route:** Provide to all portions of buildings required to be accessible, to accessible building entrances, connecting accessible pedestrian walkways, and the public way.			
	Exception: Except in offices of health-care providers, transportation facilities and airports, and Group M with 5 or more tenants, floors above and below accessible levels 3,000 sf (279 m²) or less and with 50 or less occupants need not be served by accessible route from accessible level.			
	Accessible Route: When floor levels are required to be connected by accessible route, and an interior path of travel is provided between levels, provide an interior accessible route of travel between levels.			
	Do not pass through kitchens, storage rooms, toilet rooms, bathrooms, or closets except accessible routes may pass through kitchen or storage rooms in Type A units.			
	Accessible Site Route: Provide accessible route to all accessible buildings on a site and connect such buildings with an accessible route.			
	Group R-1 Apartments Exception: A vehicular route with parking at accessible buildings may be provided in place of accessible route when slope of finish grade exceeds 1:12 (8.33%) or when physical barriers prevent accessible route.			
1103.2.3	**Accessible Entrances:** Make 50% of entrances to each building and each separate tenancy accessible, but not less than 1.			
	Exceptions: Entrances used only for loading and service.			
	Entrances to nonaccessible spaces.			
	When building entrances normally serve accessible parking, transportation facilities, passenger loading zones, taxi stands, public streets and sidewalks, or accessible interior vertical access, make at least 1 such entrance serving each such function accessible.			
	Locate primary entrance to Type A or Type B unit on accessible route from public or common areas; primary entrance may not be to a bedroom.			
1104.1.1	**Means of Egress:** At least 1 accessible exit or exit-access door from required accessible spaces.			
	When more than 1 exit or exit-access door is required from accessible space, provide each accessible portion with at least 2 means of egress.			
	Make each accessible means of egress continuous from each required accessible occupied area to public way and include accessible routes, ramps, exit stairs, elevators, horizontal exits, or smoke barriers.			

Code Ref.	Code Compliance Item	OK	NA	ID
1104.1.2	**Stairways:** 48" (1219 mm) clear width between handrails where part of accessible means of egress.			
	Area of Refuge: Provide area of refuge in enlarged story-level landing, or access stair from area of refuge or horizontal exit.			
	Exceptions: Exit stairways serving single dwelling units or guest rooms.			
	Exit stairways serving fully sprinklered buildings.			
	48" (1219 mm) clear width between handrails not required for exit stairways accessed from horizonal exit.			
	Areas of refuge not required in open parking garages.			
1104.1.3	**Elevators:** Provide to floors 4 or more stories above or below level of exit discharge serving such floor.			
	Exception: Elevators need not be provided to floors provided with a horizontal exit and located at or above level of exit discharge in fully sprinklered buildings.			
	Access to Elevators Part of Accessible Means of Egress: Access from area of refuge or horizontal exit.			
	Exceptions: In fully sprinklered buildings.			
	Areas of refuge not required in open parking garages.			
1104.1.4	**Platform Lifts:** Shall not serve as an accessible means of egress except within a dwelling unit.			
1104.2.1	**Areas of Refuge:** **Access:** Provide accessible egress into area of refuge; provide direct access to stair or elevator.			
1104.2.2	**Pressurization:** When elevator lobby is used as area of refuge, pressurize elevator shaft and lobby for smoke control.			
	Exception: Elevators in area of refuge formed by horizontal exit or smoke barrier.			
1104.2.3	**Size:** Accommodate at least 1 wheelchair space of 30" (762 mm) by 48" (1219 mm) for each 200 occupants or portion thereof based on area served by area of refuge.			
	Do not reduce required exit width or interfere with access to or use of fire department hose connections and valves.			
	Access to wheelchair spaces shall not be obstructed by more than 1 adjoining wheelchair space.			
1104.2.4	**Construction:** Separate from other spaces with 1-hour smoke barrier except when located within stairway enclosure.			

Code Ref.	Code Compliance Item	OK	NA	ID
1105.1	**Facility Accessibility:** Provide accessible facilities when building or portions of building are required to be accessible.			
	Design Standard: CABO/ANSI A117.1-1992.			
	Comply with 1106 below for Type B dwelling units.			
1105.2.1	**Bathing Facilities:** Make at least 1 of each type of fixture accessible.			
	Exception: Private single occupancy bathing facilities may be adaptable.			
	Recreational Facilities: Provide accessible unisex bathing room where separate sex bathing facilities are provided.			
	Exception: Unisex room not required where separate sex facilities have only 1 shower.			
1105.2.2	**Toilet Facilities:** When located in accessible dwelling units, guest rooms, and congregate residences comply with CABO/ANSI A117.1.			
	In other occupancies, make each toilet room accessible, making at least 1 of each type of fixture or element accessible.			
	Toilet Stalls: Make at least 1 stall wheelchair accessible in each facility.			
	6 or More Stalls: Make at least 1 additional stall ambulatory accessible.			
	Private Single Occupancy Toilet Rooms: May be adaptable.			
	Groups A and M: Provide accessible unisex where aggregate of 6 or more male or female toilets are provided.			
	Mixed Occupancies: Use toilets required for Group A or M to determine unisex toilet requirement.			
1105.2.3	**Elevators, Stairways, and Platform Lifts:** Make elevators on accessible routes accessible except for private elevators serving only 1 dwelling unit.			
	Comply with CABO/ANSI A117.1.			
	Platform Lifts: May be used in lieu of elevator as follows:			
	To provide accessible route to performing areas in Group A.			
	To provide unobstructed sight lines and distribution for wheelchair viewing positions in Group A.			
	To provide access to spaces with less than 5 occupants.			
	To provide access where existing site constraints or other constraints make use of ramp or elevator infeasible.			
1105.2.4.1	**Unisex Bathing and Toilet Rooms:** Comply with CABO/ANSI A117.1.			
1105.2.4.2	**Location:** On accessible route.			
	Not more than 1 story above or below separate sex facilities.			

Code Ref.	Code Compliance Item	OK	NA	ID
1105.2.4.2	**Unisex Bathing and Toilet Rooms:** **Location, Continued:** 500'-0" (152 400 mm) maximum from separate sex room to unisex room on accessible route; such route may not pass through security check points in airports or transportation facilities.			
1005.2.4.3	**Clear Floor Space:** 30" by 48" (762 mm by 1219 mm) in room beyond door swing where door swings into room.			
1005.2.4.5	**Required Fixtures:** **Unisex Toilet Rooms:** Only 1 toilet and 1 lavatory toilet, and only 1 shower where provided.			
	Unisex Bathing Rooms: Only 1 fixture; include 1 toilet and 1 lavatory.			
	Provide storage facilities in unisex bathing room where provided in separate sex bathing rooms.			
1105.4.8.1	**Assembly Areas - Stadiums, Theaters, Auditoriums - Wheelchair Spaces:** Comply with Table 11-A; removable seats permissible in wheelchair spaces.			
	Seating Capacity over 300: Provide wheelchair spaces in more than 1 location on an accessible route of travel.			
	Disperse spaces based on availability of various seating areas and levels.			
	Provide services in accessible areas identical to inaccessible areas.			
1105.4.8.2	**Assistive Listening Systems - Group A and Assembly Spaces in Groups B, E, and M:** Provide in stadiums, theaters, auditoriums, and lecture halls with fixed seats and where audible communication is integral to use as follows:			
	Areas with 50 or more occupants.			
	Areas where audio-amplification system is used.			
	Receivers: Rate of 4% of seats, 2 minimum.			
	In spaces not equipped with audio amplification, or with 50 or less occupants, provide permanent assistive listening system or provide electrical outlets or other supplementary wiring necessary to support portable system.			
	Signage: Provide signage indicating availability of listening system.			
1106.2.1	**Type B Dwelling Units:** **Accessible Route:** Connect all dwelling unit spaces and elements with at least 1 accessible route.			
	Where only 1 accessible route is provided, do not pass through bathrooms, closets, or similar spaces.			
	Exceptions: One of the following is not required to be on accessible route:			
	Raised floor area in portion of living, dining, or sleeping room.			
	Sunken floor area in portion of living, dining, or sleeping room.			
	Mezzanine not having pluming fixtures or enclosed habitable space.			

Code Ref.	Code Compliance Item	OK	NA	ID
1106.2.2	**Type B Dwelling Units, Continued:** **Clear Width:** 36" (914 mm) minimum.			
1106.2.3	**Changes in Level:** **1/2" (12.7 mm) or less:** Comply with CABO/ANSI A117.1.			
	More than 1/2" (12.7 mm): Provide ramp, elevator, or wheelchair lift.			
1106.4	**Primary Entrance Door:** Comply with Section 4.13 of CABO/ANSI A117.1.			
	Exception: Maneuvering clearances not required on dwelling side.			
	Other Doors: **Minimum Clear Width:** 32" (813 mm) measured from face of open door and stop; 1/4" (6.4 mm) permitted.			
	Double Leaf Doors: Provide minimum clear width at active leaf.			
1106.5	**Kitchens:** **Clearances:** 40" (1016 mm) minimum clearance between opposing countertops, base cabinets, appliances, or walls.			
	60" (1524 mm) minimum between countertops, base cabinets, appliances, or walls on 3 sides.			
	Clear Floor Space: 20" by 48" (762 mm by 1219 mm) minimum at sink and each appliance.			
	Exception: Sinks per Section 4.33.4.5 of CABO/ ANSI A117.1.			
	Space at sink may be parallel approach.			
	Extend space 15" (381 mm) minimum each side of sink center line.			
	Provide parallel or front approach for dishwasher, range, cooktop, oven, refrigerator/freezer, and trash compactor.			
1106.6.1	**Toilet and Bath Facilities:** Make accessible as follows, except in dwelling units on levels not required to be accessible.			
1106.6.2	**Clear Floor Space:** Do not swing doors into clear floor space required for any fixture except where 30" by 48" (762 mm by 1219 mm) is provided in room beyond door swing.			
	May include knee and toe clearances.			
	Clear floor space and clearances may overlap.			
1106.6.4.1	**Type B Dwelling Unit - Toilet and Bathing Fixtures - Option A:** **Lavatory:** 30" by 48" (762 mm by 1219 mm) minimum clear space parallel approach, extending 15" (381 mm) minimum each side of sink center line.			
	Exception: Lavatory per Section 4.20, CABO/ANSI A117.1.			
	Water Closet: 18" (457 mm) minimum from toilet center line to bathtub, lavatory, or wall on 1 side, 15" (381 mm) minimum on the other.			
	Locate grab bar on 18" (457 mm) side.			

Code Ref.	Code Compliance Item	OK	NA	ID
1106.6.4.1	**Type B Dwelling Unit - Toilet and Bathing Fixtures - Option A:** **Water Closet, Continued:** **Parallel Approach Clearances:** 56" (1422 mm) minimum from wall behind toilet.			
	48" (1219 mm) minimum from point 18" (457 mm) from toilet center line on side for grab bars.			
	Forward Approach Clearances: 66" (1676 mm) minimum from wall behind toilet.			
	48" (1219 mm) minimum from point 18" (457 mm) from toilet center line on side for grab bars.			
	Vanities or lavatories on wall behind water closet permitted to overlap clear floor space.			
	Parallel or Forward Approach: 56" (1422 mm) minimum from wall behind toilet.			
	66" (1676 mm) minimum from point 18" (457 mm) from toilet center line on side for grab bars.			
	Bathing Fixtures: **Parallel Approach Bathtubs:** 30" (762 mm) wide by 60" (1524 mm) long minimum adjacent to bathtub.			
	Lavatory may extend into clearance at control end of tub if 30" by 48" (762 mm by 1219 mm) clearance remains.			
	Lavatories per CABO/ANSI A117.1 permitted in clearance.			
	Forward Approach Bathtubs: 48" (1219 mm) wide by 60" (1524 mm) long minimum adjacent to bathtub.			
	Toilet may be placed at control end of tub.			
	Showers: **Shower Stall:** 36" by 36" (914 mm by 914 mm) minimum.			
	Clear Floor Space: 30" (762 mm) perpendicular to stall by 48" (1219 mm) parallel to shower head wall.			
1106.6.4.2	**Type B Dwelling Unit - Toilet and Bathing Fixtures - Option B:** **General:** Provide accessible fixtures in single toilet/bathing area.			
	Lavatory: 30" by 40" (762 mm by 1219 mm) minimum clear space parallel approach, extending 15" (381 mm) minimum each side of sink center line; fixture rim 34" (864 mm) maximum above floor.			
	Exception: Lavatory per Section 4.20, CABO/ANSI A117.1.			
	Water Closet: 18" (457 mm) minimum from toilet center line to bathtub, lavatory, or wall on 1 side, 15" (381 mm) minimum on the other.			
	Locate grab bar on 18" (457 mm) side.			

Code Ref.	Code Compliance Item	OK	NA	ID
1106.6.4.2	**Type B Dwelling Unit - Toilet and Bathing Fixtures - Option B:** **Water Closet, Continued:** **Parallel Approach Clearances:** 56" (1422 mm) minimum from wall behind toilet.			
	48" (1219 mm) minimum from point 18" (457 mm) from toilet center line on side for grab bars.			
	Vanities or lavatories on wall behind water closet permitted to overlap clear floor space.			
	Forward Approach Clearances: 66" (1676 mm) minimum from wall behind toilet.			
	48" (1219 mm) minimum from point 18" (457 mm) from toilet center line on side for grab bars.			
	Vanities or lavatories on wall behind water closet permitted to overlap clear floor space.			
	Parallel or Forward Approach: 56" (1422 mm) minimum from wall behind toilet.			
	66" (1676 mm) minimum from point 18" (457 mm) from toilet center line on side for grab bars.			
	Bathing Fixtures: At least 1 bathing fixture shall comply with the following:			
	Bathtubs: 30" by 48" (762 mm by 1219 mm) minimum for parallel approach adjacent to bathtub.			
	Align front edge of clear space with control end of tub.			
	Shower Stall: 36" by 36" (914 mm by 914 mm) minimum if only bathing fixture.			
	Clear Floor Space: 30" (762 mm) perpendicular to stall by 48" (1219 mm) parallel to shower head wall.			

Interior Environment

UBC Chapter 12

Code Ref.	Code Compliance Item	OK	NA	ID
1203.4.2	**Group R - Yards:** 3'-0" (914 mm) wide minimum for 1-story and 2-story buildings, plus additional 1'-0" (305 mm) for each additional story.			
	Where 14 stories or more, provide 15'-0" (4570 mm) minimum width.			
1203.4.3	**Group R - Courts:** 3'-0" (914 mm) wide minimum, or 6'-0" (1829 mm) wide minimum where windows are on both sides.			
	Where bounded on 3 sides by building walls, 10'-0" (3048 mm) long minimum unless bounded on 1 end by public way or yard.			
	For 1-story and 2-story buildings, add additional 1'-0" (305 mm) width and 2'-0" length for each additional story.			
	Where 14 stories or more, provide minimum width and length for 14 stories.			
	Access: Provide access for cleaning.			
	Ventilation: Provide horizontal air intake at bottom of 10 sf (0.93 m^2) minimum, leading to exterior of building unless court abuts yard or public way.			
	Construct as required for court walls of building but not less than 1-hour rated.			
1204	**Group R - Eaves Over Required Windows:** 30" (762 mm) minimum from side and rear property lines.			

Roofing and Roof Structures

UBC Chapter 15

Code Ref.	Code Compliance Item	OK	NA	ID
1511	**Penthouse and Roof Structure Height:** 28'-0" (8534 mm) maximum above roof surface, except in Type I construction.			
	Penthouse and Roof Structure Area: Do not exceed 33-1/3% of area of supporting roof.			
	Penthouse and Roof Structure - Prohibited Uses: Only allowed to shelter mechanical equipment and related vertical shaft openings in roof.			
	Other purposes require compliance with requirements for additional story.			
1512	**Towers and Spires:** When enclosed, provide exterior walls as required for building.			
	When unenclosed and extending more than 75'-0" (22 860 mm) above grade, provide iron, steel, or reinforced concrete structure.			
	Area: Not more than 1/4 of street frontage of building and not exceeding 1,600 sf (149 m^2) unless conforming to type of construction requirements and height limitations for building.			
	When area exceeds 100 sf (9.29 m^2) at any point, extend supporting frame to ground.			
	Roof Covering: Comply with requirements for building.			
	Skeleton Towers for Radio Masts: Use noncombustible materials and directly support on noncombustible frame work to the ground when more than 25'-0" (7620 mm) high and placed on roof of buildings.			
1513	**Access to Rooftop Equipment:** Comply with Mechanical Code.			

Wood

UBC Chapter 23

Code Ref.	Code Compliance Item	OK	NA	ID
2307	**Wood Supporting Masonry or Concrete:** Do not use wood members to permanently support the dead load of masonry or concrete.			
	Exceptions: Masonry or concrete nonstructural floor or roof surfacing 4" thick maximum;			
	Wood pile foundations;			
	Exterior veneer of brick, concrete, or stone may be supported by treated wood foundations when the maximum height of the veneer does not exceed 30'-0" above the foundation.			
	Interior veneer of brick, concrete, or stone may be supported on wood floors designed to support the additional load, and designed to limit deflection and shrinkage to 1/600 of the span.			
	Glass block with installed weight of 20 psf (97.6 kg/m^2) or less complying with UBC Table 21-O; limit deflection of wood floors supporting glass block to 1/600 of the span.			
2308	**Wall Framing:** Do not support more than 2 floors and a roof with wood stud framing unless an analysis satisfactory to the building official shows that shrinkage of wood framing will not have adverse effects on the structure or building systems.			
2315.2	**Wood Combined with Masonry or Concrete - Horizontal Forces:** Do not use wood members to resist horizontal forces contributed by masonry or concrete construction in buildings over 1 story.			
	Exceptions: Horizontal wood floor and roof trusses and diaphragms resisting forces imposed by wind, earthquake, or earth pressure, provided such forces are not resisted by rotation of the truss or diaphragm.			
	Vertical plywood-sheathed shear walls providing resistance to wind or earthquake forces in 2-story buildings of masonry or concrete construction, where story-to-story wall heights do not exceed 12'-0", forces are not resisted by rotation or cantilever action, deflections are limited to 0.005 times each story height, unsupported diaphragm edges are blocked, and no out-of-plane horizontal offsets between first and second story of shear walls.			

Refrigeration Machinery Rooms

UBC Section 2802

Code Ref.	Code Compliance Item	OK	NA	ID
2802	**Refrigeration Machinery Rooms:** Locate on property as required for Group H-7 per UBC Table 3-B; horizontal separation may be limited to floor area of machinery room.			
	1-hour occupancy separation from remainder of building.			
	Protect supporting structural elements as required for type of construction, not occupancy separation.			

Plumbing Systems

UBC Chapter 29

Code Ref.	Code Compliance Item	OK	NA	ID
2902.2	**Minimum Number of Fixtures - Group A:** 1 lavatory for every 2 toilets for each sex.			
	1 drinking fountain at each floor except in drinking or dining establishments.			
2902.3	**Minimum Number of Fixtures - Groups B, F, H, M and S:** Provide at least 1 toilet In buildings or portions of buildings where persons are employed.			
	Provide separate facilities for each sex when more than 4 employees.			
	May be in adjacent building on same property.			
	When in food prep, food storage, or food serving areas, provide non-absorbent interior finishes, handwashing facilities, and separate from food prep or storage rooms with tight-fitting door.			
2902.4	**Minimum Number of Fixtures - Group E:** Provide on following ratios: **Elementary Schools:** 1:100 for boys, 1:35 for girls. **Secondary Schools:** 1:100 for boys, 1:45 for girls.			
	Urinals: 1:30 for boys in elementary and secondary.			
	Lavatories: 1 for every 2 urinals or toilets.			
	Drinking Fountains: 1 on each floor.			
2902.5	**Minimum Number of Fixtures - Group I:** Provide at least 1 toilet In buildings or portions of buildings where persons are employed.			
	Provide separate facilities for each sex when more than 4 employees.			
	May be in adjacent building on same property.			
	When in food prep, food storage, or food serving areas, provide non-absorbent interior finishes, handwashing facilities, and separate from food prep or storage rooms with tight-fitting door.			
	Provide additional facilities for other occupants when employees' facilities are not accessible to other occupants.			

Code Ref.	Code Compliance Item	OK	NA	ID
2902.6	**Minimum Number of Fixtures - Group R:** 1 toilet.			
	Hotels: At least 1 separate facility for each sex with at least 1 toilet each, identified for male and female.			
	Provide additional toilets on each floor for each sex at rate of 1 for every 10 additional guests, or fraction of 10, in excess of 10.			
	Hotel Guest Rooms: May have 1 unidentified toilet facility.			
	Dwelling Units: Provide kitchen with a kitchen sink.			
	Provide bathroom with a toilet, lavatory, and either shower or tub.			
	Provide each sink, lavatory, tub, and shower with hot and cold running water.			
2903	**Alternate Number of Fixtures:** Use Appendix Chapter 29 when adopted by local jurisdiction.			
2904	**Water Closet Minimum Clear Space:** 30" (762 mm) wide, 24" (610 mm) in front.			

Elevators

UBC Chapter 30

Code Ref.	Code Compliance Item	OK	NA	ID
3002	**Elevator Shaft Enclosures:** Provide rated construction per UBC Table 6-A.			
	Where nonrated, may be constructed with laminated glass meeting UBC Standard 24-2.			
	Elevator Lobbies: Provide at least 1 means of egress not requiring keys, tools, special knowledge, or effort.			
3003.1	**Number of Elevator Cars in Hoistway:** **1 to 3 Cars in Building:** May all be in same hoistway enclosure.			
	4 Cars in Building: Provide at least 2 separate hoistway enclosures.			
	More than 4 Cars in Building: Not more than 4 cars may be in single hoistway enclosure.			
3003.3	**Standby Power:** When required in high rise office buildings and Group R-1, connect to at least 1 elevator in each bank.			
	Use self-contained generator set with automatic operation upon loss of electrical power, located in room separated from building areas with 1-hour occupancy separation.			
3303.4.1	**Size of Cab:** Accommodate a wheelchair in at least 1 cab where serving 3 or more stories.			
	68" by 54" (1727 mm by 1372 mm) minimum between wall and wall, or wall and door, excluding return panels.			
	51" (1295 mm) minimum between wall to return panel.			
3303.5	**Stretcher Requirements:** Where serving 4 or more stories, accommodate an ambulance-type stretcher in at least 1 cab.			
	80" by 54" (2032 mm by 1372 mm) minimum between walls or between walls and door, excluding return panel.			
	51" (1295 mm) minimum between wall to return panel.			
	Door Width: 42" (1067 mm) minimum.			

Construction in the Public Right of Way

UBC Chapter 32

Code Ref.	Code Compliance Item	OK	NA	ID
3201	**Projections Beyond the Property Line:** Not permitted except in compliance with this chapter. Horizontal distance from property line to outermost point.			
3202	**Projections into Alleys:** Not permitted except for curbs projecting 9" (229 mm) maximum, 9" (229 mm) maximum above grade.			
	Footings at least 8'-0" (2438 mm) below grade may project 12" (305 mm) maximum.			
3203	**Space below Sidewalks on Public Property:** May be used and occupied where allowed by the public agency.			
	Footings at least 8'-0" (2438 mm) below grade may project 12" (305 mm) maximum.			
3204	**Projection of Balconies, Sun-Control Devices, and Appendages:** Not permitted less than 8'-0" (2438 mm) above grade.			
	Permitted over 8'-0" (2438 mm) above grade; 1" (25 mm) for every 1" (25 mm) additional clearance, 4'-0" (1219 mm) maximum projection.			
3205	**Marquees - Projection and Clearance:** 2'-0" (610 mm) minimum horizontal clearance from curb line.			
	12'-0" (3658 mm) minimum vertical clearance when projecting more than 2/3 the distance from property line to curb line.			
	8'-0" (2438 mm) minimum vertical clearance when projecting less than 2/3 the distance from property line to curb line.			
3205.3	**Marquee Length:** 25'-0" (7620 mm) maximum when projecting more than 2/3 the distance from property line to curb line.			
3205.4	**Marquee Height:** 3-0"' (914 mm) maximum when projecting more than 2/3 the distance from property line to curb line.			
	9'-0" (2743 mm) maximum when projecting less than 2/3 the distance from property line to curb line.			

Group I-3
(Detention and Correctional Facilities)

UBC Appendix Chapter 3, Division I

When adopted by the governing jurisdiction, Appendix Chapter 3, Division I may be used as alternative provisions to requirements of Chapter 3. When used for design purposes, all requirements in this appendix chapter shall be used. Chapter 3 provisions may be used if not specifically noted in this appendix chapter.

Code Ref.	Code Compliance Item	OK	NA	ID
316.2	**Exceptions to Table 6-A:** Nonbearing cell walls in cell complexes may be non-rated, noncombustible construction if cell complex is separated from other areas of building, including corridors connecting to the complex, by construction and opening protection as required for corridors.			
	Do not consider open spaces in front of cell tiers not more than 2 tiers high a vertical shaft whether extending from floor to ceiling or from floor to underside of roof.			
317	**Compartmentation:** Divide stories with more than 50 inmates into at least 2 approximately equal compartments by 1-hour smoke barriers.			
	Protection may be accomplished with horizontal exits; see UBC Section 1008.			
	Unrestricted number of glazed openings area is permitted in smoke barriers in restraint areas if vision panels comply are fire tested.			
318	**Occupancy Separations:** Regardless of UBC Table 3-B, 3-hour occupancy separations may be used between Group I-3 and Group B-1 used only for parking vehicles used to transport inmates if no repair work is performed.			
	If B-1 occupancy is not enclosed with walls and roof, no separation is required.			
321.1	**Automatic Sprinkler Systems:** Provide in buildings or portions of buildings housing 6 or more inmates.			
324.1	**Number of Means of Egress:** Minimum of 2 from multiple occupancy rooms and day rooms of 1-hour construction with more than 20 occupants.			
	Restraint Areas: Determine occupant load from UBC Table 10-A, provide means of egress per UBC Section 1003.1.			

Code Ref.	Code Compliance Item	OK	NA	ID
324.1	**Means of Egress in Restraint Areas:** At least 2 when occupant load is more than 20.			
	Restraint areas are cells, day rooms, cell tiers, and cell complexes.			
324.2	**Means of Egress Through Adjoining or Accessory Areas:** Permitted if such adjoining room is accessory to area served and provides direct means of egress to corridor, exit, or exterior exit balcony.			
	Do not pass through kitchens, storerooms, restrooms, closets, or similar spaces.			
	Spaces in front of cells normally called a day room and used for access to means of egress shall not be considered an adjoining or accessory area if individual cells open directly into the space.			
324.3	**Minimum Cell Door Dimensions:** 2'-0" (610 mm) wide, 6'-0" (1829 mm) high.			
324.5	**Dead-end Exit-Access Balconies:** 50'-0" (15 240 mm) maximum beyond exit stairway when serving cell tiers.			
	See Section 1004.2.3 for number of means of egress.			
325	**Fenced Enclosures:** When building exits terminate in fenced enclosures, provide safe dispersal areas at least 50'-0" (15 240 mm) from building.			
	Provide 3 sf (0.28 m^2) per occupant.			
	Provide gates from dispersal area for relocation of occupants.			
	Provide at least 2 means of egress from when fenced enclosures are without safe dispersal areas.			
	Fenced Enclosures on Roofs: At least 2 means of egress for buildings regardless of occupant load.			

Agricultural Buildings

UBC Appendix Chapter 3, Division II

When adopted by the governing jurisdiction, Appendix Chapter 3, Division II may be used as alternative provisions to requirements of Chapter 3. When used for design purposes, all requirements in this appendix chapter shall be used. Chapter 3 provisions may be used if not specifically noted in this appendix chapter.

Code Ref.	Code Compliance Item	OK	NA	ID
327.1	**General:** Classify as Group M-3 (storage, livestock and poultry; milking barns; shade structures; horticulture structures, greenhouse and crop protection).			
	Area and Height: Comply with UBC Table A-3-A.			
327.2	**Special Provisions - 1-Story Building Area:** Not limited when entirely surrounded and adjoined by public ways or yards 60'-0" (18 288 mm) wide minimum.			
	Special Provisions - 2-Story Building Area: Not limited when entirely surrounded and adjoined by public ways or yards 60'-0" (18 288 mm) wide minimum and fully sprinklered.			
	Plastics: When using plastics, comply with Type V-N.			
	Area of plastic skylights and roofs is not limited.			
328	**Occupancy Separations:** Comply with UBC Table A-3-B and Section 302.			
329	**Exterior Wall Protection:** 1-hour minimum when less than 20'-0" (6096 mm) from property line unless UBC Table 6-A is more restrictive.			
	Exterior Wall Opening Protection: 3/4-hour when less than 20'-0" (6096 mm) from property line.			
330	**Means of Egress:** Comply with UBC Chapter 10.			
	Maximum Travel Distance: 300'-0" (91 440 mm).			
	Means of Egress: At least 1 for every 15,000 sf (1394 m²) or fraction thereof.			
	Minimum Dimensions: 2'-6" (763 mm) wide, 6'-8" (2032 mm) high.			

Group R-4
(Group Care Facilities)

UBC Appendix Chapter 3, Division IV

When adopted by the governing jurisdiction, Appendix Chapter 3, Division IV may be used as alternative provisions to requirements of Chapter 3. When used for design purposes, all requirements in this appendix chapter shall be used. Chapter 3 provisions may be used if not specifically noted in this appendix chapter.

Code Ref.	Code Compliance Item	OK	NA	ID
333.3.2	**General:** Classify as Group R-4 (residential group care for ambulatory, non-restrained persons who may have mental or physical impairment).			
	Each facility shall accommodate at least 5 and not more than 16 residents, excluding staff.			
334.1	**Construction:** May be of any materials allowed by code.			
	Height: 2 stories maximum; do not locate above second story in any building. Comply with UBC Section 506.			
	Area: 3,000 sf (279 m^2) maximum per story except where increase in area is permitted by UBC Sections 504 and 505.			
334.2	**Special Provisions:** Provide 1-hour construction for facilities more than 3,000 sf (279 m^2) and located above first story.			
334.3	**Mixed Occupancies:** Separate from Group H by 4-hour occupancy separation.			
	Separate from all other occupancies with 1-hour occupancy separation.			
	No separation required between R-4 and carports with no enclosed space above where carport is open on 2 or more sides.			
335	**Location on Property - Exterior Walls:** 1-hour and no openings permitted when less than 3'-0" (914 mm) from property line.			

Code Ref.	Code Compliance Item	OK	NA	ID
336	**Exits:** Provide per UBC Chapter 10 and as follows:			
	Number of Exits: At least 2 exits or exit-access doors from every story, basement, or portion thereof.			
	Basements used only for service may have 1 exit or exit-access door (do not consider storage, laundry rooms, or maintenance offices as service rooms).			
	Storage rooms, laundry rooms, and maintenance offices 300 sf (27.9 m^2) may have 1 exit or exit-access door.			
	Distance to Exits: Reduce maximum length allowed in UBC Chapter 10 by 50%.			
	Corridor Width: 3'-0" (914 mm) minimum.			
	Stairways: Construct as required by UBC Section 1006 except that existing stairways may have 8" (203 mm) maximum rise and 9" (229 mm) minimum run and be 30" (762 mm) wide.			
339	**Minimum Ceiling Heights:** 7'-6" (2286 mm) in habitable spaces.			
	7'-0" (2134 mm) to lowest projection in kitchens, halls, bathrooms, toilet compartments.			
	At exposed beams, measure from bottom of exposed beams where beams are less than 48" (1219 mm) on center or from bottom of deck where beams are more than 48" (1219 mm) on center; 7'-0" minimum from bottom of beams.			
	Minimum Ceiling Height - Sloped Ceiling: Minimum height required in half of room only. Do not include areas with ceiling less than 5'-0" (1524 mm) in minimum area computations.			
	Minimum Ceiling Height - Furred Ceilings: 7'-0" (2134 mm) in not more than 1/3 of room area.			
	Floor Area - Dwelling Units and Congregate Residences: Minimum of 1 room not less than 120 sf (11.2 m^2).			
	Other Habitable Rooms: 70 sf (6.5 m^2) minimum, except kitchens.			
	Room Dimensions - Width: Except for kitchens, 7'-0" (2134 mm) minimum in any dimension.			

Aviation Control Towers

UBC Appendix Chapter 4, Division II

Appendix Chapter 4, Division II may be used when adopted by the governing jurisdiction.

Code Ref.	Code Compliance Item	OK	NA	ID
422	**General:** Applies to control towers 1,500 sf (139.35 m²) maximum per floor and includes airport traffic control cab, electrical and mechanical equipment rooms, airport terminal radar and electronics rooms, office spaces incidental to tower operations, lounges for employees, including sanitary facilities.			
	Occupancy Classification: B-2.			
423	**Construction:** Type I-FR, II 1-hour, II-N, or III 1-hour construction.			
	Height: Comply with UBC Table A-4-A.			
	Area: 1,500 sf (139.35 m²) maximum.			
424	**Means of Egress:** Single stair permitted in towers of any height for occupant loads of 15 maximum.			
	Separate access to stair and elevator by at least half the length of maximum diagonal dimension of area served.			
	Stair and elevator hoistway may be in common enclosure if a 4-hour separation is provided between them, no openings permitted; stair need not extend to roof. Section 403 does not apply.			
	Provide pressurized stairway.			
425	**Fire Alarms:** Provide smoke detectors in all occupied levels, connected to fire alarm system.			
	Provide audible alarms on all levels.			
426	**Accessibility:** Control towers need not be accessible.			
427	**Standby Power and Emergency Generation Systems:** Provide for towers over 65'-0" (19 812 mm) high.			
	Connect to pressurized enclosure, mechanical system and lighting, elevator operational power, and smoke detection system.			

Site Accessibility

UBC Appendix Chapter 11, Division I

Appendix Chapter 11, Division I may be used when adopted by the governing jurisdiction.

Code Ref.	Code Compliance Item	OK	NA	ID
1107.1	**General:** Provide accessible exterior routes from public transportation stops, accessible parking, accessible passenger loading zones, and public sidewalks to accessible building entrances they serve.			
	Provide at least 1 accessible route to all buildings on a site, connecting accessible elements, facilities, and building entrances by the most practical direct route.			
1107.3	**Design and Construction Standards:** CABO/ANSI A117.1.			
1108.1	**Accessible Parking:** Comply with UBC Table A-11-A.			
	Exceptions: Groups I-1.1 and I-2 (Treatment of mobility-impaired persons): 20% accessible.			
	Groups I-1.1, I-1.2, and B-2 (Outpatient medical care): 10% accessible.			
	Group R-1 (Apartment building with accessible or adaptable dwelling units): 2% accessible.			
	Where parking is provided within or under buildings, provide accessible parking within or under buildings.			
	Accessible Van Spaces: Provide 1 accessible van space for every 8 accessible spaces or fraction thereof.			
	Accessible Space Location: Locate on shortest possible accessible route to an accessible entrance.			
	Disperse accessible spaces to be near multiple accessible entrances.			
	In multilevel parking structures, van spaces may be located on 1 level.			
	In parking facilities not related to a particular building, locate accessible spaces on the shortest accessible route to an accessible pedestrian entrance to parking facility.			
1108.3	**Signage:** Comply with CABO/ANSI A117.1.			
1109	**Passenger Loading Zones:** Locate on an accessible route.			

Accessibility for Existing Buildings

UBC Appendix Chapter 11, Division II

Appendix Chapter 11, Division II may be used when adopted by the governing jurisdiction.

Code Ref.	Code Compliance Item	OK	NA	ID
1110	**Scope:** Defines minimum standards for removing architectural barriers in existing buildings.			
1112.1.1	**Compliance:** Do not reduce accessibility, provide access to the maximum feasible extent.			
1112.1.2	**Existing Elements:** Make altered elements comply with CABO/ANSI A117.1, including alterations of existing elements, spaces, essential features, or common areas.			
	Accessible means of egress required by Section 1104 need not be provided in alterations of existing buildings and facilities.			
	When altering an area of primary function, make accessible route to such area accessible; include toilet facilities or drinking fountains serving such function.			
	Exceptions: Costs of providing accessible route need not exceed 20% of costs of alterations affecting area of primary function.			
	Alterations to windows, hardware, operating controls, electrical outlets and signs.			
	Alterations to mechanical systems, electrical systems, installation or alteration of fire-protection systems, and abatement of hazardous materials.			
	Alterations undertaken primarily for increasing accessibility of existing buildings.			

Code Ref.	Code Compliance Item	OK	NA	ID
1112.2.2	**Modifications - Hotel Guest Rooms:** When compliance with CABO/ANSI A117.1 is technically infeasible, provide at least 1 room in 25 accessible, with audio/visual alarm indicating appliances.			
	Provide at least 1 additional room in 25 with visible and audible alarms for persons with hearing impairments.			
	Number of accessible guest rooms and guest rooms accessible to persons with hearing impairments need not exceed Section 1103.1.9.3.			
1112.2.3	**Modifications - Performance Areas:** When it is technically infeasible to alter performance areas to be on an accessible route, make at least 1 of each type of performance area accessible.			
1112.2.4	**Modifications - Platform Lifts:** May be used when installation of elevators is technically infeasible.			
1112.2.5	**Modifications - Toilet Rooms:** When technically infeasible to alter existing toilet and bathing facilities to be accessible, provide 1 accessible unisex toilet accessible to occupants on the same floor.			
	Locate on the same floor and in the same area as existing toilet facilities.			
	Provide 1 accessible toilet and lavatory; provide privacy lock on door.			
	Provide directional signs indicating location of nearest accessible toilet or bathing facility when existing toilet facilities are altered but not made accessible.			
1112.2.6	**Modifications - Assembly Areas:** Seating shall adjoin an accessible route that also serves as a means of egress.			
	When technically infeasible to disperse accessible seating throughout altered assembly area, accessible seating may be clustered.			
	Provide for companion seating with each accessible seating area.			
1112.2.7	**Modifications - Dressing Rooms:** When technically infeasible to provide accessible dressing rooms in each group of rooms, provide 1 accessible dressing room for each sex or 1 accessible unisex dressing room on each level.			

Minimum Plumbing Fixtures

UBC Appendix Chapter 29

Appendix Chapter 29 may be used when adopted by the governing jurisdiction.

Code Ref.	Code Compliance Item	OK	NA	ID
2905	**Minimum Plumbing Fixtures:** Comply with UBC Table A-29-A.			
	Number of fixtures is assumed to be 50% male, 50% female. Obtain approval from building official for adjustments to male/female ratio.			

Membrane Structures

UBC Appendix Chapter 31, Division II

Appendix Chapter 31, Division II may be used when adopted by the governing jurisdiction.

Code Ref.	Code Compliance Item	OK	NA	ID
3111.2	**Scope:** Applies to air-supported, air-inflated, and membrane-covered cable or frame structures erected for 180 days or longer.			
	Water storage facilities, water clarifiers, water treatment plants, sewer plants, aquaculture pond covers, residential and agricultural greenhouses, and similar structures not used for human occupancy need only meet requirements of UBC Section 3112.2.			
3112.1	**Type of Construction:** Classify combustible structures as Type V-N, non-combustible may be Type II-N.			
	A noncombustible membrane structure used exclusively as a roof and located more than 25'-0" (7620 mm) above any floor, balcony, or gallery is deemed to comply with the roof construction requirements for Type I and Type II-FR if such structure complies with UBC Section 3112.			
3112.2	**Membrane Material:** Provide noncombustible or flame retardant conforming to UBC Standard 31-1.			
	Plastic less than 20 mils (0.51 mm) thick used in greenhouses and for aquaculture pond covers need not be flame retardant.			
3112.3	**Other Code Provisions:** Meet other provisions of the code except as specifically required by this section.			
	Provide fire retardant roof coverings.			
	Roof coverings for Group M-1 not exceeding 1,000 sf (93 m²) need not be fire retardant.			
3112.4	**Allowable Floor Area:** Comply with UBC Table 5-B.			
3112.5	**Maximum Height:** 1 story; do not exceed height limitations of UBC Table 5-B.			
	Does not apply to membrane structures serving as roof only.			
3115	**Engineering Analysis:** Use methods acceptable to building official.			

Life Safety for Existing Buildings

UBC Appendix Chapter 34, Division I

Appendix Chapter 34, Division I may be used when adopted by the governing jurisdiction.

Code Ref.	Code Compliance Item	OK	NA	ID
3407.1	**Number of Means of Egress:** Provide minimum of 2 exits for each floor above the first floor.			
	1 such means of egress may be exterior fire escape per Section 3412.4.			
	1 means of egress permitted in second stories with 10 or less occupants.			
3407.1	**Ladder Devices Used as Means of Egress:** May be used in lieu of exterior fire escape if approved by building official; comply with UBC Standard 10-3 and the following:			
	Serves 10 or less occupants or single dwelling unit or guest room.			
	Building is 3 stories or less.			
	Access is adjacent to an opening as required for emergency egress or rescue or from a balcony.			
	Does not pass in front of any building opening below unit served.			
	Activating device for ladder is accessible only from opening or balcony served.			
	Ladder used is at least 6'-0" (1829 mm) away from exposed electrical wiring.			
3407.2	**Stair Construction:** 9" (229 mm) minimum run, 8" (203 mm) maximum rise, 30" (762 mm) minimum width exclusive of handrails.			
	Provide at least 1 handrail.			
	Landings: 30" (762 mm) minimum in direction of travel at each access to stair.			
	Exterior Stairs: Provide noncombustible construction;			
	Exterior stairs on Types III, IV, and V buildings may be of wood, 2" (51 mm) minimum nominal thickness.			

Code Ref.	Code Compliance Item	OK	NA	ID
3407.3	**Corridors in Groups A, B, E, F, H, I, M, R-1, and S:** Provide 1-hour walls and ceilings where serving 30 or more occupants.			
	Permitted Existing Corridor Construction: 1/2" (13 mm) gypsum board, wood lath and plaster, and openings with fixed wire glass in steel frames.			
	Corridor Doors: 20-minute fire assemblies or solid core wood, 1-3/4" (44 mm) minimum thickness, self-closing or automatic-closing by smoke detection.			
	Existing Corridor Door Frames: Where 1-3/4" (44 mm) thick door cannot be accommodated, provide 1-3/8" (35 mm) solid-bonded wood-core or insulated steel door.			
	Transoms and Openings other than Doors: Limit to 25% of area of room/corridor wall, 3/4-hour rated.			
	Corridor Wall Exception: Noncompliant corridor walls, ceilings, and openings may be permitted in fully sprinkled buildings.			
3407.4	**Fire Escapes:** May be used as 1 required exit when complying with Section 3407.4, but fire escapes shall not take the place of stairways required by code under which building was constructed.			
3408	**Enclosure of Vertical Shafts, Stairways, Elevator Hoistways:** 1-hour construction.			
	Enclosure not required for openings serving only 1 adjacent floor except in Group I.			
	Continuous vertical shafts not required at stairways if each story is separated from other stories by 1-hour construction or approved wire glass in steel frames.			
	Provide sprinkled exit corridors and provide at least 1 sprinkler head above corridor openings on the tenant side of openings between corridor and occupant space.			
	Protection for vertical openings not required when building is fully sprinklered.			
	Opening Protection: 1-hour assemblies, self-closing or automatic-closing by smoke detection.			
3412	**Separation of Occupancies:** Comply with UBC Section 302.			
	Existing wood lath and plaster in good condition or 1/2" (13 mm) gypsum board may be acceptable when approved by building official.			

Life Safety for Existing High-Rise Buildings

UBC Appendix Chapter 34, Division II

Appendix Chapter 34, Division II may be used when adopted by the governing jurisdiction.

Code Ref.	Code Compliance Item	OK	NA	ID
3413	**Scope:** Applies to high-rise buildings housing Group B offices or Group R-1 with occupied floors more than 75'-0" (22 860 mm) above lowest level of fire department access.			
3414	**General:** Modify buildings as required below per UBC Table A-34-A.			
3418.1.1	**Type of Construction:** Fully sprinkle Type II-N, III-N, or V-N buildings.			
3418.1.7	**Vertical Shaft, Stairway, and Elevator Enclosure:** 1-hour enclosure for openings through 2 or more floors when not enclosed with existing construction.			
	1-hour enclosure for piping, duct, vent, dumbwaiter, rubbish chute, or linen chute openings through 2 or more floors.			
	Openings for piping, ducts, gas vents, dumbwaiters, and rubbish and linen chutes of copper or ferrous construction are permitted without shaft enclosure if floor openings are firestopped at each floor level.			
3418.1.8	**Vertical Shaft Opening Protection:** 1-hour assemblies in new vertical shaft enclosures, 20-minute in existing vertical shaft enclosures, except for elevator doors.			
	Elevator Lobbies: Unless building is fully sprinklered, provide elevator lobbies at elevator openings constructed as required for corridors.			
3418.1.15	**Exit Stairways:** 2 minimum.			
3418.1.16	**Corridor Construction:** 1-hour walls and ceilings when serving 30 or more occupants.			
	Permitted Existing Construction: 1/2" (13 mm) gypsum board, wood lath and plaster in good condition.			

Code Ref.	Code Compliance Item	OK	NA	ID
3418.1.19	**Corridor Dead Ends:** 20'-0" (6096 mm) maximum when serving more than 30 occupants.			
3418.2	**Sprinkler Alternatives:** Requirements of Table A-34-A may be modified in fully sprinkled existing buildings of Types I, II-FR, II 1-Hour, III 1-hour, IV, or V 1-hour construction as follows:			
	Item 7: Vertical enclosures may be nonrated construction for required exit stairs.			
	Vertical shaft enclosures for openings in floors provided for elevators, escalators, and supplemental stairs is not required when such openings are protected with a curtain board and water curtain system.			
	Item 16: Existing corridor construction need not be altered.			
	Item 19: Length of existing deadend corridors is not limited.			

Part 3: Detailed Construction Requirements

Uniform Building Code Compliance Manual
1997 Uniform Building Code

Group A Occupancies

UBC Section 303

Code Ref.	Code Compliance Item	OK	NA	ID
303.2.1	**Interior Wall Covering - Gymnasiums 3,200 sf (297 m²) or Less:** May be 1" (25 mm) nominal thickness tight T&G boards, or 3/4" (19 mm) plywood in lieu of fire-resistive plaster.			
	Gymnasiums - Floors: May be wood or unprotected steel or iron.			
303.2.2.3	**Group A-4 Bleacher Materials:** Seatboards, toeboards, bearing or base pads, and footboards may be combustible material.			
303.9	**Fire Alarm System:** Provide in Groups A-1, A-2, and A-2.2.			

Group B Occupancies

UBC Section 304

Code Ref.	Code Compliance Item	OK	NA	ID
304.6	**Escalator Enclosure:** Not required in fully sprinkled buildings where 12" (305 mm) draft curtain is provided around perimeter of floor opening.			
	Sprinklers: Provide around perimeter of opening within 24" (610 mm) of draft curtain; 6" (1829 mm) maximum spacing.			
304.8	**Special Hazards:** Locate devices generating a glow, spark, or flame capable of igniting flammable vapors such that sources of ignition are at least 18" (457 mm) above floor of any room in which Class I flammable liquids or flammable gases are used or stored.			

Group E Occupancies

UBC Section 305

Code Ref.	Code Compliance Item	OK	NA	ID
302.5	**Heating Equipment Room Doors:** On interior pairs of doors, provide self-closing active leaf with astragal and inactive leaf secured in closed condition, openable only by tool.			
305.2.3	**Group E-3 Day Care Rooms Above First Story - Fire Alarm:** Provide manual fire alarm and smoke detection system throughout entire story.			
	Initiating device actuation shall sound audible alarm throughout entire story. Alarm signals shall sound in the daycare to indicate fire alarm or sprinkler flow elsewhere in the building.			
	Connect alarm system to building fire alarm system when provided.			
	Group E-3 Day Care Rooms Above First Story - Smoke Compartment Separation Walls: 1-hour smoke barriers.			
	Doors: Smoke/draft control assemblies, 20-minute rating minimum, tight-fitting with gaskets at sides and top, and automatic closing by actuation of sprinklers, fire, or smoke alarm systems.			
	HVAC and Duct Penetrations: Provide Class I, 250°F (121°C) fire dampers which close upon activation of fire alarm or detection of smoke by duct-mounted detector.			
305.2.4	**Special Hazards:** Equipment in rooms sharing common atmosphere where flammable liquids, combustible dust, or hazardous materials are used, stored, or developed shall comply with Fire Code.			
305.9	**Fire Alarm System:** Required when occupant load is 50 or more.			
	Sprinkler or fire detection systems shall automatically activate fire alarm system, including exterior alarm mounted on each building.			

Group F Occupancies

UBC Section 306

Code Ref.	Code Compliance Item	OK	NA	ID
306.6	**Escalator Enclosure:** Not required in fully sprinkled buildings where 12" (305 mm) draft curtain is provided around perimeter of floor opening.			
	Sprinklers: Provide around perimeter of opening within 24" (610 mm) of draft curtain; 6" (1829 mm) maximum spacing.			
306.8	**Special Hazards:** Locate devices generating a glow, spark, or flame capable of igniting flammable vapors such that sources of ignition are at least 18" (457 mm) above floor of any room in which Class I flammable liquids or flammable gases are used or stored.			

Group H Occupancies

UBC Section 307

Code Ref.	Code Compliance Item	OK	NA	ID
307.1.3	**Shelves, Racks, and Wainscoting:** **Liquid Use, Dispensing, and Mixing Rooms:** Noncombustible construction or wood 1" (25 mm) minimum nominal thickness.			
307.1.4	**Storage Rooms for Class I, II, and III-A Flammable or Combustible Liquids:** Noncombustible construction or wood 1" (25 mm) minimum nominal thickness.			
307.1.5	**Storage Warehouses for Class I, II, and III-A Flammable or Combustible Liquids:** Noncombustible construction or wood 1" (25 mm) minimum nominal thickness.			
307.2.2	**Floors:** Noncombustible liquid-tight construction (except for surfacing) in areas containing hazardous materials or where motor vehicles, boats, helicopter, or airplanes are stored, repaired, or operated.			
	Groups H-4 and H-5 With No Repair Work: Asphalt paving permitted.			
307.2.3.1	**Spill Control and Secondary Containment for Storage of Hazardous Materials Liquids and Solids:** Provide when required by Fire Code.			
	See Fire Code for outdoor storage.			
307.2.3.2	**Spill Control in Hazardous Materials Storage Areas:** Provide in rooms, areas, or buildings used for storage of hazardous material liquids in individual vessels more than 55 gal (208.2 L) or aggregate capacity of multiple vessels exceeds 1,000 gal (3785 L).			
	Design: Prevent flow of liquids to adjoining areas, contain spill from single largest vessel by 1 of following:			
	Liquid-tight sloped or recessed floors,			
	Liquid-tight floors with liquid-tight raised or recessed sills or dikes,			
	Sumps and collections systems.			
	Construction: Noncombustible materials (except for floor surfacing) with liquid-tight seal compatible with materials stored.			
	Sills may be omitted at doors when open-grate trenches connected to drainage system are provided.			

Code Ref.	Code Compliance Item	OK	NA	ID
307.2.3.3	**Secondary Containment in Hazardous Materials Storage Areas:** When required by Fire Code, provide secondary containment when capacity of individual vessels or aggregate capacity of multiple vessels exceeds following:			
	Liquids: Individual vessels more than 55 gal (208.2 L) or aggregate capacity of multiple vessels exceeds 1,000 gal (3785 L).			
	Solids: Individual vessels more than 550 lbs (248.8 kg) or aggregate capacity of multiple vessels exceeds 10,000 lbs (4524.8 kg).			
	Construction: Building, room, or area shall contain or drain hazardous materials and fire protection water by 1 of following methods:			
	Liquid-tight sloped or recessed floors,			
	Liquid-tight floors provided with liquid-tight raised or recessed sills or dikes,			
	Sumps and collections systems.			
	Drainage systems to approved location.			
	Incompatible Materials: Separate from each other in secondary containment system.			
	Size: Sufficient for spill from single largest container plus volume of fire-protection water over minimum design area, or area of room or storage area, whichever is smaller, for 20 minutes.			
	Monitoring System: Provide system to detect hazardous materials in secondary containment.			
	Provide for visual inspection of primary or secondary containment, or other approved means.			
	When secondary containment is subject to water intrusion, provide monitoring system to detect water.			
	Connect monitoring devices to distinct visual or audible alarms.			
	Drainage System: Comply with Plumbing Code.			
	Slope to drains 1% minimum.			
	Size drains for volume of fire-protection water over minimum design area, or area of room or storage area, whichever is smaller, for 20 minutes.			
	Provide drainage system materials compatible with hazardous materials.			
	Separate incompatible materials from each other in drainage system.			
	Terminate drains at location away from buildings, valves, means of egress, fire-access roadways, adjoining property and storm drains.			

Code Ref.	Code Compliance Item	OK	NA	ID
307.2.4.1.1	**Spill Control in Hazardous Materials Use or Dispensing Areas - Open Containers and Systems:** When required by Fire Code, provide spill control in rooms, areas, or buildings used for dispensing and use of hazardous material liquids in individual vessels more than 1.1 gal (4 L) or where aggregate capacity of multiple vessels exceeds 5.3 gal (20 L).			
	Provide spill control per 307.2.3.2 above.			
307.2.4.1.2	**Secondary Containment in Hazardous Materials Use or Dispensing Areas - Open Containers and Systems:** When required by Fire Code, provide secondary containment in rooms, areas, or buildings used for dispensing and use of hazardous material liquids in individual vessels more than 1.1 gal (4 L) or where aggregate capacity of multiple vessels exceeds 5.3 gal (20 L).			
	Provide secondary containment per 307.2.3.3 above.			
307.2.4.2.1	**Spill Control in Hazardous Materials Use or Dispensing Areas - Closed Containers and Systems:** When required by Fire Code, provide spill control in rooms, areas, or buildings used for dispensing and use of hazardous material liquids in individual vessels is more than 55 gal (208.2 L).			
	Provide spill control per 307.2.3.2 above.			
307.2.4.2.2	**Secondary Containment in Hazardous Materials Use or Dispensing Areas - Open Containers and Systems:** When required by Fire Code, provide secondary containment in rooms, areas, or buildings used for dispensing and use of hazardous material liquids in individual vessels is more than 55 gal (208.2 L) or where aggregate capacity of multiple vessels exceeds 1,000 gal (3785 L).			
	Provide secondary containment per 307.2.3.3 above.			
307.2.5	**Smoke and Heat Vents - Group H-4:** Comply with Fire Code.			
307.2.6	**Standby Power:** Provide in Groups H-1 and H-2, and in H-3 where Class I or II organic peroxides are stored.			
	Automatically provide power to required electrical equipment upon interruption of normal power; comply with Electrical Code.			
307.2.7	**Emergency Power:** Provide in Groups H-6 and H-7.			
	Automatically supply power to required electrical equipment upon interruption of normal power; comply with Electrical Code.			
	Exhaust System: May operate at not less than half speed on emergency power when demonstrated that safe atmosphere will be provided.			
307.2.8	**Group H-1:** **Roof Construction:** Provide lightweight construction insulated to prevent sensitive materials from reaching decomposition temperature.			
	Materials both Health and Physical Hazards: Where such materials are in quantities exceeding UBC Table 3-E, comply with requirements for Group H-1 and H-7.			

Code Ref.	Code Compliance Item	OK	NA	ID
307.2.9	**Water-Reactive Materials in Groups H-2 and H-3:** Provide water-resistant construction.			
	Do not route liquids piping over or through areas containing water-reactive materials unless isolated by liquid-tight construction.			
	Fire-protection piping may be routed over reactives without isolation.			
307.6	**Group H-4 - Automobile Ramp Enclosure Doors:** Equip with automatic-closing devices.			
307.8	**Groups H-4 and H-5 - Special Hazards:** Locate devices generating a glow, spark, or flame capable of igniting flammable vapors such that sources of ignition are at least 18" (457 mm) above floor of any room in which Class I flammable liquids or flammable gases are used or stored.			
307.9	**Fire Alarm Systems:** Provide in Group H rooms used to manufacture organic coatings; comply with Fire Code.			
	Provide in aerosol storage warehouse per Fire Code.			
	Automatic Smoke Detection System: Provide in rooms used for storage, dispensing, use, and handling of hazardous materials when required by Fire Code.			
307.10	**Explosion Control - Separation:** Provide walls, floors, and roofs to separate uses from explosion exposure; resist 100 psf (4.79 kPa) minimum internal pressure.			
	Explosion Vents: Provide one or any combination of the following to relieve at maximum internal pressure of 20 psf (958 Pa), but not less than other required design loads:			
	Walls of lightweight material.			
	Lightly fastened hatch covers.			
	Lightly fastened, outward opening swinging doors in exterior walls.			
	Lightly fastened walls or roof.			
	Explosion Vent Discharge: Design discharge vertically or directly to unoccupied yards not less than 50'-0" (15 240 mm) in width on same lot.			
	Locate release device discharge end not less than 10'-0" (3048 mm) vertically and 20'-0" (6096 mm) horizontally from window openings or exits in same or adjoining buildings or structures.			
	Always direct exhaust toward the least exposure and never into interior of building unless suitably designed shaft with exterior discharge is provided.			

Group H-6 Occupancies

UBC Section 307.11

Code Ref.	Code Compliance Item	OK	NA	ID
307.11.2.1	**Doors in Fabrication Area Occupancy Separations:** 3/4-hour rated, self-closing, including doors into corridors.			
	Windows between Fabrication Area and Corridors: Fixed glazing, 3/4-hour, not exceeding 25% of wall area of room/corridor wall.			
307.11.2.2	**Fabrication Area Floors:** Provide noncombusible construction, except for surfacing.			
	When forming occupancy separation, make floors liquid-tight.			
307.11.2.3	**Fabrication Area Shaft and Exit Enclosures:** Mechanical, duct, and piping penetrations may extend through not more than 2 floors within a fabrication area.			
	Seal floor level annular space around penetrations for cables, cable trays, tubing, piping, conduit, or ducts to restrict air movement.			
	Consider fabrication area, including areas ductwork and piping pass-through, as single conditioned environment.			
307.11.2.5	**Transporting Hazardous Production Materials:** Provide enclosed piping or tubing systems, complying with Section 307.11.6 below, through service corridors, or corridors where permitted by Section 307.11.3.			
307.11.2.6	**Fabrication Area Electrical Equipment:** Comply with Electrical Code.			
	When average air change is at least 4 cfm/sf (1.76 L/s/m^2), hazardous location requirements need not apply.			
	When average air change is at least 3 cfm/sf (1.32 L/s/m^2) and 3 times that required by Fire Code, hazardous location requirements need not apply.			

Code Ref.	Code Compliance Item	OK	NA	ID
307.11.2.6	**Fabrication Area Electrical Equipment, Continued:** Electrical equipment and devices within 5'-0" (1524 mm) of work stations in which flammable or pyrophoric gases or flammable liquids are used shall be Class I, Division 2 hazardous locations.			
	Do not energize work stations without adequate exhaust ventilation.			
	Class I, Division 2 hazardous electrical requirements not needed when air removal from work station or dilution provides nonflammable atmospheres on continuous basis.			
307.11.3	**HPM Piping over Corridors:** Do not use corridors for transport of HPM materials except as provided in Section 307.11.6.2 below.			
	Exception: Building official may allow hazardous material piping and tubing above existing corridors subject to Fire Code and as follows:			
	In exit-access corridors adjacent to altered fabrication area, comply with Section 1004.3.4 for the length of common wall of corridor and fabrication area, and for the distance along corridor to point of entry of HPM into corridor serving fabrication area.			
	Provide emergency telephone, local alarm manual pull station, or signal device corridor at 150'-0" (45 720 mm) intervals maximum and at each stair doorway; relay signal to emergency control station and a local signal device.			
	Provide sprinklers per UBC Standard 9-1 for Ordinary Hazard, Group 3; when 1 row of sprinklers is used, only 13 need be calculated.			
	Provide 1-hour self-closing doors separating pass-throughs from existing corridors; construct pass-throughs as per corridors; sprinkle pass-through.			
307.11.4	**Service Corridor Doors:** Self-closing.			
	Service Corridor Ventilation: Provide exhaust at rate of 1 cfm/sf (0.044 L/s/m^2) or 6 air changes per hour, whichever is greater.			
307.11.5.1	**Liquid Storage and HPM Room Construction:** Noncombustible liquid-tight.			
	Raised Grating: Noncombustible.			
307.11.5.4	**Liquid Storage Rooms, HPM Rooms, and Gas Rooms - Mechanical Ventilation:** Exhaust at 1 cfm/sf (0.044 L/s/m2) or 6 air changes per hour, whichever is greater, all material categories.			
	Operate at negative pressure and direct ventilation to exhaust system.			
307.11.5.5	**Fire and Emergency Alarm:** Provide manual fire alarm system throughout Group H-6.			
	Liquid Storage Rooms, HPM Rooms, and Gas Rooms: Provide initiating device outside each interior door.			
	Activation of alarm-initiating device sounds local alarm and sends signal to emergency control station.			

Code Ref.	Code Compliance Item	OK	NA	ID
307.11.5.6	**Electrical Wiring in Liquid Storage Rooms, HPM Rooms, and Gas Rooms:** Comply with Electrical Code.			
307.11.6.1	**HPM Piping and Tubing in Service Corridors:** Expose to view.			
307.11.6.2	**HPM Piping and Tubing in Corridors and Above Other Occupancies:** Do not locate piping and tubing in corridors or above areas not classified as H-6 except as permitted below.			
	HPM piping and tubing may be installed in space defined by walls of corridors and roof or floor above, or in concealed spaces above other occupancies when the following are provided:			
	Sprinklers in the space unless space is less than 6" (152 mm) in least dimension.			
	Ventilation of at least 6 air changes per hour. Do not use space to convey air from any other area.			
	Provide receptor below piping or tubing transporting HPM liquids designed to collect all discharge or leakage and drain to approved location. Do not use 1-hour enclosure as part of receptor.			
	Separate all HPM supply piping and tubing HPM non-metallic waste lines from exit corridor or other occupancies other than H-6 by 1-hour construction. Gypsum board joints on the piping side of enclosure need not be taped when occurring over framing. Protect enclosure access openings with rated assemblies.			
	Provide readily accessible manual or automatic remotely activated fail-safe emergency shutoff valves on piping and tubing other than waste lines at branch connections into fabrication areas and entries to exit corridors.			
	Provide excess flow valves per Fire Code.			

Group I Occupancies

UBC Section 308

Code Ref.	Code Compliance Item	OK	NA	ID
308.2.2.1	**Group I-1.1 - Doors in Smoke Barriers:** Tight-fitting draft-control assemblies, not less than 20-minute rated, minimum of 44" (1118 mm) for passage of beds and equipment and 32" (813 mm) for other exits.			
	Provide pair of opposite-swinging doors without center mullion or horizontal sliding doors per with UBC Standard 7-8 when installed across corridors.			
	Provide vision panels when installed across corridors.			
	Provide close fit, minimum clearances for operation, no cutouts, louvers, or grilles.			
	Provide stops at heads and jambs, rabbets or astragals at meeting edges of opposite-swinging doors.			
	Provide positive latching, except on doors installed across corridors.			
	Provide automatic closing.			
	Where installed across corridors, activate by smoke detectors with listed hold-open device which releases or closes the door upon power failure at device.			
	Doors on floor or in affected zone shall automatically close upon activation of fire alarm or sprinklers.			
	Provide sign adjacent to self-closing doors stating that they are to be maintained in closed position.			
308.2.2.1	**Group I-1.1 - Smoke Control Zone Exit or Exit-Access Doors:** Provide vision panels.			
308.2.2.2	**Group I-3 - Floor Surfaces:** Noncombustible in rooms occupied by inmates or patients whose personal liberties are restrained.			
308.8	**Specific Use Separation Doors:** Self-closing or automatic-closing by actuation of smoke detector.			

Code Ref.	Code Compliance Item	OK	NA	ID
308.9	**Fire Alarm Systems:** Provide manual and automatic system.			
	Patient Areas: Audible alarms.			
	Nonpatient Areas: Visible or audible alarms.			
308.10	**Smoke Detectors:** Install in patient sleeping rooms of hospital and nursing homes; connect to primary building power.			
	Detector actuation shall cause visual display on corridor side of room and audible/visual alarm at nurses' station.			
	Nurse call system may be combined with single-station detectors and related devices when listed for such use.			
	Smoke detectors (on room side) integral with automatic door closers may substitute for room smoke detector provided it performs required alarm functions.			

Group M Occupancies

UBC Section 309

Code Ref.	Code Compliance Item	OK	NA	ID
309.6	**Escalator Enclosure:** Not required in fully sprinkled buildings where 12" (305 mm) draft curtain is provided around perimeter of floor opening.			
	Sprinklers: Provide around perimeter of opening within 24" (610 mm) of draft curtain; 6" (1829 mm) maximum spacing.			
309.8	**Special Hazards:** Locate devices generating a glow, spark, or flame capable of igniting flammable vapors such that sources of ignition are at least 18" (457 mm) above floor of any room in which Class I flammable liquids or flammable gases are used or stored.			

Group R Occupancies

UBC Section 310

Code Ref.	Code Compliance Item	OK	NA	ID
302.4.3. Exception 3	**Minimum Group R-3 and Group U Separation Requirements:** 1-hour construction on garage side.			
	Doors: Self closing, tight-fitting door; solid wood or 20 minute; 1-3/8" (35 mm) thick.			
	Ducts: 26 gage (0.48 mm) thick, galvanized steel with no openings into Group U, need not have fire dampers when passing through walls, floors, or ceilings forming separation.			
310.4	**Emergency Escape or Rescue Window Dimensions:** Net clear openable area: 5.7 sf (0.53 m²) minimum. Net clear openable height: 24" (610 mm) minimum. Net clear openable width: 20" (508 mm) minimum. Maximum sill height: 44" (1118 mm) above floor.			
	Make operable from inside to provide full opening without use of special tools.			
310.4	**Escape and Rescue Windows - Security Bars, Grilles, or Grates:** May be provided if openable from inside without key, special knowledge, or effort and if smoke detectors are provided throughout building in accordance with Section 310.9 below.			
310.8	**Nonsprinklered R-1 Separation:** When serving 10 or more occupants, separate from corridors and other spaces by not less than fixed wire glass in steel frames or 20-minute smoke and draft control assemblies which are automatic-closing by smoke detection.			
310.9.1.1	**Smoke Detectors - General:** Provide in dwelling units, congregate residences, and hotel or lodging guest rooms used for sleeping.			
310.9.1.2	**Smoke Detectors - Group R Additions, Alterations, and Repairs:** Provide when required by building official; may be battery powered only.			
310.9.1.3	**Smoke Detectors - Power Source:** Hardwire to building power system without disconnect switch (except for overcurrent protection) and provide battery back-up.			

Code Ref.	Code Compliance Item	OK	NA	ID
310.9.1.4	**Smoke Detectors - Dwelling Units:** Locate in each sleeping room and at a centrally located point in corridors or areas giving access to sleeping areas.			
	In multistory dwelling units, locate detector on each story and in basements.			
	Where stories are split into 2 or more levels, locate detector in upper level. When sleeping rooms are located on lower level, locate detectors in both levels. When sleeping rooms are located on upper level, place detector at ceiling of upper level in close proximity to stairway.			
	Where ceiling height of a room open to hallway serving bedrooms exceeds that of hallway by 24" (610 mm) or more, provide detectors in hallway and adjacent room.			
310.9.1.5	**Smoke Detectors - Efficiency Dwelling Units, Congregate Residences, and Hotels:** Locate on ceiling or wall of main room or each sleeping room.			
	When sleeping rooms are on upper level, locate detector on ceiling of upper level in close proximity to stairway.			
310.10	**Fire Alarm System - Group R-1:** Provide manual and automatic fire alarm system in apartment houses 3 or more stories high or containing more than 15 dwelling units; in hotels over 2 stories or containing 20 or more guest rooms; and in congregate residences over 2 stories or with 20 or more rooms.			
	Exceptions: Manual fire alarm not required in 1 or 2 story buildings when dwelling units and contiguous attic and crawl spaces are separated from each other and public or common areas by 1-hour occupancy separation and each dwelling unit or guest room has exit directly to a public way, exit court, or yard.			
	Separate fire alarm system not required in buildings with supervised sprinkler system throughout with a local alarm to notify occupants.			
	Fire Alarm and Communication System: Provide in Group R-1 located in high rise buildings.			
	Fire Alarm System - Signal Sound Pressure Level: Minimum of 15 decibels above equivalent sound level in room or space, or exceed any maximum sound level with 30 second duration by minimum of 5 decibels.			
	Maximum Sound Level: 120 decibels.			
310.11	**Heating:** Heat habitable spaces to 70°F (21°C) minimum at +3'-0" (914 mm) above floor.			
310.12	**Group R-1 - Doors into Class I Flammable Liquid Storage Rooms:** 1-hour, self-closing doors.			
	Provide sign on each side of door in 1" (25.4 mm) high letters stating: FIRE DOOR - KEEP CLOSED.			

Group S Occupancies

UBC Section 311

Code Ref.	Code Compliance Item	OK	NA	ID
311.2.3.1	**Floor Materials - Group S-3 and S-5:** Noncombustible and nonabsorbent in areas where motor vehicles, boats, or airplanes are stored, and in motor vehicle fuel-dispensing stations and repair garages.			
	Floors may be asphaltic paving where motor vehicles or airplanes are stored or operated.			
	Floor Drainage - Group S-3 and S-5: Drain floors to oil separator or trap discharging to sewers; comply with Plumbing Code.			
311.2.3.2 2603.13	**Marine or Motor Vehicle Fuel Dispensing Stations:** Canopies with plastic panels may be erected over pumps as follows:			
	Separation: 10'-0" (3048 mm) minimum to any other building; face yards or streets at least 40'-0" (12 192 mm) wide on the other sides.			
	Maximum Panel Area: 100 sf (9.3 m^2).			
	Aggregate Areas of Panels: 1,000 sf (93 m^2).			
311.2.3.3	**Parking Garage - Minimum Headroom:** 7'-0" (2134 mm) to any ceiling, beam, pipe, or similar obstruction, except for wall-mounted shelves, storage surfaces, racks, or cabinets.			
311.2.3.5	**Parking Garage - Vehicle Barriers:** Provide in parking areas more than 5'-0" (1524 mm) above adjacent grade except in Group U-1 parking garages.			
311.6	**Escalator Enclosure:** Not required in fully sprinkled buildings where 12" (305 mm) draft curtain is provided around perimeter of floor opening.			
	Sprinklers: Provide around perimeter of opening within 2'-0" (610 mm) of draft curtain; 6'-0" (1829 mm) maximum spacing.			
311.8	**Special Hazards:** Locate devices generating a glow, spark, or flame capable of igniting flammable vapors such that sources of ignition are at least 18" (457 mm) above floor of any room in which Class I flammable liquids or flammable gases are used or stored.			
	High Piled Combustible Stock or Aerosols: Comply with Fire Code.			
	Storage of Flammable and Combustible Liquids: Comply with Fire Code.			

Atria

UBC Section 402

Code Ref.	Code Compliance Item	OK	NA	ID
402.2	**Smoke Control System:** Provide system in atrium areas and areas opening into atrium which will operate automatically upon actuation of sprinkler system in atrium or areas open to atrium and as required by Section 905.9.			
402.3	**Atria Enclosure - Doors:** Minimum 20-minute, tight fitting, smoke and draft control assemblies without louvers.			
	Nonrated tight-fitting doors may be used when sprinkler system is equipped with quick-response sprinklers and wets entire door surface when actuated.			
	Atria Enclosure - Fixed Glazing: 3/4-hour fire windows, not exceeding 25% of area of common wall between atrium and room.			
	Exceptions: Openings in R-1 may be unprotected when area of guest room, congregate residence, or dwelling unit does not exceed 1,000 sf (93 m^2) and each room or unit has exit not entering atrium.			
	Fixed wire glass set in steel frame may be used to separate atrium from guest rooms, congregate residences, or dwelling units.			
	Tempered glass, laminated glass, or glass block may be used as follows:			
	Provide sprinkler system equipped with quick-response sprinklers which completely wet entire surface of glass when actuated (both surfaces when walking surfaces are on both sides).			
	Set tempered or laminated glass in gasketed frame so glazing system may deflect without breaking (loading) the glass before sprinklers go off.			
	Glass block: 3/4-hour assembly.			
	Curtain rods, drapery traverse rods, curtains, drapes, or similar obstructions not permitted between sprinklers and glass.			
402.7	**Standby Power:** Provide standby power for atrium and for smoke-control system for tenant space conforming to Section 905.8.			
402.8	**Interior Finish - Walls and Ceilings:** Provide Class I with no reduction for sprinkler protection in atria and unseparated tenant spaces.			

High-Rise Buildings

(Group B Office and Group R-1)

UBC Section 403

Code Ref.	Code Compliance Item	OK	NA	ID
403.2	**Sprinkler System:** Provide sprinkler system throughout building.			
	Sprinkler riser may be combined with standpipe riser.			
	Provide shutoff valves and water flow device on each floor.			
	Sprinkler System in Seismic Zones 2, 3, and 4: In addition to main water supply, provide secondary on-site supply equal to calculated sprinkler design plus 100 gpm (378.5 L/min) additional for total standpipe system for duration of 30 minutes.			
	Make secondary supply automatically available if principal supply fails.			
403.2.2.3	**Fire Dampers:** Not required except where protecting rated floor-ceilings.			
403.3	**Smoke Detection:** Provide detectors connected to fire alarm system.			
	Actuation of Smoke Detectors: Activates emergency voice/alarm signaling system and smoke control system.			
	Smoke Detector Locations: In every mechanical equipment, electrical, transformer, telephone equipment, elevator machine, or similar room.			
	In elevator lobbies; connect to alarm verification zone or provide door releasing device.			
	In main return-air and exhaust-air plenums located in serviceable area downstream of last duct inlet.			
	At each connection to a vertical duct or riser serving 2 or more stories from return-air duct or plenum.			
	In Group R-1, detector may be used in each return-air riser carrying not more than 5,000 cfm (2360 L/s) and serving not more than 10 air inlet openings.			
	In Group R-1 interior means of egress corridors serving occupant load of 10 or more.			

Code Ref.	Code Compliance Item	OK	NA	ID
403.4	**Smoke Control:** Provide system complying with Chapter 9.			
403.5.2	**Emergency Voice Alarm Signaling System:** Operation of any fire detector, sprinkler or water-flow device automatically sounds alert tone followed by voice instruction giving information and direction on a general or selective basis to following areas:			
	Elevators.			
	Elevator lobbies.			
	Corridors.			
	Exit stairways.			
	Rooms and tenant spaces exceeding 1,000 sf (93 m^2).			
	Dwelling units in apartment houses.			
	Guest rooms or suites in hotels.			
	Areas of refuge.			
	Provide manual override for all paging zones.			
403.5.3	**Fire Department Communication System:** Provide 2-way communication between central control station and elevators, elevator lobbies, emergency and standby power rooms, and at entries into enclosed stairways.			
403.6.1	**Central Control Station Equipment:** Voice alarm and public address system panels.			
	Fire department communication panel.			
	Fire-detection and alarm annunciator panels.			
	Annunciator visually indicating location of elevators and if they are operational.			
	Status indicators and controls for air-handling systems.			
	Controls for unlocking all stairway doors simultaneously.			
	Sprinkler valve and water-flow detector display panels.			
	Emergency and standby power status indicators.			
	Telephone for fire department use with controlled access to public telephone system.			
	Fire pump status indicators.			
	Schematic building plans indicating typical floor plan and detailing building core, means of egress, fire-protection systems, fire-fighting equipment, and fire department access.			
	Work table.			

Code Ref.	Code Compliance Item	OK	NA	ID
403.6.2	**Central Control Station Annunciation Identification:** Permanently identify control panels as to function.			
	Central Control Station Alarm Annunciation: Provide audible and visual indicators for alarm, supervisory, and trouble signals for fire-detection and alarm annunciator panels and for sprinkler valve and water-flow detector display panel; comply with Fire Code.			
	Annunciation Zones: When system serves more than 1 building, consider each building separately.			
	Consider each floor a separate zone.			
	When 1 or more sprinkler riser serves same floor, consider each riser a separate zone except when more than 1 riser serves the same system on the floor.			
403.7	**Elevators:** **Elevator Lobby Doors:** Minimum 20-minute, tight-fitting, smoke and draft control assemblies without louvers.			
	Elevator Lobby Fixed Glazing: 3/4-hour rated, not exceeding 25% of area of common wall between atrium and room.			
	Elevator Lobby Smoke Detectors: Provide detector on each lobby ceiling.			
	When detector is activated, elevator doors shall not open and cars serving that lobby shall return to main floor and be under manual control only.			
	If main floor detector of a transfer floor detector is activated, all cars serving main floor or transfer floor shall return to location approved by fire department and building official and be under manual control only.			
	Detector may serve to close lobby doors and smoke dampers serving lobby.			
	Hoistway Venting: Do not vent through an elevator machine room.			
	Smoke Control: Treat each elevator machine room as separate smoke-control zone.			
403.8.1	**Standby Power:** Provide generator set complying with Electrical Code to simultaneously power smoke detection system, smoke control system, fire alarm system, emergency voice/alarm signaling system, fire department communication system, elevators, standby lighting, exit signs and means of egress illumination, fire pumps required to maintain pressure, central control station lighting, and mechanical equipment room lighting.			
	Provide set supervision with manual start and transfer override features in central control station.			

Code Ref.	Code Compliance Item	OK	NA	ID
403.8.1	**Standby Power, Continued:** Provide on-premises fuel supply sufficient for not less than 2 hour's full-demand operation of system.			
	Capacity need not be sized to operate all connected electrical equipment simultaneously.			
403.8.2	**Standby Lighting:** Provide separate circuits and fixtures to provide light of not less than 1 footcandle at floor level in corridors, stairways, pressurized enclosures, elevator cars, elevator lobbies, and other areas which are clearly part of escape route.			
	Provide separate circuits for central control station and mechanical room lighting.			
403.8.3	**Emergency Systems:** Exit sign, means of egress illumination and elevator car lighting shall operate within 10 seconds of failure of normal power supply.			
403.9	**Means of Egress:** Provide capability of simultaneously unlocking stairway doors locked on stairway side without unlatching upon signal from central control station.			
	Provide continuously operating telephone or 2-way communication system connected to emergency service not less than every fifth floor in required stairways where code permits door to be locked.			
403.10	**Seismic Considerations - Zones 2, 3, and 4:** Verify that mechanical and electrical equipment required for life-safety systems, including fire pumps and elevator drive and suspension systems have been anchored for seismic forces.			

Covered Mall Buildings

UBC Section 404

Code Ref.	Code Compliance Item	OK	NA	ID
404.3.1	**Sprinkler System:** Provide sprinkler system throughout.			
	Provide electronic supervision by central, proprietary, or remote station or a local alarm service which will give audible signal at constantly attended location.			
	Provide mall sprinklers independent from tenant spaces. Tenant spaces may be supplied from same system if they can be independently controlled.			
404.3.2	**Standpipes:** Provide combined Class I standpipe outlet at the most hydraulically remote outlet, sized to deliver 250 gpm (946.4 L/min).			
	Supply outlet from mall zone sprinkler system.			
	Outlets: Provide outlets: Within mall at entrance to each exit passage or corridor.			
	At each floor-level landing within enclosed stairways.			
	At exterior public entrances to mall.			
404.3.3	**Smoke Control System:** Provide smoke control system except when mall is 1 story and gross leasable area does not exceed 24,000 sf (2230 m^2).			
404.3.4	**Fire Department Access to Rooms:** Identify rooms containing controls for HVAC systems, sprinkler systems, and other detection, suppression, or control elements.			
404.3.6	**Public Address System:** Provide in covered malls over 50,000 sf (4645.2 m^2) for fire department use.			
	When provided in covered mall less than 50,000 sf (4645.2 m^2), make system accessible for use by fire department.			

Code Ref.	Code Compliance Item	OK	NA	ID
404.3.7	**Plastic Panels and Plastic Signs Limitations:** Limit size and location in every story or level and from side wall to side wall of tenant spaces or mall as follows:			
	Plastics: Self ignition temperature of 650°F (343°C) or greater per UBC Standard 26-6, maximum smoke density rating of 450 tested per UBC Standard 8-1 in manner used or 75 per UBC Standard 26-5 in thickness intended for use.			
	Classify as CC1 or CC2 per UBC Standard 26-7.			
	Foam Plastics: Maximum heat release rate of 150 kw per approved recognized standards, 20 pcf (320.4 kg/m^3) minimum density, and 1/2" (12.7 mm) maximum thickness.			
	Do not exceed 20% of wall area facing mall.			
	Do not exceed height of 36" (914 mm) except if sign is vertical, in which case do not exceed height of 96" (2438 mm).			
	Do not exceed width of 36" (914 mm).			
	Locate 18" (457 mm) minimum from adjacent tenants.			
404.3.10	**Standby Power - Covered Mall Buildings over 50,000 sf (4645.2 m^2):** Provide system to operate public address system, smoke control activation system, and smoke control equipment.			
404.4.8	**Horizontal Sliding or Vertical Rolling Security Grilles and Doors:** When part of required means of egress, comply with the following:			
	Shall remain secured in full open position during occupancy by general public.			
	Shall not be closed when more than 10 persons occupy spaces served by 1 exit or 50 persons occupy spaces served by more than 1 exit.			
	Shall be openable from within without use of special knowledge or effort when space is occupied.			
	When 2 or more exits are required, not more than half of exits may be equipped with horizontal sliding or vertical rolling grilles or doors.			

Stages and Platforms

UBC Section 405

Code Ref.	Code Compliance Item	OK	NA	ID
405.1.3	**Design:** Indicate all assumed live loads on drawings.			
405.2	**Temporary Platforms:** Construct of any material permitted by code.			
	Do not use space between floor and platform for any purpose except electrical wiring or plumbing to platform equipment.			
	Permanent Platforms: Construct of materials required for type of construction.			
	Provide 1-hour floor construction when space between floor and platform is used for storage or any purpose other than platform equipment wiring or plumbing.			
	Space Below Platforms: When space is only used for platform equipment wiring or plumbing, construct permanent platforms of any material permitted by code and firestop space between floor and platforms.			
	Floor Finish: May be of wood in all types of construction.			
405.3.1	**Stage Floor:** May be of wood in all types of construction.			
	Stage Floor Construction: May be unprotected noncombustible or heavy timber construction with 1-1/2" (38 mm) thick wood deck when permitted by construction type or where stage is separated from other areas by 2-hour occupancy separation.			
	Stage Floor: When required to be 1-hour construction, floor may be unprotected when space below stage is sprinkled throughout.			
405.3.3	**Emergency Ventilation:** Provide for all stage areas over 1,000 sf (93 m^2) or stage height greater than 50'-0" (15 240 mm) to remove smoke and combustion gases directly outside during fires.			
	Provide ventilation by smoke control or roof vents, or by combination of both.			

Code Ref.	Code Compliance Item	OK	NA	ID
405.3.3	**Emergency Ventilation, Continued:** **Smoke Control:** Provide means to maintain smoke level not less than 6'-0" above highest level of seating or above top of proscenium opening where proscenium wall and opening protection is required.			
	System shall activate independently by activation of stage area sprinkler system and by manually operated switch at approved location.			
	Connect smoke control system to both normal and standby power. Locate and protect fan power wiring and ducts to a provide a minimum of 20 minutes of operation after activation.			
	Roof Vents: Locate 2 or more labeled vents near center of and above highest part of stage area; provide net free vent area equal to 5% of stage area.			
	Provide net free vent area equal to 5% of stage area.			
	Vents shall open automatically by heat-activated devices; provide means for manual operation of vents from stage floor.			
405.3.4	**Proscenium Opening:** Where 2-hour proscenium wall protection is required, protect opening by fire curtain or water curtain complying with UBC Standard 4-1.			
	Fire curtain shall close automatically upon automatic detection of fire and upon manual activation, and shall resist passage of smoke or flame for 20 minutes between stage area and audience area.			
405.3.5	**Gridirons, Fly Galleries, and Pinrails:** Provide materials permitted by type of construction for beams used only for attachment of portable or fixed equipment, gridirons, galleries and catwalks; fire rating not required.			
	Gallery and Catwalk Floors: May be of combustible materials.			

Motion Picture Projection Rooms

UBC Section 406

Code Ref.	Code Compliance Item	OK	NA	ID
406.1.2	**Electrical Equipment:** Locate rheostats, transformers, and generators in projection room or in adjacent room of equivalent construction.			
	Projection Room Door Sign: Post sign outside each projection room door and within projection room itself stating: SAFETY FILM ONLY PERMITTED IN THIS ROOM; 1" (25.4 mm) block letters.			
406.5.2.1	**Projection Booth Ventilation - Supply Air:** Provide amount of air equivalent to that exhausted by projection equipment.			
406.5.2.2	**Projection Booth Ventilation - Exhaust Air:** May be through lamp exhaust system. Interconnect with lamp so lamp will not operate unless air flow is sufficient for lamp.			
	Terminate ducts at exterior of building, located to prevent recirculation of exhaust air into air-supply system.			
	Provide each projection machine with rigid duct to exterior.			
	Exhaust systems may be combined with other machine exhaust systems but may not be interconnected with any other exhaust air or return system.			
406.5.3.1	**Projection Equipment Ventilation:** Provide rigid exhaust duct for each machine.			
406.5.3.2	**Electric Arc Projection Equipment:** 200 cfm (94.4 L/s) per lamp minimum or exhaust as required by equipment manufacturer.			
406.5.3.3	**Xenon Projection Equipment:** 300 cfm (142 L/s) per lamp minimum or exhaust as required by equipment manufacturer.			

Amusement Buildings

UBC Section 408

Code Ref.	Code Compliance Item	OK	NA	ID
408.4	**Automatic Sprinkler System:** Fully sprinkle amusement buildings.			
	Provide system with electrically supervised main water-flow switch.			
	Supervise sprinkler main cutoff valve.			
408.5.1	**Smoke Detection:** Provide smoke detection system per Fire Code.			
	Provide alternate type of detector where ambient conditions will cause a smoke detector to alarm.			
408.5.2	**Alarm System:** Activate alarm system by smoke detectors, sprinkler system, or other fire-detection device.			
	Activation shall sound immediate alarm at constant supervised location from which manual operation of required automatic response may be initiated.			
408.5.3	**Alarm System Response:** Activation of 2 or more smoke detectors, a single detector monitored by alarm verification zone, sprinkler system, or fire detectors shall automatically:			
	Stop confusing sounds and visual effects, and			
	Activate directional exit marking, and			
	Cause illumination of means of egress, 1 footcandle (10.76 lx) minimum at walking surface.			
408.5.4	**Public Address System:** Provide system audible throughout building; public address system may also serve as alarm system.			

Medical Gas Systems in Groups B and I

UBC Section 410

Code Ref.	Code Compliance Item	OK	NA	ID
410	**General:** Comply with Fire Code and this Section.			
	Enclosure: Provide 1-hour enclosure for nonflammable supply gas cylinders located inside buildings.			
	Gas Cylinder Storage Room Doors: Self-closing, smoke/draft assemblies, 1-hour rated.			
	Vents: Provide 2 vents through exterior wall not less than 36" (0.023 m²) per vent. 1 vent within 6" (152 mm) of floor and 1 within 6" (152 mm) of ceiling.			
	Sprinkler System: Where room is not on exterior wall, provide sprinkler system in room and vent room through ducting in 1-hour enclosure.			
	Mechanical Ventilation: Provide 6 air changes per hour when exterior wall is not provided for gas cylinder storage rooms.			

Area Separation Walls

UBC Section 504.6

Code Ref.	Code Compliance Item	OK	NA	ID
504.6.3	**Extensions Beyond Exterior Walls:** Extend area separation walls horizontally to outside edges of horizontal projecting elements such as balconies, roof overhangs, canopies, marquees, or architectural projections extending beyond floor area.			
	Exceptions: Terminate at exterior wall when horizontal projections do not have concealed spaces.			
	When horizontal projections have concealed spaces, extend through concealed space to outer edge of projection.			
	When either exception above is used, provide 1-hour exterior walls and projecting elements, and 3/4-hour opening protection, for a distance not less than the depth of the projecting elements on both sides of separation wall.			
504.6.4	**Vertical Terminations:** Extend vertically from foundation to 30" (762 mm) minimum above roof.			
	May terminate at underside of roof sheathing, deck, or slab of 2-hour rated roof-ceiling assembly.			
	2-hour area separation walls may terminate at underside of roof sheathing, deck, or slab when:			
	Roof-ceiling framing elements parallel to walls are 1-hour rated for at least 5'-0" (1524 mm) on each side of wall.			
	Roof-ceiling framing elements not parallel to walls are 1-hour rated for entire span.			
	Roof openings are not closer than 5'-0" (1524 mm).			
	Roof is minimum of Class B.			
	2-hour separation walls may terminate at underside of noncombustible roof sheathing, deck or slabs of noncombustible construction provided:			
	Roof openings are not closer than 5'-0" (1524 mm).			
	Roof is Class B minimum.			

Code Ref.	Code Compliance Item	OK	NA	ID
504.6.5	**Parapet Faces:** Noncombustible for top 18" (457 mm).			
504.6.6	**Buildings of Different Heights:** Terminate 30" (762 mm) above lower roof level if exterior wall is 1-hour rated for 10'-0" (3048 mm) above lower roof with 3/4-hour opening protection.			
	Exception: 2-hour area separation walls may terminate at underside of roof sheathing, deck, or slab of lower roof when:			
	Roof-ceiling framing elements parallel to the walls are 1-hour rated for at least 10'-0" (3048 mm) on each side of wall at lower roof.			
	Lower roof-ceiling framing elements not parallel to the wall are 1-hour rated for entire span.			
	Roof openings are not closer than 10'-0" (3048 mm).			
504.6.7	**Combustible Framing:** Provide 4" (102 mm) minimum separation between combustible members entering masonry area separation walls from opposite sides.			
	Where combustible members frame into hollow walls or walls of hollow units, solidly fill hollow spaces for full thickness of wall and at least 4" (102 mm) above, below, and between structural members with noncombustible fireblocking materials.			

Guardrails

UBC Section 509

Code Ref.	Code Compliance Item	OK	NA	ID
509.1	**Guardrails:** Provide at unenclosed floor and roof openings, open and glazed sides of stairways, landings and ramps, balconies or porches more than 30" (762 mm) above grade or floor below, and roofs used for other than service of building.			
	Provide at ends of aisles terminating fascia of boxes, balconies, and galleries.			
	Guardrails Not Required: On loading sides of loading docks.			
	On auditorium side of stages, raised platforms, runways, ramps, and side stages used for entertainment or presentation; along sides of elevated walking surfaces when used for normal functioning of special lighting or for access and use of special equipment; and at vertical openings in performance areas of stages.			
	Along vehicle service pits not accessible to public.			
509.2	**Minimum Guardrail Height:** 42" (1067 mm).			
	Exceptions: 36" (914 mm) in R-3, M-1, R-3 congregate residences, and R-1 guest rooms.			
	26" (660 mm) at balconies immediately in front of first row of seats which are not at end of aisles.			
	As required for handrails at stairways, exclusive of landings.			
	26" (660 mm) above aisle floor where elevation change of 30" (762 mm) or less occurs between aisle parallel to seats (cross aisle) and adjacent floor or grade below.			
	Exception: Guardrail not required where backs of seats along front of aisles project 24" (610 mm) or more above floor of aisle.			

Code Ref.	Code Compliance Item	OK	NA	ID
509.2	**Minimum Guardrail Height Exceptions, Continued:** Extend tops of guardrails full width of aisle at ends of aisles terminating at fascia of boxes, balconies, and galleries.			
	Make rail 42" (1067 mm) minimum to closest surface of aisle where there are steps and 36" (914 mm) otherwise.			
509.3	**Guardrail Openings:** Provide intermediate rails or ornamental pattern such that a sphere 4" (102 mm) in diameter cannot pass through.			
	Exceptions: May be 12" (305 mm) sphere at commercial and industrial occupancies not accessible to public.			
	May be 6" (152 mm) sphere at triangular openings formed by riser, tread, and bottom element of guardrail at open side of stair.			

Types of Construction

UBC Chapter 6

Code Ref.	Code Compliance Item	OK	NA	ID
601.5.2.1	**Exceptions to UBC Table 6-A:** **Fixed Partitions - Stores and Offices:** Interior nonload-bearing partitions dividing portions of stores, offices, or similar places occupied by 1 tenant and which do not establish corridor serving occupant load requiring rated construction may be of:			
	Noncombustible materials.			
	Fire-retardant treated wood.			
	1-hour rated construction.			
	Wood panels or similar construction up to 3/4 height of room; when more than 3/4 height, construct upper portion of glass.			
601.5.2.2	**Fixed Partitions - Hotels and Apartments:** Interior nonload-bearing partitions within dwelling units in apartment houses and guest rooms in hotels, when such dwelling units, guest rooms, or suites are separated from each other and from corridors by at least 1-hour construction may be:			
	Noncombustible materials or fire-retardant treated wood in buildings of any type of construction.			
	Combustible framing with noncombustible finish materials in Type III or V.			
	Opening to such corridors shall be equipped with doors conforming to Section 1004.3.4.3.2 regardless of occupant load.			
601.5.3	**Folding, Portable, or Moveable Partitions:** Need not be rated when:			
	They do not block required exits or exit-access doors (without providing alternative conforming exits or exit-access doors) and do not establish a corridor.			
	Location is restricted by permanent tracks or guides.			
	Flammability is limited to that allowed by UBC Table 8-B for room or area.			

Code Ref.	Code Compliance Item	OK	NA	ID
601.5.4	**Exceptions to Table 6-A, Continued:** **Walls Fronting on Streets or Yards:** Elements of walls fronting on streets or yards with width of 40'-0" (12 192 mm) may be:			
	Bulkheads below shop windows, show-window frames, aprons, and showcases may be of noncombustible materials provided height does not exceed 15'-0" (4572 mm).			
	Wood veneer boards not less than 1" (24 mm) nominal thickness, or exterior panels not less than 3/8" (9.5 mm) nominal thickness may be applied to walls provided veneer does not exceed 15'-0" (12 192 mm) and veneer is placed either directly against noncombustible surfaces or furred out from such surfaces not to exceed 1-5/8" (41 mm) with concealed spaces fire-blocked.			
	Height of fire-retardant treated wood veneer suitable for exterior exposure may be 35'-0" (10 668 mm).			
601.5.5	**Trim:** Trim, picture molds, chair rails, baseboards, handrails, and show-window backing may be of wood.			
	Doors and windows may be unprotected except where openings are required to be rated.			
	Foam plastic trim covering not more than 10% of wall or ceiling may be used provided such trim has density of at least 20 pcf (320.4 kg/m^3), has maximum thickness of 1/2" (12.7 mm) and maximum width of 4" (102 mm), and flame spread rating of no greater than 75.			
601.5.6	**Exterior Loading Platforms:** Noncombustible construction or heavy-timber with wood floors not less than 2" (51 mm) nominal thickness. Do not carry such construction through exterior walls.			
601.5.7	**Combustible Insulating Boards:** May be used under finished flooring.			
601.5.8	**Walls in Health-care Suites:** Where suite meets Group I egress requirements, interior noncombustible nonload-bearing partitions may be nonrated.			
	Combustible Buildings: Interior nonload-bearing construction within suites may be combustible framing covered with noncombustible materials having thermal barrier with index of 15 per UBC Standard 26-2.			
605.6	**Heavy-Timber Construction:** **General:** Framed sawn timbers or structural glued-laminated timber. All dimensions below are nominal.			
605.6.5	**Floors:** No concealed spaces allowed.			
	Lay lumber such that a continuous line of joints only occurs over points of support.			
	Do not extend floors closer than 1/2" (13 mm) to walls. Cover such space with molding, allow for swelling or shrinkage. Corbeling of masonry walls under floors may be used in place of molding.			

Code Ref.	Code Compliance Item	OK	NA	ID
605.6.6	**Heavy-Timber Construction, Continued:** **Roof Decks:** No concealed spaces allowed.			
605.6.7	**Construction Details:** Provide wall plate boxes or hangers where beams, girders, or trusses rest on masonry or concrete walls.			
	Closely fit girders and beams around columns and cross tie or intertie adjoining ends.			
	Wood bolsters may be placed on columns supporting roof loads only.			
	Rest intermediate beams supporting floors on top of girders, or support by ledgers or blocks on sides of girders, or support by closely fitting metal hangers.			
	Anchor roof girders and at least every other roof beam to supporting members.			
	Anchor roof decks supported by walls at 20'-0" (6096 mm) intervals.			
605.6.9	**Partitions:** 1-hour rated construction or solid wood of at least 2 layers of 1" (25 mm) matched boards or laminated construction of 4" (102 mm) thickness.			

Fire-Resistant Materials and Construction

UBC Chapter 7

Code Ref.	Code Compliance Item	OK	NA	ID
704.2.1	**Protective Coverings - Thickness:** UBC Table 7-A.			
704.2.2	**Masonry Protection at Steel Columns:** Embed metal ties in transverse joints.			
704.2.3	**Concrete Protection over Steel Columns:** Reinforce edges with wire ties 0.18" (4.6 mm) minimum diameter wound around columns at pitch of 8" (203 mm) maximum or by equivalent reinforcement.			
704.2.4	**Embedment of Pipes:** Do not embed in required fire protection of members.			
704.2.5	**Column Jacketing:** Protect rated coverings where exposed to injury from vehicles and material handling.			
704.2.6	**Ceiling Membrane Protection:** Individual protection of structural members is not required where ceilings form protective membrane except where such members support a floor and roof or more than 1 floor.			
704.2.7	**Plaster Application:** Finish coat may be omitted where plaster mix complies with UBC Tables 7-A, 7-B, and 7-C.			
704.2.8	**Truss Protection:** Where rated protection is required, enclose trusses for entire length and height.			
704.3.1	**Attached Metal Members on Protected Members:** Edges of attached lugs, brackets, rivets, and bolt head may extend to within 1" (25 mm) of surface of protection.			
704.3.2	**Concrete Cover for Reinforcement:** Measure from outside of reinforcement.			
	Stirrups and spiral reinforcement ties may project 1/2" (12.7 mm) into protection.			

Code Ref.	Code Compliance Item	OK	NA	ID
704.3.3	**Concrete Cover for Bonded Prestressed Concrete Tendons:** For single tendon or more than 1 tendon installed with equal concrete cover, measure from nearest surface; UBC Table 7-A.			
	For multiple tendons with variable concrete cover, provide average coverage not less than UBC Table 7-A. Refer to Section 704.3.3 for detailed coverage measurement requirements.			
704.4	**Members Carrying Masonry or Concrete:** In buildings 2 stories or more, provide 1-hour protection or rating requirement of wall, whichever is greater.			
704.5	**Fire-resistive Material Omitted:** Protection not required on bottom flange of lintels spanning 6'-0" (1829 mm) or less, shelf angles, or plates not part of structural frame.			
705	**Projections:** Cornices, eave overhangs, exterior balconies, similar architectural appendages extending beyond floor area:			
	Type I or II construction: Noncombustible materials.			
	Type III, IV, or V construction: noncombustible or combustible materials.			
	For combustible projections over walls where openings are not permitted or where protection is required, provide 1-hour or heavy-timber construction.			
706.1	**Building Movement Joints:** Protect joints in rated walls, floors, and floor-ceiling assemblies with rated joint assemblies matching rating of floor or wall.			
	Exception: Rated joint systems not required in following locations: Floors in single dwelling unit.			
	Floors where joint is protected by shaft enclosure.			
	Floor with atriums where space adjacent to atrium is included in volume of atrium for smoke control purposes.			
	Floors in malls.			
	Floor in open parking structures.			
	Mezzanine floors.			
	Wall permitted to have unprotected openings.			
	Roof where openings are permitted.			
708.1	**Fire Blocks and Draft Stops:** Provide in combustible construction to cut off concealed vertical and horizontal draft openings, form barriers between floors, top stories and roofs or attic spaces, and subdividing concealed attic spaces, roof spaces and floor-ceiling assemblies.			
708.2.1	**Fire Blocks Required:** In concealed spaces of stud walls and furred spaces, at floor and ceiling levels, and at 10'-0" (3048 mm) intervals, vertical and horizontal.			
	Exception: Omit fire blocks at floor and ceiling when smoke-actuated fire dampers are installed at floor and ceiling.			

Code Ref.	Code Compliance Item	OK	NA	ID
708.2.1	**Fire Blocks Required, Continued:** At interconnections between concealed vertical and horizontal spaces which occur at soffits, drop ceilings, and cove ceilings.			
	In concealed spaces between stair stringers at top and bottom of run and between studs along and in line with run of stairs if walls under stairs are unfinished.			
	Around vents, pipes, ducts, chimneys, fireplaces, and similar openings providing passage for fire at ceiling and floor levels; use noncombustible materials.			
	At openings between attics and chimney chases for factory-built chimneys.			
	Wood Flooring on Rated Masonry or Concrete Floors: Divide open spaces between sleepers into spaces not more than 100 sf (9.3 m^2) and fill space under partitions with noncombustible materials or fire blocking.			
	Exceptions: Not required in gym floors at or below grade.			
	In bowling lanes, fire blocks only required at juncture of alternate lanes and at lane ends.			
708.2.2	**Fire Block Construction:** 2" (51 mm) lumber, 2 thicknesses of 1" (25 mm) lumber with staggered lap joints, 23/32" (18.3 mm) structural panel with joints backed by same material, or 3/4" (19.1 mm) Type 2-M particleboard with joints backed by same material.			
	Gypsum board, mineral fiber, glass fiber securely fastened in place. Do not use loose insulation materials unless specifically fire tested in form and manner intended for use.			
	Sound Walls with Parallel or Staggered Studs: Mineral or glass fiber batts or blankets or other flexible materials.			
708.3.1.1	**Draft Stops Required - Floor-Ceiling Assemblies:** **Single-family Dwellings:** Where useable space is above and below floor-ceiling, subdivide concealed spaces into areas not exceeding 1,000 sf (93 m^2), dividing area approximately equally.			
	Buildings with 2 or More Dwelling Units and Hotels: Provide in line with walls separating units from each other and other areas.			
	Other Occupancies: Subdivide into areas not exceeding 1,000 sf (93 m^2), maximum horizontal dimension between draft stops of 60'-0" (18 288 mm).			
	Where sprinklers are provided in concealed spaces, subdivide into areas not exceeding 3,000 sf (279 m^2), maximum horizontal dimension between draft stops of 100'-0" (30 480 mm).			

Code Ref.	Code Compliance Item	OK	NA	ID
708.3.1.2	**Draftstops Required - Attics, Mansards, Overhangs, and False Fronts set out from Building:** **2 or More Dwelling Units and Hotels:** Provide draft stops in line with walls separating units from each other and from other areas.			
	Draft stops may be omitted along 1 corridor wall provided stops at walls separating units and other areas extend to remaining corridor draft stop. In sprinklered buildings see exception below.			
	Other Occupancies: **Nonsprinkled Buildings:** Subdivide into areas 3,000 sf (279 m²) or less, maximum horizontal dimension between stops of 60'-0" (18 288 mm).			
	Sprinkled Buildings: Subdivide onto areas 9,000 sf (836 m²) or less, maximum horizontal dimension between stops of 100'-0" (30 480 mm).			
708.3.1.3	**Draft Stop Construction:** 1/2" (12.7 mm) gypsum board, 3/8" (9.5 mm) wood structural panel, or 3/8" (9.5 mm) Type 2-M particle board.			
708.3.1.3	**Draft Stop Openings:** Provide doors constructed as required for draft stops, self-closing with automatic latches.			
708.4	**Fire Blocks in Other Locations:** Fireblock behind veneers on noncombustible walls, at 10'-0" (3048 mm) intervals, vertical and horizontal.			
	Fire block behind ceilings applied against noncombustible construction, at 8'-0" (2438 mm) intervals, vertical and horizontal; maximum furring depth of 1-3/4" (44 mm).			
709.1	**Rated Walls and Partitions:** Provide in accordance with UBC Table 7-B and provide assembly numbers on drawings.			
709.3.2.1	**Rated Exterior Walls:** Extend rated construction through attic areas and other concealed spaces.			
	Do not add construction materials to floor/ceiling and roof/ceiling assemblies which affect dissipation of heat within assembly which have not been tested as part of the assembly.			
709.3.2.3	**Vertical Fire Spread at Exterior Walls:** Seal voids created at intersections of exterior rated walls and rated floors or floor-ceilings with fire/smoke stopping.			
	Vertical Fire Spread at Exterior Walls - Exterior: Where exterior openings are above and within 5'-0" (1524 mm) laterally of opening in story below, separate such openings with horizontal flame barrier extending 30" (762 mm) beyond exterior wall at floor or vertical flame barrier 3'-0" (914 mm) high beginning at top of lower opening; all flame barriers 3/4-hour rated.			
	Exceptions: Flame barriers not required: In fully sprinklered buildings.			
	In buildings 3 stories or less.			
	On Group S-4 occupancies.			

Code Ref.	Code Compliance Item	OK	NA	ID
709.4.2	**Parapet Construction:** Match rating required for wall below, with noncombustible face on roof surface side for top 18" (457 mm).			
709.6.1	**Through Penetrations at Rated Walls:** Provide rated penetration assemblies or protect penetrations with firestop system with F rating matching rating of wall.			
	Exception: Where penetrating items are steel, ferrous, or copper pipes or steel conduits, annular space permitted to be protected as follows:			
	Concrete, grout or mortar full thickness of wall in concrete or masonry walls where penetrating items are 6" (152 mm) maximum diameter and opening is 144 si (92 903 mm^2) maximum.			
	Material shall prevent passage of flame and hot gases sufficient to ignite solid cotton waste; UBC Standard 7-1.			
709.7	**Membrane Penetrations of Rated Walls:** Comply with requirements for through-penetrations above.			
	Exceptions: Steel electrical boxes 16 si (10 323 mm^2) maximum, where area of openings is 100 si for any 100 sf (694 mm^2/m^2) wall area. Separate boxes on opposite sides of wall by 24" (610 mm) minimum.			
	Annular space at sprinkler penetration permitted to be unprotected where covered by metal escutcheon plates.			
710.1	**Rated Floor-Ceilings or Roof-Ceilings:** Provide assemblies per UBC Table 7-C and provide assembly numbers on drawings.			
	Do not add construction materials to floor/ceiling and roof/ceiling assemblies which affect the dissipation of heat within the assembly which have not been tested as part of the assembly.			
710.2	**Through-Penetrations of Rated Floor-Ceilings or Roof-Ceilings:** Provide rated shaft enclosures, rated penetration assemblies, or protect penetrations with firestop system with F rating and T rating matching rating of assembly.			
	Exceptions: Steel, ferrous, or copper conduits, pipes, tubes, vents, concrete or masonry penetrating items penetrating single rated floor assembly where annular space is protected with materials that prevent passage of flame and hot gases sufficient to ignite solid cotton waste; UBC Standard 7-1.			
	Penetrating items with 6" (152 mm) maximum diameter not limited to penetration of single rated floor assembly provided area of penetration does not exceed 144 si (92 903 mm^2) in 100 sf (9.3 m^2) of floor area.			
	Penetration of single concrete floor by steel, ferrous, or copper conduits, pipes, tubes, or vents with 6" (152 mm) maximum diameter provided concrete, grout, or mortar is installed full thickness of floor or thickness to provided required rating.			

Code Ref.	Code Compliance Item	OK	NA	ID
710.2	**Through-Penetrations of Rated Floor-Ceilings or Roof-Ceilings: Exceptions, Continued:** Penetrating items with 6" (152 mm) maximum diameter not limited to penetration of single rated floor assembly provided area of penetration does not exceed 144 si (92 903 mm^2) in 100 sf (9.3 m^2) of floor area.			
	Floor penetrations within cavity of wall do not require T rating.			
710.3	**Membrane Penetrations of Rated Floor-Ceilings or Roof-Ceilings:** Comply with requirements for through-penetrations above.			
	Exceptions: Membrane penetrations of steel, ferrous, or copper conduits, electrical outlet boxes, pipes, tubes, vents, concrete, or masonry items where annular space is protected per Section 710.2 above or is protected to prevent passage of flame and products of combustion. Do not exceed aggregate area of 100 si for any 100 sf (694 mm^2/m^2) in assemblies tested without penetrations.			
	Annular space at sprinkler penetration permitted to be unprotected where covered by metal escutcheon plates.			
710.4	**Rated Roofs:** May have unprotected openings.			
711.3	**Shaft Enclosures - Special Provisions:** In other than Group I, openings penetrating only 1 floor and not connected with openings communicating with other stories or basements and not concealed in construction assemblies need not be enclosed.			
	In 1- and 2-story buildings other than Group I, gas vents, ducts, piping and factory-built chimneys extending through not more than 2 floors need not be enclosed where penetrations are fire stopped at each floor.			
	Exception: Listed BW gas vents.			
	Walls containing gas vents and noncombustible piping passing through 3 floors or less need not be rated as shaft enclosures if annular space around vents or piping is filled with noncombustible materials.			
	Exception: Listed BW gas vents.			
	Floor penetrations for cables, cable trays, conduit, pipes or tubing protected by fire stops matching rating of floor construction need not be enclosed.			
711.4	**Shaft Enclosures - Opening Protection:** Self-closing or automatic closing by smoke or heat detector; 1-hour in 1-hour walls, 1-1/2 hour in 2-hour walls.			
	Exceptions: Openings to exterior may be unprotected per UBC Table 5-A.			
	Openings protected by through-penetration fire stops to provide same degree of fire resistance as shaft enclosure.			
	Noncombustible ducts, vents, or chimneys used to convey vapors, dusts, or combustion products may penetrate enclosure at bottom.			

Code Ref.	Code Compliance Item	OK	NA	ID
711.4	**Shafts Penetrating Smoke Barrier - Opening Protection:** In addition to fire dampers, provide smoke dampers.			
	Exceptions: At exhaust-only openings serving continuously operating fans protected as required by Chapter 9.			
	Where damper operation would interfere with smoke control system.			
711.6	**Chute and Dumbwaiter Shafts - Type V Construction:** Where not more than 9 sf (0.84 m²) in area, inside layers of rated construction may be replaced with 26 gage sheet metal with joints locklapped.			
	Openings: Self-closing, solid wood door, 1-3/8" (35 mm) thick.			
712	**Useable Space Under First Floor:** Enclose on useable side as required for 1-hour construction.			
	Exceptions: Groups R-3 and U.			
	Basements of 1-story Group S-1 parking garages where 10% or more of area of floor-ceiling is open to first floor.			
	Fully sprinklered under-floor spaces.			
	Doors: Self-closing, tight-fitting solid wood, 1-3/8" (35 mm) thick, 20-minute rated.			
713.6.1	**Rated Door Assemblies - Closing Devices:** **3-hour Rated Doors:** Automatic closing by smoke or heat detection.			
	Automatic Closing by Heat Detection: 1 detector on each side of wall at top of opening, or 1 detector on each side of wall at ceiling height when ceiling is more than 3'-0" (914 mm) above top of opening.			
	1-1/2 hour, 1-hour, and 3/4-hour Doors: Automatic closing by smoke or heat detector or self-closing.			
	Automatic Closing by Heat Detection: 1 detector on each side of wall at top of opening, or 1 detector on each side of wall at ceiling height when ceiling is more than 3'-0" (914 mm) above top of opening, or provide single fusible link in automatic closer.			
	Rated Doors across Corridors: Automatic closing by smoke detector.			
	Hold-open device shall release upon power failure at device.			
	Automobile Ramp Enclosure Doors: Automatic closing.			
	Automatic Closing by Smoke Detection: 10 second maximum closing or reclosing delay.			

Code Ref.	Code Compliance Item	OK	NA	ID
713.6.2	**Rated Swinging Door Assemblies:** **Hinges:** Provide not less than 2, provide 1 additional for each 30" (762 mm) over 60" (1524 mm) or fraction thereof.			
	Provide ball bearing or anti-friction type hinges, except for spring hinges.			
713.6.3	**Latch:** Provide automatic latch to secure door when closed on single doors and both leaves of double doors, unless specifically permitted otherwise.			
713.7	**Glazing in Rated Doors:** **3-hour Rated Doors:** No glazing permitted.			
	1-1/2 hour and 1-hour Rated Doors: 100 si (64 500 mm^2) maximum, 4" (102 mm) minimum dimension.			
	100 si (64 500 mm^2) maximum each leaf in pair of doors.			
	3/4-hour Rated Doors: Maximum 1,296 si (0.84 m^2) per light.			
713.8	**Rated Interior Windows:** Limit to area and size tested.			
	Rated Exterior Windows: Maximum 84 sf (7.8 m^2), width or height not to exceed 12'-0" (3658 mm).			
713.10	**Smoke Dampers:** Provide and make accessible for service at ducted and unducted air openings at following locations:			
	Area or occupancy separation wall penetrations.			
	Horizontal exit wall penetrations and means of egress corridor penetrations.			
	Smoke dampers not required where ducts penetrating rated corridors have no openings serving the corridor.			
	Shaft enclosure penetrations.			
	Smoke barrier penetrations.			
	Elevator lobby penetrations.			
	Area of refuge penetrations except for emergency outside air ventilation systems in areas of refuge.			
713.10	**Smoke Damper Activation:** Close damper by actuation of smoke detector by 1 of following methods:			
	Damper in Duct: Smoke detector in duct within 5'-0" (1524 mm) of damper; no air outlets or inlets between damper and detector; detector listed for air velocity, temperature, and humidity anticipated.			
	Damper in Unducted Wall Opening: Spot-type smoke detector listed for releasing service within 5'-0" (1524 mm) horizontally of damper.			
	Damper in Ceiling: Spot-type smoke detector on ceiling listed for releasing service within 5'-0" (1524 mm) horizontally of damper.			

Code Ref.	Code Compliance Item	OK	NA	ID
713.10	**Smoke Damper Activation, Continued:** **Damper in Corridor Wall or Ceiling:** May be controlled by smoke-detection system in corridor.			
	Total-Coverage Smoke-Detection System: When system is provided throughout areas served by HVAC system, dampers may be controlled by smoke-detection system.			
713.11	**Fire Dampers:** Provide and make accessible for service at ducted and unducted air openings at following locations:			
	Area or occupancy separation wall penetrations.			
	Horizontal exit wall and means of egress corridor penetrations.			
	Exception: Fire dampers not required where ducts penetrating rated corridors have no openings serving the corridor.			
	Shaft enclosure penetrations.			
	Exceptions: Fire dampers not required in penetrations of exhaust air subducts extending vertically at least 22" (559 mm) above top of opening in vented shaft where air flow is upward.			
	Fire dampers not required in penetrations of rated floors forming base of shaft enclosure where damper is rated for horizontal.			
	Penetrations of rated roof-ceiling and floor-ceiling assemblies.			
	Atrium enclosure penetrations.			
	Rated exterior wall penetrations where rated due to location on property.			
	Area of refuge penetrations except for emergency outside air ventilation systems in areas of refuge.			

Interior Finishes

UBC Chapter 8

Code Ref.	Code Compliance Item	OK	NA	ID
801.1	**Scope - Applies to:** Exposed interior wall and ceiling finish, including fixed or moveable walls and partitions, wainscoting, paneling, or finish applied structurally or for decoration, acoustical correction, surface insulation, sanitation, or fire resistance.			
	Does Not Apply to: Trim defined as picture molds, chair rails, baseboards, and handrails; doors and windows or their frames; or to materials less than 1/28" (0.9 mm) thick applied directly to surface of walls or ceilings.			
803	**Interior Finishes Applied to Rated or Noncombustible Construction:** Apply directly to such construction or to furring not more than 1-3/4" (44 mm) thick applied directly to such construction.			
	Fire block furring at 8'-0" (2438 mm) intervals in any direction.			
	Where walls and ceilings are required to be rated or noncombustible and walls are set out or ceilings are dropped more than 1-3/4" (44 mm), provide Class I materials except when protected on both sides by sprinkler systems.			
	Provide noncombustible hangers and members of such dropped ceilings except in Type III or V where fire-retardant treated wood may be used.			
	Class I, II, or III materials may be installed over wood decking/planking of heavy-timber construction, or to wood furring 1-3/4" (44 mm) thick maximum applied to wood decking/furring.			
	Fire block furring at 8'-0" (2438 mm) intervals in any direction.			
	Apply interior wall or ceiling finishes less than 1/4" (6.4 mm) thick directly against noncombustible materials except for Class I materials or tested assemblies.			

Code Ref.	Code Compliance Item	OK	NA	ID
804	**Interior Finish Materials:** Meet flame spread ratings in Table 8-A, smoke density not greater than 450.			
	Except in Group I and in enclosed vertical exits, Class III may be used in means of egress and rooms as wainscoting extending not more than 48" (1219 mm) above floor and for tack and bulletin boards of 5% of gross wall area of room maximum.			
	Flame spread class may be reduced by 1 when building is fully sprinklered, Class III minimum.			
	Exposed faces of heavy-timber structural members, decking, and planking.			
804.2	**Carpeting on Ceilings:** Provide Class I.			
805	**Textile Wall Coverings:** Provide Class I and protect with sprinkler system or provide tested assembly meeting UBC Standard 8-2.			
807.1.1	**Toilet Compartment and Shower Floors:** Smooth, hard, nonabsorbent surface extending up walls at least 5" (127 mm).			
807.1.2	**Toilet Compartment Walls:** Smooth, hard, nonabsorbent surface to +48" (1219 mm) where within 24" (610 mm) of front and sides of toilets and urinals.			
	Not required in dwelling units and guest rooms.			
	Not required in toilet rooms not accessible to public with only 1 toilet.			
	Seal toilet accessories to protect structural elements from moisture.			
807.1.3	**Showers:** Finish walls with smooth, hard, nonabsorbent surface to +70" (1778 mm) above drain inlet.			

Fire-Protection Systems

UBC Chapter 9

Code Ref.	Code Compliance Item	OK	NA	ID
904.1.1	**Fire Department Connection:** Obtain fire department approval for location.			
904.1.2	**Standards:** UBC Standard 9-1 or 9-2.			
	System may be connected to domestic water-supply main if supply is of adequate pressure, capacity, and size for combined domestic/sprinkler requirements.			
	Connect between public water main or meter and building shut-off valve; no intervening valves or connections allowed.			
904.2.2	**Sprinkler Heads in Rubbish and Linen Chutes:** Provide access for servicing heads.			
904.2.3.6	**Amusement Buildings - Sprinkler System:** Provide electrically supervised main water-flow switch and main cutoff valve.			
904.2.3.7	**Stages - Sprinkler System:** Sprinklers not required for stages 1,000 sf (93 m^2) or less and 50'-0" (15 240 mm) high or less where curtains, scenery, or combustible hangings are not retracted vertically.			
	Limit combustible hangings to single main curtain, borders, legs, and a single backdrop.			
	Sprinklers under Stage: Not required under stage areas less than 48" (1219 mm) clear height used only for chair/table storage and lined with 5/8" (16 mm) Type X gypsum board.			
904.2.6.3	**Group H-6 - Sprinkler Systems:** Provide for hazard classification as follows: Location — Occupancy Hazard Classification Fabrication Areas — Ordinary Hazard Group 3 Service Corridors — Ordinary Hazard Group 3 Storage Rooms without Dispensing — Ordinary Hazard Group 3 Storage Rooms with Dispensing — Extra Hazard Group 2 Exit Corridors — Ordinary Hazard Group 3			

Code Ref.	Code Compliance Item	OK	NA	ID
904.2.7	**Groups I-1.1 and I-2:** Provide quick response or residential sprinklers throughout patient sleeping areas.			
	Exception: Dry piping system may be used in jails, prisons, and reformatories.			
	Provide manually operated valve at continuously monitored location; opening of valve charges piping system.			
	Provide heads equipped with fusible elements or design as deluge system.			
904.2.9	**Group R-1 - Sprinkler Systems:** Provide residential or quick-response standard sprinklers in dwelling units and guest rooms.			
904.3.1	**Sprinkler System Monitoring and Alarms:** Electrically monitor all valves controlling water supply and water-flow switches where number of sprinklers is: 20 or more in Group I-1.1 and I-1.2. 100 or more in all other occupancies.			
	Monitoring not required for underground key or hub valves in roadway boxes provided by municipalities or public utilities.			
	Provide distinct difference between valve monitoring and water-flow alarm and trouble signals.			
	Automatically transmit signal to central, remote, or proprietary monitoring station.			
904.3.2	**Sprinkler Flow Alarms:** Provide audible alarm on building exterior and on the interior in a normally occupied location.			
904.5.3	**Class I Standpipes:** Provide 1 outlet above roof line when roof slope is less than 4:12 (33.3%).			
	Interconnect standpipes at bottom when more than 1 is provided.			
	Protect risers and laterals not in exit enclosure with same rating as required for shaft enclosures; enclosure not required in fully sprinklered buildings.			
904.5.4	**Class II Standpipes:** Fire protection of risers and laterals not required.			
904.5.5	**Class III Standpipes:** Interconnect standpipes at bottom when more than 1 is provided.			
	Protect risers and laterals not in exit enclosure with same rating as required for shaft enclosures; enclosure not required in fully sprinklered buildings.			
	Laterals for Class II outlets on Class III systems need not be protected.			
905.2.3	**Smoke Barrier Construction:** Construct and seal to limit smoke leakage, exclusive of protected openings.			
905.2.4	**Smoke Barrier Opening Protection:** Automatic closing actuated by required controls for mechanical smoke-control system.			
	Passive smoke-control systems may have openings controlled by spot-type detectors.			
	Airflow method may be used to protect fixed openings between zones.			

Code Ref.	Code Compliance Item	OK	NA	ID
905.2.4	**Smoke Barrier Opening Protection, Continued:** Tight-fitting, smoke/draft assemblies, 20-minute rated, self-closing or automatic closing by smoke detector.			
	Exceptions: **Group I - Smoke Barrier Doors across Corridors:** Provide pair of opposite swing doors without center mullion; no undercuts, louvers, or grilles; provide head and jamb stops and automatic closing devices; no need for positive latching; provide vision panels not exceeding size tested.			
	Requirements do not apply to Group I-3 occupancies.			
	Provide smoke gaskets at door heads, jambs, and sill.			
	Louvers not permitted.			
	Smoke Barrier Duct and Air Openings: Provide Class II, 250°F (121°C) smoke dampers.			
905.2.5	**Duration of Smoke-Control System Operation:** Make all portions of system capable of continuous operation after fire detection for at least 20 minutes.			
905.3.1	**Smoke Control System:** **Pressurization Method:** Primary means of controlling smoke.			
905.4.1	**Airflow Method:** May be used to prevent smoke migration through permanent openings between smoke-control zones.			
905.5.1	**Exhaust Method:** May be used for large enclosed volumes.			
905.7.4	**Smoke Control System Air Inlets and Outlets:** Locate outside air inlets to minimize reintroduction of smoke or flame into building.			
	Locate exhaust outlets to minimize reintroduction of smoke and limit exposure of building or adjacent buildings to additional fire hazard.			
905.8.1	**Smoke Control System - Power Systems:** Primary power from building power system and secondary power from standby power system per Electrical Code.			
	Transfer to full standby power automatically within 60 seconds of power failure.			
	Locate standby power source and transfer switches in separate room from normal power transformers and switchgear; 1-hour enclosure.			
	Locate secondary power source and transfer switches in separate room from normal power system and equipment; 1-hour separation.			
	Ventilate secondary power source room to and from exterior.			
	Distribute secondary power independent from normal power.			
905.8.2	**Smoke Control System Power Sources:** Provide uninterruptable power for smoke-control system elements relying on volatile memories for 15-minute primary power interruption.			

Code Ref.	Code Compliance Item	OK	NA	ID
905.8.2	**Smoke Control System Power Surges:** Provide conditioner or suppressors for smoke control elements susceptible to power surges.			
905.9.1	**Detection and Control System Supervision:** Supervise fire detection and control systems for mechanical smoke control systems per Fire Code.			
	Provide positive confirmation of actuation, testing, manual override, and presence of power downstream of all disconnects.			
	When supervision requires sensing damper position, use limit or proximity switches.			
	When supervision requires sensing of airflow, use differential pressure transmitters.			
	Indicate required supervision at fire fighter's control panel.			
905.9.2	**Smoke Control System Wiring:** Place in conduit, regardless of voltage.			
905.9.3	**Smoke Control Detection and Control System Activation:** **Mechanical System - Pressurization Method:** Provide automatic control of pressurized stairways in buildings with no occupied floors 300'-0" (91 440 mm) above or 75'-0" (22 860 mm) below exit grade.			
	All other portions of system may be manual except in Group I where entire system shall be completely automatic.			
	Mechanical System - Pressurization Method: Provide completely automatic control in buildings with occupied floors more than 300'-0" (91 440 mm) above or 75'-0" (22 860 mm) below exit grade.			
	Mechanical System - Airflow or Exhaust Methods: Provide completely automatic control.			
	Passive System: Control by spot-type smoke detectors for release devices.			
905.9.4	**Automatic Control:** Initiate automatic control sequences from sprinkler system or from total coverage smoke detection system.			
906.1	**Smoke and Heat Venting:** **Single-story Groups B, F, M, and S:** Provide in buildings with over 50,000 sf (4645 m²) in undivided area.			
	Not required in office building and retail sales areas where storage does not exceed 12'-0" (3658 mm) height.			
	Not required in fully sprinkled Group S-2 used for bulk frozen food storage.			
	Groups H-1, H-2, H-3, H-4, or H-5: Provide in buildings over 15,000 sf (1394 m²) in any single floor area.			
	High Piled Combustible Stock: Comply with Fire Code.			

Code Ref.	Code Compliance Item	OK	NA	ID
906.3	**Smoke and Heat Venting, Continued:** **Vent Location:** Not closer than 20'-0" (6096 mm) from property line.			
	Vent Types: Fixed open or automatic opening by heat activation, open automatically in event of fire.			
	Locate heat detectors at near highest elevation of ceiling, not lower than upper 1/3 of smoke curtains.			
906.5.1	**Vent Size:** Not less than 16 sf (1.5 m^2) effective vent area, 4'-0" (1219 mm) minimum dimension, excluding ribs and gutters of 6" (152 mm) maximum width.			
906.5.2	**Vent Spacing - Groups B, F, M, and S:** 120'-0" (36 600 mm) maximum.			
	Vent Spacing - Groups H: 100'-0" (30 480 mm) maximum.			
906.5.3	**Venting Ratio:** Vent opening to floor area: **Groups B, F, M, and S:** 1:100. **Group H:** 1:50.			
906.6	**Smoke and Heat Venting - Curtain Boards:** Subdivide smoke/heat vented buildings with curtain boards not exceeding 250'-0" (76 200 mm) in any direction; curtained area 50,000 sf (4645 mm) maximum.			
	Group H: Subdivide buildings not exceeding 100'-0" (30 480 mm) in any direction; curtained area 15,000 sf (1394 m^2) maximum.			
	Curtain Board Location and Depth: Extend down from ceiling 6'-0" (1829 mm) minimum, but no closer than 8'-0" (2438 mm) to floor.			
	Group H: Extend down from ceiling 12'-0" (3660 mm) minimum, but need not be closer than 8'-0" (2438 mm) to floor if curtain is at least 6'-0" (1829 mm) deep.			
	Curtain Board Construction: Sheet metal, lath and plaster, gypsum board; joints and connections smoke tight.			

Means of Egress

UBC Chapter 10

Code Ref.	Code Compliance Item	OK	NA	ID
1003.2.8.2	**Exit Signs Required:** Place exit signs to identify path of exit travel to and within exits.			
	Locate signs to clearly indicate direction of egress travel.			
	No point shall be more than 100'-0" (30 480 mm) from nearest visible sign.			
	Exit Signs Not Required: At main exit doors obviously and clearly identifiable as exit doors.			
	Rooms or areas requiring only 1 exit or exit access.			
	In Group R-3 and individual units in R-1.			
	At exits from rooms or areas with less than 50 occupants in Group I-1.1, I-1.2, I-2, or E-3 day-care.			
1003.2.8.3	**Exit Sign Graphics:** Contrast color and design of lettering, arrow and symbols with background; 6" (152 mm) high block letters, 3/4" (19 mm) stroke.			
	Letters 2" (51 mm) wide minimum, 3/8" (9.5 mm) minimum space between letters.			
1003.2.8.4	**Exit Sign Illumination:** Internally illuminated, or externally illuminated by 2 lamps with minimum luminance of 5.0 footcandles (53.82 lx).			
	Self-luminous signs with 0.06 foot lambert (0.21 cd/m^2) minimum permitted.			
1003.2.8.5	**Exit Sign Power Supply:** Supply 1 lamp from building power system and 1 lamp from batteries, unit equipment, or on-site generator set.			
	Self-luminous signs permitted.			
1003.2.9.1	**Exit Illumination:** Illuminate means of egress at all times building is occupied by 1 footcandle (10.76 lx) at floor except in Group R-3 and R-1 dwelling units, guest rooms, and sleeping rooms.			
	Illumination level may be reduced to 0.2 footcandle (2.15 lx) during performances in auditoriums, theaters, and concert or opera halls. Restore required illumination automatically upon activation of fire alarm system, when such system is provided.			

Code Ref.	Code Compliance Item	OK	NA	ID
1003.2.9.2	**Exit Illumination - Power Supply:** Provide normal power from building power system.			
	Upon failure of normal power, provide automatic emergency system in Group I-1.1, I-1.2, and occupancies where exit system serves 100 or more occupants.			
1003.3.1.1	**Means of Egress Doors - General:** Make exit doors easily recognizable as exit doors; do not use mirrors or reflecting materials.			
1003.3.1.2	**Power Operated Exit Doors:** Provide 2 guide rails on swing side projecting from jambs at least dimension of widest door leaf.			
	Exceptions: Guide rails not required when walls meeting guide rail criteria are provided.			
	Industrial or commercial occupancies not accessible to public may use guide rails constructed to limit openings to 12" (305 mm) sphere.			
	Power Operated Doors Swinging toward Traffic Flow: Not permitted for use by untrained traffic unless actuating devices start to function at least 8'-11" (2718 mm) beyond door in open position and guide rails extend 6'-5" (1956 mm) beyond door in open position.			
	Guide Rail Construction and Height: Solid or mesh panels, minimum of 30" (762 mm) high to prevent penetration into door swing, able to resist 50 plf (730 N/m) at top.			
	Guide Rail Clearances: 6" (152 mm) maximum between rails and leading edge of door at closest point in arc of travel.			
	6" (152 mm) maximum between rails and door in open position.			
	2" (51 mm) minimum between rail at hinge side and door in open position.			
	2" (51 mm) maximum between free-standing rails and jamb or other surfaces.			
1003.3.1.5	**Door Opening Force:** Maximum of 30 lbs (133.45 N) applied to latch side. See Chapter 11 for doors required to be accessible.			
	Exceptions: Door opening force above not required in Group I-3 detention areas; doors in or serving individual dwelling units; and revolving, sliding, or overhead doors.			
	Double Acting Doors: Provide view panel; minimum 200 si (0.129 m^2).			
1003.3.1.6	**Floor Level at Doors:** Not less than 1/2" (13 mm) lower than threshold of doorway when accessibility is required, not less than 1" (25 mm) lower when accessibility is not required.			
	Landing Slope: Level except slope of 1/4:12 (2%) permitted at exterior.			

Code Ref.	Code Compliance Item	OK	NA	ID
1003.3.1.8	**Exit Door Locks and Latches:** Make openable from inside without key or special knowledge or effort.			
	Exceptions: **Groups B, F, M, and S:** Key locks may be used on main exit when consisting of single door or pair of doors with sign is provided stating, "THIS DOOR MUST REMAIN UNLOCKED DURING BUSINESS HOURS."			
	1" (25 mm) high letters on contrasting background.			
	When unlocked, doors must be free to swing without latching.			
	Exit doors from dwelling units, Group R-3 congregate residences, and Group R guest rooms having occupant load of 10 or less may be provided with night latch, deadbolt, or security chain if such devices are openable from inside without key or tool and mounted at +48" (1219 mm) maximum.			
1003.3.1.8	**Flush Bolts:** Manual flush bolts prohibited.			
	Automatic flush bolts allowed on 1 leaf of pairs of doors; no knob or surface hardware permitted on such leaf; single operation unlatching required.			
	Manual Flush Bolts Permitted: In Group R-3 residences, and on inactive leaf of pairs of doors serving rooms required for moving equipment from normally occupied rooms.			
1003.3.1.9	**Panic Hardware:** Mount activating member at +30" (762 mm) minimum to +44" (1118 mm) maximum; 15 lbs (66.72 N) maximum unlatching force.			
	Balanced Doors: When panic hardware required, push-pad may not extend across more than 1/2 door width.			
1003.3.1.10	**Special Time-delay Egress Control Devices:** May be used in Groups B, F-1, I-2, M, and R-1 congregate residence groupcare facilities, when building is fully sprinkled and has automatic smoke-detection system throughout. Comply with following:			
	Automatically deactivate egress control device upon activation of sprinklers or detection systems.			
	Automatically deactivate egress control device upon loss of power to egress control device, smoke detection system, or exit illumination system.			
	Capable of deactivation from remote master switch.			
	Initiate irreversible process deactivating egress control devices whenever 15 lbs (66.72 N) maximum manual force is applied for 2 seconds to panic bar or door latching hardware.			
	Initiation deactivates device in 15 seconds maximum.			
	Time delay not field adjustable.			
	Actuation of panic bar or latching hardware activates audible alarm at door.			
	Unlatching requires only 1 operation.			

Code Ref.	Code Compliance Item	OK	NA	ID
1003.3.1.10	**Special Time-delay Egress Control Devices, Continued:** **Sign:** Provide on door within 12" (305 mm) of panic bar stating, "KEEP PUSHING. THIS DOOR WILL OPEN IN _____ SECONDS. ALARM WILL SOUND."			
	1" (25 mm) minimum letter height, 1/8" (3.2 mm) minimum stroke.			
	Relocking of Special Egress Control Devices: By manual means only at door.			
1003.3.1.11	**Glass Door Identification:** Make doors readily identifiable from adjacent construction.			
1003.1.2	**Gates in Fences:** Comply with requirements for doors where a part of means of egress system.			
	Exception: Gates surrounding stadiums may be horizontally sliding or swinging type, and may be more than 48" (1219 mm) wide.			
1004.3.3.2	**Hallway Width:** Provide unobstructed width except that handrails, and doors when fully opened, shall not reduce width by more than 7" (178 mm).			
	Other nonstructural projections such as trim may project into width 1-1/2" (38 mm) on each side.			
1004.3.3.3	**Hallway Construction:** **Type I and II Construction:** Noncombustible, except where combustible materials are permitted in building elements.			
	Type III, IV, or V Construction: Combustible or noncombustible.			
	Wall Height: Any height permitted.			
	Partitions, rails, counters, and similar space dividers not over 6'-0" (1829 mm) shall be construed to form hallway.			
	Openings: Not restricted as to type or number unless protection is required by other sections.			
1004.3.4.2	**Corridor Width:** Provide unobstructed width except that handrails, and doors when fully opened, shall not reduce width by more than 7" (178 mm).			
	Other nonstructural projections such as trim may project into width 1-1/2" (38 mm) on each side.			
1004.3.4.3	**Corridor Construction:** **Corridor Floors:** Rated construction not required unless required by other sections.			
	Type I and II Construction: Noncombustible, except where combustible materials are permitted in building elements.			
	Type III, IV, or V Construction: Combustible or noncombustible.			
	Fire Resistive Materials: Provide rated materials on both sides of wall.			

Code Ref.	Code Compliance Item	OK	NA	ID
1004.3.4.3	**Corridor Construction, Continued:** **Corridor Walls:** Extend walls to floor/ceiling or roof/ceiling as follows:			
	Terminate corridor side wall membrane at corridor ceiling membrane constructed for 1-hour floor/ceiling or roof/ceiling assembly to include suspended ceilings, dropped ceilings, and lay-in roof/ceiling panels part of rated assembly.			
	Terminate room side wall membrane at underside of a floor or roof constructed of materials for 1-hour assembly.			
	Exception: Where corridor ceiling is element of at least 1-hour rated floor/ceiling or roof/ceiling assembly at entire story, both sides of corridor walls may terminate at ceiling membrane.			
	Corridor Ceilings: May be constructed of materials for rated wall assembly.			
	Where constructed per rated wall assembly, corridor side wall membrane may terminate at lower ceiling membrane, and room side wall membrane may terminate at upper ceiling membrane.			
	Noncombustible ceilings may be suspended below rated ceiling.			
1004.3.4.3 .2.1	**Corridor Doors:** 20-minute, tight-fitting smoke/draft assembly, self-closing or automatic closing by smoke detector.			
	No louvers or mail slots permitted.			
	Provide smoke gasket at top and sides.			
1004.3.4.3 .2.2	**Corridor Windows:** 3/4-hour rated, limit aggregate area to 25% of area of room/corridor wall of any room.			
1005.3.5.2	**Horizontal Exit Construction:** Continuous from exterior wall to exterior wall and from floor to underside of floor or roof above.			
	Structural Supports: Protect with rated construction.			
	Type I and II Construction: Noncombustible, except where combustible materials are permitted in building elements.			
	Type III, IV, or V Construction: Combustible or noncombustible.			
1005.3.5.3	**Horizonal Exit Openings:** 1-1/2 hour rated, self-closing or automatic closing by smoke detector.			
	Hold-opens: Close or release fire assembly to closed position in power failure.			
	Maximum Transmitted End Point: 450°F (232°C) above ambient at end of 30 minutes; UBC Standard 7-2.			
1006.3.2.3	**Exterior Exit Balcony Construction:** **Type I and II Construction:** Noncombustible, except where combustible materials are permitted in building elements.			
	Type III, IV, or V Construction: Combustible or noncombustible.			

Code Ref.	Code Compliance Item	OK	NA	ID
1006.3.2.3	**Exterior Exit Balcony Construction, Continued:** **Groups R-1 and I:** 1-hour walls and ceilings.			
	Exceptions: Exterior sides of exterior exit balconies.			
	Roof assembly may be heavy-timber without concealed spaces except in Type I or II construction.			

Stairs and Ramps

UBC Sections 1003.3.3 and 1003.3.4

Code Ref.	Code Compliance Item	OK	NA	ID
1003.3.3.1	**Stairway Width:** Handrails may project into width 3-1/2" (89 mm) each side.			
	Stringers and trim may project into width 1-1/2" (38 mm) each side.			
1003.3.3.3	**Stairway Tread and Riser Dimensional Uniformity:** 3/8" (9.5 mm) maximum difference between smallest and largest within any flight.			
1003.3.3.4	**Stairway Headroom:** 6'-8" (2032 mm) minimum measured from plane parallel and tangent to tread nosings to soffit above.			
1003.3.3.5	**Stairway Landings:** Make level.			
	Exterior landings may slope 1/4:12 (2%) maximum.			
1003.3.3.6	**Stairway Handrails:** Provide on each side of stair.			
	Only 1 handrail required on stairs less than 44" (1118 mm) wide or stairs serving individual dwelling units in Groups R-1, R-3, and R-3 congregate residence.			
	Only 1 handrail required on private stairs less than 30" (762 mm) high.			
	No handrails required on stairs with less than 4 risers and serving 1 dwelling unit in Groups R-1, R-3, R-3 congregate residences, and U.			
	Intermediate Handrails: Where stair is required to be more than 88" (2235 mm) wide, provide intermediate handrail for each 88" (2235 mm) of required width, spaced approximately equally across width of stairway.			
	Handrail Height: Place top of handrail and extensions at 34"-38" (864 - 965 mm) above nosing of treads and landings.			
	Handrail Extensions: Continue handrail full length of stairs and extend in direction of travel minimum of 12" (305 mm) beyond top and bottom risers.			
	Handrail Terminations: Return to wall or terminate in newel post or safety terminals.			
	Handrail Shape and Size: Minimum 1-1/4" (32 mm), maximum 2" (51 mm) for handgrip portion or equivalent shape.			
	Smooth surface with no sharp corners.			
	Minimum 1-1/2" (38 mm) between wall and handrail.			

Code Ref.	Code Compliance Item	OK	NA	ID
1003.3.3.9	**Interior Stairway Construction:** When stair is not enclosed, provide 1-hour construction for walls and soffits enclosing space under stair.			
	1-hour construction for walls and soffits enclosing useable space under stairs.			
	Buildings 4 Stories or More: When stairs exit directly to building exterior, provide fire department access for emergency entry.			
1003.3.3.12	**Roof Hatches - Buildings 4 Stories or More:** Provide roof hatch at highest point of enclosure where stairs extend to roof, 16 sf (1.5 m^2) minimum, 24" (610 mm) minimum dimension.			
	No hatch required in pressurized enclosures or in stairs extending to roof which open onto roof.			
1003.3.3.13	**Stairway Identification - Buildings 4 Stories or More:** In enclosed stairways, provide a sign at each floor level which identifies stairway and indicates floor level, upper and lower terminus, if it provides roof access.			
	Locate sign 5'-0" (1524 mm) above floor, readily visible when door is open or closed; comply with UBC Standard 10-2.			
1003.3.4.2	**Ramp Width - Projections:** Handrails may project 3-1/2" (89 mm) each side. Trim may project 1-1/2" (38 mm) each side.			
1003.3.4.5	**Ramp Handrails:** Provide on ramps steeper than 1:20 (5%) as required for stairs, except intermediate handrails are not required.			
	Ramped aisles do not need handrails on sides serving fixed seats.			
1003.3.4.6	**Ramp Guardrails:** Provide where ramps are open on 1 or both sides more than 30" (762 mm) above floor or finished grade.			
1003.3.4.7	**Ramp Construction:** As required for stairways.			
1003.3.4.8	**Ramp Surface:** Slip resistant.			

Exit Enclosures and Passageways

UBC Sections 1005.3.3 and 1005.3.4

Code Ref.	Code Compliance Item	OK	NA	ID
1005.3.3.4	**Stairways to Basements:** Provide barrier to prevent persons from accidentally continuing below grade level exit into basement; provide exit signs per 1003.2.8.			
1005.3.3.5	**Stair and Ramp Enclosures - Doors:** Self-closing or automatic closing by smoke detector.			
	1-hour doors in 1-hour enclosures.			
	1-1/2 hour doors in 2-hour enclosures.			
	Hold-opens: Close or release fire assembly to closed position in power failure.			
	Maximum Transmitted End Point: 450°F (232°C) above ambient at end of 30 minutes; UBC Standard 7-2.			
	Stair, Ramp, and Escalator Enclosures - Other Openings: Other openings not permitted except for ductwork and equipment necessary for pressurization, sprinkler piping, standpipes, and electrical conduit serving stairway.			
1005.3.3.7	**Pressurized Stair Enclosures:** Activate pressurization automatically by activation of fire alarm system.			
	In nonsprinkled buildings, activation may be by spot-type smoke detector installed within 5'-0" (15 234 mm) of each vestibule entry.			
	Relief Vent: Provide controlled relief vent through roof discharging at least 2,500 cfm (1180 L/s) at design pressure difference.			
	Pressurized Stair Enclosures - Doors: Self-closing or automatic closing by smoke detector.			
	1-1/2 hour door from building into vestibule.			
	20-minute smoke/draft control door from vestibule into stair.			

Code Ref.	Code Compliance Item	OK	NA	ID
1005.3.3.7	**Pressurized Stair Enclosures - Doors, Continued:** **Hold-opens:** Close or release fire assembly to closed position in power failure.			
	Maximum Transmitted End Point: 450°F (232°C) above ambient at end of 30 minutes; UBC Standard 7-2.			
	Minimum Pressure Differences: With doors closed, 0.05" water gage (12.44 Pa) positive pressure relative to fire floor and 0.05" water gage (12.44 Pa) negative pressure relative to exit enclosure, no pressure difference required relative to nonfire floor.			
	Standpipes: Provide fire department connections and valves serving floor within vestibule.			
	Locate to not obstruct egress where hose lines are connected and charged.			
1005.3.4.4	**Exit Passageway - Openings:** Self-closing or automatic-closing by smoke detector.			
	Hold-opens: Close or release fire assembly to closed position in power failure.			
	Maximum Transmitted End Point: 450°F (232°C) above ambient at end of 30 minutes; UBC Standard 7-2.			
	Penetrations: Not permitted except for sprinkler piping, standpipes, and electrical conduit serving passageway terminating in listed junction box, 16 si (10323 mm^2) maximum.			

Aisles

UBC Section 1004.3.2

Code Ref.	Code Compliance Item	OK	NA	ID
1004.3.2.2	**Aisle Width:** Keep minimum width unobstructed.			
	Exception: Handrails and doors, when fully opened, may reduce width 7" (178 mm) maximum.			
	Doors may not reduce required width by more than 1/2 in any position.			
	Decorative features and trim may project 1-1/2" (38 mm) maximum each side.			
1004.3.2.5	**Aisle Steps - Riser and Tread Variations:** 3/16" (4.8 mm) maximum variation permitted.			
	Provide contrasting marking stripe on each tread at nosing making tread readily apparent when viewed in decent; 1" (25 mm) wide minimum, 2" (51 mm) wide maximum.			
	Riser and Tread Variations: When slope of aisle steps and adjoining seating area is the same, riser heights may be increased to 9" (229 mm) and may be non-uniform only to extent necessary by changes in slope of adjoining seating area to maintain adequate sight lines.			
	Variations may exceed 3/16" (4.8 mm) between risers provided location is identified by marking stripe on tread at nosing or leading edge adjacent to non-uniform riser.			
	Mark variations with stripe on each tread at nosing or leading edge adjacent to non-uniform risers; make distinctly different from normal marking stripe.			
1004.3.2.7	**Aisle Handrails:** Provide on each side or in aisle width of ramped aisles with slope steeper than 1:15 (6.7%) and aisle stairs (2 or more adjacent steps).			
	Handrails not required on ramped aisles not more than 1:8 (12.5%) with fixed seating on both sides of aisle.			
	Handrails not required when guardrail is at side of aisle which conforms to handrail size and shape.			
	Handrail Height: Place top of handrail and extensions at +34"-38" (864 - 965 mm) above nosing of treads and landings or ramped aisle surface.			

Code Ref.	Code Compliance Item	OK	NA	ID
1004.3.2.7	**Handrail Size and Shape:** Minimum 1-1/4" (32 mm), maximum 2" (51 mm) for handgrip portion or equivalent shape.			
	Provide smooth surface with rounded terminations and bends; no sharp corners.			
	Projection: Handrails may project into aisle width 3-1/2" (89 mm).			
	Handrails in Aisle Width: Provide gaps or breaks at intervals not exceeding 5 rows; minimum clear width 22" (9559 mm), maximum 36" (914 mm).			
	Provide additional handrail at 12" (305 mm) below main handrail.			

Means of Egress
Groups A, E, H, I, and R

UBC Section 1007

Code Ref.	Code Compliance Item	OK	NA	ID
1007.2.5	**Group A - Panic Hardware:** No lock or latch permitted on exit or exit-access doors from rooms with 50 or more occupants except for panic hardware.			
	Exceptions: Panic device may be omitted in Group A-3 and churches when main exit consists of single door or pair of doors.			
	Key lock may be used if sign is provided stating, "THIS DOOR MUST REMAIN UNLOCKED DURING BUSINESS HOURS."			
	Letters 1" (25 mm) high on contrasting background.			
	When unlocked, doors must be free to swing without latching device.			
	On pairs of doors, provide 1 leaf without locks and latch second leaf into first leaf and frame such that single unlocking action will unlock both leaves simultaneously.			
	Flush, edge, or surface bolts used to close or restrain door other than by operation of locking device are prohibited.			
	Panic hardware may be omitted on gates surrounding stadiums when gates are under constant immediate supervision when public is present.			
	Provide safe dispersal areas based on 3 sf (0.28 m^2) per occupant located between stadium and fence, not less than 50'-0" (15 240 mm) from stadium.			
	Gates may be sliding or swinging and may exceed 4'-0" (1219 mm) width limitation.			
1007.2.6	**Assembly Rooms - Posting of Room Capacity:** Provide sign indicating maximum number of occupants permitted in rooms with 50 or more occupants without fixed seating; post in conspicuous place on sign near main exit or exit-access doorway.			

Code Ref.	Code Compliance Item	OK	NA	ID
1007.2.7	**Amusement Building Exit Marking:** Provide exit marking and exit signs.			
	Provide low-level directional markings and exit signs +8" (203 mm) maximum at exit path to indicate path of travel, activated by amusement building smoke detectors, sprinklers, or fire detector.			
	At exit or exit-access doors, provide low-level sign on door or adjacent to door with closest edge of sign within 4" (102 mm) of door frame.			
1007.3.4	**Group E - Exit Travel through Intervening Rooms:** Where only 1 exit access is required from interior room and path of travel is through adjoining or intervening room, provide smoke detectors throughout common atmosphere of exit access.			
	Smoke Detector Alarms: Make audible in interior room and connect to school fire alarm system.			
	Exceptions: Smoke detectors not required when: Aggregate occupant load of interior room is 10 or less.			
	Enclosures forming interior rooms are less than 2/3 of floor to ceiling height and 8'-0" (2438 mm) maximum.			
	Rooms used only for mechanical or public utility service to building.			
1007.3.10	**Group E - Panic Hardware:** No lock or latch permitted on exit or exit-access doors from rooms with 50 or more occupants except for panic hardware.			
1007.3.11	**Group E - Fences and Gates:** Do not equip gates with locks unless safe dispersal areas are provided, at least 50'-0" (15 240 mm) from buildings, 3 sf (0.28 m^2) minimum per occupant.			
1007.4.3	**Group H - Corridor Doors:** 3/4-hour minimum, self-closing or automatic closing by heat or smoke detector.			
	May have 100 si (0.06445 m^2) maximum wire glass lite set in steel frames.			
1007.4.5	**Group H - Panic Hardware:** No lock or latch permitted on exit or exit-access doors from Groups H-1, H-2, H-3, H-6 or H-7 except for panic hardware.			
1007.4.6	**Group H - Incinerator Rooms:** Interior openings between Group H and an incinerator room prohibited.			
1007.5.4	**Group I-1.1 Hospitals and Nursing Homes - Corridor Exceptions:** Sleeping and treatment room doors do not need closers in fully sprinkled buildings.			
	Fixed tempered or laminated glazing may be used in wood or metal frames where glazed area does not exceed 25% of area of corridor wall of room.			
	Total glazing area in corridor walls not limited with 1/4" (6.4 mm) thick wire glass set in steel frames; individual panels of 1,296 si (0.836 m^2) maximum.			
	Corridor doors, except those required to be rated in Section 308.8, or for enclosing vertical openings or exits, are not required to be rated if doors are tight-fitting smoke/draft assemblies and positive latching.			

Code Ref.	Code Compliance Item	OK	NA	ID
1007.5.8	**Group I:** **Panic Hardware:** No lock or latch permitted on exit or exit-access doors from rooms with 50 or more occupants except for panic hardware.			
	Patient Room Doors: Openable from either side without key.			
	Exceptions: **Group I-1.1 Hospitals and Nursing Homes:** Lock may be used on patient room doors if readily openable from patient room side and readily operable from staff side. Locate keys on floor involved at prominent location accessible to staff.			
	Group I-1.3: Locks or safety devices permitted where personal liberties are forcibly restrained.			
1007.6.1	**Group R Hallways:** Construct as required for corridors where serving 10 or more occupants.			
1007.6.2	**Floor Level Exit Signs - Group R-1:** Provide in addition to other required exit signs in exit corridors serving guest rooms of hotels.			
	Internally or externally illuminated, photoluminescent, or self-luminous.			
	Location: Bottom of sign at +6" (152 mm) minimum and +8" (203 mm) maximum from floor.			
	At exit or exit-access doors, provide low-level sign on door or adjacent to door with closest edge of sign within 4" (102 mm) of door frame.			

Grandstands and Bleachers

UBC Section 1008

Code Ref.	Code Compliance Item	OK	NA	ID
1008.5.6	**Stair and Ramp Handrails:** Provide as normally required for stairs and ramps.			
	Where stair or ramp serves as aisle at right angles, provide handrails at 1 side or along centerline.			
	Aisle Stairways with Center Handrail: 48" (1219 mm) minimum clear width between seats.			
	Provide additional handrail at 12" (305 mm) below main handrail.			
	Aisle Stairways with Center Handrail - Seating on Both Sides: Provide gaps or breaks in handrail at intervals not exceeding 5 rows; minimum clear width 22" (559 mm), maximum 36" (914 mm).			
	Handrail Height: Place top of handrail and extensions at +34"-38" (864 - 965 mm) above nosing of treads and landings or ramped aisle surface.			
	Handrail Dimensions: Minimum 1-1/4" (32 mm), maximum 2" (51 mm) for handgrip portion or equivalent shape.			
	Provide smooth surface; no sharp corners; rounded terminations and bends.			
	Projection: 3-1/2" (89 mm) maximum into aisle width.			
1008.5.7	**Guardrails:** Provide at portions of elevated seating more than 30" (762 mm) above grade or floor below.			
	Guardrail Height: Not less than 42" (1067 mm) above rear of seat board or rear of steps in aisle when guardrail is parallel and adjacent to aisle.			
	Height may be 26" (660 mm) where in front of front row seats and not located at end of aisle where there is not a cross aisle; need not meet 4" (102 mm) sphere spacing; provide midrail.			
1008.5.8	**Toeboards:** Provide 4" (102 mm) high vertical barrier along edge of walking platforms whenever guardrails are required.			
	Toeboards not required at ends of footboard.			
1008.5.9	**Footboards:** Provide for all seat rows above third row or beginning at such point where seat is more than 24" (610 mm) above grade or floor.			
	When platform is used for seating and footrests, footrests not required if each level or platform is 24" (610 mm) wide minimum.			

Accessibility

UBC Chapter 11

Code Ref.	Code Compliance Item	OK	NA	ID
1101.2	**Design Standard:** CABO/ANSI A117.1-1992.			
	Comply with Section 1106 below for Type B dwelling units.			
1103.1.9.2	**Guest Rooms for Hearing Impaired:** Provide audio/visual alarm devices, activated by in-room smoke detector and building fire protective signaling system.			
1103.2.4.1	**International Symbol of Accessibility:** Identify following with international symbol of accessibility:			
	Accessible parking spaces, except where total spaces provided are 5 or less.			
	Accessible areas of refuge.			
	Accessible passenger loading zones.			
	Accessible toilet and bathing facilities.			
1103.2.4.2	**Other Signs:** Identify inaccessible entrances, public toilets and bathing facilities, and elevators not on accessible route with signage indicating route to nearest similar accessible element.			
	Assembly Areas: Provide signs at ticket offices and similar locations notifying general public of availability of assistive listening systems.			
	Doors to Exit Stairways: Provide tactile sign with raised letters and Braille stating, "EXIT."			
	Elevators and Exits Serving Required Accessible Route: When such elements do not provide accessible means of egress, provide sign indicating location of accessible means of egress.			
	Unisex Toilets or Bathing Rooms: In addition to symbol of accessibility, identify room with tactile sign with raised letters and Braille.			
	Provide directional signage at separate-sex toilets or bathing facilities indicating location of unisex room.			
1104.1.3	**Standby Power:** Provide to elevators part of an accessible means of egress.			

Code Ref.	Code Compliance Item	OK	NA	ID
1104.2.4	**Areas of Refuge:** **Construction:** 1-hour smoke barrier separation from other spaces extending to roof or floor deck above, except where located in stairway enclosure.			
	Doors: Tight-fitting, smoke/draft control assemblies, 20-minute rated, self-closing or automatic closing by smoke detection.			
	Smoke Dampers: Provide at each duct penetration.			
1104.2.5	**2-way Communication System:** Provide system for communication between area of refuge and central control point approved by fire department, except in buildings 4 stories or less.			
	When central control point is not constantly attended, also provide controlled access to public telephone system.			
1104.2.6	**2-way Communication System Instructions:** Post instructions beside the system, including:			
	Directions to other exits;			
	Advice that persons able to use stairways do so as soon as possible, unless assisting others;			
	Information of planned availability of assistance in use of stairs or supervised operation of elevators and how to summon assistance;			
	Directions for use of communication system.			
1104.2.7	**Identification:** Tactile sign at each door providing access to area of refuge stating "AREA OF REFUGE," along with international symbol of accessibility.			
	Illuminate as required for exit signs when exit sign illumination is required.			
1105.2.3	**Lavatories, Mirrors, and Towel Fixtures:** Make at least 1 accessible in each toilet facility.			
1105.4.1	**Drinking Fountains:** Make at least 50% accessible, but not less than 1.			
1105.4.2	**Fixed or Built-in Seating or Tables:** Make at least 5% accessible, but not less than 1; distributed throughout dining and drinking establishments.			
1105.4.3	**Storage Cabinets, Closets, Lockers, and Drawers:** Make at least 1 of each type accessible in accessible or adaptable spaces.			
1105.4.4.1	**Dressing and Fitting Rooms:** Make at least 5% accessible, but not less than 1, in each group serving distinct and different functions.			
1105.4.4.2	**Counter and Windows:** Provide accessible portion of counter or at least 1 accessible window.			
1105.4.4.3	**Checkout Aisles:** Comply UBC Table 11-C.			
	Traffic control devices, security devices, and turnstiles in such aisles shall be accessible.			
1105.4.5	**Controls, Operating Mechanisms, and Hardware:** Make accessible in accessible spaces and along accessible routes.			

Code Ref.	Code Compliance Item	OK	NA	ID
1105.4.6	**Alarms:** Provide audio/visual type alarm systems.			
	Provide in hotel guest rooms; accessible public and common-use areas including toilet rooms and bathing facilities, hallways, and lobbies.			
1105.4.7	**Rail Transit Platforms:** Provide detectable warnings when bordering a drop-off and not protected by screens or guardrails.			
1106.3.1	**Dwelling Unit Type B - Operating Controls:** **General:** Applies to lighting controls, electrical receptacles, environmental controls, and user controls for security or intercom.			
	Exceptions: Electrical receptacles serving dedicated use.			
	Appliance-mounted controls or switches.			
	Single receptacle located above portion of countertop uninterrupted by sink or appliance provided:			
	At least 1 receptacle complying with this section is provided for portion of countertop and			
	All other receptacles provided for portion of countertop comply with this section.			
	Floor electrical receptacles.			
	Plumbing fixture controls.			
	Clear Floor Space: 30" by 48" (762 by 1219 mm) minimum for forward or parallel approach at each control.			
	Where parallel approach is provided at control located above obstruction, make offset between center line of floor space and control 12" (305 mm) maximum.			
	Height: 48" (1219 mm) maximum, 15" (381 mm) minimum.			
1106.6.3	**Type B Dwelling Unit - Grab Bar and Seat Reinforcement:** Provide reinforcement to support wall-mounted grab bars and seats.			

Interior Environment

UBC Chapter 12

Code Ref.	Code Compliance Item	OK	NA	ID
1202	**Light:** Provide natural or artificial light in normally occupied spaces.			
	Ventilation: Provide natural or artificial ventilation in normally occupied spaces.			
1202.1	**Minimum Window Size:** In rooms without natural light, 1/10 floor area.			
1202.2	**Minimum Natural Ventilation:** Openable exterior openings, 1/20 floor area, opening onto public way, yard, or court.			
	Minimum Artificial Ventilation: 15 cfm (7 L/s) outside air per occupant.			
	Where velocity at register exceeds 10 fps (3 m/s), place register at least 8'-0" (2438 mm) above floor.			
	Toilet Rooms - Ventilation Window: Minimum 3 sf (0.28 m^2).			
	Toilet Rooms - Ventilation Duct: 100 si (64 500 mm^2) vertical duct for first toilet, 50 si (32 258 m^2) for each additional toilet.			
	Toilet Room - Mechanical Ventilation: 1 complete air change every 15 minutes, ducts connected directly to outside, point of discharge 3'-0" (914 mm) minimum from openings allowing re-entry of exhaust air.			
1202.2.2	**Group B - Mechanical Ventilation for Class I, II, or III-A Liquids:** 6 air changes per hour minimum.			
	Take exhaust from a point at or near floor level.			
1202.2.3	**Group H- Ventilation:** Mechanically ventilate spaces where explosive, corrosive, combustible, flammable, or highly toxic dusts, mists, fumes, vapors, or gases are or may be emitted due to processing, use, handling, or storage.			
	Extend ducts conveying explosive or flammable vapors, fumes, or dusts directly to exterior without entering other spaces.			
	Do not extend exhaust ducts into or through ducts and plenums.			
	Ducts conveying vapor or fumes having flammable constituents less than 25% of their lower flammability limit may pass through other spaces.			

Code Ref.	Code Compliance Item	OK	NA	ID
1202.2.3	**Group H Ventilation:** Confine emissions generated at work stations to the area where generated.			
	See Mechanical and Fire Codes for location of supply and exhaust openings.			
	Provide manual shutoff for Group H ventilation equipment outside room and adjacent to principal access door; break-glass type, labeled VENTILATION SYSTEM EMERGENCY SHUTOFF.			
1202.2.4	**Group H-4 Motor Vehicle Repair and Handling - Mechanical Ventilation:** Provide exhaust of 1 cfm per sf (5.1 L/s/m^2) of floor area minimum.			
	Equip each repair stall with exhaust pipe extension duct extending outside building.			
	When such duct is over 10'-0" (3048 mm), provide 300 cfm (141.6 L/s) mechanical exhaust.			
	Provide offices and waiting areas with conditioned air under positive pressure.			
	Exception: Ventilating equipment may be omitted when repair garages, enclosed heliports, and aircraft hangars have well-distributed unobstructed openings sufficient for necessary ventilation.			
1202.2.5	**Group H-6 - Mechanical Exhaust Ventilation:** Provide throughout fabrication areas at minimum 1 cfm per sf (0.044 L/s/m^2) of floor area.			
	Do not connect to other duct systems outside that fabrication area.			
	Comply with Mechanical Code except that automatic shutoffs are not required on air-moving equipment.			
	Provide smoke detectors in circulating airstream to initiate signal at emergency control station.			
	Provide at least 1 manual remote control switch to shut down fabrication area ventilation system at location outside fabrication area; not required on exhaust systems.			
	Ventilation System: Provide to capture and exhaust fumes and vapors at work stations.			
	Do not connect 2 or more operations when either one or combination of substances removed could constitute a fire, explosion or hazardous reaction within exhaust duct system.			
	Contain exhaust ducts penetrating occupancy separations in shaft matching rating of separation.			
	Exhaust ducts shall not penetrate area separation walls.			
	Do not install fire dampers in exhaust ducts.			
1202.2.6	**Group S-3 Repair/Storage Garages and S-5 Aircraft Hangars - Mechanical Ventilation:** May be omitted when unobstructed openings to outside are sufficient to provide necessary ventilation.			

Code Ref.	Code Compliance Item	OK	NA	ID
1202.2.7	**Group S-3 Parking Garages - Mechanical Ventilation:** Except in open parking garages and loading platforms in bus terminals, provide minimum of 1.5 cfm/sf (0.71 L/s) gross floor area.			
	Alternate System: Exhaust 14,000 cfm (6608 L/s) for each operating vehicle; base system on instantaneous movement rate of vehicles, but not less than 2.5% (or 1 vehicle) of garage capacity.			
	Carbon Monoxide Sensing Devices: May be used to modulate ventilation system to maintain maximum average carbon monoxide concentration of 50 parts per million during any 8-hour period, and maximum concentration of 200 parts per million for 1-hour maximum.			
	Accessory Spaces: Provide connecting offices, waiting rooms, and ticket booths with conditioned air under positive pressure.			
1203.1	**Group R - Ventilation and Light Openings:** Open to public way, yard, or court except:			
	Required exterior openings may open into a roofed porch where porch abuts a public way, yard, or court; has a ceiling height of 7'-0" (2134 mm) minimum; and has a longer side at least 65% open and unobstructed.			
	Skylights.			
1203.2	**Group R - Light in Guest Rooms and Habitable Rooms in Dwelling Units and Congregate Residences:** Provide exterior glazed openings not less than 10% of floor area of rooms with minimum of 10 sf (0.93 m^2), except kitchens may be provided with artificial light.			
1203.3	**Group R - Ventilation in Guest Rooms and Habitable Rooms in Dwelling Units and Congregate Residences:** Provide openable exterior openings not less than 1/10 of floor area, 5 sf (0.46 m^2) minimum, or provide mechanical ventilation of 2 air changes per hour in guest rooms, dormitories, habitable rooms, and public corridors with 15 cfm (7 L/s) outside air per occupant.			
	Consider room in question as part of adjoining room when 1/2 of area of common wall is open and unobstructed and provides minimum opening of 1/10 floor area of interior room or 25 sf (2.3 m^2), whichever is greater.			
	Group R - Ventilation in Bathrooms, Toilet Rooms, and Laundry Rooms: Provide openable exterior openings not less than 1/20 of floor area, minimum 1-1/2 sf (0.14 m^2), or provide mechanical ventilation of 5 air changes per hour, ducted directly to exterior.			
	Connect ducts directly to exterior and at least 3'-0" away from openings allowing air entry into occupied portions of building.			

Solar Energy Collectors

UBC Chapter 13

Code Ref.	Code Compliance Item	OK	NA	ID
1301	**Solar Collectors:** When located above or on roof, do not reduce required fire rating or fire retardancy class of roof covering materials.			
	Exceptions: Collectors on 1- and 2-family dwellings.			
	Noncombustible collectors on buildings 3 stories or or less or more than 9,000 sf (836 m²).			
	Solar collectors having noncombustible sides and bottoms may be equipped with plastic covers on buildings not over 3 stories or 9,000 sf (836 m²) if such cover is approved for use when over 0.010" (0.3 mm) thick and area does not exceed 33-1/3% of roof area for CC1 materials and 25% for CC2.			
	Plastic covers 0.010" (0.3 mm) thick or less may be of any plastic if total area of collectors does not exceed 33-1/3% of roof area.			

Exterior Wall Coverings

UBC Chapter 14

Code Ref.	Code Compliance Item	OK	NA	ID
1402.1	**Weather-resistive Barriers:** Provide on all weather-exposed surfaces to protect interior wall covering; equal to UBC Standard 14-1 for kraft waterproof paper or asphalt-saturated rag felt.			
	May be omitted: When exterior covering is weatherproof panels.			
	In back-plastered construction.			
	Where there is no human occupancy.			
	Over water-repellent panel sheathing.			
	Under paperbacked metal or wire fabric lath.			
	Behind lath and cement plaster on underside of roof and eave projections.			
1402.2	**Flashing and Counterflashing:** Flash exterior openings to make waterproof.			
	Minimum Flashing Thickness: 0.019" (0.48 mm) 26 gage corrosion-resistant metal.			
1402.3	**Waterproofing Weather-exposed Areas:** Waterproof underneath balconies, landings, exterior stairways, and occupied roofs exposed to weather; slope 1:12 (2%) minimum.			
1402.4	**Dampproofing Foundation Walls:** Dampproof basement walls below grade.			
1402.5	**Window Wells:** Extend below window sill.			
1403.1.2	**Veneer on Wood Frame:** 30'-0" (9144 mm) maximum height above non-combustible foundation, except when special construction is designed to provide for differential movement.			
1403.4.1	**Veneer Design - General:** Do not support any loads but veneer weight and dead load of veneer above.			
	Design backing surfaces and foundations to support vertical and lateral loads imposed by veneer.			
	Consider differential movement of supports, including termperature changes, shrinkage, creep, and deflection.			

Code Ref.	Code Compliance Item	OK	NA	ID
1403.4.2	**Adhered Veneer - Design:** Except for ceramic tile, design veneer and backing to bond to supporting element for minimum shear stress of 50 ksi (345 kPa).			
1403.4.3	**Anchored Veneer - Design:** Design to resist horizontal force equal to at least 2 times weight of veneer.			
1403.5.1	**Adhered Veneer - Permitted Backing:** Continuous; of any material permitted by code, surfaces prepared to secure and support loads imposed by veneer.			
	Exterior Veneers: Provide weatherproof covering.			
1403.5.2	**Adhered Veneer - Area Limitations:** Unlimited except as required in 1403.1.2 above and as required to control expansion and contraction.			
1403.5.3	**Adhered Veneer - Unit Sized Limitations:** 36" (914 mm) maximum in greatest dimension or more than 720 si (0.46 m^2) total area.			
	15 psf (73.2 kg/m^2) maximum weight.			
	Units weighing 3 psf (14.6 kg/m^2) are not limited in dimension or area.			
1403.5.4	**Adhered Veneer - Application:** In lieu of designed application required by 1403.4.1 and 1403.4.2, apply veneer using construction methods listed in Section 1403.5.4.			
1403.6.1	**Anchored Veneer - Permitted Backing:** Any material permitted by code.			
	Exterior Veneers: Provide weatherproof covering.			
1403.6.2	**Anchored Veneer - Height and Support Limitations:** Support on footings or noncombustible supports.			
	Seismic Zones 2, 3, and 4: Support weight of veneers over 30'-0" (9144 mm) high above foundation with noncombustible, corrosion resistant structural framing.			
	Provide horizontal supports for such framing spaced not more than 12'-0" (3658 mm) vertically above initial 30'-0" (9144 mm) height.			
	Vertical spacing may be increased when special design techniques are used.			
	Provide noncombustible, noncorrosive lintels and noncombustible supports over all openings where veneer is not self-spanning. Limit deflections to 1/600 maximun under full veneer load.			
1403.6.3	**Anchored Veneer - Area Limitations:** Unlimited except as required in 1403.1.2 above and as required to control expansion and contraction.			
1403.6.4.1	**Anchored Veneer - Application:** In lieu of designed application required by 1403.4.1 and 1403.4.3, apply veneer using construction methods listed in Section 1403.6.4.2, 1403.6.4.3, 1403.6.4.4, and 1403.6.4.5.			
1404.1	**Vinyl Siding:** Where complying with UBC Standard 14-2, may be used on Type V buildings where wind speeds do not exceed 80 mph (129 km/h) and building height is less than 40'-0" (12 192 mm).			
1404.2	**Vinyl Siding Application:** Apply over sheathing.			

Roofs and Roof Structures

UBC Chapter 15

Code Ref.	Code Compliance Item	OK	NA	ID
1503	**Roof-Covering Requirements:** Comply with Table 15-A.			
	Provide either fire-retardant roof assemblies or noncombustible coverings.			
1504	**Roof-Covering Classification:** **Fire-retardant Roofing:** Assemblies meeting UBC Standard 15-2 and listed as Class A, B, or C roof.			
	Noncombustible Roof Covering: Cement shingles or sheets, exposed concrete slab roof, ferrous or copper shingles or sheets, slate shingles, or clay or concrete roofing tile.			
	Nonrated Roofing: Approved material not listed as Class A, B, or C assembly.			
1505.1	**Attic Access:** Provide in combustible buildings; access not required for attics with maximum vertical height of less than 30" (762 mm).			
	Locate in corridor, hallway, or readily accessible location.			
	Minimum Opening Dimensions: 22" by 30" (559 mm by 762 mm).			
	Minimum Headroom Clearance above Access: 30" (762 mm).			
1505.3	**Attic Ventilation:** Provide ventilation for enclosed attics and each enclosed rafter space where ceilings are applied to underside of rafters.			
	Protect vent openings from entrance of rain or snow.			
	Do not block flow of air with insulation.			
	Provide 1" (25 mm) minimum air space between insulation and roof sheathing.			
	Net Free Ventilating Area: Minimum 1/150 of area of ventilated space.			

Code Ref.	Code Compliance Item	OK	NA	ID
1505.3	**Attic Ventilating Area Exceptions:** Area may be 1/300 when 50% of required ventilating area is located in upper portion of attic space, at least 3-0"' (914 mm) above eave or cornice vents.			
	Area may be 1/300 when attic is provided with vapor retarder, transmission rate not more than 1 perm (5.7×10^{-11} kg/Pa·s·m^2) on warm side of insulation.			
	Attic Ventilation Openings: Cover with corrosion-resistant metal mesh, 1/4" (6.4 mm) openings each dimension.			
1506.1	**Roof Drainage:** Provide minimum 1/4:12 (2%) roof slope unless structure is designed to support ponding water.			
1506.2	**Roof Drains:** Provide at low points unless roof drains over edges, sized and discharged in compliance with Plumbing Code.			
1506.3	**Secondary Roof Drains:** Provide either overflow drains or scuppers as follows: **Overflow Drains:** Provide at roof drains with same size and inlet flow located 2" above roof low point.			
	Connect overflow drains to storm sewer independent of roof drain lines.			
	Scuppers: Provide scuppers of 3 times size of roof drains.			
	4" (102 mm) minimum opening height.			
	Locate in parapet walls adjacent to roof drains, inlet flow line 2" above roof low point.			
1506.4	**Concealed Piping:** Install in compliance with Plumbing Code.			
1506.5	**Roof Drainage over Public Property:** Not permitted except for R3 and U occupancies.			
1511.4	**Penthouse and Roof Structure Construction:** Construct as required for building.			
	Exceptions: Types I and II-FR may have 1-hour noncombustible exterior walls and roofs when at least 5'-0" (1524 mm) away from adjacent property line.			
	Types III and IV may have 1-hour noncombustible walls when at least 5'-0" (1524 mm) away from adjacent property line.			
	Mechanical equipment enclosures located at least 20'-0" (6096 mm) from adjacent property line may be unprotected noncombustible construction.			
	Unroofed mechanical equipment screens, fences, and similar enclosures on 1-story buildings may be combustible construction when located at least 20'-0" (6096 mm) from adjacent property line and not more than 4'-0" (1219 mm) above roof surface.			

Glass Unit Masonry

UBC Section 2110

Code Ref.	Code Compliance Item	OK	NA	ID
2110.1	**Minimum Thickness:** 3" (76 mm).			
2110.2	**Mortar Joints:** 1/4" (6.4 mm) minimum, 3/8" (9.5 mm) maximum, completely filled.			
2110.3	**Lateral Support:** Provide panel anchors in mortar joints along each end of panel, 16" (406 mm) maximum spacing; resist horizontal design forces or 200 plf (2920 Nlm), whichever is greater.			
2110.4	**Joint Reinforcement:** Space 16" (406 mm) on center maximum, extend full length of panel.			
	Place in mortar beds immediately below and above openings.			
2110.5	**Exterior Panel Size:** 144 sf (13.4 m^2) maximum unsupported wall surface, or 15'-0" (4572 mm) in any direction.			
	Interior Panel Size: 250 sf (232 m^2) maximum of unsupported area or 25'-0" (7620 mm) in any direction.			
2110.6	**Expansion Joints:** Provide along both sides and top.			
	Provide thickness to accommodate structural displacements, 3/8" (9.5 mm) minimum.			
	Keep free of mortar and fill joint with resilient material.			
2110.7	**Reuse of Units:** Do not reuse units removed from existing construction.			

Wood

UBC Chapter 23

Code Ref.	Code Compliance Item	OK	NA	ID
2306.3	**Under-floor Access:** Provide access when wood joists are 18" (457 mm) or more above earth or girders are 12" (305 mm) or more above earth.			
	Minimum 18" by 24" (457 mm by 610 mm) access opening, screened or covered, unobstructed by pipes or ducts.			
2306.7	**Under-floor Ventilation:** Mechanical means or openings in exterior foundation walls.			
	Area of Openings: 1 sf net area for each 150 sf (0.067 m² for each 10 m²) of underfloor area.			
	Location: As close to corners as practical, provide cross ventilation on at least 2 opposite sides.			
	Cover: Corrosion-resistant wire mesh with openings of 1/4" (6.4 mm).			
	Building official may allow operable louvers and may allow required net area of vent openings to be reduced to 10% of the above if moisture due to climate and groundwater conditions are not considered excessive and if under-floor ground surface area is covered with vapor retarder.			
2306.8	**Wood Earth Separation:** Provide treated or decay-resistant wood where located nearer than 6" (152 mm) to earth.			
	Treated or decay-resistant wood where wood rests on concrete slabs on earth.			
	2" (51 mm) air space between planter boxes and wood stud walls. Provide exterior wall covering on wood stud wall; provide flashing and air circulation when air space is less than 6" (152 mm).			
2306.12	**Weather Exposure:** Provide treated or decay-resistant wood for structural members exposed to weather without overhead protection.			
2306.13	**Water Splash:** Protect wood frame walls and partitions covered on the interior with plaster, tile, or similar materials and are subject to water splash with approved waterproof paper.			

Glass and Glazing

UBC Chapter 24

Code Ref.	Code Compliance Item	OK	NA	ID
2401.1	**Scope:** Applies to all glass and glazing except for Groups R and U not over 3 stories and located in areas with minimum basic wind speed of less than 80 mph (129 km/h).			
2401.1	**Support:** Support glass firmly on all 4 edges unless of approved design otherwise.			
2403	**Area Limitations:** Withstand loads for cladding in UBC Chapter 16, Part II.			
	Area of Individual Glass Lites: Graph 24-1 and Table 24-A.			
	Design glass or glazing subject to ice or snow loads per Chapter 16.			
2404.2	**Framing Member Deflection:** 1/175 or 3/4" (19.1 mm) maximum perpendicular to glass, positive or negative.			
2405	**Louvered Windows and Jalousies:** 3/16" (4.76 mm) minimum glass thickness, 48" (1219 mm) maximum glass length; exposed edges smooth.			
	Do not use wired glass with wire exposed on longitudinal edges.			
2406.4	**Hazardous Locations:** Provide safety glazing in the following locations:			
	Glazing in ingress and egress doors except jalousies and assemblies of leaded, faceted, or carved glass when used for decorative purposes.			
	Glazing in fixed and sliding panels of sliding door assemblies and panels in swinging doors other than wardrobe doors except for assemblies of leaded, faceted, or carved glass when used for decorative purposes.			
	Glazing in storm doors.			
	Glazing in all unframed swinging doors.			
	Glazing in doors and enclosures for hot tubs, whirlpools, saunas, steam rooms, bathtubs, and showers; glazing in walls enclosing these compartments where bottom exposed edge of glazing is less than 60" (1524 mm) above standing surface and drain inlet; except for assemblies of leaded, faceted, or carved glass used for decorative purposes.			

Code Ref.	Code Compliance Item	OK	NA	ID
2406.4	**Hazardous Locations, Continued:** Glazing in individual fixed or operable panels adjacent to doors where nearest exposed edge of glazing is within 24" (610 mm) arc of either vertical edge of door in closed position and where bottom exposed edge of glazing is less than 60" (1524 mm) above walking surface.			
	Exceptions: Safety glazing not required when: An intervening wall or other permanent barrier exists between door and glazing.			
	Decorative assemblies of leaded, faceted, or carved glass.			
	Glazing in individual fixed or operable panels where exposed area of individual pane is greater than 9 sf (0.84 m^2), exposed bottom edge is less than 18" (457 mm) above floor, exposed top edge is greater than 36" (914 mm) above floor, and 1 or more walking surfaces is within 36" (914 mm) horizontally of plane of glazing.			
	Exceptions: Safety glazing not required when: Protective bar is provided on accessible sides of glazing 34" (864 mm) to 38" (965 mm) above floor; bar height 1-1/2" (38 mm) minimum, withstanding 50 plf (729 N/m) horizontal force without contacting glass.			
	Outboard pane of insulating glass and in other multiple panels when bottom exposed edge of glass is 25'-0" (7620 mm) above grade, roof, walking surface or other horizontal or sloped (within 45° of horizontal) surface adjacent to glass exterior.			
	Glazing in railings regardless of height above walking surface including structural baluster panels and nonstructural infill panels.			
	Glazing in walls and fences used as barriers for pools and spas when the bottom edge of glazing is less than 5'-0" (1524 mm) above pool side of glazing and glazing is within 5'-0" (1524 mm) of water's edge.			
	Glazing in walls enclosing stair landings or within 5'-0" (1524 mm) of bottom and top of stairs where bottom edge of glass is less than 5'-0" (1524 mm) above a walking surface.			
2406.4	**Hazardous Locations - Safety Glazing Not Required In:** Openings in doors through which 3" (76 mm) diameter sphere will not pass.			
	Curved panels of revolving door assemblies.			
	Doors of commercial refrigerated cabinets.			
	Glass block panels.			
2406.6	**Glass Railings:** Single pane of fully tempered glass, laminated fully tempered glass, or laminated heat strengthened glass designed for loads in UBC Table 16-A, with a safety factor of 4.			
	Minimum Thickness: 1/4" (6.4 mm).			

Code Ref.	Code Compliance Item	OK	NA	ID
2406.6	**Glass Railings, Continued:** Support handrail or guardrail sections by at least 3 glass balusters or otherwise support so that rail remains in place in case 1 baluster panel fails.			
	Do not install glass panels without handrail or guardrail attached.			
	Glass rails not permitted in parking garages except where rail is not exposed to vehicle impact.			
2407	**Hinged Shower Doors:** Open outward.			
2409.1	**Sloped Glazing and Skylights:** Glass or glazing material installed at slope of 15° or more from vertical plane, including skylights, roofs, and sloped walls.			
2409.2	**Sloped Glazing and Skylights - Allowable Glazing Materials:** **Single Layer Materials:** Laminated glass with 0.015" (0.38 mm) minimum polyvinyl butyral interlayer for panes 16 sf (1.5 m²) or less and 12'-0" (3658 mm) maximum above walking surface or 0.030" (0.76 mm) for larger or higher panes, wired glass, heat strengthened glass, fully tempered glass, or rigid plastic per UBC Section 2603.7.			
	Multiple Layer Systems: Each lite of materials allowed above.			
2409.3	**Sloped Glazing and Skylights - Screening:** **Single Layer Glazing:** Provide screens below heat-strengthened glass and tempered glass, capable of supporting weight of glass, and installed below and within 4" (102 mm) of glass.			
	Screening for Multiple-Layer Glazing: Provide screens below heat-strengthened glass and tempered glass when used as bottom layer, capable of supporting weight of glass, and installed below and within 4" (102 mm) of glass.			
	Screening Materials: Noncombustible, not thinner than 0.08" (2.3 mm), mesh not more than 1" by 1" (25 mm by 25 mm), noncorrosive.			
	Screening Exceptions: Screen not required under:			
	Fully tempered glass located between intervening floors at a slope of 30° or less from vertical plane if highest point of glass is 10'-0" (3048 mm) or less above walking surface.			
	Glazing materials, including annealed glass, if walking surface or any other accessible area below glazing is permanently protected from falling glass for a minimum horizontal distance equal to twice the height.			
	Glazing materials, including annealed glass, in sloped glazing systems of commercial or detached greenhouses used exclusively for growing plants and not intended for use by the public, provided height of the greenhouse at the ridge does not exceed 20'-0" (6096 mm) above grade.			
	Fully tempered glass in dwelling units when area of each pane (single glass) or unit (insulating glass) is not more than 16 sf (1.5 m²) or less and 12'-0" (3658 mm) maximum above walking surface or other accessible area, and nominal thickness of each pane is 3/16" (4.76 mm) maximum.			

Code Ref.	Code Compliance Item	OK	NA	ID
2409.4	**Sloped Glazing and Skylights - Framing:** Provide noncombustible materials in Types I and II construction except in foundries or buildings where acid fumes deleterious to metals are incidental to the use of the building where pressure-treated woods or other noncorrosive materials may be used.			
	Mount skylights set at an angle of less than 45° from the horizontal plane at 4" (102 mm) minimum above plane of roof on a curb constructed of materials as required for frame.			
	Skylights may be installed in plane of roof when roof slope is 45° or more from horizontal.			
2409.5	**Sloped Glazing and Skylights - Design Loads:** Design to withstand tributary loads required by UBC Section 1605. Sizing limitations of Graph 24-1 and Table 24-A may be used if design loads are increased by factor of 2.67.			
2409.6	**Sloped Glazing and Skylights - Floors and Sidewalks:** Support glazing in floors or sidewalks by metal or reinforced concrete frames.			
	Minimum Thickness: 1/2" (13 mm).			
	Glazing Materials: Wire glass or wire screen under glass panels over 16 si (0.1 m²).			
	Provide strength of glazing as required for sidewalks or floors except where glazing is surrounded by railings 42" (1067 mm) high, in which case design construction for not less than roof loads.			

Gypsum Board and Plaster

UBC Chapter 25

Code Ref.	Code Compliance Item	OK	NA	ID
2503	**Vertical Assemblies - Wood Framing:** Minimum 2" (51 mm) nominal in least dimension except that 1" by 2" (25 mm by 51 mm) furring strips may be used over solid backing.			
	Studless Partitions: 2" (51 mm) minimum thickness.			
2504.2	**Horizontal Assemblies - Wood Framing:** Minimum 2" (51 mm) nominal in least dimension except that 1" by 2" (25 mm by 51 mm) furring strips may be used over solid backing.			
2504.3	**Horizontal Assemblies - Hangers for Suspended Ceilings:** Size per UBC Table 25-A and fasten to or embed in structural framing, masonry, or concrete.			
	Saddle tie hangers around main runners. Bolt lower ends of flat hangers to runner channels with 3/8" (9.5 mm) bolts or bend tightly around runners and bolt to main part of hanger.			
2504.4	**Horizontal Assemblies - Runners and Furring:** Size per UBC Table 25-A.			
	Securely attach cross furring to main runners by saddle tying with minimum of 1 strand of 0.051" (1.30 mm) (16 AW gage) or 2 stands of 0.04" (1.02 mm) (18 AW gage) tie wire or equivalent attachment.			
2505.1	**Interior Lath - General:** Where wood stud walls are subject to water splash, provide moisture barrier behind lath.			
2505.2 2506.5	**Lath Supports:** Space supports per UBC Tables 25-B and 25-C.			
2506.3	**Exterior Lath - Permitted Backing:** Do not use gypsum lath or gypsum board, except on ceilings or roof soffits as backing for metal lath or wire fabric lath and cement plaster.			

Code Ref.	Code Compliance Item	OK	NA	ID
2506.4	**Exterior Lath - Weather-Resistive Barriers:** Provide on all weather-exposed surfaces to protect interior wall covering; equal to UBC Standard 14-1 for kraft waterproof paper or asphalt-saturated rag felt.			
	Weather-resistive barrier may be omitted under paperbacked metal or wire fabric lath, behind lath and cement plaster on underside of roof and eave projections			
2506.5	**Weep Screeds:** Provide at or below foundation plate line on all exterior stud walls, 3-1/2" (89 mm) minimum vertical flange.			
	Place screed minimum of 4" (102 mm) above earth and 2" (51 mm) above paved areas.			
	Provide type that allows water to drain to exterior.			
	Lap weather-resistive barrier over and terminate exterior lath on attachment flange.			
2507.1	**Interior Plaster:** Do not apply directly over fiber insulation board.			
	Do not apply cement plaster directly to gypsum lath, gypsum masonry, or gypsum plaster except on horizontal ceilings or roof soffits.			
	Minimum Thickness: See UBC Table 25-D.			
2507.4	**Interior Acoustical Plaster Finish:** May be applied over any base coat plaster, clean masonry, or concrete.			
2509.5	**Exposed Aggregate Plaster:** May be applied over concrete, masonry, cement plaster base coats, or gypsum plaster base coats.			
2511.1	**Gypsum Board - General:** Do not install on building exteriors.			
2511.2	**Gypsum Board Supports:** Space per UBC Table 25-G for single-ply application or 25-H for 2-ply application.			
2512	**Gypsum Board in Showers and Water Closets:** Provide water-resistant type when used as a base for tile or wall panels for tubs, shower, or water closet compartment walls.			
	Do not install water-resistant board over a vapor barrier, in areas subject to continuous high humidity such as saunas, steam rooms, or gang shower rooms; or on ceilings where framing exceeds 12" (305 mm) on center.			

Plastic

UBC Chapter 26

Code Ref.	Code Compliance Item	OK	NA	ID
2602.4	**Foam Plastic Insulation - Thermal Barriers:** Separate building interiors from foam plastic insulation by thermal barrier, index of 15 when tested per UBC Standard 26-2.			
	Install thermal barrier to remain in place for the duration of time of index classification.			
2602.4	**Thermal Barriers Not Required:** For siding backer board if the foam plastic insulation is maximum of 2,000 Btu per sf (22.7 MJ/m^2) per UBC Standard 26-1 and when separated from building interior by at least 2" (51 mm) of mineral fiber insulation, or applied as re-siding over existing walls.			
	For walk-in cooler/freezer units less than 400 sf (37.2 m^2).			
	In masonry or concrete wall, floor, or roof systems when foam plastic insulation is covered by 1" (25 mm) minimum thickness of masonry or concrete. Loose fill shall meet index of 15 when tested in accordance with UBC Standard 26-2.			
	Within attic or crawl space where entry is made only for service of utilities, and when foam plastic insulation is covered by material such as 1-1/2" (38 mm) thick mineral fiber insulation; 1/4" (6.4 mm) plywood, hardboard, or gypsum board; corrosion-resistant sheet metal of 0.016" (0.4 mm) base thickness.			
	In cooler and freezer walls when foam plastic insulation has flame-spread rating of 25 or less, has flash and self-ignition temperatures of less than 600°F and 800°F (316°C and 427°C) respectively, is covered by 0.032" (0.8 mm) thick aluminum or corrosion-resistant steel of 0.016" (0.4 mm) base thickness, and is protected by an automatic sprinkler system. When such cooler or freezer is located in a building, that portion of building where it is located shall also be sprinkled.			

Code Ref.	Code Compliance Item	OK	NA	ID
2602.5.2.1	**Foam Plastic Insulation in Noncombustible Exterior Walls - 1-story Buildings:** May be used when:			
	Building is protected throughout with automatic sprinklers.			
	Insulation has a flame-spread rating of 25 or less and smoke developed rating of 450 or less per UBC Standard 8-1.			
	Maximum thickness of 4".			
	Thermal barrier may be omitted when foam plastic insulation is covered by 0.032" (0.8 mm) thick aluminum or corrosion-resistant steel of 0.016" (0.4 mm) base thickness.			
	When wall is rated substantiate that rating is maintained per UBC Standard 7-1.			
2602.5.2.2	**Foam Plastic Insulation in Noncombustible Exterior Walls - Buildings of Any Height:** Comply with the following:			
	When wall is rated substantiate that rating is maintained per UBC Standard 7-1.			
	Foam plastic insulation is separated from building interiors by thermal barrier with index of 15 when tested per UBC Standard 26-2.			
	Combustible content of plastic insulation in any portion of wall is maximum of 6,000 Btu per sf (22.7 MJ/m^2) of wall area per UBC Standard 26-1.			
	Wall assembly is tested per UBC Standard 26-4 or 26-9.			
	Foam plastic insulation, exterior coatings, and facings tested separately, shall have flame spread rating of 25 or less and smoke developed rating of 450 or less per UBC Standard 8-1, tested with thickness intended for use.			
2602.5.3	**Foam Plastic Insulation in Roofing:** Flame-spread rating of 75 or less and smoke-developed rating of 450 or less, when used with thermal barrier per UBC Section 2602.4, and when listed as part of Class A, B, or C roof covering assembly.			
	Foam insulation need not meet the flame-spread and smoke-developed ratings above and need not have thermal barrier when part of a Class A, B, or C roof assembly which passes the test for insulated decks.			
2602.5.4	**Foam Plastic Insulation in Nonrated Doors:** May be used as core material, flame-spread rating of 75 or less, when door facing is 0.032" (0.8 mm) thick aluminum or steel of 0.016" (0.4 mm) base thickness; no thermal barrier required.			
2603.1.4	**Light-Transmitting Plastics - Combination of Glazing and Exterior Wall Panels:** Combinations of plastic glazing and plastic exterior wall panels are subject to area, height, percentage, and separation requirements applicable to class of plastics prescribed for wall panel installation.			

Code Ref.	Code Compliance Item	OK	NA	ID
2603.1.5	**Light-Transmitting Plastics - Combination of Roof Panels and Skylights:** Combination of plastic roof panels and skylights are subject to area, percentage, and separation requirements applicable to roof panel installation.			
2603.3.2	**Light-Transmitting Plastics - Fastenings:** Provide for design loads; provide for expansion and contraction of plastic materials and other materials used in conjunction.			
2603.4	**Plastic Glazing of Unprotected Openings - Type V Construction:** May be glazed with plastic materials.			
	Plastic Glazing of Unprotected Openings - Other Types of Construction: May be glazed with plastic materials when:			
	Total area of plastic glazing does not exceed 25% of wall area of any wall face of story in which installed and area of any single pane installed above first story does not exceed 16 sf (1.5 m²) and when vertical dimension of any single pane does not exceed 48" (1219 mm).			
	Exception: Area of plastic glazing may be increased to 50% when building is fully sprinklered, no limits on maximum dimensions of single panes.			
	Flame barriers extending 30" (762 mm) beyond exterior wall in plane of the floor or vertical panels 48" (1219 mm) minimum high are provided between glazed units in adjacent stories.			
	Do not install plastic panels more than 65'-0" (19 812 mm) above grade level.			
2603.5	**Light-Transmitting Exterior Wall Panels - Type V Construction:** May be used in nonrated exterior walls of Type V construction.			
	Light-Transmitting Exterior Wall Panels - Other Types of Construction: May be used in nonrated exterior walls when:			
	Panels are not installed more than 40'-0" (12 192 mm) above grade.			
	Panels are not installed in exterior walls located less than 10'-0" (3048 mm) from property line.			
	Area and size of panels complies with UBC Table 26-A.			
	Exceptions: No vertical separation at floor required when flame barriers extending 30" (762 mm) beyond exterior wall at plane of floor except the thickness of the flame barrier.			
	In fully sprinklered buildings, maximum percentage of plastic panels may be increased 50%, maximum area of any panel may be increased 50%, and horizontal and vertical separation may be reduced by 50%.			
2603.6	**Plastic Roof Panels:** May be used in nonrated roof assemblies as follows:			
	Separate individual panels by 48" (1219 mm) minimum horizontally.			
	Do not install plastic roof panels within the distance to property line or public way where openings are prohibited or required to be protected.			

Code Ref.	Code Compliance Item	OK	NA	ID
2603.6	**Plastic Roof Panels, Continued:** Limit area of Class CC1 plastics to 150 sf (13.9 m^2), limit total aggregate area of panels to 33-1/3% of floor area of room or space sheltered.			
	Limit area of Class CC2 plastics to 100 sf (9.3 m^2), limit total aggregate area of panels to 25% of floor area of room or space sheltered.			
	Exception: Swimming pool shelters under 5,000 sf (464.5 m^2) and not closer than 10'-0" (3048 mm) to property line or adjacent building.			
2603.7	**Light-Transmitting Plastics in Skylights:** Mount plastics 4" (102 mm) minimum above plane of roof by curb consistent with type of construction requirements.			
	Curbs may be omitted on roofs of Group R-3 with 3:12 (25%) minimum slope when using self-flashing skylights.			
	Slope flat or corrugated plastic skylights 4:12 (33-1/3%) minimum.			
	Dome shaped skylights shall rise above mounting flange a minimum distance equal to 10% of maximum span of dome, 5" (127 mm) minimum, except for skylights passing Class B Burning Brand Test of UBC Standard 15-2.			
	Protect edges of plastic lights or domes by metal or noncombustible materials; protection not required where nonrated roof coverings permitted.			
	Maximum area within the curb for skylights with CC2 material is 100 sf (9.3 m^2), for CC1 material is 200 sf (18.6 mm).			
	Exceptions: Maximum area is not limited if building is 1 story, has exterior separation from other buildings of 30'-0" (9144 mm) minimum, and room or space sheltered is not a Group I-1.1, I-1.2, or I-3 occupancy.			
	Except in Groups A-1, A-2, I, H-1.1, H-1.2, and H-2, maximum area within curb is not limited where skylights serve as a fire venting system or building is fully sprinklered.			
	Maximum aggregate area of skylights on a roof with CC2 material is 25% of floor area, for CC1 material is 33-1/3%.			
	Separate skylights from each other at least 48" (1219 mm) horizontally.			
	Exceptions: Except in Groups A-1, A-2, I, H-1.1, H-1.2, and H-2, separation not required where skylights serve as fire venting system or building is fully sprinklered.			
	Separation not required for multiple skylights above same room or space with combined area not exceeding CC2 material is 100 sf (9.3 m^2) for CC2 material or 200 sf (18.6 mm) for CC1 material.			
	Do not install skylights in portions of roof within the distance to property line or public way where openings are prohibited or required to be protected.			
2603.7.2	**Plastics over Stair Shafts:** Plastics which do not automatically vent but which are able to be vented may be used.			

Code Ref.	Code Compliance Item	OK	NA	ID
2603.8	**Light Diffusing Systems:** Support directly or indirectly by noncombustible hangers.			
	Comply with UBC Chapter 8 or meet the following:			
	Diffusers shall fall from mountings at ambient temperature of at least 200°F (93°C) below ignition temperature of plastic material.			
	Diffusers shall remain in place at ambient room temperature of 175°F (79°C) for at least 15 minutes.			
	10'-0" (3048 mm) maximum panel length, 30 sf (2.8 m^2) maximum panel area.			
	When used in required means of egress, do not exceed 30% of aggregate area of ceiling in which installed; aggregate area not limited in fully sprinklered building.			
	Do not install in sprinklered areas if system prevents effective operation of sprinklers and unless sprinklers are located both above and below light-diffusing system.			
2603.10	**Light-Transmitting Plastics in Partitions:** Permitted per other requirements.			
2603.13	**Light-Transmitting Plastics in Canopies:** May be used over motor vehicle fuel dispensing stations fuel dispensers when panels are 10'-0" (3048 mm) minimum from any other building and face yards or streets at least 40'-0" (12 192 mm) wide on the other sides.			
	Maximum Panel Area: 100 sf (9.3 m^2).			
	Aggregate Areas of Panels: 1,000 sf (93 m^2).			
2603.14	**Light-Transmitting Plastics in Solar Collectors:** May be used with collectors having noncombustible sides and bottoms on buildings 3 stories or 9,000 sf (836 m^2) maximum, provided plastic cover, when more than 0.010" (0.3 mm) thick is of approved material and total area does not exceed 25% of roof area with CC2 material and 33-1/3% of roof area with CC1 material.			
	Plastic cover 0.010" (0.3 mm) thick or less may be of any plastic provided total area does not exceed 33-1/3% of roof area.			
2605	**Interior Plastic Veneers:** UBC Chapter 8.			
	Exterior Plastic Veneers: Use approved materials.			
	Do not attach to exterior walls over 50'-0" (15 240 mm) above grade.			
	Do not exceed area of 300 sf (27.9 m^2) per section and separate sections by 48" (1219 mm) minimum vertically.			
	Area and separation requirements do not apply to Type V buildings if walls are nonrated.			

Elevators

UBC Chapter 30

Code Ref.	Code Compliance Item	OK	NA	ID
3003.6	**Emergency Signs:** Except at main entrance level, provide sign indicating that in case of fire, elevator will not operate and exit stairs should be used.			
3004	**Hoistway Venting:** Vent when extending through 3 or more stories. Do not interconnect separate hoistways for venting purposes.			
	Minimum Vent Area: 3-1/2% of elevator shaft area, minimum of 3 sf (0.28 m^2) per elevator.			
3005	**Elevator Machine Room Ventilation:** Provide independent ventilation or air conditioning system to prevent overheating, meet the elevator equipment manufacturer's requirements.			
	When standby power is connected to elevators, connect air conditioning system to standby power.			
	Pressurization: When serving a pressurized elevator hoistway, pressurize machine room upon activation of heat or smoke detector located in machine room.			

Chimneys and Fireplaces

UBC Section 3102

Code Ref.	Code Compliance Item	OK	NA	ID
3102.3.1	**Chimney Support:** Do not support any structural load other than its own weight.			
3102.3.2	**Chimney Construction:** Convey flue gases per UBC Table 31-B.			
	Produce drafts not less than that required for safe operation.			
3102.3.3	**Chimney Clearance to Combustible Material:** UBC Table 31-B.			
3102.3.4	**Chimney Lining:** When required by UBC Table 31-B, provide fireclay flue tile, firebrick, or molded refractory units 5/8" (16 mm) thick minimum.			
	Bed in medium-duty refractory mortar, smooth joints on inside.			
3102.3.5	**Chimney Passageway Area:** Not smaller than vent connection on appliance, not less than required by UBC Table 31-A.			
	Flue Area: UBC Figure 31-A.			
	Chimney Height: Measure from firebox floor to top of last chimney flue tile.			
3102.3.6	**Chimney Height and Termination:** Extend above roof and highest elevation of building as required by UBC Table 31-B.			
	Consult building official for elevations over 2,000'-0" (610 m) to determine height of chimney.			
3102.3.7	**Chimney Cleanouts:** Provide within 6" (152 mm) of chimney base.			
3102.3.8	**Chimney Spark Arresters:** Provide when required by building official or where sparks would create hazard.			
	Net Free Area of Spark Arrester: At least 4 times chimney outlet.			
	Screen Openings: 1/2" (13 mm) maximum opening size, 3/8" (9.5 mm) minimum opening size.			
	Materials: Corrosion-resistant, 0.109" (2.77 mm) (#12 BW gage) wire, 0.042" (1.07 mm) (#19 BW gage) galvanized wire, or 0.022" (0.56 mm) (#24 BW gage) stainless steel.			

Code Ref.	Code Compliance Item	OK	NA	ID
3102.3.8	**Spark Arrester - Solid or Liquid Fuel Appliances:** Comply with Fire Code unless chimneys are 200'-0" (60 960 mm) from any mountainous, brush-covered, or forest covered land or land covered with flammable material and are not attached to structures with less than Class C roof covering.			
3102.4.2	**Masonry Chimney Walls:** UBC Table 31-B.			
3102.4.3	**Masonry Chimney Reinforcing and Seismic Anchorage:** In Seismic Zones 2, 3, and 4, provide 4-#4 bars extending full height of chimney, with 1/2" (13 mm) minimum grout or mortar cover.			
	Horizontal Ties: Minimum 1/4" (6.4 mm) diameter spaced at 18" (457 mm) on center maximum; provide 2 ties at each bend in vertical bars.			
	Provide 2 additional bars where chimney exceeds 40" (1016 mm) wide; provide 2 additional bars for each additional flue or each additional 40" (1016 mm) in width or fraction thereof.			
	Anchorage: Anchor masonry and concrete chimneys at each floor or ceiling above 6' (1829 mm) above grade.			
	Provide two 3/16" by 1" (4.8 mm by 25 mm) steel straps cast 12" (305 mm) minimum into chimney with 180° bend with 6" (152 mm) extension around vertical bars in outer face of chimney.			
	Fasten straps to structure with two 1/2" (13 mm) diameter bolts per strap.			
3102.4.4	**Maximum Masonry Chimney Offsets:** 4" in 24" (102 mm in 610 mm), but not more than 1/3 of dimension of chimney in the direction of offset.			
	Transition fireplace to chimney 2:1 (200%) slope maximum.			
3102.4.5	**Change in Masonry Chimney Size or Shape:** Do not make change within 6" (152 mm) above or below combustible floor, ceiling, or roof component.			
3102.4.6	**Masonry Flue Separation:** Minimum 4" (102 mm) thick masonry.			
3102.4.7	**Masonry Chimney Inlets:** 1/8" (3.2 mm) minimum thick metal or 5/8" (16 mm) minimum thick refractory material.			
	Where no other inlets are provided except cleanout, provide masonry plug 16" (406 mm) maximum below inlet and locate cleanout above plug.			
	Inlet may serve as cleanout when plug is located less than 6" (152 mm) below inlet.			
3102.5.3	**Factory-built Chimneys and Fireplaces - Multiple Vents in Vertical Shafts:** When used with listed factory-built fireplaces may be used in common shaft of required fire rating.			
3102.5.4	**Metal Chimneys:** Anchor at each floor and roof with two 1-1/2" by 1/8" (38 mm by 3.2 mm) metal straps looped around outside of chimney and nailed with at least six 8d nails per strap at each joist.			
3102.7.1	**Masonry and Concrete Fireplaces and Barbeques - Support:** Provide designed foundations or provide foundations 12" (305 mm) thick minimum, extending at least 6" (152 mm) outside fireplace wall, and projecting below natural grade in accordance with UBC Table 18-I-D.			

Code Ref.	Code Compliance Item	OK	NA	ID
3102.7.3	**Masonry and Concrete Fireplaces and Barbeques - Wall Thickness:** **Fireplace:** Minimum 8" (203 mm) thick masonry.			
	Firebox: 10" (254 mm) thick except 8" (203 mm) where firebrick lining is used.			
3102.7.4	**Masonry and Concrete Fireplaces and Barbeques - Metal Hoods:** Minimum 0.036" (0.92 mm) (#19 carbon sheet steel gage) copper, galvanized steel, or corrosion-resistant ferrous metal, with smoke-proof seams and connections.			
	Slope hoods at 45° or less from vertical and extend horizontally at least 6" (152 mm) beyond fire box limits.			
	Keep minimum of 18" (457 mm) from combustible materials unless approved for reduced clearances.			
3102.7.6	**Smoke Chamber:** **Front and Side Walls:** 8" (203 mm) minimum thickness.			
	Back Walls: 6" (152 mm) minimum thickness.			
3102.7.8	**Masonry and Concrete Fireplaces and Barbeques - Clearance to Combustible Materials:** 2" (51 mm) minimum from fireplace, smoke chamber, or chimney walls; 6" (152 mm) from fireplace opening.			
	Combustible Projections within 12" (305 mm) of Fireplace Opening: Not more than 1/8" (3 mm) for each 1" (25 mm) clearance from opening.			
	Hoods: Not closer than 18" (457 mm) to combustible materials.			
3102.7.9	**Areas of Flues, Throats, and Dampers:** UBC Figure 31-A or Table 31-A.			
	Throat: 8" (203 mm) minimum above fireplace opening.			
	Dampers: 0.097" (2.46 mm) (#12 carbon sheet metal gage) minimum thickness.			
	Damper Opening: 90% of required flue area when fully opened.			
3102.7.10	**Lintels**: Noncombustible or self-supporting masonry.			
3102.7.11	**Hearth:** Provide brick, concrete, stone, or approved noncombustible hearth slab; 4" (102 mm) minimum thickness, supported by noncombustible materials or reinforced to carry its own weight and imposed loads.			
3102.7.12	**Hearth Extensions:** 16" (406 mm) minimum from front, and 8" (203 mm) minimum beyond each side of fireplace opening.			
	Where fireplace opening is 6 sf (0.56 m^2) or larger, provide extension 20" (508 mm) minimum in front and 12" (305 mm) minimum beyond each side of fireplace opening.			

Construction in the Public Right of Way

UBC Chapter 32

Code Ref.	Code Compliance Item	OK	NA	ID
3205.5	**Marquee Construction:** Support entirely from building; noncombustible construction.			
	1-hour construction when on Type V building.			
3205.6	**Marquee Roof Construction:** May be a skylight if lights are laminated or wire glass, or plastic complying with UBC Section 2603.7.			
	Slope roofs and skylights to drains; direct drains under sidewalk, do not drain onto sidewalk.			
3205.7	**Marquee Location:** Do not interfere with exterior standpipes or obstruct means of egress.			
3206.2	**Awning Construction:** Noncombustible frames with combustible coverings permitted.			
	Do not obstruct required means of egress.			
3206.3	**Awning Projections:** May extend over public property 7'-0" (2134 mm) maximum from face of building, 2'-0" (610 mm) minimum to face of curb.			
	Do not extend more than 2/3 the distance from property line to curb.			
3206.4	**Awning Clearances:** 8'-0" (2438 mm) minimum.			
	Awning Valances: 7'-0" (2134 mm) minimum clearance, 12" (305 mm) maximum valance length below awning roof.			
3207	**Power Operated Doors:** Do not project power operated doors or their guide rails over public property.			
	Swinging Doors: Do not project doors more than 12" (305 mm) maximum over public property when in open position.			
	No projection permitted beyond property line in alleys.			

Site Work

UBC Chapter 33

Code Ref.	Code Compliance Item	OK	NA	ID
3301.1	**Excavation and Fills:** Do not exceed 1:2 (50%) slope for permanent fills or excavations unless permitted by soils investigation.			
	Backfill: Do not place fill or surcharge loads adjacent to buildings unless building or structure is capable of withstanding additional fills or surcharge loads.			
	Existing Footings: Underpin and protect existing footings or foundations from settlement or lateral movement caused by adjacent excavation.			

Group I-3 Occupancies
(Detention and Correctional Facilities)
UBC Appendix Chapter 3, Division I

When adopted by the governing jurisdiction, Appendix Chapter 3, Division I may be used as alternative provisions to requirements of Chapter 3. When used for design and construction purposes, all requirements in this appendix chapter shall be used. Chapter 3 provisions may be used if not specifically noted in this appendix chapter.

Code Ref.	Code Compliance Item	OK	NA	ID
319	**Glazing - Restraint Areas:** In fully sprinkled buildings, glazing area in 1-hour corridor walls not restricted where glazing is 1/4" (6.4 mm) thick wired glass or fire-tested glazing set in steel frames.			
	Wired Glass: In lieu of limiting aggregate area to 25% of area of room/corridor wall, comply with Sections 713.7 and 713.8.			
	Fire-Tested Glazing Materials: Do not exceed size and area of test.			
320	**Electrical:** Provide special electrical systems, exit illumination, power installations, and alternate on-site electrical supplies for every building or portion of a building housing 10 or more inmates.			
321.1	**Automatic Sprinkler Systems:** Provide in buildings or portions of buildings housing 6 or more inmates.			
	Sprinkler Control Valves: Provide electric supervision so that at least a local alarm will sound at a constantly attended location when valves are closed.			
	Sprinklers and Piping in Cells: May be imbedded in concrete construction.			
	Pressurized Enclosures: Not required in fully sprinklered buildings.			
	Pressurize required stairways to 0.15" water column (37.3 Pa) upon actuation of smoke detection system.			
321.2	**Wet Standpipe Systems:** Provide Class II standpipes with hoses in every building in facilities housing 50 or more inmates.			
	Locate in cell complexes and other cell areas of buildings.			
	Locate Class II standpipes such that hoses will not be required to be extended through interlocking security doors, exit doors in smoke partitions, or horizontal exit walls.			

Code Ref.	Code Compliance Item	OK	NA	ID
321.3	**Dry Standpipe Systems:** Provide Class I standpipes regardless of height or number of stories.			
	Fire Department Connections: May be located inside security walls or fences when acceptable to fire department.			
	Standpipes may be placed in secured pipe chases in cell complexes.			
322	**Fire Alarm System:** Comply with Fire Code.			
323.2	**Smoke Management System:** **Zones:** Not more than 1 smoke compartment per zone, except cell zones.			
	Operation: Operate system at 100% exhaust from any zone of smoke generation and at 100% supply to all floors with returns closed in adjacent zones of smoke generation at 8 air changes per hour minimum.			
323.3	**Initiation:** Automatically initiate system upon actuation of zoned sprinkler flow indicators or smoke detectors or both.			
323.4	**Manual Controls:** Provide zone operation status indicators and manual controls capable of overriding automatic controls in location approved by fire department.			
323.5	**Intake Location:** Place exhaust discharges and fresh air intake to prevent reintroduction of smoke.			
323.6	**Plans:** Indicate required fire dampers and smoke/fire dampers.			
323.7	**Fire Damper Omission:** Omit required fire dampers which interfere with operation of smoke management system except for those required to maintain rating of floor/ceiling assemblies.			
323.8	**Duct Materials:** Safely convey heat, smoke, and toxic gases; withstand positive/negative pressures, maintain structural integrity in fire exposure.			
324.4	**Electrically Controlled and Operated Sliding Doors:** May be used as exit doors regardless of occupants served.			
	Provide for manual operation by staff during power failure.			
324.6	**Electrically Operable Exit Doors:** Provide electric operation, from facility control center, for all means of egress doors (except those opening directly to exterior) and doors from cells and holding rooms.			
	Electric operation shall override any manual device.			

Group R-4 Occupancies
(Group Care Facilities)

UBC Appendix Chapter 3, Division IV

When adopted by the governing jurisdiction, Appendix Chapter 3, Division IV may be used as alternative provisions to requirements of Chapter 3. When used for design purposes, all requirements in this appendix chapter shall be used. Chapter 3 provisions may be used if not specifically noted in this appendix chapter.

Code Ref.	Code Compliance Item	OK	NA	ID
334.3	**Mixed Occupancies:** At separation with U-1 occupancy, only 1-hour construction on garage side required; provide self-closing, tight-fitting door, 1-3/8" (35 mm) thick.			
	Steel ducts, 26 gage (0.48 mm) thick, galvanized steel with no openings into Group M need not have fire dampers when passing through walls, floors, or ceilings forming separation.			
336	**Means of Egress:** Provide per UBC Chapter 10 and as follows:			
	Emergency Means of Egress Illumination: Provide storage batteries or on-site generator set to automatically provide emergency power upon power failure.			
	Emergency Escape or Rescue Window: Provide in sleeping rooms as follows:			
	Net clear openable area: 5.7 sf (0.53 m2) minimum.			
	Net clear openable height: 24" (610 mm) minimum.			
	Net clear openable width: 20" (508 mm) minimum.			
	Maximum sill height: 44" (1118 mm) above floor.			
	Make operable from inside without use of special tools.			
	Security Bars, Grilles, or Grates: May be provided if openable from inside without key, special knowledge, or effort and if smoke detectors are provided throughout building per Section 310.9.			
341	**Fire Alarm Systems:** Provide automatic and manual fire alarm system.			
342	**Heating:** Heat habitable spaces to 70°F (21°C) minimum at +3'-0" (914 mm) above floor.			
343	**Special Hazards:** Permanently install heating equipment.			

Basement Pipe Inlets

UBC Appendix Chapter 9

Appendix Chapter 9 may be used when adopted by the governing jurisdiction.

Code Ref.	Code Compliance Item	OK	NA	ID
907.2	**Where Required:** Provide in first floor of every store, warehouse, or factory having basements.			
	Exceptions: Where basements are fully sprinklered or where basement is used for storage of permanent archives or valuables such as safe deposit vaults or similar uses adversely affected by water.			
907.3	**Location:** As required by fire department.			
907.4	**Detailed Requirements:** Cast iron, steel, brass, or bronze with lids of cast brass or bronze.			
	Provide sleeve 8" (203 mm) minimum diameter extending through floor and terminating flush with or through basement ceiling.			
	Provide a top flange flush with finish floor surface.			
	Provide lid of solid casting with lift recessed in top and cast-in sign reading "FIRE DEPARTMENT ONLY, DO NOT COVER."			
	Provide for easy removal of lid from flange shoulder.			

Ventilation

UBC Appendix Chapter 12, Division I

When adopted by the governing jurisdiction, Appendix Chapter 12, Division I may be used as alternative provisions to requirements of Chapter 12.

Code Ref.	Code Compliance Item	OK	NA	ID
1207.1	**General:** Ventilate enclosed portions of buildings with natural ventilation by means of openable exterior openings with area of not less than 1/20 of floor area of such portions, or with mechanically operated system providing ventilation per UBC Table A-12-A while building is occupied.			
1207.2	**Register Velocity - Assembly Educational and Institutional Occupancies:** Place registers more than 8'-0" (2438 mm) above floor when velocity exceeds 10 fps (3.048 m/s).			
1207.3	**Toilet Rooms:** Provide fully openable exterior window of 3 sf (0.28 m^2) minimum, or a vertical duct of 100 si (0.064 516 m^2) minimum for first toilet facility, with 50 si (0.032 mm^2) for each additional facility; or mechanically operated system exhausting 50 cfm (23.6 L/s) for each water closet or urinal, connected directly to exterior with point of discharge 3'-0" (914 mm) minimum from openable window.			
1207.4	**Ventilation in Hazardous Locations:** Mechanically ventilate spaces in which explosive, corrosive, combustible, flammable, or highly toxic dusts, mists, fumes, vapors, or gases are or may be emitted due to processing, use, handling, or storage of materials.			
	Confine emissions to area where generated per Fire Code and Mechanical Code.			
	Provide supply and exhaust openings per Mechanical Code; treat toxic exhaust air per Mechanical Code.			
	Provide mechanical shutoff control for ventilation equipment outside room and adjacent to principal access door; provide switch of break-glass type and label "VENTILATION SYSTEM EMERGENCY SHUTOFF."			
1207.5	**Groups B, F, M, and S:** Provide mechanical exhaust from spaces where Class I, II, or III-A liquids are used; provide 6 air changes per hour; take exhaust from a point at or near floor level.			

Code Ref.	Code Compliance Item	OK	NA	ID
1207.6	**Group S Parking Garages:** In parking garages used for storing or handling of automobiles operating under their own power and on loading platforms in bus terminals, provide exhaust of 1.5 cfm/sf (0.708 L/s/m^2) of gross floor area or 14,000 cfm (6608 L/s) for each operating vehicle (based on anticipated instantaneous movement rate, but not less than 2.5% or 1 vehicle of the garage capacity).			
	Carbon monoxide sensors may be used to modulate system to maintain maximum average concentration of 50 parts per million during any 8-hour period, with maximum concentration not greater than 200 parts per million for 1 hour.			
	Provide conditioned air under positive pressure to connecting offices, waiting rooms, ticket booths, and similar uses.			
	Exception: Ventilation system may be omitted in Group B-1 repair garages and motor vehicle fuel-dispensing stations without lubrication pits, storage garages, and aircraft hangars when unobstructed openings are provided to outer air sufficient to provide required ventilation.			
1207.6	**Group H-4 Occupancies:** Provide mechanical ventilation from spaces used for repair or handling of motor vehicles operating under their own power exhausting 1.5 cfm/sf (7.62 L/s/m^2) of floor area.			
	Provide each engine repair stall with exhaust pipe extension duct, extending to exterior, which, if over 10'-0" (3048 mm) long, shall exhaust 300 cfm (141.6 L/s).			
	Provide conditioned air under positive pressure to connecting offices and waiting rooms.			
	Exception: Ventilation system may be omitted in aircraft hangars and repair garages when unobstructed openings are provided to outer air sufficient to provide required ventilation.			

Sound Transmission Control
(Group R Occupancies)
UBC Appendix Chapter 12, Division II

When adopted by the governing jurisdiction, Appendix Chapter 12, Division II may be used for design and construction purposes.

Code Ref.	Code Compliance Item	OK	NA	ID
1208	**General:** Provide sound control assemblies for all wall and floor-ceiling assemblies separating dwelling units or guest rooms from each other and from public space such as interior corridors and service areas.			
1208.2	**Minimum Airborne Sound Insulation - Wall and Floor-ceiling Assemblies:** STC 50 (STC 45 if field tested).			
	Seal, line, insulate, or treat penetrations for piping, electrical devices, recessed cabinets, bathtubs, soffits, of HVAC ducts to maintain sound rating.			
	Entrance Doors: Provide minimum STC 26, including perimeter seals.			
1208.3	**Impact Sound Insulation - Floor-ceiling Assemblies:** IIC 50 (IIC 45 if field tested); floor covering may be included in assembly.			

Reroofing

UBC Appendix Chapter 15

When adopted by the governing jurisdiction, Appendix Chapter 15 may be used for design and construction purposes.

Code Ref.	Code Compliance Item	OK	NA	ID
1515.1	**Approval:** Building official may allow existing roof to remain when:			
	Roof structure is sufficient to support additional dead load of new roof.			
	There is only 1 existing roof covering on the structure.			
	Existing roof drains and drainage prevent extensive accumulation of water.			
	Existing roof is securely attached to deck.			
	Roof deck is structurally sound.			
	Existing insulation is not water soaked.			
	Fire retardant requirements are maintained.			
1516.1	**Reroofing Overlays Allowed:** UBC Table A-15-A.			
1516.2	**Overlay on Built-up Roofs:** When existing roofing is removed and existing nailable deck has residual bitumen adhering to it, provide rosin-sized or other dry sheet under base sheet prior to installation of new roof.			
	Gravel-surfaced Roof: Clean of all loose gravel and debris; cut all blisters, buckles, and other irregularities and make smooth and secure; provide 3/8" (9.5 mm) minimum thickness insulation board nailed or cemented over existing surface with hot bitumen; install new roof.			
	Smooth or Cap-sheet Roof: Cut all blisters, buckles, and other irregularities and make smooth and secure; spot cement base sheet over existing surface; apply new roof.			
	Intersection Walls: Clean and prime concrete and masonry walls; remove surface materials on vertical walls to 6" (152 mm) minimum above deck surface to receive new roofing and flashing.			
	Replace all rotted wood.			
	Replace or reinstall surfacing material.			

Code Ref.	Code Compliance Item	OK	NA	ID
1516.2	**Overlay on Built-up Roofs:** **Parapets of Area Separation Walls:** Provide noncombustible faces, including counterflashing and coping; combustible roofing may extend 7" (178 mm) above roof surface.			
	Cant Strips: Provide at all angles; flash with at least 2 layers more than in new roof with exposed layer of inorganic felt or mineral surfaced cap sheet.			
	Asphalt and Wood Shingle Application: Not more than 1 overlay of asphalt shingles over 1 existing built-up roof on slopes 2:12 (16.7%) or greater.			
	Not more than 1 overlay of wood shingles over 1 existing built-up roof on slopes 3:12 (25%) or greater.			
	Clean roof of all gravel and debris; cut all blisters, buckles, and other irregularities and make smooth and secure; provide Type 30 nonperforated felt underlayment prior to reroofing.			
	Spray-applied Polyurethane Foam Applications: May be applied directly to existing built-up roof systems when completed assembly is Class A, B, or C covering.			
	When applied over a rated roof-ceiling assembly, substantiate that required fire-resistive time period is not reduced.			
	Base Sheets or Dry Sheets: Not required.			
	Miscellaneous Materials: Provide adhesives, elastomeric caulking, metal, vents, and drains as a composite part of roof system.			
1516.3	**Overlay on Existing Wood Roofs or Asphalt Shingle Roofs:** Apply only fire-retardant assemblies or noncombustible coverings over existing wood shakes per manufacturer's listing or installation instructions.			
	Where new roofing creates a combustible concealed space, cover entire existing surface with gypsum board, fiber, or glass fiber secured in place.			
	Remove hip and ridge covers prior to reroofing.			
	Asphalt Shingle Application: Maximum 2 overlays of asphalt shingles over existing asphalt or wood shingles.			
	Asphalt Shingles over Wood Shingles: Provide Type 30 nonperforated felt underlayment over wood shingles.			
	Wood Shake Application: Maximum 1 overlay of wood shakes over existing asphalt or wood shingles on slopes 4:12 (33%) or greater; with 1 layer 18" (457 mm) Type 30 nonperforated felt interlaced between each layer of shakes.			
	Wood Shingle Application: Maximum 1 overlay of wood shingles over existing wood or asphalt shingles.			
	Wood Shingles over Asphalt Shingles: Provide Type 30 nonperforated felt underlayment over asphalt shingles.			

Code Ref.	Code Compliance Item	OK	NA	ID
1517	**Tile Roofing:** Permitted over existing roofing on slopes of 4:12 (33%) or greater per UBC Table A-15-A.			
	Provide report indicating that existing or modified framing system is adequate to support additional load.			
1518	**Metal Roof Covering:** Permitted over existing roofing per UBC Table A-15-A.			
1520	**Flashing and Edging:** Repair or replace missing, rusted, or damaged flashing and counterflashing, vent caps, and metal edging.			
	Where existing flashings remain, remove and clean.			
	Prime prior to reroofing installation.			

Waterproofing and Dampproofing Foundations

UBC Appendix Chapter 18

When adopted by the governing jurisdiction, Appendix Chapter 18 may be used for design and construction purposes.

Code Ref.	Code Compliance Item	OK	NA	ID
1829	**Scope:** Waterproof or dampproof walls retaining earth and enclosing interior spaces and floors below grade except walls enclosing crawl spaces.			
1831	**Dampproofing Required:** Dampproof walls retaining earth and enclosing interior spaces, and floors below grade where hydrostatic pressure will not occur, except for wood foundations.			
1832	**Floor Dampproofing:** Provide between floor and base materials.			
	Dampproofing may be on top of slab where separate floor is provided above slab.			
	Minimum Floor Dampproofing Materials: 6 mil (0.152 mm) polyethylene.			
	4 mil (0.1 mm) or mopped-on bitumen when permitted on top of slab.			
1833	**Wall Dampproofing:** Provide on exterior surface of walls, extending from 6" (152 mm) above grade down to top of footing.			
	Wall Dampproofing Materials: Bituminous material, acrylic modified cement base coating, or other approved material.			
	Where materials are not approved for direct application to masonry, parge exterior below grade masonry surfaces with 3/8" (9.5 mm) minimum thickness portland cement mortar.			
1834.1	**Dampproofing - Subsoil Drainage System:** Provide base materials and foundation drains when floor dampproofing is required.			
	Where finished ground level is below floor level for more than 25% of building perimeter, base material is not required and foundation drains are only required around portions of building where floor level is below ground level.			
1834.2	**Dampproofing - Underfloor Base Material:** 4" (102 mm) minimum thickness gravel or crushed stone with a maximum of 10% passing No. 4 (4.75 mm) sieve.			

Code Ref.	Code Compliance Item	OK	NA	ID
1834.3	**Dampproofing - Foundation Drain:** Gravel, crushed stone, or drain tile.			
	Gravel or Crushed Stone: Extend drain 12" (305 mm) minimum beyond outer edge of footing; ensure that bottom of drain is higher than bottom of floor base material or that top of drain is at least 6" (152 mm) above top of footing.			
	Cover top of drain with filter fabric.			
	Drain Tile or Perforated Pipe: Do not set invert of pipe above floor level.			
	Cover top of joints or perforations with filter fabric.			
	Place pipe on minimum 2" (51 mm) of gravel or crushed stone and cover with minimum 6" (152 mm) of gravel or crushed stone.			
1834.4	**Drainage Disposal:** Discharge floor base material and foundation drain by gravity or mechanical means to drainage system unless soil is well-drained gravel or sand-gravel mixture.			
1835	**Waterproofing Required:** Waterproof walls retaining earth and enclosing interior spaces, and floors below grade where hydrostatic pressure caused by water table does exist.			
	Exceptions: Dampproofing may be used where groundwater table can be lowered and maintained at least 6" (152 mm) below bottom of lowest floor or where wood foundations are used.			
1836	**Floor Waterproofing:** Provide concrete floors designed for hydrostatic pressure.			
	Floor Waterproofing Materials: Rubberized asphalt, polymer-modified asphalt, butyl rubber, neoprene, or 6 mil (0.15 mm) minimum thickness polyvinylchloride or polyethylene capable of bridging cracks.			
1837	**Wall Waterproofing - General:** Provide concrete or masonry walls designed to withstand hydrostatic pressure and other lateral loads.			
	Where Required: Apply from 12" (305 mm) above maximum elevation of groundwater table down to top of footing. Provide dampproofing on remainder of walls below grade.			
1838.1	**Placement of Backfill Against Dampproofing or Waterproofing:** Use fill material free of organic material, construction debris, and large rocks.			
1838.2	**Site Grading:** Slope ground away from foundations at least 1:12 (8.3%) for 6'-0" (1829 mm) minimum from face of wall or provide alternate method of diverting water away from foundation. Consider possible settlement of backfill.			
1838.3	**Erosion Protection:** Provide protection from soil erosion where water impacts ground from edge of roof, downspouts, valleys, or rainwater collection device; direct water away from foundation.			

Flood-Resistant Construction

UBC Appendix Chapter 31, Division I

When adopted by the governing jurisdiction, this section may be used for design and construction purposes.

Code Ref.	Code Compliance Item	OK	NA	ID
3106	**Protection of Mechanical and Electrical Systems:** Place such systems above base flood elevation or protect to prevent water from entering or accumulating within system components during floods up to the base flood elevation.			
	Electrical Systems Below Base Flood Elevation: Conform to wet locations requirements in Electrical Code.			
3107.1	**Flood Hazard Zones - A Zones:** Areas prone to flooding, waves not more than 3'-0" (914 mm) high.			
3107.2	**A Zones - Elevation:** Locate lowest floor, including basement floors, at or above base flood elevation **(BFE).**			
	Exceptions: Any occupancy may have floors below BFE except Group R.			
	Floors used only for access, means of egress, foyers, storage and parking garages may be below BFE per UBC Section 3107.3 below.			
3107.3	**A Zones - Enclosures below BFE:** Do not use except for access, means of egress, foyers, storage and parking garages.			
	Provide vents, valves, or openings in enclosed spaces to automatically equalize lateral pressure of water acting on exterior walls; minimum of 2 per building or 1 for each enclosure below BFE.			
	Openings: 1 si/sf (0.007 m^2/1 m^2) or 4 sf (0.37 m^2) minimum; bottom of opening 12" (305 mm) maximum above finish grade.			
3107.4	**A Zone - Flood-Resistant Construction:** Occupancies other than Group R may have occupied floors below BFE as follows:			
	Waterproof walls and floors below BFE.			
	Design to resist hydrostatic and hydrodynamic forces, including buoyancy.			
	Watertight closures for openings below BFE designed to resist flood loads.			
	Seal plumbing, HVAC, and electrical penetrations; provide closures on sewer and storm drain openings below BFE to prevent backwater flow during flooding.			

Code Ref.	Code Compliance Item	OK	NA	ID
3108.1	**Coastal High Hazard Zones - V Zones:** Areas subject to waves more than 3'-0" (914 mm) high or subject to high-velocity wave run-up or wave-induced erosion.			
3108.2	**V Zones - Elevation:** Locate lowest portion of horizontal structural members, except for footings, mat or raft foundations, pile caps, columns, grade beams, and bracing, at or above BFE.			
3108.3	**V Zones - Enclosures Below BFE:** Spaces below BFE shall be free of obstructions.			
	Exceptions: Footings, mat or raft foundations, pile caps, columns, grade beams, and bracing.			
	Structural systems of entrances and required exits.			
	Storage of portable or mobile items moved during storms.			
	Walls may enclose all or part of the space if walls are not part of structural support of building and are designed to break away under high tides or wave action without damaging structure of building; screens or lattices which allow passage of water may be used.			
3108.4	**V Zones - Foundations:** Support buildings on piles or columns.			
	Piles: Provide soil penetration to resist combined wave and wind loads during floods equal to BFE.			
	Mat or Raft Foundations: Locate at a depth to protect from erosion or scour.			
3109	**Elevation Certification:** Provide certification by land surveyor that actual elevation of lowest floor (if in flood hazard zone) or lowest horizontal structural member (if in coastal high hazard zone) in relation to mean sea level meets code requirements.			

Membrane Structures

UBC Appendix Chapter 31, Division II

When adopted by the governing jurisdiction, this section may be used for design and construction purposes.

Code Ref.	Code Compliance Item	OK	NA	ID
3113.1	**Inflation Systems:** Provide primary and auxiliary inflation systems for air-supported and air-inflated structures.			
3113.2	**Air Inflation System Equipment Requirements:** Provide blowers and automatic control to maintain required inflation pressures and prevent overpressurization.			
	Auxiliary Inflation System Required: In buildings over 1,500 sf (193.4 m²), provide auxiliary system to automatically maintain inflation in case of primary system failure. Provide automatic operation.			
	Blower Equipment: Power by continuous rated motors at maximum power required for any flow condition required by structural design.			
	Provide inlet screens, belt guards, and protective devices to prevent injury.			
	House in weather-protecting structure.			
	Equip with back-draft check dampers to minimize air loss when inoperative.			
	Locate inlets to protect from air contamination.			
3113.3	**Inflation Systems - Emergency Power:** Provide emergency power generator set for auxiliary inflation systems, with automatic starting upon normal electrical system failure and automatic transfer and operation of required electrical functions at full power within 60 seconds of normal service failure.			
	Provide generator capable of operating independently for 4 hours minimum.			
3114	**Section Provisions:** Provide system capable of supporting membrane in event of deflation in air-supported and air-inflated structures with 50 or more occupants or when covering a swimming pool.			
	Maintain membrane 7'-0" (2134 mm) minimum above floor, seating, or water surface.			
	Maintain membranes used for roofs in Type I or Type II-FR construction 25'-0" (7620 mm) above floor or seating areas.			

Patio Covers

UBC Appendix Chapter 31, Division III

When adopted by the governing jurisdiction, this section may be used for design and construction purposes.

Code Ref.	Code Compliance Item	OK	NA	ID
3116	**Patio Cover Definition:** 1-story, 12'-0" (3657 mm) high maximum.			
	Enclosure Wall Openings: Provide open area of longer wall and 1 additional wall equal to 65% of area below 6'-8" (2032 mm) minimum of each wall.			
	Opening Coverings: Insect screen or removable transparent or translucent plastic, 0.125" (3.2 mm) minimum thickness.			
3117	**Design Loads:** Support dead loads plus 10 psf (0.48 kN/m^2), or use snow loads where it exceeds this minimum.			
	Wind Loads: UBC Table A-31-A.			
	Uplift Loads: When 12'-0" (3657 mm) high or less, use load equal to wind load; when 10'-0" (3048 mm) high or less, use 3/4 of wind load.			
	When Enclosed with Screen or Plastic: Apply wind loads to structure, assuming full enclosure.			
3119	**Footings:** Cover may be supported on 3-1/2" (89 mm) minimum thickness concrete slab without footings provided supported dead and live load is 750 lb (3.34 kN) maximum per column.			

Life Safety for Existing Buildings

UBC Appendix Chapter 34, Division I

When adopted by the governing jurisdiction, this section may be used for design and construction purposes.

Code Ref.	Code Compliance Item	OK	NA	ID
3407.4	**Fire Escapes:** May be used as 1 required exit when complying with the following, but fire escapes shall not take the place of required stairways under code which building was constructed:			
	Access from a corridor shall not be through an intervening room.			
	Protect openings within 10'-0" (3048 mm) with 3/4-hour assemblies; provide 1-hour enclosure walls around openings located in recesses or vestibules.			
	Provide egress opening with minimum dimension of 29" (737 mm), openable from inside without use of key or special knowledge or effort; 30" (762 mm) maximum sill height.			
	Provide top and intermediate handrails on each side of stairs and balconies.			
	60° maximum stairway pitch, 18" (457 mm) minimum width, 4" (102 mm) minimum tread, 10" (254 mm) maximum riser.			
	44" (1118 mm) minimum balcony width, no floor openings greater than 5/8" (16 mm) other than stairway opening.			
	22" by 44" (559 mm by 1118 mm) minimum stairway opening.			
	36" (914 mm) minimum balcony balustrade height, 9" (229 mm) maximum between balusters.			
	Extend fire escapes to roof or provide gooseneck ladder between top landing and roof on buildings over 3 stories with roof slope of less than 4:12 (33.3%).			
	22" (559 mm) minimum width, located within 12" (305 mm) of building.			
	3/4" (19.1 mm) diameter ladder rungs spaced at 12" (305 mm) on center.			
	Where ladder passes through cornice or overhang, provide 30" by 33" (838 mm by 762 mm) minimum opening.			
	Maximum height of lowest balcony is 18'-0" (5486 mm) above grade. Extend fire escape from balcony to ground with counterbalanced stairs.			

Code Ref.	Code Compliance Item	OK	NA	ID
3407.5	**Exit and Fire Escape Signs:** When 2 or more exits are required from story, provide at stair enclosure doors, horizontal exits, and other required exits.			
	When 2 or more exits are required from room or area, provide exit signs at required exits and as otherwise needed to indicate egress direction.			
	Provide fire escape sign at doors and windows giving access to fire escapes.			
3408	**Enclosure of Vertical Shafts, Stairways, Elevator Hoistways:** 1-hour construction.			
	Enclosure not required for openings serving only 1 adjacent floor except in Group I.			
	Continuous vertical shafts not required at stair if each story is separated from other stories by 1-hour construction or approved wire glass in steel frames.			
	Provide sprinkled exit corridors and provide at least 1 sprinkler head above corridor openings on the tenant side of openings between corridor and occupant space.			
	Opening Protection: 1-hour assemblies, self-closing or automatic-closing by smoke detection.			
3409	**Basement Access or Sprinkler Protection:** Provide sprinkler system in basements or stories more than 1,500 sf (139.3 m^2) not having minimum of 20 sf (1.86 m^2) opening above adjoining ground level in each 50'-0" (15 240 mm) or fraction thereof of exterior wall on at least 1 side of building.			
	Provide openings with 30" (762 mm) minimum clear opening dimensions.			
	Fully sprinkle basements with spaces over 75'-0" (22 860 mm) from required openings.			
3410	**Standpipes:** Class I or Class III system in buildings of 4 or more stories.			
3411.1	**Smoke Detectors:** Provide in rooms used for sleeping in dwelling units or hotel or lodging house guest rooms.			
	Power Source: May be wired to commercial source or battery operated; no disconnect permitted except for overcurrent protection.			
	Location - Dwelling Units: Wall or ceiling mounted centrally in corridor or area giving access to each separate sleeping area.			
	Upper Level Sleeping Rooms: Mount in center of ceiling above stair.			
	Basements: Provide when stair opens from basement into dwelling.			
	Alarm: Audible in all sleeping areas.			
	Location in Efficiency Dwelling Units and Hotels: Ceiling or wall mounted in main room or hotel sleeping room.			
	Upper Level Sleeping Rooms: Mount in center of ceiling above stair.			
	Alarm: Audible in sleeping area.			

Life Safety for Existing High-Rise Buildings

UBC Appendix Chapter 34, Division II

When adopted by the governing jurisdiction, Appendix Chapter 34, Division II may be used for design and construction purposes.

Code Ref.	Code Compliance Item	OK	NA	ID
3413	**Scope:** Applies to Group B-2 or R-1 occupancies having occupied floors 75'-0" (22 860 mm) above lowest level of fire department vehicle access.			
3414	**General:** Do not eliminate fire protection systems or reduce the level of fire safety provided in existing buildings in conformance with previously adopted codes.			
3418.1.1	**UBC Table A-34-A - Type of Construction:** Fully sprinkle Types II-N, III-N, or V-N.			
	Meters and backflow preventors are not required unless required by local authority having jurisdiction.			
3418.1.2	**UBC Table A-34-A - Automatic Sprinklers:** Fully sprinkle required corridors, stairwells, elevator lobbies, public assembly areas with 100 or move occupants, and commercial kitchens.			
	Provide at least 1 sprinkler on room side of every corridor opening.			
	Sprinkler may be omitted in noncombustible stairwells.			
3418.1.3	**UBC Table A-34-A - Fire Department Communication System:** Provide system acceptable to fire department when portable system is determined not effective.			
3418.1.4	**UBC Table A-34-A - Single-station Smoke Detectors:** Provide in all dwelling units or guest rooms.			
	Dwelling Units: Mount in wall or in center of ceiling of corridor or area giving access to each separate sleeping area.			

Code Ref.	Code Compliance Item	OK	NA	ID
3418.1.4	**UBC Table A-34-A - Single-station Smoke Detectors, Continued:** **Upper Level Sleeping Rooms:** Mount in center of ceiling directly above stairway.			
	Efficiency Dwelling Units, Hotel Suites, Hotel Guest Rooms: Mount on ceiling or wall of main room or sleeping room.			
	Alarm: Provide alarm audible in sleeping area.			
	Battery operation permitted.			
3418.1.5	**UBC Table A-34-A - Manual Fire Alarm System:** Provide and connect to central, proprietary, or remote station; or provide audible signal at constantly attended location.			
3418.1.6	**UBC Table A-34-A - Occupant Voice Notification System:** Provide to at least all normally occupied areas from a location approved by the fire department.			
	System may be combined with fire alarm system if approved and listed for such use.			
	Sounding of fire alarm in any location shall not prohibit voice communication to other areas or floors.			
	Design system to permit voice transmission to override fire alarm signal, but such signal shall not terminate in less than 3 minutes.			
3418.1.7	**Permitted Existing Shaft Construction:** 1/2" (13 mm) gypsum board, wood lath and plaster in good condition, and openings with fixed 1/4" (6.4 mm) thick wire glass in steel frames.			
3418.1.8	**UBC Table A-34-A - Vertical Shaft Opening Protection:** 1-hour assemblies in new vertical shaft enclosures.			
	20-minute in existing vertical shaft enclosures, except for elevator doors.			
	1-3/4" (44 mm) solid wood door or equivalent, self-closing or automatic closing and self-latching.			
3418.1.9	**UBC Table A-34-A - Manual Shutoff of HVAC Systems:** Provide manual shutoff controls in location approved by fire department.			
3418.1.10	**UBC Table A-34-A - Automatic Elevator Recall System:** Provide as required by UBC Section 403.7, Item 2.			
3418.1.11	**UBC Table A-34-A - Unlocked Stairway Doors:** Maintain exit doors into exit stairways unlocked from stairway side on at least every fifth level.			
	Provide a sign at each unlocked door stating "ACCESS TO FLOOR THIS LEVEL."			
3418.1.11	**UBC Table A-34-A - Locked Stairway Doors:** Permitted when all doors locked from stairway side can be unlocked simultaneously by signal from approved location without unlatching; and continuously operating 2-way communication system connected to approved location is provided at not less than every fifth floor.			

Code Ref.	Code Compliance Item	OK	NA	ID
3418.1.12	**UBC Table A-34-A - Stair Shaft Ventilation:** Vent shafts which extend to roof with manually openable hatch to exterior; 16 sf (1.486 m^2) minimum area, 24" (610 mm) minimum dimension in any direction.			
	Exceptions: Ventilation not required in pressurized stair enclosures .			
3418.1.13	**UBC Table A-34-A - Elevator Shaft Ventilation:** Vent to exterior all shafts which extend to roof; minimum vent area is 3-1/2% of shaft area or 3 sf (0.28 m^2).			
	Automatic venting by actuation of elevator lobby detector or power failure may be provided in pressurized hoistways.			
3418.1.14	**UBC Table A-34-A - Posting of Elevators:** Provide sign in elevator cab adjacent to floor status indicator and at each elevator call station reading "IN FIRE EMERGENCY, DO NOT USE ELEVATOR - USE EXIT STAIRS."			
	Sign may be omitted at main entrance levels.			
3418.1.17	**UBC Table A-34-A - Exit Corridor Opening Protection:** 1-3/8" (35 mm) solid-bonded wood-core doors, 1/4" (6.4 mm) thick wire glass, fire dampers, or equivalent.			
	Fix transoms closed and cover with 1/2" (13 mm) Type X gypsum board on both sides of opening.			
3418.1.18	**UBC Table A-34-A - Exit-Access Door Closers:** Self-closing devices or automatic closing by actuation of smoke detector.			
	When spring hinges are used, provide 2 minimum on each door leaf.			
3418.1.20	**UBC Table A-34-A - Interior Finish:** Comply with UBC Chapter 8 for corridors, exit stairs and extensions thereof.			
3418.1.21`	**UBC Table A-34-A - Exit Stair Illumination:** Provide 1 footcandle (10.81 lx) minimum at floor when building is occupied.			
	Provide battery pack or on-site generator as alternate source of power.			
3418.1.22	**UBC Table A-34-A - Corridor Illumination:** Provide 1 footcandle (10.81 lx) minimum at floor when building is occupied.			
	Provide battery pack or on-site generator as alternate source of power.			
3418.1.23	**UBC Table A-34-A - Exit Stair Exit Signs:** Provide illuminated exit signs at exit stairs.			
	Provide battery pack or on-site generator as alternate source of power or self-illuminating sign.			
3418.1.24	**UBC Table A-34-A - Exit Signs:** Provide illuminated exit signs in all means of egress and locations to clearly indicate direction of egress.			
	Provide battery pack or on-site generator as alternate source of power or self-illuminating sign.			

Code Ref.	Code Compliance Item	OK	NA	ID
3418.2	**Sprinkler Alternatives:** Requirements of UBC Table A-34-A may be modified in fully sprinkled existing buildings of Types I, II-FR, II 1-Hour, III 1-Hour, IV, or V 1-hour construction as follows:			
	Item 5: Manual fire warning system not required.			
	Item 6: Occupant voice notification not required. If building is equipped with public address system, it shall be available for use as a voice notification system.			
	Item 7: Vertical enclosures may be nonrated construction for required exit stairs.			
	Vertical shaft enclosures for openings in floors provided for elevators, escalators, and supplemental stairs is not required when such openings are protected with a curtain board and water curtain system.			
	Item 8: Openings in vertical shaft enclosures may be nonrated but shall be at least 1-3/4" (44 mm) thick solid-wood door; self-closing and latching.			
	Item 10: Automatic elevator recall system not required.			
	Item 12: Stair shaft ventilation not required.			
	Item 16: Existing corridor construction need not be altered.			
	Item 17: Door openings into corridors may be protected by assemblies other than those required by UBC Section 3418.1 if effective smoke barrier is maintained.			
	Provide self-closing and latching hardware.			
	Duct penetrations protection not required.			
	Item 19: Length of existing deadend corridors is not limited.			
	Item 20: Interior finish in means of egress may be reduced by 1 classification, but not less than Class III.			
	Meters or backflow preventors not required unless required by other regulations of governing jurisdiction.			

Part 4: Structural Documentation Requirements

Uniform Building Code Compliance Manual
1997 Uniform Building Code

Foundations and Retaining Walls

UBC Chapter 18

Code Ref.	Code Compliance Item	OK	NA	ID
1803 1804.1	**Classify soils** for foundation and lateral pressures according to UBC Table 18-I-A and UBC Standard 18-1; see Foundation Investigation/Geotechnical Soils Report where provided.			
	Determine expansive characteristics of soils according to UBC Standard 18-2 and UBC Tables 18-I-B and 18-I-C; see Foundation Investigation/Geotechnical Soils Report where provided.			
1804.2	**Foundation Investigation:** Provide soils classification, foundation pressure, lateral pressure, the effect of moisture on bearing capacity, compressibility, liquefaction, and expansiveness.			
	Seismic Zones 3 and 4: When required by the building official, evaluate potential for liquefaction and soil instability except where:			
	Building official waives evaluation based on written opinion of geotechnical engineer or geologist that liquefaction is not probable.			
	Building is single-story, detached, Group R-3 with or without attached garages.			
	Building is Group U-1.			
	Fences.			
1804.3	**Soil Classification and Bearing Capacity:** Indicate on plans unless foundations conform to UBC Table 18-I-D.			
1804.4	**Expansive Soils:** When present, provide design and construction to safeguard against damage.			
1804.5	**Liquefaction Potential and Strength Loss:** Design to consider differential settlement, lateral movement, or reduction of soil bearing capacity.			
1804.7	**Drainage:** Provide control and drainage of surface water around buildings.			

Code Ref.	Code Compliance Item	OK	NA	ID
1805	**Foundation and Lateral Pressure:** Do not exceed values in UBC Table 18-I-A unless substantiated by foundation investigation.			
	UBC Table 18-I-A: May be used for design of foundations on rock or nonexpansive soils for Types II 1-hour, II-N, and V buildings not exceeding 3 stories or for structures having continuous footings with load of less than 2,000 plf (29.2 kN/m) and isolated footings with loads less than 50,000 lbs (222.4 kN/m).			
1806.1	**Footings:** Construct of solid masonry or concrete, or treated wood.			
	Extend below frost line.			
	Where supporting wood, extend 6" (152 mm) minimum above adjacent finish grade.			
	Provide minimum depth indicated in UBC Table 18-I-D unless recommended otherwise by foundation investigation.			
1806.3	**Footings - Bearing Walls:** Unless otherwise designed, provide foundations in accordance with UBC Table 18-I-D.			
	Exceptions: 1-story wood or metal frame building not for human occupancy and not over 400 sf (37.2 m^2) may have walls supported on wood foundation plate.			
	Buildings supported by posts embedded in earth per Section 1806.7.			
1806.4	**Footings - Stepped Foundations:** When ground slopes more than 1:10 (10%), provide level foundation or step such that top and bottom of foundation are level.			
1806.5	**Building Clearance from Ascending Slopes:** UBC Figure 18-1.			
	Footing Setback from Descending Slope: UBC Figure 18-1.			
	Pools: Provide 1/2 of setback distances required by UBC Figure 18-1.			
	Where pool walls are within 7'-0" (2134 mm) of top of slope, that portion shall be constructed to support water without soil support.			
	Foundation Elevation: Set top of foundation minimum of 12" (305 mm) plus 2% above street gutter elevation at point of discharge, or storm drain inlet.			
1806.6	**Foundation Plates and Sills:** Bolt to foundation with steel anchor bolts. **Bolts in Seismic Zones -0 - 3:** 1/2" (13 mm) diameter minimum.			
	Bolts in Seismic Zone 4: 5/8" (16 mm) diameter minimum.			
	Bolt Embedment: 7" (178 mm) minimum into concrete or masonry.			
	Bolt Spacing: 72" (1829 mm) maximum spacing, with nut and washer.			
	Number of Bolts: Provide minimum of 2 bolts per piece, located within 12" (305 mm) of each end.			

Code Ref.	Code Compliance Item	OK	NA	ID
1806.6.1	**Additional Bolting Requirements in Seismic Zones 3 and 4:** Specifically design sill bolt spacing and diameter for 3-story raised wood floor buildings.			
	Provide 2" by 2" by 3/16" (51 mm by 51 mm by 4.8 mm) plate washers on each bolt.			
1806.7.1	**Additional Foundation Requirements in Seismic Zones 3 and 4:** **Foundations with Stem Walls**: Provide ome #4 bar at top of wall and 1-#4 bar at bottom of footing.			
	Slabs with Turned-Down Footings: Provide one #4 bar at top and bottom.			
	Slabs cast monolithically with footing may have one #5 bar at either top or bottom.			
1806.8.3	**Backfill Around Columns:** When not embedded in footings, backfill columns with:			
	2,000 psi (13.79 Mpa) concrete; provide 2" minimum concrete cover at bottom of column.			
	Clean sand, compacted in 8" (203 mm) lifts.			

Pile Foundations

UBC Sections 1807 and 1808

Code Ref.	Code Compliance Item	OK	NA	ID
1807.1	**General:** Review foundation investigation and comply with recommended pile types, driving criteria, and installation procedures.			
1807.2	**Pile Caps:** Interconnect piles and caissons when subject to seismic forces.			
1808.1	**Wood Piles:** Use treated piles; untreated allowed only when the cutoff is below lowest groundwater level assumed for life of building.			
1808.4.2	**Precast Concrete Piles - Spirals:** 3" (76 mm) maximum spacing for 24" (610 mm) from ends, 8" (203 mm) maximum spacing elsewhere.			
	Minimum Tie and Spiral Gage: **Piles 16" (406 mm) diameter or less:** 0.22" (5.6 mm) (#5 BW gage) wire.			
	Piles 16" (406 mm) to 20" (508 mm) diameter: 0.238" (6 mm) (#4 BW gage) wire.			
	Piles 20" (508 mm) diameter and larger: 1/4" (6.4 mm) round or 0.259" (6.6 mm) (#3 BW gage) wire.			
1808.5	**Precast Prestressed Concrete Piles - Spirals:** 3" (76 mm) maximum spacing for 24" (610 mm) from ends, 8" (203 mm) maximum spacing elsewhere.			
	At each end of pile, space first 5 spirals or ties 1" (25 mm) on center.			
	Minimum Tie and Spiral Gage: **Piles 24" (610 mm) diameter or less:** 0.22" (5.6 mm) (#5 BW gage) wire.			
	Piles 24" (610 mm) to 36" (914 mm) diameter: 0.238" (6 mm) (#4 BW gage) wire.			
	Piles 36" (914 mm) diameter and larger: 1/4" (6.4 mm) round or 0.259" (6.6 mm) (#3 BW gage) wire.			
1808.6	**Structural Steel Piles:** 8" (203 mm) minimum nominal depth, 3/8" minimum flange and web thickness.			
	Flange Projection: Not more than 14 times flange or web thickness; flange widths not less than 80% of section depth.			
	Steel Pipe Piles: 10" (254 mm) minimum nominal diameter, 1/4" (6.4 mm) minimum wall thickness.			
1808.7	**Concrete Filled Steel Pipe Piles:** 8" (203 mm) minimum nominal diameter.			

Treated Wood Foundations

UBC Section 1810-1814

Code Ref.	Code Compliance Item	OK	NA	ID
1811.7	**Treated Wood:** Provide for all exterior foundation lumber and plywood (except upper top plate), interior bearing wall framing and sheathing, posts and wood supports in crawl spaces;			
	Sleepers, joists, blocking, and plywood subflooring used in basement floors;			
	Plates, framing, and sheathing in the ground or in direct contact with concrete;			
	Exterior wall framing less than 6" (152 mm) above grade.			
1812.2	**Area Drainage:** Slope finish grade minimum of 1/2" (13 mm) in 12" (305 mm) for 6'-0" (1829 mm).			
1812.3	**Subgrade Drainage:** Minimum 4" (102 mm) layer of gravel, crushed stone, or sand beneath basement floor slabs and wall footings.			
	MH and CH Soils: Minimum 6" (152 mm) layer of gravel, crushed stone, or sand beneath basement floor slabs and wall footings.			
	Basements below Grade: Provide sump to drain gravel layer except when foundation is in GW, GP, SW, SP, GM, or SM soils.			
	Sump Dimensions: Minimum 24" (610 mm) diameter or 20" (508 mm) square; extend minimum 24" (610 mm) below basement floor slab.			
	Provide positive gravity or mechanical drainage from sump.			
1812.4	**Basement Floor Sheeting:** 6 mil polyethylene sheeting over gravel layer and under concrete slabs or wood floor systems.			
	Place sheeting over wood sleepers supporting joists; do not extend beneath wood footing plate.			

Code Ref.	Code Compliance Item	OK	NA	ID
1812.4	**Basement Wall Sheeting:** 6 mil polyethylene sheeting over below-grade portion of walls.			
	Set top of sheeting in sealant and cover with treated lumber or plywood strip extending minimum 2" (51 mm) above grade and minimum 5" (127 mm) below grade; set strip in sealant along edge.			
	Extend sheeting to bottom of wood plate but do not overlap or extend into gravel footing.			
1812.5	**Perimeter Drainage Control - Backfill:** Provide gravel backfill 1/2 height of excavation.			
	GW, GP, SW, SP, GM, and SP Soils - Backfill: Gravel backfill to 12" (305 mm) above footing.			
	Cover gravel with 6 mil polyethylene, Type 30 felt, or filter fabric lapped 6".			
1812.6	**Alternate Drainage - Concrete Footings:** Place footings on 4" (102 mm) thick layer of gravel, crushed stone, or sand.			
	Provide for drainage of water from outside footing to granular layer under slab or provide drain tiles through foundation wall spaced at 72" (1829 mm) on center around the foundation.			
1812.7	**Wall Insulation:** Provide blocking at bottom of insulation where insulation does not continue down to bottom plate.			
1814.4	**Wood Footing Assembly:** Treated wood footing plate on layer of gravel, coarse sand, or crushed stone.			
	Footing Design - Granular Layer: **Minimum width:** 2 times footing width.			
	Minimum depth: 3/4 times footing width.			
	Confine granular layer by backfill, granular fill, undisturbed soil, or foundation wall.			
1814.4	**Footing Design - Frost Depth:** Extend wood footing plate below frost depth or extend granular layer to frost depth.			
	When granular layer extends to frost depth, connect to positive mechanical drainage or gravity drainage (to sump) at or below frost line unless installed in GW, GP, SW, SP, GM where permanent water table is below frost line.			
	Where bottom of wood footing is above frost line, cover top of granular layer with 6 mil polyethylene, Type 30 felt, or filter fabric lapped 6".			
	Granular Layer Protection: Provide protection against erosion when footing is close to finish grade.			

Concrete

UBC Chapter 19

Code Ref.	Code Compliance Item	OK	NA	ID
1903.5.2	**Welded Reinforcing:** Indicate type and location of welded splices and other welding of reinforcing bars.			
1905.1.3	**Compressive Strength Test Age:** Show on drawings.			
	Compressive Strength: Show for each part of structure.			
1906.3.1	**Conduits and Pipes Embedded in Concrete:** Conduit and pipes may be embedded when materials are not harmful to concrete and provided they are not considered to replace structurally the displaced concrete.			
1906.3.2	**Conduits and Pipes Embedded in Concrete:** Coat aluminum materials to prevent reaction or electrolytic reaction.			
1906.3.4	**Conduits and Pipes Embedded in Concrete Columns:** Do not displace more than 4% of cross section area required for strength or for fire protection.			
1906.3.5	**Conduits and Pipes Embedded in Concrete Slab, Wall, or Beam:** No larger in outside diameter than 1/3 thickness of slab, wall, or beam.			
	Spaced not closer than 3 diameters or widths on center.			
	Do not impair strength of construction.			
1906.3.6	**Conduits, Pipes, and Sleeves:** May be considered as structurally replacing in compression the displaced concrete when:			
	Not exposed to rusting.			
	Uncoated or galvanized iron or steel not thinner than standard schedule 40 steel pipe.			
	Nominal outside diameter not over 2" (51 mm) and are spaced at least 3 diameters on center.			
1906.3.9	**Pipes in Slabs:** Place between top and bottom reinforcing unless for radiant heat.			
1906.3.10	**Concrete Cover for Pipes, Conduits, and Fittings:** 1-1/2" (38 mm) minimum where exposed to earth or weather.			
	3/4" (19 mm) where not exposed to earth or weather.			

Code Ref.	Code Compliance Item	OK	NA	ID
1906.4.3	**Construction Joints:** Do not impair strength of structure; transfer shear and other forces through joint.			
1906.4.4	**Construction Joints in Supported Floors:** Locate within middle third of span of slabs, beams, and girders.			
	Construction Joints in Girders: Offset from joints in supported floors minimum of 2 times width of intersecting beams.			
1907.1 1921.1	**Reinforcing Hooks and Bends:** Show detail indicating applicable requirements of UBC Sections 1907.1, 1907.2, and 1921.1.			
1907.7	**Concrete Protection for Reinforcement:** Provide concrete cover complying with UBC Sections 1907.			
1908.11	**Joist Construction - Minimum Rib Width:** 4" (102 mm).			
	Maximum Rib Height: 3-1/2 times rib width.			
	Clear Spacing Between Ribs: 30" (762 mm) maximum.			
1912.14	**Splices in Reinforcement:** Provide typical splice details on drawings complying with structural calculations.			
	Welded Splices: UBC Standard 19-2.			
1914.3.4	**Wall Reinforcement - Walls 10" (254 mm) and Thicker:** Provide reinforcing in both directions on both wall faces.			
	Outer Reinforcing: 1/2 to 2/3 of required reinforcing each way; place 2" (51 mm) minimum and 1/3 wall thickness maximum from exterior surface.			
	Inner Reinforcing: Balance of reinforcing each way; place 3/4" (19 mm) minimum and 1/3 wall thickness maximum from interior surface.			
1914.3.5	**Wall Reinforcement - Maximum Spacing:** 3 times wall thickness or 18" (457 mm) either way.			
1914.3.7	**Reinforcing Around Windows and Doors:** Provide 2 - #5 bars on all sides of opening in addition to minimum reinforcing; extend bars 24" (610 mm) beyond opening corners.			
1915.7	**Minimum Footing Depth:** **Bearing on Soil:** 6" (152 mm) minimum above reinforcing.			
	Bearing on Piles: 12" (305 mm) minimum above reinforcing.			
1924.4	**Shotcrete:** **Reinforcing - Size:** #5 bar maximum size unless preconstruction tests show adequate encasement is provided.			
	Minimum Clearance: **#5 and smaller:** 2-1/2" (64 mm) between parallel bars.			
	#6 and larger (where permitted): 6 bar diameters.			
	Where 2 curtains are used, provide minimum of 12 bar diameters on curtain nearest nozzle and 6 bar diameters on other steel.			

Code Ref.	Code Compliance Item	OK	NA	ID
1925.1	**Reinforced Gypsum Concrete:** **Minimum Thickness:** 2" (51 mm).			
	Thickness may be reduced to 1-1/2" (38 mm) provided following are met:			
	Overall thickness including form board is 2" (51 mm) minimum.			
	Clear span of gypsum concrete between supports is 2'-9" (838 mm) maximum.			
	Diaphragm action is not required.			
	Design live load is 40 psf (195 kg/m^2) maximum.			

Masonry - General

UBC Section 2106

Code Ref.	Code Compliance Item	OK	NA	ID
2106.1.4	**Stack Bond:** Consider as stack bond if less than 75% of units in any transverse vertical plane lap the ends of the units below a distance less than 1/2 the height of the unit, or less than 1/4 the length of the unit.			
2106.1.5.2	**Wall Ties in Cavity Wall Construction:** Provide ties of sufficient length to engage all wythes; completely embed in mortar or grout where within wythe.			
	Tributary Area: One 3/16" (4.8 mm) tie for each 4.5 sf (0.42 m^2) wall area.			
	Cavity Walls: One 3/16" (4.8 mm) tie for each 3 sf (0.28 m^2) wall area where cavity is more than 3" (75 mm) and less than 4-1/2" (115 mm) wide.			
	Spacing: 24" (610 mm) maximum vertical, 36" (914 mm) maximum horizontal.			
	Stagger alternate courses.			
	Adjustable Ties: **Tributary Area:** One tie for each 1.77 sf (0.16 m^2) wall area.			
	Spacing: 16" (406 mm) maximum horizontal and vertical.			
	Bed Joint Misalignment: 1-1/4" (32 mm) maximum.			
	Connecting Part Clearance: 1/16" (1.6 mm) maximum. Pintle ties shall have at least two 3/16" (4.8 mm) pintle legs.			
2106.1.5.3	**Grouted Multi-wythe Walls - Wall Ties:** One 3/16" (4.8 mm) tie for each 2 sf (0.19 m^2) wall area			
2106.1.5.4	**Multi-wythe Walls - Joint Reinforcement:** Provide at least one 9 gage steel cross wire for every 2 sf (0.19 m^2) of wall area.			
	Vertical Spacing: 16" (406 mm) maximum on center.			
2106.1.6	**Vertical Supports:** Provide for minimum 1/4" (6.4 mm), 1" (25 mm) maximum bed joint; noncombustible materials.			
2106.1.7	**Lateral Support:** Cross walls, columns, pilasters, counterforts, or buttresses for horizontal spans; floors, beams, girts, or roofs for vertical spans.			
	Lateral Support Maximum Spacing: 32 times least width of compression area.			

Code Ref.	Code Compliance Item	OK	NA	ID
2106.1.8	**Protection of Ties and Joint Reinforcement:** 5/8" (16 mm) minimum mortar cover at exposed faces.			
	Minimum Joint Thickness: 1/4" (6.4 mm).			
2106.1.9	**Pipes and Conduit in Masonry:** Do not reduce required strength or fire protection.			
	May be placed in unfilled cores of hollow units.			
	Electrical conduit may be embedded in structural masonry when location is specifically detailed.			
	Pipes and conduits may pass through masonry using sleeves large enough to pass hubs or couplings through; space sleeves no closer than 3 diameters, center to center.			
2106.1.12.3	**Special Provisions - Seismic Zone 2:** Reinforce walls and columns per structural calculations.			
	Vertical Wall Reinforcing: At each corner, each side of openings, wall ends, and at maximum spacing of 48" (1219 mm) horizontally.			
	Horizontal Wall Reinforcing: At top and bottom of openings extending 24" (610 mm) minimum or 40 bar diameters beyond opening;			
	Continuously at structurally connected roof and floor levels and tops of walls;			
	At bottoms of walls or in top of foundations when doweled in walls;			
	At 10'-0" maximum vertical spacing or evenly spaced joint reinforcing.			
	Stack Bond: Evenly spaced joint reinforcing or horizontal bars at 48" (1219 mm) maximum.			
2106.1.12.4	**Special Provisions - Seismic Zones 3 and 4:** Reinforce walls and columns per Seismic Zone 2 above and per structural calculations.			
2106.2.14	**Anchor Bolts - Configuration:** 90° bend, diameter of 3-bolt diameters, 1-1/2 bolt diameter extension; standard bolt head; or plate welded to shank.			
	Placement: Grout in place, minimum of 1" (25 mm) grout between bolt and masonry.			
	1/4" (6.4 mm) diameter bolts may be placed in 1/2" (13 mm) bed joints.			
	Edge Distance: 1-1/2" (38 mm) from edge of masonry to edge of bolt.			
	Minimum Embedment Depth: 4 bolt diameters or 2" (51 mm) minimum.			
	Minimum Spacing: 4 bolt diameters.			

Masonry - Empirical Design

UBC Section 2109

Code Ref.	Code Compliance Item	OK	NA	ID
2109.1	**Scope:** This section may be used for masonry structures in Seismic Zones 0 and 1 where basic wind speed is less than 80 mph.			
2109.2	**Maximum Height:** 35'-0" (10 688 mm) where masonry walls provide lateral load resistance.			
2109.3	**Lateral Stability - Minimum Shear Wall Thickness:** 8" (203 mm).			
	Minimum Shear Wall Length: 0.4 times longest building dimension; length calculation shall not include openings.			
	Maximum Shear Wall Spacing: UBC Table 21-L.			
2109.5	**Lateral Support:** UBC Table 21-O for vertical and horizontal support.			
	Support Elements: Cross walls, pilasters, buttresses, or structural framing members horizontally; floors, roof, or structural framing members vertically.			
	Cantilever Walls - Height to Thickness Ratio: Maximum of 6 for solid masonry, 4 for hollow masonry.			
2109.6.1	**Minimum Thickness - Bearing Walls:** **1-story Buildings:** 8" (203 mm).			
	Solid Masonry, 1-story Buildings: 6" (152 mm), maximum 9'-0" (2743 mm) high. 6'-0" (1829 mm) may be added in gables.			
2109.6.2	**Variation in Thickness:** Carry greatest thickness requirement up to higher floor level.			
2109.6.3	**Decrease in Thickness - Hollow Masonry:** Provide solid masonry course at change in thickness.			
2109.6.4	**Minimum Parapet Thickness:** 8" (203 mm), but not thinner than wall below.			
	Maximum Parapet Height: 3 times thickness.			

Code Ref.	Code Compliance Item	OK	NA	ID
2109.6.5	**Foundation Wall Construction:** Comply with UBC Table 21-P when height of unbalanced fill and height of wall between lateral supports is 8'-0" (2438 mm) maximum, and when equivalent fluid weight of unbalanced fill does not exceed 30 pcf (480 kg/m^2).			
2109.7.2	**Bond - Masonry Headers:** When used to bond facing and backing, provide headers at 4% minimum of wall surface of each face, extending 3" (76 mm) minimum into backing.			
	24" (610 mm) maximum spacing between headers, horizontal and vertical.			
	Where a single header cannot extend through wall, overlap with header from opposite side by 3" (76 mm) minimum.			
	Where 2 or more hollow units make up wall, bond stretcher courses at 34" (864 mm) maximum vertical spacing by lapping 3" (76 mm) minimum over unit below, or by lapping at vertical units not more than 17" (432 mm) maximum vertical spacing with units at least 50% greater in thickness than units below.			
2109.7.3	**Bond - Wall Ties:** When used to bond facing and backing, provide 3/16" (4.8 mm) diameter ties embedded in joints.			
	Maximum Tie Spacing: 1 tie for every 4-1/2 sf (0.42 m^2) wall area, staggered in alternate courses; 24" (610 mm) vertical, 36" (914 mm) horizontal maximum spacing.			
	Ties in Hollow Masonry: Rectangular shape.			
	Ties in Other Masonry Walls: Provide 90° bend each end with 2" (51 mm) long hooks.			
	Additional Ties at Openings: Space at 36" (914 mm) on center around perimeter of opening, within 12" (305 mm) of opening.			
	Wall Ties - Joint Reinforcement: When used for bonding facing and backing, provide 9 gage cross wire every 2-2/3 sf (0.25 m^2) of wall area; embed in mortar joint.			
	Joint Reinforcement Spacing: 16" (406 mm) on center maximum.			
2109.7.4	**Longitudinal Bond:** Offset head joints in running bond at least 1/4 of unit length or provide longitudinal reinforcing complying with Section 2106.1.12.3.			
2109.8.1	**Intersecting Wall Anchorage:** Where lateral support is required, provide anchorage by 1 of following methods:			
	Overlap 50% of units at intersection, minimum 3" (76 mm) bearing on units below.			
	1/4" x 1-1/2" (6.4 mm x 38 mm) steel connectors with ends bent up 2" (51 mm) minimum, 24" (610 mm) long; spaced 48" (1219 mm) maximum vertically.			

Code Ref.	Code Compliance Item	OK	NA	ID
2109.8.1	**Intersecting Wall Anchorage (continued):** Joint reinforcing with 9 gage rods, spaced 8" (203 mm) maximum vertically and extending 30" (762 mm) minimum in either direction at intersection.			
	Joint reinforcing or 1/4" (6.4 mm) mesh galvanized hardware cloth, 16" (406 mm) maximum vertical spacing, at interior nonbearing walls only.			
	Other metal ties, joint reinforcing, or anchors providing equivalent area of anchorage required above.			
2109.8.2	**Floor and Roof Anchorage:** Connect to masonry walls by 1 of following methods:			
	Anchor wood floor joists bearing on wall with metal strap anchors, 6'-0" (1829 mm) maximum spacing.			
	Anchor parallel joists with metal strap anchors, 6'-0" (1829 mm) maximum spacing, extending over and under and secured to at least 3 joists; provide blocking at each strap.			
	Anchor steel floor joists with #3 bars or equivalent, 6'-0" (1829 mm) maximum spacing. Anchor parallel joists at joist cross bridging.			
	Anchor roof structures with 1/2" (13 mm) diameter bolts at 6'-0" (1829 mm) on center maximum or equivalent; 15" (381 mm) minimum bolt embedment.			
	Bolts may hook or weld to bond beam reinforcement placed 6" (152 mm) maximum from top of wall.			
2109.8.3	**Walls Adjoining Structural Framing:** Anchor walls to structural frame where needed for lateral support with metal anchors or keyed construction.			
	Metal Anchors: 1/2" (13 mm) diameter bolts at 48" (1219 mm) on center maximum, embedded 4" (102 mm) minimum.			
2109.9	**Unburned Clay Masonry:** Do not use in buildings over 1 story.			
	Maximum Unsupported Height: 10 times wall thickness.			
	Minimum Bearing Wall Thickness: 16" (406 mm).			
	Footing/Foundation Walls: Extend 6" (152 mm) minimum above grade.			
2109.10	**Stone Masonry** **Ashlar Bond:** Provide bond stones at rate of 10% minimum of area.			
	Rubble Bond 24" (610 mm) Thick or Less: Provide bond stones at 36" (914 mm) vertically and horizontally.			
	Rubble Bond More than 24" (610 mm) Thick: Provide bond stones for each 6 sf (0.56 m²) of wall surface, both sides.			
	Minimum Bearing Wall Thickness: 16" (406 mm).			

Steel Joists and Girders

UBC Section 2219

Code Ref.	Code Compliance Item	OK	NA	ID
2221	**Standards:** Standard Specification for Steel Joists, K-Series, LH-Series, DLH-Series and Joist Girders published by Steel Joist Institute.			

Structural Steel

UBC Chapter 22

Code Ref.	Code Compliance Item	OK	NA	ID
2206	**Design and Construction Standards:** AISC Load and Resistance Factor Design Specification for Structural Steel Buildings (AISC LRFD).			
2208	AISC Specification for Structural Steel Buildings - Allowable Stress Design and Plastic Design (AISC ASD).			
2210	AISC Seismic Provisions for Structural Steel Buildings.			

Wood

UBC Chapter 23

Code Ref.	Code Compliance Item	OK	NA	ID
2306	**Decay and Termite Protection:** **Wood Supports Embedded in Ground or Supported on Ground:** Use ground-contact treated wood unless continuously below groundwater line or continuously submerged in fresh water.			
	Use ground-contact treated wood where embedded in concrete or masonry exposed to weather.			
	Under-Floor Clearance: Use treated or decay-resistant wood for posts, girders, joists, and subfloor when bottom of joists, or wood structural floors without joists, are closer than 18" (457 mm) to exposed earth, or wood girders are closer than 12" (305 mm) to exposed earth.			
	Plates, Sills, and Sleepers: Provide treated wood or foundation redwood where resting on concrete or masonry slabs in direct contact with the earth or on concrete or masonry foundations.			
	Columns and Posts: Where on concrete or masonry floors or decks exposed to weather or water splash, or in basements, support on concrete piers or metal pedestals or provide treated or decay-resistant wood.			
	Project concrete or masonry piers 8" (203 mm) minimum above exposed earth.			
	Project metal pedestals a 6" (152 mm) minimum above exposed earth or 1" above concrete or masonry floors.			
	Girders in Masonry or Concrete Walls: Provide 1/2" air space on tops, sides, and ends or provide treated or decay resistant wood.			
	Wood Supporting Roofs and Floors: Use treated or decay-resistant wood where floors or roofs are moisture-permeable, such as concrete or masonry slabs, unless protected by membrane.			
	Weather Exposure: Use treated or decay-resistant wood for wood members forming structural support of buildings, balconies, porches, or similar building appurtenances exposed to weather without adequate protection from a roof, eave, overhang.			

Code Ref.	Code Compliance Item	OK	NA	ID
2312.2	**Roof Sheathing Nailing:** UBC Table 23-II-B-2.			
2315.1	**Wood Shear Walls and Diaphragms:** Shape and size per UBC Table 23-II-G.			
2315.3.1	**Diagonally Sheathed Diaphragms:** 1" (25 mm) nominal minimum thickness sheathing boards at 45° to supports.			
	Minimum Nailing: 2-8d nails for 6" (152 mm) nominal boards. 3-8d nails for boards 8" (203 mm) or wider. 3-8d nails for 6" (152 mm) boards at diaphragm boundaries. 4-8d nails for 8" (203 mm) boards at diaphragm boundaries.			
	Separate end joints in adjacent boards by at least 1 joist or stud space. Separate end joints on the same joist or stud by at least 2 boards.			
2315.3.3	**Vertical Structural Panel Diaphragms - Minimum Thickness:** 5/16" (7.9 mm) for studs spaced 16" (406 mm) on center, 3/8" (9.5 mm) for studs spaced 24" (610 mm) on center.			
	Horizontal Structural Panel Diaphragms - Minimum Thickness: Comply with UBC Tables 23-II-E-1 and 23-II-E-2.			
	Bear panel edges on framing members and butt along center lines.			
	Place nails for not less than 3/8" (9.5 mm) from panel edge and space 6" on center maximum along panel edge bearings.			
	Unblocked shear panels less than 12" (305 mm) wide permitted.			
2315.4	**Particleboard Diaphragms:** Place nails not less than 3/8" (9.5 mm) from panel edge and spaced 6" on center maximum along panel edge bearings.			
	Bear panel edges on framing members and butt along center lines.			
	Unblocked panels less than 12" (305 mm) wide permitted.			
2315.5.3	**Shear Walls and Diaphragms in Seismic Zones 3 and 4:** **Wood Structural Panels:** 48" by 96" (1219 mm by 2438 mm) minimum sheet size.			
	24" (610 mm) minimum sheet dimension at boundaries and changes in framing unless edges are supported by framing members or blocking.			
	Provide framing or blocking at all edges of panel.			
2315.5.5	**Particleboard Diaphragms:** 48" by 96" (1219 mm by 2438 mm) minimum sheet size except at boundaries and changes in framing.			
2315.6	**Fiberboard Sheathing Diaphragms:** 48" by 96" (1219 mm by 2438 mm) sheets vertically to studs spaced 16" on center maximum.			
	Nailing: Comply with UBC Table 23-II-J.			
	Blocking: Provide at horizontal joints when wall height exceeds length of sheathing panel			

Code Ref.	Code Compliance Item	OK	NA	ID
2315.6	**Fiberboard Sheathing Diaphragms, Continued:** **Nailing:** Comply with UBC Table 23-II-J at perimeter and intermediate studs.			
	Nail panel to blocking with nails sized per UBC Table 23-II-J spaced 3" (76 mm) on center each side of joint.			
	Space perimeter nails 3/8" (9.5 mm) minimum from edges and ends.			
	Anchor end studs of shear walls to resist forces.			
	Maximum height-to-width ratio: 1-1/2:1.			
2318	**Fasteners:** Indicate the required length, center-to-center spacing, edge distance, and end distance of nails, screws, lag bolts, and other timber connectors.			
	Nailing Schedule: Comply with UBC Table 23-II-B-1.			

Conventional Light-Frame Construction

UBC Section 2320

Code Ref.	Code Compliance Item	OK	NA	ID
2320.1	**Conventional Light-Frame Construction Provisions - Scope:** Applies to: Group R occupancies of 1, 2, or 3 stories.			
	1-story Occupancy Category 4 buildings (UBC Table 16-K), slab on grade floor.			
	Group U occupancies.			
	Top story walls and Roofs of 1 or 2 story wood-framed Occupancy Category 4 (UBC Table 16-K) buildings.			
	Interior nonload-bearing partitions, ceilings, and curtain walls in all occupancies.			
2320.4	**Seismic Zone 0, 1, 2, and 3 Requirements:** **Braced Wall Lines - Basic Wind Speed Less than 80 mph (129 km/h):** Provide interior and exterior braced wall lines at 34'-0" (10 363 mm) on center maximum in both directions in each story.			
	Braced Wall Lines - Basic Wind Speed More than 80 mph (129 km/h): Provide interior and exterior braced wall lines at 25'-0" (7620 mm) on center maximum in both directions in each story.			
	Exception - Group R-3 - 1 and 2 Story Buildings: Spacing may be 34'-0" (10 363 mm) for 1 single room in each dwelling unit of 900 sf (83.61 m²) maximum.			
	Veneer Thickness: 5" (127 mm) maximum.			
	Unusually Shaped Buildings in Seismic Zone 3: Provide designed lateral force resisting system under conditions stated in Section 2320.5.4.			

Code Ref.	Code Compliance Item	OK	NA	ID
2320.5	**Seismic Zone 4 Requirements:** **Braced Wall Lines:** Provide interior and exterior braced wall lines at 25'-0" (7620 mm) on center maximum in both directions in each story.			
	Exception - Group R-3 - 1 and 2 Story Buildings: Spacing may be 34'-0" (10 363 mm) for 1 single room in each dwelling unit of 900 sf (83.61 m²) maximum.			
	Designed Lateral Force Resisting System: Provide as required below or provide structurally designed system.			
	Veneer Thickness: 5" (127 mm) maximum.			
	Unusually Shaped Buildings: Provide designed lateral force resisting system under conditions stated in Section 2320.5.4.			
	Lumber Roof Decks: Use solid sheathing.			
2326.5.6	**Seismic Zone 4 Requirements - Interior Braced Wall Support:** **Braced Walls in 1-story Buildings:** Support on continuous foundations at 50'-0" (15 240 mm) maximum intervals.			
	Braced Walls in Multistory Buildings: Support on continuous foundations.			
	Exception: 2-story buildings may have interior braced wall lines supported on continuous foundations at 50'-0" (15 240 mm) maximum intervals provided:			
	Cripple wall height is 4'-0" (1219 mm) maximum;			
	First-floor braced wall panels are supported on doubled floor joists, continuous blocking, or floor beams; and			
	Distance between braced lines does not exceed twice building width parallel to braced wall line.			
2320.6	**Foundation Plates or Sills:** Secure to concrete or masonry with 1/2" (13 mm) minimum diameter bolts, embedded into concrete or masonry 7" (182 mm) minimum, spaced at 72" (1829 mm) maximum.			
	Provide 2 bolts per piece minimum, with 1 bolt located within 12" (305 mm) of each end of each piece.			
2320.7	**Girders - Single Story:** 4 x 6 (102 mm x 153 mm) minimum for 6'-0" (1829 mm) spans or less, spaced 8'-0" (2438 mm) on center maximum.			
	Girders Splices over Supports: Tie together.			
	Bearings: 3" (76 mm) minimum on masonry or concrete.			
2320.8.1	**Floor Joists - Size and Spacing:** UBC Tables 23 -IV-J-1 and 23-IV-J-2.			
2320.8.2	**Floor Joists - Bearing:** 1-1/2" minimum at joist ends when bearing on wood or metal, 3" where bearing on masonry, or 1 x 4 (25 mm by 102 mm) ribbon strip and nailed to adjoining studs.			

Code Ref.	Code Compliance Item	OK	NA	ID
2320.8.3	**Floor Joists - Framing Details:** Support laterally at ends and supports by full depth solid blocking unless nailed to header, band or rim joist, or adjoining stud.			
	Lap joists framing from opposite sides of beams or partitions 3" (76 mm) minimum or tie ends together.			
	Support joists framed into beams by framing anchors or ledger strips, 2 x 2 (51 mm by 51 mm) minimum.			
	End Notches: 1/4 of joist depth maximum.			
	Top or Bottom Notches: 1/6 of joist depth maximum, do not locate in middle third of span.			
	Bored Holes: Not permitted within 2" (51 mm) of top or bottom of joist; do not exceed diameter of 1/3 of depth of joist.			
2320.8.4	**Floor Joists - Opening Framing:** Double trimmer and header joists where span exceeds 4'-0" (1219 mm).			
	Support ends of header joists over 6'-0" (1829 mm) long with framing anchors or joist hangers unless bearing on beam or partition.			
	Support tail joists over 12'-0" (3658 mm) long by framing anchors or ledger strips, 2 x 2 (51 mm by 51 mm) minimum.			
2320.8.5	**Floor Joists - Supporting Bearing Partitions:** Do not offset bearing partitions perpendicular to joists more than joist depth from supporting girders or walls.			
	Double joists under parallel bearing partitions.			
2320.9.1	**Lumber Subfloor:** UBC Tables 23-II-D-1 and 23-I-D-2.			
	Subflooring may be omitted where joist spacing is 16" (406 mm) maximum and 1" (25 mm) nominal tongue and groove floor is perpendicular to joists.			
2320.9.3	**Wood Structural Panel Subfloor:** UBC Tables 23-II-E-1 and 23-II-E-2.			
	Combination Subfloor-Underlayment: UBC Table 23-II-F-1.			
2320.9.3	**Plank Flooring Subfloor:** 2" (51 mm) nominal thickness; UBC Table 23-IV-A.			
	Joints may be random-spaced provided system spans at least 4 supports, planks are center matched and end matched or splined, each plank bears on at least 1 support and joints are separated by at least 24" (610 mm) in adjacent pieces.			
	Finish Floor over Random-length Decking: 1x strip square-edge flooring.			
	1/2" (13 mm) T&G flooring applied at right angles to span of planks.			
	3/8" (9.5 mm) plywood with face grain at right angles to span of planks.			
	3/8" (9.5 mm) particleboard.			

Code Ref.	Code Compliance Item	OK	NA	ID
2320.11.1	**Wall Framing - Size, Height, and Spacing:** UBC Table 23-IV-B.			
	Utility Grade Studs: Do not exceed 8'-0" (2438 mm) high exterior walls or bearing walls, 10'-0" (3048 mm) high interior nonload-bearing walls, 16" (406 mm) spacing, and do not support more than a roof and ceiling.			
2320.11.2	**Wall Framing Details:** Provide 3 studs at each exterior wall corner.			
	Top Plate - Exterior and Bearing Walls: Double top plates with overlapping corners and intersections with other partitions; offset end joints 48" (1219 mm) minimum.			
	Where 2 x 4 (52 mm by 102 mm) bearing studs are spaced 24" (610 mm) and supported floor joists, floor trusses, or roof trusses are spaced at more than 16" (406 mm), locate such supported joists or trusses within 5" (127 mm) of studs beneath or provide third plate.			
	Stud Bearing: 2" (51 mm) minimum on plate or sill of same width as stud.			
2320.11.3 2320.11.4	**Wall Framing - Bracing:** Brace exterior walls and main cross-stud partitions to resist wind and seismic forces in accordance with assemblies detailed in Sections 2320.11.3 and 2320.11.4.			
2320.11.5	**Cripple Walls:** Match stud size above, 14" minimum length, or frame with solid blocking.			
	Frame walls over 48" (1219 mm) high with studs sized for an additional story; consider as first-story walls for bracing requirements of Section 2320.11.3.			
2320.11.7	**Pipes in Walls:** Space wall studs and floor joists to clear piping.			
	Provide double joists beneath parallel partitions containing piping and space to permit passage of pipes and provide bridging.			
	Where piping necessitates cutting of top or bottom plates, provide metal ties not less than (3.2 mm by 38 mm) wide across the cut and fastened to each side with not less than 4-16d nails.			
2320.11.8	**Bridging:** When not covered by interior or exterior wall covering or sheathing, provide full depth bridging in stud walls having a height-to-least thickness ratio exceeding 50.			
2320.11.9	**Cutting and Notching - Exterior Bearing Walls:** Do not cut or notch wood studs more than 25% of stud depth.			
	Cutting and Notching - Interior Nonbearing Partitions: Do not cut or notch more than 40% of stud depth.			
2320.11. 10	**Bored Holes - Wall Studs:** Do not bore holes greater in diameter than 40% of stud width, no closer than 5/8" (16 mm) from edge of stud.			
	Bored holes not greater than 60% of stud width permitted in nonbearing partitions or in any wall where bored stud is doubled provided not more than 2 such successive doubled studs are bored.			
	Do not locate bored holes in same section of stud as cut or notch.			

Code Ref.	Code Compliance Item	OK	NA	ID
2320.12.1	**Roof and Ceiling Framing:** Section applies to roofs 3:12 (25%) minimum. For lesser slopes, design roof members as beams.			
2320.12.2	**Ceiling Joist Spans:** UBC Tables 23-IV-J-3 and 23-IV-J-4.			
	Rafter Spans: UBC Tables 23 -IV-R-1 through 23-IV-R-12.			
2320.12.3	**Roof Ridge Board:** 1" (25 mm) minimum nominal thickness, as deep as cut rafter ends.			
	Valley and Hip Rafters: 2" (51 mm) minimum nominal thickness, as deep as cut rafter ends.			
2320.12.4	**End Notches:** 1/4 maximum of rafter or joist depth.			
	Top or Bottom Notches: 1/6 maximum of joist or rafter depth maximum, do not locate in middle third of span.			
	Notch of 1/3 maximum of joist or rafter depth permitted when located not further than depth of member from face of support.			
	Bored Holes: Not permitted in 2" of top or bottom of joist; do not exceed diameter of 1/3 of depth of joist.			
2320.12.5	**Roof and Ceiling Framing - Openings:** Double trimmer and header rafters when the span of header exceeds 4'-0" (1219 mm).			
	Support the ends of rafters more than 6'-0" (1829 mm) long by framing anchors or hangers unless bearing on beam, partition, or wall.			
2320.12.6	**Rafter Ties:** Nail rafters to adjacent ceiling joists to form continuous tie when rafters are parallel to joists.			
	Where rafters are perpendicular to ceiling joists, provide cross ties of minimum 1 x 4 (25 mm by 102 mm) spaced at 4'-0" (1219 mm) on center.			
2320.12.7	**Purlins:** Where used, support by struts to bearing walls.			
	Maximum Spans: **2 x 4 (51 mm by 102 mm):** 4'-0" (1219 mm). **2 x 6 (51 mm by 152 mm):** 6'-0" (1829 mm).			
	Strut Size: 2 x 4 (51 mm by 102 mm) minimum.			
	Unsupported Strut Length: 8'-0" (2438 mm) maximum at 45° minimum from horizontal.			
2320.12.8	**Roof and Ceiling Blocking:** Support rafters, roof trusses, and ceiling joists laterally to prevent rotation.			
2320.13	**Exit Facilities:** In Seismic zones 3 and 4, connect exterior exit balconies, stairs, and similar exit facilities to structure at 8'-0" (2438 mm) on center maximum. Do not use toe nails or nails in withdrawal.			

Gypsum Board and Plaster

UBC Chapter 2513

Code Ref.	Code Compliance Item	OK	NA	ID
2513.1	**Shear Resisting Construction with Wood Frame:** Cement plaster, gypsum lath and plaster, gypsum sheathing, and gypsum wall board may be used on wood studs for vertical diaphragms.			
	Do not use to resist forces imposed by masonry or concrete construction.			
2513.3	**Wall Framing:** Conform to UBC Section 2326.11 for bearing walls; space studs not more than 16" (406 mm) on center.			
2513.4	**Maximum Height-to-Length Ratio:** 2:1.			
	Where walls with height-to-length ratio of more than 1-1/2:1, block all edges.			
2513.5	**Application:** Stagger end joints of adjacent panels.			
	Blocking at Panel Edges: UBC Table 25-I.			
	Nails: Size and spacing per UBC Table 25-I; space 3/8" (9.5 mm) minimum from panel edges and ends.			
	Gypsum Lath: Apply perpendicular to studs.			
	Gypsum Sheathing: Apply 48" (1219 mm) wide pieces parallel or perpendicular to studs; apply 24" (610 mm) wide pieces perpendicular to studs.			
	Gypsum Wall Board or Veneer Base: Apply perpendicular or parallel to studs.			

Masonry Construction in High-Wind Areas

UBC Appendix Chapter 21

When adopted by the governing jurisdiction, this section may be used for design and construction purposes.

Code Ref.	Code Compliance Item	OK	NA	ID
2112.2	**Scope:** Chapter applies when all of the following are met:			
	Building is located in area with basic wind speed from 80-100 mph (129-177 km/h).			
	Building is located in Seismic Zone 0, 1, or 2.			
	Building is 1 or 2 stories.			
	Floor and roof joists are of wood, steel, or precast hollow core planks, maximum span of 32'-0" (9754 mm) between bearing walls. Masonry walls shall support steel joists or concrete planks.			
	Building is of regular shape.			
2112.3	**General:** Comply with UBC Chapter 21 except where specifically modified below or use other methods designed in compliance with UBC Chapter 16.			
	Wood Floors, Roofs and Interior Walls: UBC Appendix Chapter 23.			
	Wind Speeds above 100 mph (177 km/h): Requires structural design.			
	Buildings of Unusual Shape: Requires structural design.			
2112.5	**Construction Requirements:** Follow UBC Section 2104 for grouted cavity wall and block wall construction.			
	Do not use unburned clay masonry or stone.			

Code Ref.	Code Compliance Item	OK	NA	ID
2112.6	**Foundations - Footings:** 8" (203 mm) minimum thickness; follow UBC Tables A-21-A-1 and A-21-A-2 for width, follow UBC Figure A-21-1 for details.			
	Extend footings 18" (457 mm) below undisturbed ground surface or frost depth, whichever is greater.			
	Stem Walls: Same width as walls supported; reinforce to match walls supported.			
	Basements and other Below Grade Walls: UBC Table A-21-B.			
2112.7	**Drainage:** Provide 4" (102 mm) minimum diameter footing drain per UBC Table A-21-A and Figure A-21-3 at basement walls retaining more than 3'-0" (914 mm) of earth and enclosing interior spaces or floors below grade.			
	Slope finish grades away from building minimum of 1/4:12 (2%).			
2112.8.1	**Wall Construction - Minimum Thickness:** **Reinforced exterior walls:** 8" (203 mm).			
	Interior masonry nonbearing walls: 6" (152 mm).			
	Unreinforced grouted brick walls: 10" (254 mm).			
	Unreinforced hollow-unit and solid masonry walls: 8" (203 mm).			
	Minimum Wall Thickness Exceptions: 8" (203 mm) in buildings not over 2 stories or 26'-0" (7924.8 mm).			
	6" (152 mm) solid masonry when not over 9'-0" (2743 mm) in 1-story buildings; may extend maximum 6'-0" (1829 mm) additional to peak of gable.			
2112.8.2	**Wall Construction - Lateral Support:** Support all walls at top and bottom.			
	Maximum Unsupported Height of Masonry Walls: 12'-0" (3658 mm); 15'-0" (4572 mm) at peak of gable end walls.			
	Wood-framed Gable End Walls: UBC Table A-21-A and UBC Figures A-21-17 or A-21-18.			
2112.8.3	**Walls in Seismic Zone 2 and Stack Bond:** UBC Figure A-21-B as a minimum; design stack bond walls.			
2112.8.4	**Wall Construction - Lintels:** Maximum span 12'-0" (3658 mm); reinforce all lintels and fully grout cells; UBC Table A-21-E.			
	Extend bars 24" (610 mm) minimum past edge of opening and into lintel supports.			
2112.8.5	**Wall Construction - Reinforcement:** UBC Tables A-21-C-1 through A-21-C-5 and Figure A-21-2.			
2112.8.6	**Wall Construction - Anchorage of Walls to Floors and Roofs:** Embed anchors in grouted cells or cavities; UBC Section 2112.9.			
2112.9	**Wood Roof Systems Supported on Masonry Walls:** UBC Sections 2337.5.1 and 2337.5.8 and UBC Table A-21-D and UBC Figure A-21-7.			

Code Ref.	Code Compliance Item	OK	NA	ID
2112.9	**Wood Roof and Floor Systems Supported on Ledgers:** UBC Table A-21-D, Part I.			
	Ends of Joist Girders: Extend 6" (152 mm) minimum over masonry or concrete supports and attach to steel plate. Locate plate 1/2" (13 mm) maximum from face of wall, plate width 9" (229 mm) minimum perpendicular to girder.			
	Attach ends of joist girders to steel plate or to steel supports with minimum of two 1/4" (6.4 mm) fillet welds 2" (51 mm) long or with two 3/4" (19 mm) bolts.			
	In steel frames, field bolt joist girders to columns to provide lateral stability during construction.			
	Steel Joist Roof and Floor Systems: Anchor per UBC Table A-21-H.			
	Table A-21-D, Part II - Wall Ties: Connect to framing or blocking at roofs and walls; extend into grout cells. Provide ties of 1-1/8" (29 mm) minimum width, 0.036" (0.91 mm) (No. 20 galvanized steel gage) sheet steel.			
	Hollow-core Precast Plank Roof and Floor Systems: Anchor per UBC Table A-21-G.			
	Roof Uplift Anchorage: UBC Tables A-21-C-1 through A-21-C-5 and UBC Figure A-21-7.			
2112.10.1	**Complete Load Path and Uplift Resistance:** UBC Figure A-21-8.			
2112.10.2	**Floor and Roof Diaphragms:** Connect to masonry walls per UBC Table A-21-F, Part II.			
	Tie gabled and sloped roof members not supported at ridge by ceiling joists or equivalent lateral ties located as close to roof member bearing as possible and spaced at 48" (1219 mm) on center maximum. (UBC Figure A-21-17 and A-21-1).			
2112.10.3	**Walls:** Provide masonry walls around all sides of floor and roof systems following UBC Figures A-21-9 and UBC Table A-21-F.			
	Cumulative Length of Exterior Masonry Walls: At least 20% of parallel dimension of each side of floor or roof system.			
	Required Elements: No openings permitted; minimum 48" (1219 mm) long.			
2112.10.3	**Interior Nonbearing Cross Walls:** Provide at right angles to bearing walls when length of building perpendicular to span of floor or roof framing exceeds twice the distance between shear walls or 32'-0" (9754 mm), whichever is greater; follow UBC Section 2112.10.4.			
2112.10.4	**Interior Masonry Cross Walls:** When required by UBC Table A-21-F, Part I, provide cross walls 6'-0" (1829 mm) long minimum; reinforce with 9 gage wire joint reinforcement spaced at 16" (406 mm) on center maximum.			
	Comply with Footnote 3 of UBC Table A-21-F, Part I.			

Code Ref.	Code Compliance Item	OK	NA	ID
2112.10.4	**Interior Wood Stud Cross Walls:** May be used to resist wind loads from 1-story masonry buildings in areas where basic wind speed is 100 mph (161 km/h), Exposure C or less, and 110 mph (177 km/h), Exposure B as follows:			
	Perpendicular to exterior masonry walls and spaced at 15'-0" (4572 mm) on center maximum.			
	Minimum of 8'-0" (2438 mm) long without openings and sheathed on at least 1 side with 15/32" (12 mm) wood structural panel nailed with 8d common or galvanized box nails at 6" (152 mm) on center edge and field nailing.			
	Block all unsupported panel edges.			
	Connect to wood blocking or floor joists below with two 16d nails at 16" (406 mm) on center through sill plate. Connect to footings with 1/2" (13 mm) bolts at 42" (1067 mm) on center.			
	Connect to roof system per UBC Table A-21-F, Part II, as a cross wall.			
	Block all unsupported wood structural panel sheathing.			

Light-Frame Construction in High-Wind Areas

UBC Appendix Chapter 23

When adopted by the governing jurisdiction, this section may be used for design and construction purposes.

Code Ref.	Code Compliance Item	OK	NA	ID
2337.2	**Scope:** Chapter applies when all of the following are met:			
	Basic wind speed is from 80-100 mph (129- 177 km/h).			
	Building is 3 stories maximum and of conventional light-frame construction.			
	Building is of regular shape with wood structural members spanning 32'-0" (9.75 m) maximum.			
	Exception: Detached carports and garages not exceeding 600 sf (55.7 m^2) and accessory to R-3 occupancies need only comply with roof-member-to-wall-tie requirements of UBC Section 2337.5.8.			
2337.5.1	**Complete Load Path and Uplift Ties:** UBC Figure A-23-1.			
	Tie Straps: 1-1/8" (28.6) by 0.036" (0.91 mm) (No. 20 gage) sheet steel, corrosion-resistant.			
2337.5.2	**Walls-to-Foundation Tie:** Tie exterior walls to continuous foundation per UBC Section 2365.10.			
2337.5.3	**Sills and Foundation Tie:** Bolt foundation plates to concrete or masonry with 1/2" (13 mm) minimum anchor bolts with 7" (178 mm) embedment into foundation.			
	Where basic wind speed is 90 mph (145 km/h) or greater, space bolts at 48" (1219 mm) on center.			
	Where basic wind speed is less than 90 mph (145 km/h) space bolts at 60" (1524 mm) on center.			

Code Ref.	Code Compliance Item	OK	NA	ID
2337.5.4	**Floor-to-Foundation Tie:** Connect lowest level exterior wall studs to foundation plate or elevated foundation system with bent tie straps spaced at 48" (1219 mm) on center maximum.			
	Nail tie straps per UBC Table A-23-B and UBC Figure A-23-1.			
2337.5.5	**Wall Framing Details - 2 x 4 Wall Stud Spacing:** 16" (406 mm) on center maximum in areas with basic wind speed of 90 mph (145 km/h) or greater.			
	Interior Main Cross-Stud Partitions: Provide approximately perpendicular to exterior wall when length of structure exceeds width.			
	Securely fasten to exterior walls at point of intersection; UBC Table 23-I-B-1.			
	Maximum distance between cross-stud partitions shall not exceed width of structure.			
2337.5.6	**Wall Sheathing:** Sheath exterior walls and required interior main cross-stud partitions; UBC Table A-23-A.			
	Sheath main cross-stud partitions on both sides.			
	Provide a total width of sheathing of at least 50% of exterior wall length and at least 60% of main cross-stud partitions.			
	Extend exterior wall sheathing from foundation sill plate or girder to top plates at roof level.			
	Provide a minimum of 48" (1219 mm) wide sheathed element at each corner or as near the corner as possible.			
	Provide minimum 48" (1219 mm) wide sheathed element for every 20'-0" (6096 mm) of wall length.			
	Height-to-length ratio of required sheathed elements shall not exceed 3 for wood structural panel or particleboard sheathing and 1-1/2" (38 mm) for other sheathing materials listed in UBC Table A-23-A.			
2337.5.7	**Floor-to-Floor Tie:** Align and connect upper-level exterior wall studs to wall studs below with tie straps required by UBC Table A-23-B.			
2337.5.8	**Roof-Member-to-Wall Tie:** Provide tie straps from side of roof framing member to exterior studs, posts, or other supporting members below roof.			
	Align wall studs with roof framing members where tied and connect following UBC Table A-23-B.			
	Eave Overhang: Do not exceed 36" (914 mm) unless designed for wind uplift.			
	Wall Openings: Where over 6'-0" (1829 mm) wide, double tie straps at each edge of opening and connect to doubled full-height wall stud.			
	Where over 12'-0" (3658 mm) wide design ties to prevent uplift.			
2337.5.9	**Ridge Ties:** Align opposing rafters at ridge and connect with tie straps following UBC Table A-23-C.			
2337.6	**Masonry Veneer:** Space anchor ties to provide support for 1-1/3 sf (860 mm^2) maximum but not more than 12" (305 mm) on center vertically.			

Code Ref.	Code Compliance Item	OK	NA	ID
2337.7	**Roof Sheathing:** 15/32" (11.9 mm) wood structural panel or particleboard with long dimension perpendicular to supporting rafters. Stagger panel end joints and support with blocking or framing members.			
2337.8	**Gable End Walls:** 24" (610 mm) maximum overhang unless designed for uplift.			
	Provide studs continuous between lateral supports perpendicular to wall.			
2337.9	**Roof Covering:** Fasten asphalt strip shingles with at least 6 fasteners and hand seal in area of 90 mph (145 km/h) basic wind speed.			
2337.10	**Elevated Foundations - General:** May support 1 story maximum.			
	Material: Treated wood for all exposed wood framing members; corrosion-resistant metal connectors and fasteners in exposed locations.			
	Wood Pile Spacing: 8'-0" (2438 mm) on center maximum.			
	Square Wood Piles: 10" (254 mm) minimum.			
	Tapered Piles - Tip: 8" (203 mm) minimum.			
	Embedment - 10" (254 mm) Square Piles: 10'-0" (3048 mm) minimum with 8'-0" (2438 mm) maximum projection above undisturbed ground surface.			
	Embedment - Tapered Piles: 14'-0" (4267 mm) minimum with 7'-0" (2134 mm) maximum projection above undisturbed ground surface.			
	Girders: Solid sawn timbers, built-up 2" (51 mm) thick lumber, or trusses.			
	Locate splices over wood piles.			
	Span in direction parallel to potential flood water and wave action.			
	Connections: Wood piles may be notched to provide shelf for supporting floor girders.			
	Do not exceed 50% of pile cross section.			
	Provide connections with 1/4" (6.4 mm) thick corrosion-resistant steel plates and 3/4" (19.1 mm) bolts.			
	Connect each end of girder to piles with at least two 3/4" (19.1 mm) bolts.			

Part 5: Specification Requirements

Uniform Building Code Compliance Manual

1997 Uniform Building Code

Quality Requirements

CSI Section 01400

Code Ref.	Code Compliance Item	OK	NA	ID
704.6	**Spray-applied Fireproofing:** Determine density and thickness in accordance with UBC Standard 7-6.			
1701.3	**Duties and Responsibilities of Special Inspector:** Observe work specified for conformance with the Contract Documents approved by the governing code jurisdiction.			
	Furnish inspection reports to the building official, architect or engineer of record, and other designated persons.			
	Bring discrepancies to immediate attention of the Contractor for correction. Notify architect or engineer of record and building official if not corrected.			
	Submit final signed report stating whether work requiring special inspection was, to the best of the inspector's knowledge, in conformance with the Contract Documents approved by the governing code jurisdiction and the applicable workmanship provisions of the governing building code.			
1701.5	**Special Inspection - Concrete:** Inspect taking of test specimens and placing of reinforced concrete.			
	Exceptions: Special inspection not required for: Concrete foundations per UBC Table 18-I-C or for Group R-3 or U-1.			
	Foundation concrete, other than cast-in-place drilled piles or caissons, where structural design is based on 2,500 psi compressive strength maximum.			
	Nonstructural slabs on grade, including prestressed slabs on grade, where effective prestress is less than 150 psi (1.03 MPa).			
	Sitework concrete supported on earth and concrete where no special hazard exits.			
	Bolts installed in Concrete: Inspect prior to and during placement of concrete.			

Code Ref.	Code Compliance Item	OK	NA	ID
1701.5 1921.9	**Special Inspection - Special Moment-Resisting Concrete Frames in Seismic Zones 3 and 4:** Continuously inspect placement of reinforcement and concrete.			
	Reinforcing Steel and Prestressing Steel Tendons: Inspect during stressing and grouting of tendons in prestressed concrete.			
	Inspect during placing of reinforcing steel and prestressing tendons for all concrete requiring special inspection. (Consult with the structural engineer for exceptions to concrete inspection.)			
	Continuous inspection is not required if inspector has inspected for conformance prior to closing of forms or delivery of concrete.			
1701.5	**Special Inspection - Structural Welding:** Inspect during welding of members or connections designed to resist code required loads and forces.			
	Exceptions: Inspection not required for welding completed in fabrication shops meeting UBC Section 1701.7.			
	Continuous inspection not required during welding of following items if materials, qualifications of welding procedures, and welders are verified prior to start of work; periodic inspections are made of work in progress; and visual inspection of all welds is made prior to completion or shipment of shop- welded work:			
	Single pass fillet welds not exceeding 5/16" (7.9 mm).			
	Floor and roof deck welding.			
	Welded studs when used for structural diaphragm or composite systems.			
	Welded sheet steel for cold-formed steel framing such as studs and joists.			
	Welding of stairs and railing systems.			
	Welding of Special Moment-Resisting Steel Frames: Inspect during welding of steel frames; provide nondestructive testing.			
	Welding of Reinforcing Steel: Inspect during welding of reinforcing steel.			
	Exception: Continuous inspection not required during welding of ASTM A706 reinforcing steel not larger than No. 5 bars used for embedments, if materials, qualifications of welding procedures and welders are verified prior to start of work; periodic inspections are made of work in progress; and visual inspection of all welds is made prior to completion or prior to shipment of shop welding.			
1701.5	**Special Inspection - High-Strength Bolting:** Periodically inspect installation of high-strength A325 or A490 Bolts per nationally recognized standards.			
	While work is in progress, determine requirements for bolts, nuts, washers, and paint; bolted parts; and installation and tightening are met.			

Code Ref.	Code Compliance Item	OK	NA	ID
1701.5	**Special Inspection - High-Strength Bolting, Continued:** Observe calibration procedures when calibration is required by plans or specifications and monitor installation of bolts to determine that plies of connected materials have been drawn together and bolt tightening procedure is properly used.			
1701.5	**Special Inspection - Structural Masonry:** **Fully Grouted Open-end Hollow Unit Masonry:** Inspect during preparation and taking of required prisms or test specimens, at start of laying units, after placement of reinforcing, inspection of grout space prior to each grouting operation, and during grouting operations.			
	Other Masonry: Inspect during preparation and taking of required prisms or test specimens, after placement of reinforcing, inspection of grout space, immediately prior to closing of cleanouts, and during grouting operations.			
1701.5	**Special Inspection - Reinforced Gypsum Concrete:** Inspect during mixing and placement of cast-in-place Class B material.			
1701.5	**Special Inspection - Insulating Concrete Fill:** Inspect during placement when used as part of structural system.			
	Inspection may be limited to initial inspection to check deck surface, placement of reinforcing, and supervision of test specimen preparation.			
1701.5	**Special Inspection - Sprayed Applied Fire-Resistive Materials:** Inspect as required by UBC Standard 7-6.			
1701.5	**Special Inspections - Piling, Drilled Piers, and Caissons:** Inspect during driving of piles and construction of cast-in-place drilled piles or caissons.			
1701.5	**Special Inspections - Shotcrete:** Inspect during taking of specimens and placement of shotcrete.			
	Visual Examination of In-Place Shotcrete: Check for reinforcing bar embedment, voids, rock pockets, sand streaks and similar deficiencies by taking at least three 3" (76 mm) cores from 3 areas chosen by the design professional which represents the worst congestion of reinforcing bars occurring on the project.			
1701.5	**Special Inspection - Special Grading, Excavation and Filling:** Inspect during earth-work excavations grading and filling operations.			
1701.5	**Special Inspection - Smoke Control Systems:** Inspect during erection of ductwork and prior to concealment for purposes of leakage testing and recording device location.			
	Inspect prior to occupancy and after sufficient completion for purposes of pressure difference testing, flow measurements, and detection and control verification.			

Code Ref.	Code Compliance Item	OK	NA	ID
1703	**Nondestructive Testing in Seismic Zones 3 and 4:** Inspect welded, fully restrained connections between primary members of ordinary moment frames and special moment resisting frames by nondestructive testing per testing program established by structural engineer of record.			
	Complete Penetration Groove Welds: Test each complete penetration groove weld in joints and splices full length of weld by ultrasonic testing or by radiography.			
1703	**Complete Penetration Groove Welds, Continued:** **Exceptions:** Nondestructive testing rate for welds made by individual welder may be reduced to 25% of welds, with approval of structural engineer of record, provided weld inspection reject rate is 5% or less based on approved sampling.			
	Nondestructive testing not required for complete penetration groove welds less than 5/16" (7.9 mm) thick, provide continuous inspection.			
	Nondestructive testing may be performed in approved fabrication shop utilizing qualified test techniques in employment of fabricator when required by plans and specifications.			
	Column Splice Welds: Test partial penetration groove welds by ultrasonic testing or radiography when required by plans and specifications; continuous inspection required.			
	Nondestructive testing not required where effective throat is less than 3/4" (19.1 mm).			
	Base Metal Testing: Test base metals thicker than 1-1/2" (38 mm) when subjected to through-thickness weld shrinkage strains by ultrasonic testing for discontinuities behind welds after joint completion.			

Temporary Facilities and Controls

CSI Section 01500

Code Ref.	Code Compliance Item	OK	NA	ID
3303.1	**General:** Do not use or occupy streets, alleys, or public sidewalks for performance of work.			
	Do not perform work adjacent to a public way in general use by the public unless pedestrian protection has been provided.			
	Adequately light all materials or structures temporarily occupying public property, including fences and ways, between sunset and sunrise.			
3303.2	**Temporary Use of Streets or Alleys:** Comply with requirements of public agency having jurisdiction.			
3303.3	**Storage on Public Property:** Do not place or store material or equipment so as to obstruct free and convenient approach to and use of fire hydrants, fire or police alarm boxes, utility boxes catch basins, or manholes.			
	Do not obstruct free water flow in street or alley gutters.			
3303.5	**Protection of Utilities:** Protect street lamps, utility boxes, fire or police alarm boxes, fire hydrants, catch basins, and manholes from damage and maintain protection for the duration of the contract. Do not obstruct the normal functioning of such devices.			
3303.6	**Walkways:** Maintain walkways of 48" (1219 mm) minimum width on sidewalks unless governing jurisdiction allows sidewalk to be fenced and closed.			
	Provide signs and railings to protect pedestrians.			
	Provide walkways with durable wearing surface and capable of supporting 150 psf (7.18 kN/m^2).			
3306.7.1 3303.7.2	**Railings for Pedestrian Protection:** Provide railings when walkways are adjacent to excavations and adjacent to the street side when walkways extend into roadways. Use materials and construction required by the building code.			
	Provide protection per UBC Table 33-A.			

Code Ref.	Code Compliance Item	OK	NA	ID
3303.7.3	**Fences for Pedestrian Protection:** 8'-0" (2438 mm) minimum height above grade, placed on edge of walk nearest building site. Extend along entire length of building and return each end to building line. Use materials and construction required by the building code.			
	Protect openings in fences by doors, normally kept closed.			
3303.7.4	**Canopies for Pedestrian Protection:** 8'-0" clear height above walkway, with solid fence along entire length on construction side using materials allowed by the building code.			
3303.8	**Maintenance and Removal of Pedestrian Protective Devices:** Maintain protection for duration of activities endangering pedestrians.			
	Remove such protection within 30 days after protection is no longer needed.			
	Do not begin demolition of any building until pedestrian protection structures are completed.			

Earthwork

CSI Section 02300

Code Ref.	Code Compliance Item	OK	NA	ID
1828.1	**Placement of Backfill Against Waterproofing or Dampproofing:** Place in lifts and compact in a manner which will not damage waterproofing or dampproofing materials.			
	Use fill material free of organic materials, construction debris, and large rocks.			
1828.2	**Grading at Foundations:** Slope finish grade away from foundations a minimum of 1:12 (8.3%).			
	Allow for settlement of final ground level adjacent to foundations due to settlement of backfill when constructing finish grades.			
3301.2	**Protection of Adjoining Property:** Follow prevailing laws.			
	At a minimum: Protect excavations 12'-0" (3658 mm) or less such that soils of adjacent properties will not cave in or settle.			
	Notify adjacent property owners at least 10 days prior to commencing excavations.			
	Provide access to excavations to owners of adjoining properties for the purpose of protecting adjoining buildings.			
3302	**Preparation of Building Site:** Remove stumps and roots from soil to a depth of 12" (305 mm) in building area.			

Piles

CSI Section 02460

Code Ref.	Code Compliance Item	OK	NA	ID
1807.8	**Jetting:** Forbidden except by written approval of the building official.			
	When used, do not impair structural capacity of existing piles and structures. After withdrawal of jet, drive piles until required resistance is obtained.			
1808.1	**Round Wood Piles:** Provide pressure-treated materials except when cutoff will be below lowest groundwater level assumed to exist during life of structure.			
1808.2	**Uncased Cast-in-Place Concrete Piles:** Use installation methods which will exclude foreign material during placement and provide full size shaft.			
	Minimum Compressive Strength: 2,500 psi (17.24 MPa).			
1808.3	**Metal-Cased Concrete Piles:** 2,500 psi (17.24 MPa) minimum compressive strength.			
	Installation: Provide sealed metal tip, 8" (203 mm) minimum diameter.			
	Drive shells full length in contact with surrounding soil and leave in place.			
	Provide shells of sufficient strength to resist collapse and sufficiently watertight to exclude water and foreign matter during concrete placement.			
	Drive piles in such order and spacing to prevent distortion or injury to previously placed piles.			
	Do not drive piles closer than 4-1/2 average pile diameters to piles with concrete placed less than 24 hours previously.			
1808.4	**Precast Concrete Piles:** 3,000 psi (20.68 MPa) prior to driving.			
	Design: Resist stresses induced by shipping and handling in addition to loads.			
1808.5	**Precast Prestressed Concrete Piles:** 5,000 psi (34.48 MPa) minimum compressive strength, 4,000 psi (27.58 MPa) minimum compressive strength prior to driving.			
	Design: Resist stresses induced by shipping and handling in addition to loads.			

Code Ref.	Code Compliance Item	OK	NA	ID
1808.6	**Structural Steel Pile Materials:** Conform to UBC Standard 22-1.			
	Identification of Structural Steel: Refer to Section 05120.			
1808.7	**Concrete-Filled Steel Pipe Pile Materials:** Conform to UBC Standard 22-1.			
	Minimum Concrete Compressive Strength: 2,500 psi (17.24 MPa).			
	Identification of Structural Steel: Refer to Section 05120.			

Concrete Forms and Accessories

CSI Section 03100

Code Ref.	Code Compliance Item	OK	NA	ID
1906.1	**Design of Formwork:** Provide final structure conforming to shapes, lines, and dimensions of members as indicated on the drawings.			
	Construct substantial and sufficiently tight to prevent leakage.			
	Brace or tie together to maintain position and shape.			
	Design and construct so as to not damage previously placed structure.			
	Design in consideration of rate and method of placing concrete, construction loads, and special construction.			
1906.1.6	**Prestressed Member Forms:** Design to prevent movement of member without damage during application of prestressing force.			
1906.2.1	**Removal of Forms and Shores:** Do not impair safety and serviceability of the structure.			
	Contractor shall develop procedure and schedule for removal of forms and installation of reshores per UBC Section 1906.2.1.			
	Do not support construction loads on any unshored portion of structure when such loads exceed combination of dead loads and design live loads.			
1906.2.4	**Prestressed Concrete Form Supports:** Apply sufficient prestressing force to enable members to carry their dead load and anticipated construction loads prior to form removal.			
1906.4.1	**Construction Joints:** Clean and remove laitance from surfaces.			
	Wet prior to concrete placement and remove standing water.			
	Locate joints so as not to impair strength of structure.			

Code Ref.	Code Compliance Item	OK	NA	ID
1906.4.1	**Construction Joints:** Locate joints in floors in middle third of spans of slabs, beams and girders. Offset joints in girders a minimum of 2 times width of intersecting beams.			
	Do not cast or erect beams or girders supported by columns or walls until concrete in vertical support members is no longer plastic.			
	Place beams, girders, haunches, drop panels, or capitals monolithically as part of slab system unless indicated otherwise on the drawings.			
3302	Remove all wood forms used in placing concrete, if within ground or between foundation sills and ground.			

Concrete Reinforcement

CSI Section 03200

Code Ref.	Code Compliance Item	OK	NA	ID
1903.5.1	**Metal Reinforcement:** Deformed type except plain may be used for spirals or tendons.			
	Welded Reinforcement: Submit report of material properties indicating conformance with welding procedures of UBC Standard 19-2.			
1903.5.3 1903.5.4 1903.5.5	**Standards of Quality - Metal Reinforcement:** UBC Standard 19-2, Welding Reinforcing Steel, Metal Inserts, and Connections in Reinforced Concrete Construction.			
	ASTM A615, A616, A617, A706, A767, and A775, Reinforcing Bars for Concrete.			
	ASTM A184, Fabricated Deformed Steel Bar Mats.			
	ASTM A496, Steel Wire, Deformed, for Concrete Reinforcement.			
	ASTM A185, Steel Welded Wire, Fabric, Plain for Concrete Reinforcement.			
	ASTM A497, Welded Deformed Steel Wire Fabric for Concrete Reinforcement.			
	ASTM A416, Uncoated Seven-wire Stress-relieved Steel Strand for Prestressed Concrete.			
	ASTM A421, Uncoated Stress-relieved Wire for Prestressed Concrete.			
	ASTM A722, Uncoated High-strength Steel Bar for Prestressing Concrete.			
1903.5.6	**Standards of Quality - Structural Steel, Steel Pipe, or Tubing:** ASTM A36, A242, A572, and A588 for structural steel in composite compression members.			
	ASTM A53, A500, and A501 for steel pipe or tubing for composite compression members composed of a steel-encased concrete core.			

Code Ref.	Code Compliance Item	OK	NA	ID
1903.10	**Welding of Reinforcing Steel:** Comply with UBC Standard 19-1.			
1907.2	**Minimum Bend Diameters:** Comply with UBC Table 19-B.			
1907.3	**Fabrication:** Bend all reinforcing cold.			
	Do not field bend reinforcing unless so indicated on the drawings or permitted by the building official.			
1907.4	**Surface Condition:** Free from mud, oil, or nonmetallic coatings that decrease bond at time of placement.			
	Rust and Mill Scale: Acceptable provided minimum dimensions of hand-wire-brushed specimen are not less than specified requirements.			
	Prestressing Tendons: Clean and free from oil, dirt, scale, pitting, and excessive rust; light oxide is permissible.			
1907.5	**Placement:** Place accurately as indicated on the drawings.			
	Adequately support prior to concrete placement and secure against displacement.			
	Prestressed Tendons Placements: Place within tolerances specified in UBC Section 1907.5.2.			
1907.10.4.9	**Spiral Reinforcing Placement:** Hold firmly in place and true to line.			

Cast-in-Place Concrete

CSI Section 03300

Code Ref.	Code Compliance Item	OK	NA	ID
1903.2	**Standards of Quality - Cement:** ASTM C845, Expansive Hydraulic Cement. ASTM C150, Portland Cement. ASTM C595 or C1157, Blended Hydraulic Cements.			
1903.3	**Standards of Quality - Aggregates:** ASTM C33, Concrete Aggregates. ASTM C330, Lightweight Aggregates for Structural Concrete. ASTM C332, Lightweight Aggregates for Insulating Concrete.			
1903.3.2	**Maximum Aggregate Size:** 1/5 narrowest dimension of between sides and forms, 1/3 depth of slabs, 3/4 of minimum clear spacing between individual reinforcing bars or wires, bundles of bars, or prestressing tendons or ducts.			
1903.4	**Mixing Water:** Clean and free from injurious amounts of oils, acids, alkalis, salts, organic materials, or other deleterious substances.			
	Mixing Water for Prestressed Concrete: Free from deleterious amounts of chloride ions.			

Code Ref.	Code Compliance Item	OK	NA	ID
1903.6	**Standards of Quality - Admixtures:** ASTM C989, Ground-iron Blast-furnace Slag for Use in Concrete and Mortars. ASTM C260, Air-entraining Admixtures for Concrete. ASTM C494 and C1017, Chemical Admixtures for Concrete. ASTM C618, Fly Ash and Raw and Calcined Natural Pozzolans for Use as Admixtures in Portland Cement Concrete. ASTM C1240, Silica Fume for Use in Hydraulic Cement Concrete and Mortar.			
1903.6	**Admixtures:** Do not use calcium chloride or admixtures containing calcium chloride in prestressed concrete, in concrete containing embedded aluminum, or in concrete cast against stay-in-place galvanized steel forms.			
	Admixtures used in concrete containing ASTM C845 expansive cements shall be compatible with cement and produce no deleterious effects.			
1903.7	**Material Storage:** Store materials and aggregates to prevent deterioration or intrusion of foreign matter. Do not use contaminated or deteriorated materials for concrete.			
1903.8	**Standards of Quality - Concrete Testing:** ASTM C192, Making and Curing Concrete Test Specimens in the Laboratory. ASTM C31, Making and Curing Concrete Test Specimens in the Field. ASTM C42, Obtaining and Testing Drilled Cores and Sawed Beams of Concrete. ASTM C39, Compressive Strength of Cylindrical Concrete Specimens. ASTM C172, Sampling Freshly Mixed Concrete. ASTM C496, Splitting Tensile Strength of Cylindrical Concrete Specimens. ASTM C1218, Water Soluble Chloride in Mortar and Concrete.			
1903.9	**Standards of Quality - Concrete Mix:** ASTM C94, Ready-mixed Concrete. ASTM C685, Concrete Made for Volumetric Batching and Continuous Mixing. UBC Standard 19-2, Mill-mixed Gypsum Concrete and Poured Gypsum Roof Diaphragms. ASTM C109, Compressive Strength of Hydraulic Cement Mortars. ASTM C567, Unit Weight Structural Lightweight Concrete.			

Code Ref.	Code Compliance Item	OK	NA	ID
1904.1	**Water-Cement Ratio:** Calculate ratio using weight of cement meeting ASTM C150, C595, or C845 plus weight of fly ash or other pozzolans meeting ASTM C618, slag meeting ASTM C989, and silica fume meeting ASTM C1240.			
	When concrete is exposed to deicing chemicals, limit amounts of fly ash, pozzolans, silica fume, slag, or combination of such materials per UBC Table 19-A-4.			
1904.2	**Durability - Freezing and Thawing Exposures:** Specify air entrainment, water-cement ratio, minimum concrete compressive strength, cement type, maximum weight of fly ash and other pozzolans and slag in accordance with UBC Tables 19-A-1, 19-A-2, and 19-A-4.			
1904.3	**Durability - Sulfate Exposure:** Specify cement type, water-cement ratio, and minimum concrete compressive strength in accordance with UBC Table 19-A-3.			
	Calcium Chloride: Do not use in concrete exposed to severed or very-severe sulfate containing solutions.			
1904.4	**Durability - Corrosion Protection of Reinforcement:** Comply with UBC Table 19-A-5 for maximum water-soluble chloride ion concentrations in hardened concrete 28-48 days old.			
	Comply with UBC Table 19-A-2 for concrete exposed to deicing salts, brackish water, seawater, or spray from these sources.			
1905.2.1	**Selection of Concrete Proportions:** Proportion materials to provide for workability under conditions of placement without segregation or excessive bleeding, resistance to freeze/thaw, sulfate, and corrosion of reinforcement, and conformance to strength test requirements.			
	Select and evaluate proportions for each condition or element of work.			
1905.3	**Proportioning on the Basis of Field Experience and Trial Mixtures:** Submit proposed proportions based on field experience or trial mixtures in accordance with the requirements of UBC Section 1905.3, except as permitted by UBC Section 1905.4, or except as required for durability in accordance with UBC Section 1904.			
1905.6.1	**Evaluation and Acceptance of Concrete - Frequency of Testing:** Sample each class of concrete for strength tests not less than once a day, or not less than once for each 150 cy (115 m^3), or not less than once for each 5,000 sf (465 m^2) of surface area for slabs or walls.			
	When frequency of testing will provide less than 5 strength tests for a given class of concrete, conduct testing from at least 5 randomly selected batches or from each batch if fewer than 5 are used.			
1905.6.1.4	**Strength Test:** The average of 2 cylinders made from the same sample of concrete, tested at 28 days or at test age designated for determination of compressive strength.			

Code Ref.	Code Compliance Item	OK	NA	ID
1905.6.2	**Laboratory-Cured Specimens:** Laboratory-cure and test cylinders for strength tests.			
	Test Results: Consider satisfactory when average of all sets of 3 consecutive strength tests equal or exceed design compressive strength and when no individual strength test (average of 2 cylinders) falls below design compressive strength by more than 500 psi (3.45 MPa).			
1905.6.4	**Investigations of Low-Strength Test Results:** When strength tests fall below design compressive strength, investigate the concrete in question in accordance with UBC Section 1905.6.4.			
1905.7	**Preparation of Equipment and Place of Deposit:** Clean equipment for mixing and transporting concrete.			
	Remove debris and ice from spaces to be occupied by concrete.			
	Properly coat forms.			
	Drench masonry filler units in contact with concrete.			
	Clean reinforcement of ice or other deleterious materials.			
	Remove water from place of deposit prior to placement.			
	Remove laitance and unsound material prior to placement against hardened concrete.			
1905.8.1	**Mixing:** Provide uniform distribution of materials by mixing.			
1905.8.2	**Ready-Mix Concrete:** Mix and deliver in accordance with ASTM C94 or C685.			
1905.8.3	**Job-Mixed Concrete:** Comply with UBC Section 1905.8.3.			
1905.9	**Conveying:** Convey concrete to place of deposit by methods that will prevent separation or loss of materials.			
	Provide supply of concrete without interruptions sufficient to permit loss of plasticity between successive pours.			
1905.10	**Depositing:** Deposit concrete as near as practicable to its final position to avoid segregation.			
	Carry on concreting at a rate such that concrete is plastic and flows readily into spaces between reinforcement.			
	Do not deposit hardened or contaminated concrete into structure.			
	Do not use retempered concrete.			
	Carry on concreting in a continuous operation until placing of panel defined by boundaries or joints is completed.			
	Provide generally level surfaces on tops of vertically formed lifts.			
	Consolidate and thoroughly work concrete around reinforcement and embedded fixtures and into corners of forms.			

Code Ref.	Code Compliance Item	OK	NA	ID
1905.11.1	**Curing Normal Concrete:** Maintain concrete above 50°F (10.0°C) after placement and in a moist condition for at least 7 days, except when using accelerated curing.			
1905.11.2	**Curing High-Early-Strength Concrete:** Maintain concrete above 50°F (10.0°C) after placement and in a moist condition for at least 3 days, except when using accelerated curing.			
1905.11.3	**Accelerated Curing:** High-pressure steam, steam at atmospheric pressure, heat and moisture, or other accepted practices may be used to accelerate strength gain and reduce curing time.			
	Provide compressive strength at load stage equal to design strength.			
	Produce durability equivalent to normal curing methods.			
1905.12	**Cold Weather Requirements:** Heat concrete materials and protect placed concrete during freezing or near-freezing weather.			
	Concrete materials, reinforcement, forms, fillers, and ground surfaces shall be free from frost.			
	Do not use frozen materials or materials containing ice.			
1905.13	**Hot Weather Requirements:** Prevent excessive concrete temperatures or water evaporation by controlling ingredients, production methods, handling, placing, protection, and curing.			

Specially Placed Concrete

CSI Section 03370

Code Ref.	Code Compliance Item	OK	NA	ID
1924.2	**Proportions and Materials:** Select and proportion materials for placement using the selected delivery equipment and for finished hardened shotcrete complying with the building code.			
1924.3	**Coarse Aggregate:** Do not exceed 3/4" (19.1 mm) where used.			
1924.5	**Preconstruction Tests:** When required by the building official, provide a test panel representative of the project and simulate job conditions as closely as possible.			
	Reproduce the thickest and most congested area designed.			
	Shoot at same angle, using same nozzleman, using same equipment, and with same concrete mix design that will be used on the project.			
1924.6	**Rebound:** Remove rebound or loose aggregate from surface prior to placement of next layer of shotcrete. Do not reuse as aggregate.			
1924.7	**Joints:** Do not allow unfinished work to stand for more than 30 minutes unless all edges are sloped to a thin edge.			
	Clean and wet edges of previously applied shotcrete prior to placement of adjacent shotcrete.			
1924.8	**Damage:** Remove and replace shotcrete exhibiting sags, sloughs, segregation, honeycombing, sand pockets and other defects.			
1924.9	**Curing:** Maintain placed material above 40°F (4.4°C).			
	Initial Curing: Keep continuously moist for 24 hours after placement.			
	Final Curing: Fog spray or moisture-retaining cover for 7 days; 3 days for high-early strength, or until design strength is obtained.			
	Keep sections deeper than 12" (305 mm) moist for 7 days.			

Code Ref.	Code Compliance Item	OK	NA	ID
1924.10	**Strength Test Specimens:** When maximum size aggregate is larger than 3/8" (9.5 mm), provide three 3" (76 mm) diameter cores or 3" (76 mm) cubes.			
	When maximum size aggregate is 3/8" (9.5 mm) or less provide three 2" (51 mm) diameter cores or 2" (51 mm) cubes.			
	Water soak cylinders for 24 hours prior to testing.			
	Specimen Sampling: From in-place work, take 3 tests at least once each shift or take 3 tests for each 50 cy (38.2 m^2) of shotcrete.			
	Test Results: The average of 3 cores from a single panel shall equal or exceed 0.85 design compressive strength with no single core less than 0.75.			
1924.11.2	**Visual Examination for structural Soundness of In-Place Shotcrete:** Check for reinforcing bar embedment, voids, rock pockets, sand streaks and similar deficiencies by taking at least three 3" (76 mm) cores from 3 areas chosen by the design professional which represents the worst congestion of reinforcing bars occurring on the project.			

Post-Tensioned Concrete

CSI Section 03385

Code Ref.	Code Compliance Item	OK	NA	ID
1918.15	**Post-Tensioning Ducts - Grouted or Unbonded Tendons:** Mortar-tight, nonreactive with concrete, tendons, or filler materials.			
	Single Wire, Strand, or Bar Tendons: Provide minimum inside diameter of 1/4" (6.4 mm) larger than tendon diameter.			
	Grouted Multiple Wire, Strand, or Bar Tendons: Provide inside cross-sectional area at least 2 times area of tendons.			
	Maintain ducts free of water when grouted members are exposed to freezing temperatures prior to grouting.			
1918.16.2	**Grout:** Portland cement and water, or portland cement, sand, and water.			
	Portland Cement: Comply with UBC Standard 19-1			
	Water: Clean and free from injurious amounts of oils, acids, alkalis, salts, organic materials, or other deleterious substances. Free from deleterious amounts of chloride ions.			
	Sand: Modify gradation of sand for satisfactory workability.			
	Admixtures: Use only materials known to have no injurious effects on grout, steel, or concrete; do not use calcium chloride.			
1918.16.3	**Selection of Grout Proportions:** Base on results of tests of fresh hardened grout prior to grouting operations, or on prior documented experience with similar materials and equipment under similar field conditions.			
	Water-Cement Ratio: 0.45 maximum; do not add water to increase flowability due to delayed use of grout.			

Code Ref.	Code Compliance Item	OK	NA	ID
1918.16.4	**Mixing and Pumping Grout:** Use equipment providing continuous mechanical mixing and agitation for uniform distribution of materials; pass through screens and pump to completely fill tendon ducts.			
	Temperature of Members at Time of Grouting: Maintain above 35°F (1.7°C) until field cured 2" (51 mm) cubes of grout reach 800 lbs (5.52 MPa) minimum compressive strength.			
	Grout Temperature: Not above 90°F (32.2°C) during mixing and pumping.			
1918.19	**Post-Tensioning Anchorages and Couplers - Bonded and Unbonded Tendons:** Develop at least 95% of specified breaking strength of tendons, when tested in unbonded condition, without exceeding anticipated set.			
	Bonded Tendons: Locate anchorages and couplers so 100% of specified breaking strength is developed at critical sections after tendons are bonded in member.			
	Enclose couplers in housing long enough to permit necessary movements.			
	Unbonded Construction: Provide for fatigue in anchorages and couplers in subject to repetitive loads.			

Precast Concrete

CSI Section 03400

Code Ref.	Code Compliance Item	OK	NA	ID
1916.2	**Design:** Consider all loading and constraint conditions including form removal, storage, transportation, and erection.			
1916.2.4	**Shop Drawings:** Provide details of reinforcement, connections, bearing seats, inserts, anchors, concrete cover, openings, lifting devices, and fabrication and erection tolerances.			
1916.7	**Items Embedded after Concrete Placement:** Do not stab cast dowels, inserts, and other embedded items into plastic concrete unless approved in writing by the structural engineer and meeting the requirements of UBC Section 1916.7.			
1916.8	**Identification and Marking:** Mark each member to indicate location and orientation in structure, and date of fabrication.			
	Correspond identification marks to placing drawings.			
1916.9	**Handling:** Do not overstress, warp, damage, or affect camber during curing, form removal, transportation, or erection.			
	Brace and support members during erection to ensure proper alignment and structural integrity until permanent connections are complete.			
1918.14	**Prestressed Concrete - Corrosion Protection for Unbonded Prestressing Tendons:** Completely coat with material ensuring corrosion protection.			
	Provide tendon cover continuous over unbonded length; prevent intrusion of cement paste or loss of coating during concrete placement.			
1918.16.2	**Grout for Bonded Prestressing Tendons:** Portland cement and water, or portland cement, sand, and water.			
	Portland Cement: UBC Standard 19-1.			
	Water: Clean and free from injurious amounts of oils, acids, alkalis, salts, organic materials, or other deleterious substances. Free from deleterious amounts of chloride ions.			
	Sand: Modify gradation of sand for satisfactory workability.			
	Admixtures: Use only materials known to have no injurious effects on grout, steel, or concrete; do not use calcium chloride.			

Code Ref.	Code Compliance Item	OK	NA	ID
1918.16.3	**Selection of Grout Proportions:** Base on results of tests of fresh hardened grout prior to grouting operations, or on prior documented experience with similar materials and equipment under similar field conditions.			
	Water-Cement Ratio: 0.45 maximum; do not add water to increase flowability due to delayed use of grout.			
1918.16.4	**Mixing and Pumping Grout:** Use equipment providing continuous mechanical mixing and agitation for uniform distribution of materials; pass through screens and pump to completely fill tendon ducts.			
	Temperature of Members at Time of Grouting: Maintain above 35°F (1.7°C) until field cured 2" (51 mm) cubes of grout reach 800 lbs (5.52 MPa) minimum compressive strength.			
	Grout Temperature: Not above 90°F (32.2°C) during mixing and pumping.			
1918.17	**Protection for Prestressing Tendons:** Protect tendons from excessive welding temperatures, welding sparks, or ground currents.			
1918.18	**Application and Measurement of Prestressing Force:** Measure by both following methods:			
	Measure tendon elongation; determine elongation from average load-elongation curves for prestressing tendons used.			
	Observe jacking force on calibrated gauge or load cell or use calibrated dynamometer.			
	When force determination of between measurement methods exceeds 5% for pretensioned elements or 7% for post-tensioned elements, ascertain cause and correct.			
	Predetermine cutting points and cutting sequence when force transfer from bulkheads to concrete is by flame cutting prestressing tendons.			
	Cut long lengths of exposed pretensioned strand near member to minimize shock.			
	Total Loss of Prestress: 2% maximum due to unreplaced broken tendons.			

Gypsum Concrete Roof Deck

CSI Section 03510

Code Ref.	Code Compliance Item	OK	NA	ID
1925.1	**General:** UBC Standard 19-2.			
	Minimum Ultimate Compressive Strength: UBC Table 19-E.			
	Specimen Sampling: Cylinders 2" (51 mm) diameter, 4" (102 mm) long, or 2" (51 mm) cubes.			

Lightweight Concrete Roof Insulation

CSI Section 03520

Code Ref.	Code Compliance Item	OK	NA	ID
703.4	**Standards of Quality:** The following standards are part of the code: UBC Standard 7-1, Fire Tests of Building Construction and Materials. ASTM C330 and C332, Lightweight Aggregates for Insulating Concrete.			

Masonry Mortar

CSI Section 04060

Code Ref.	Code Compliance Item	OK	NA	ID
2102.2	**Standards of Quality:** ASTM C144, Aggregates for Masonry Mortar. UBC Standard 21-11, Masonry Cement (Plastic cement conforming to UBC Standard 25-1 may be used in lieu of masonry cement when it also conforms to UBC Standard 21-11). ASTM C150, Portland Cement. UBC Standard 21-14, Mortar Cement. UBC Standard 21-12, Quick Lime for Structural Purposes. UBC Standard 21-13, Hydrated Lime for Masonry Purposes. When Types N and NA hydrated lime are used in masonry mortar, they shall comply with the provisions of UBC Standard 21-15, Section 21.1506.7, excluding the plasticity requirement. UBC Standard 21-15, Mortar for Unit Masonry. UBC Standard 21-16, Field Test Specimens for Mortar. UBC Standard 21-20, Standard Test Method for Flexural Bond Strength of Mortar Cement.			
2103.2	**Cementitious Materials for Mortar:** Lime, masonry cement, portland cement, or mortar cement.			
	Epoxy resins and derivatives, phenols, asbestos fibers, or fireclays are not permitted in cementitious materials or additives.			
	Water: Clean and free of deleterious amounts of acid, alkalies, organic materials, or harmful substances.			
2103.3.2	**Mortar Mix Proportions:** UBC Table 21-A; adjust water content to provide workability under field conditions.			

Code Ref.	Code Compliance Item	OK	NA	ID
2103.5.2	**Antifreeze Compounds:** Do not use antifreeze liquids, chloride salts, or similar substances.			
2103.5.3	**Air Entraining Substances:** Do not use unless tested to determine compliance with requirements of the UBC.			
2103.5.4	**Colors:** Use only pure mineral oxide, carbon black, or synthetic colors.			
	Limit carbon black to maximum of 3% of cement weight.			
2105.4	**Mortar Testing:** UBC Standard 21-16.			
2106.1.12.4	**Special Provisions - Seismic Zones 3 & 4:** Do not use Type N mortar in vertical or lateral load resisting systems.			
2109.6.5	**Foundation Walls:** Type M or S mortar.			

Masonry Grout

CSI Section 04070

Code Ref.	Code Compliance Item	OK	NA	ID
2102.2	**Standards of Quality:** ASTM C404, Aggregates for Grout. ASTM C150, Portland Cement. UBC Standard 21-18, Method of Sampling and Testing Grout. UBC Standard 21-19, Grout for Masonry.			
2103.2	**Cementitious Materials for Grout:** Lime or portland cement.			
	Water: Clean and free of deleterious amounts of acid, alkalies, organic materials, or harmful substances.			
2103.4.1	**Grout - Minimum Compressive Strength:** 2,000 psi (14.0 Mpa) at 28 days.			
2103.4.2	**Grout Mix Proportions:** Provide mix with water content allowing flow under field conditions without segregation.			
	Submit mix proportions based on one of the following methods: Proportions required by UBC Table 21-B by grout type.			
	Proportions of ingredients and additives, in terms of parts by volume, based on laboratory or field experience with ingredients and masonry units proposed for use.			
	Minimum compressive strength providing the required prism strength.			
2103.5.2	**Antifreeze Compounds:** Do not use antifreeze liquids, chloride salts, or similar substances.			
2103.5.3	**Air Entraining Substances:** Do not use unless tested to determine compliance with requirements of the UBC.			
2105.5	**Grout Testing:** UBC Standard 21-18.			

Glass Masonry Units

CSI Section 04270

Code Ref.	Code Compliance Item	OK	NA	ID
2110.1	**Glass Masonry:** Glass block may be solid or hollow and may contain inserts.			
	Provide treatment for mortar bonding on mortared surfaces.			
2110.2	**Mortar Type:** Type S or N.			
	Mortar Joint Thickness: 1/4" (6.4 mm) minimum, 3/8" (9.5 mm) maximum.			
	Completely fill joints.			
2110.4	**Joint Reinforcement:** UBC Standard 21-10, Part I; hot-dipped galvanized for exterior walls.			
	Provide at 16" (406 mm) on center maximum, full length of wall panel.			
	Lap longitudinal wires 6" (152 mm) minimum.			
	Place in bed joints immediately above and below openings.			
2110.6	**Expansion Joints:** Keep free of mortar.			

Masonry Assemblies

CSI Section 04800

Code Ref.	Code Compliance Item	OK	NA	ID
2102.2	**Standards of Quality - Clay or Shale Masonry Units:** ASTM C34, Structural Clay Load-bearing Wall Tile. ASTM C56, Structural Clay Nonload-bearing Tile. UBC Standard 21-1, Section 21.101, Building Brick (solid units). ASTM C126, Ceramic Glazed Structural Clay Facing Tile, Facing Brick and Solid Masonry Units (Load bearing glazed brick shall comply with weathering and structural requirements of UBC Standard 21-1, Section 21.106, Facing Brick). UBC Standard 21-1, Section 21.106, Facing Brick (solid units). UBC Standard 21-1, Section 21.107, Hollow Brick. ASTM C67, Sampling and Testing Brick and Structural Clay Tile. ASTM C212, Structural Clay Facing Tile. ASTM C530, Structural Clay Non-Loadbearing Screen Tile.			
	Standards of Quality - Concrete Masonry Units: UBC Standard 21-3, Concrete Building Brick. UBC Standard 21-4, Hollow and Solid Load-bearing Concrete Masonry Units. UBC Standard 21-5, Nonload-bearing Concrete Masonry Units. ASTM C140, Sampling and Testing Concrete Masonry Units. ASTM C426, Standard Test Method for Drying Shrinkage of Concrete Block.			

Code Ref.	Code Compliance Item	OK	NA	ID
2102.2	**Standard of Quality - Masonry Units of Other Materials:** UBC Standard 21-2, Calcium Silicate Face Brick (sand-lime brick). UBC Standard 21-9, Unburned Clay Masonry Units. ACI-704, Cast Stone. UBC Standard, 21-17, Test Method for Compressive Strength of Masonry Prisms.			
	Standards of Quality - Reinforcement: UBC Standard 21-10, Part I, Joint Reinforcing for Masonry. ASTM A615, A616, A706, A767, A775, Deformed and Plain Billet-steel Bars, Rail-steel Deformed and Plain Bars, Axle-steel Deformed and Plain Bars, and Deformed Low-alloy Bars for Concrete Reinforcement. UBC Standard 21-10, Part II, Cold-drawn Steel Wire for Concrete Reinforcement.			
	Masonry Materials: Specify type, grade, and minimum compressive strength to meet project conditions; refer to UBC standards.			
2101.2.7	**Wall Ties and Anchors:** Conform to UBC Standard 21-10, Part II, for steel wire. Conform to UBC Standard 22-1, A36, for other anchors and ties.			
	Provide 30,000 psi (207 Mpa) minimum tensile yield for nonferrous ties and anchors.			
	Provide corrosion-resistant or coated materials for anchors and ties not fully embedded in mortar or grout.			
2104.2	**Materials Handling, Storage, and Preparation:** Keep materials clean and structurally suitable for use.			
	Provide materials free from loose rust and coatings which inhibit bond.			
	Prevent deterioration or intrusion of foreign materials.			
	Provide method of controlling measurement of mortar and grout materials.			
	Mix mortar or grout not less than 3 minutes and not more than 10 minutes in mechanical mixer with water content to provide desired workability. Hand mixing of small amounts of mortar is permitted.			
	Mortar may be retempered. Do not use mortar or grout which has hardened or stiffened due to hydration. Do not use mortar 2-1/2 hours, or grout 1-1/2 hours after initial mixing water has been added.			
2104.2	**Water Absorption Rate - Burned Clay or Sand Lime Units:** Do not exceed 0.035 osi (1.6 L/m²) at time of laying.			
	Do not wet concrete masonry units unless approved.			

Code Ref.	Code Compliance Item	OK	NA	ID
2104.3.1	**Cold Weather Construction - General:** Store materials to prevent wetting by capillary action, rain, and snow.			
	Cover tops of walls not enclosed or sheltered with weather-resistive material at end of each day or shutdown.			
	Cover partially completed walls at all times when work is not in progress. Drape cover over wall and down 2'-0" (610 mm) minimum each side; hold securely in place.			
2104.3.2	**Cold Weather Construction - Preparation:** Thaw ice or snow on masonry beds by application of heat until dry to touch.			
	Remove portions of masonry damaged by freezing prior to continuing work.			
2104.3.3	**Cold Weather Construction:** Do not lay wet or frozen units.			
	Heat sand and mixing water to produce mortar temperatures between 40°F and 120°F (4.5°C and 49°C). Maintain temperatures of mortar on boards above freezing.			
	Provide heat sources on both sides of walls under construction when air temperature is 25°F to 20°F (-4°C to -7°C). Use windbreaks when winds exceed 15 mph (24 km/h).			
	When air temperature is 20°F (-7°C) or below, enclose construction and maintain air temperature above freezing. Minimum temperature of units: 20°F (-7°C).			
2104.3.4	**Cold Weather Construction - Protection:** Provide protection for the following mean daily temperatures:			
	40°F to 32°F (4.5°C to 0°C): Protect from rain and snow with weather-resistive membrane for 24 hours.			
	32°F to 25°F (0°C to -4°C): Completely cover with weather-resistive membrane for 24 hours.			
	25°F to 20°F (-4°c to -7°C): Completely cover with insulating blankets for 24 hours.			
	20°F (-7°C) and below: Maintain masonry temperature above freezing for 24 hours by enclosure and supplementary heat.			
2104.3.5	**Cold Weather Construction - Placing Grout and Protection of Grouted Masonry:** Heat grout mixing water and aggregate to produce grout temperatures between 40°F and 120°F (4.5°C and 49°C) when air temperatures fall below 40°F (4.5°C).			
	Maintain grouted masonry above freezing during grout placement and for at least 24 hours after placement.			
	Enclose masonry during grout placement and for at least 24 hours after placement when temperatures fall below 20°F (-7°C).			

Code Ref.	Code Compliance Item	OK	NA	ID
2104.4.1	**Placing Masonry Units - Mortar:** Provide plastic mortar and place units with sufficient pressure to extrude mortar from joints and produce tight joints. Do not produce voids with deep furrows.			
	Initial Bed Joint Thickness: 1/4" (6.4 mm) minimum, 1" (25 mm) maximum.			
	Subsequent Bed Joint Thickness: 1/4" (6.4 mm) minimum, 5/8" (16 mm) maximum.			
2104.4.2	**Solid Masonry Units:** Provide full head and bed joints.			
2104.4.3	**Hollow Masonry Units:** Provide solid head and bed joints at least as thick as face shell.			
2104.5	**Reinforcement Placing:** Locate as indicated on the drawings.			
	Secure against displacement prior to grouting with wire positioners at 200 bar diameters maximum spacing.			
	Placement Tolerances in Walls and Flexural Members: d=8" (200 mm) or less: ± 1/2" (13 mm). d=24" (600 mm) or less but greater than 8" (200 mm): ± 1" (25 mm). d=greater than 24" (600 mm): ± 1-1/4" (32 mm).			
	Placement Tolerance in Longitudinal Location: ± 2" (51 mm).			
2104.6.1	**Grouted Masonry - General:** Construct to tie all elements of masonry together as a structural element.			
	Clean grout spaces of mortar projections over 1/2" (13 mm), mortar droppings and foreign material prior to grouting.			
	Place grout in spaces indicated on the drawings and confine grout to those spaces.			
	Fill all cells and spaces containing reinforcement with grout.			
	Control materials and water content to provide fluidity without segregation.			
	Complete grouting of any section of wall in 1 day without interruptions longer than 1 hour.			
	Horizontal Construction Joints: Stop all wythes at same elevation, stop grout a minimum of 1-1/2" (38 mm) below mortar joint, except at top of wall.			
	Stop grout a minimum of 1/2" (13 mm) below top of bond beams.			
	Grouting Limitations: Provide fine or coarse grout as determined by grout space size; comply with UBC Table 21-C for pour height.			
	Cleanouts: Provide for pours over 5'-0" (1524 mm) high, in bottom course at every vertical bar, but not more than 32" (813 mm) on center.			
	Seal after inspection and prior to grouting.			
	Where cleanouts are not provided, keep grout spaces clean and provide minimum total clear area required by UBC Table 21-C.			

Code Ref.	Code Compliance Item	OK	NA	ID
2104.6.1	**Grouted Masonry - Maximum Lift Height:** 6'-0" (1829 mm) unless method for higher lifts is approved.			
2104.6.2	**Grouted Masonry - Construction:** Place reinforcement prior to grouting. Set bolts accurately with templates and hold securely during grouting.			
	Avoid segregation of grout materials.			
	Consolidate grout by mechanical vibration prior to loss of plasticity.			
	Mortar of pouring consistency may be substituted for grout in nonstructural elements not over 8'-0" (2438 mm) above highest point of lateral support.			
	Multi-wythe Construction: Provide vertical barriers spaced 30'-0" (9144 mm) minimum horizontally in grout spaces. Complete grouting of any section between barriers in one day with no interruptions more than 1 hour.			
2104.7	**Aluminum Equipment:** Do not use aluminum handling or pumping equipment.			
2105.3	**Preconstruction Quality Assurance:** Provide preconstruction masonry testing by masonry prism testing, masonry prism test records, or the unit strength method in accordance with UBC Section 2105.3.			
2105.3	**Construction Quality Assurance:** Provide masonry testing by masonry prism testing, masonry prism test records, or the unit strength method in accordance with UBC Section 2105.3. When 1/2 of allowable masonry stresses are used in design, testing during construction is not required; provide certifications required by UBC Section 2105.3.			
2112.4.2 Appendix	**Materials for Masonry Construction in High Wind Areas:** **Exterior Concrete Block:** Minimum Grade N-II; 1,900 psi (13 091 kPa) minimum compressive strength on net area.			
	Interior Concrete Block: Grade S-II minimum; 700 psi (4823 kPa) minimum compressive strength on gross area.			
	Exterior Clay or Shale Hollow Brick: Grade MW minimum or Grade SW where subject to severe freezing; 2,500 psi (17 225 kPa) minimum compressive strength on net area.			
	Interior Clay or Shale Hollow Brick: Grade MW minimum; 2,000 psi (13 780 kPa) minimum compressive strength on net area.			
	Exterior Clay or Shale Bricks: Grade MW minimum or Grade SW where subject to severe freezing; 2,500 psi (17 225 kPa) minimum compressive strength on net area.			
	Interior Clay or Shale Bricks: 2,000 psi (13 780 kPa) minimum compressive strength.			
	Grout: 2,000 psi (13 780 kPa) minimum compressive strength.			
	Mortar for Exterior Walls and Interior Shear Walls: Type M or S.			

Masonry Veneer

CSI Section 04810

Code Ref.	Code Compliance Item	OK	NA	ID
1401.2	**Standards:** UBC Standard 14-1, Kraft Waterproof Building Paper.			
1402.1	**Building Paper and Felt Installation:** Free from tears and holes other than from fasteners.			
	Apply over studs or sheathing of all exterior walls.			
	Apply horizontally, upper layers lapped over lower not less than 2" (51 mm); lap end joints not less than 6" (152 mm).			
1403.3	**Anchors, Supports, and Ties:** Noncombustible and corrosion resistant.			
	Corrosion-resistant Materials: Equal to hot-dipped galvanized coating of 1.5 oz of zinc per sf (458 g/m^2).			
	Accessory Materials: Provide corrosion-resistant screws, nails, dowels, bolts, nuts, washers, shims, anchors, ties, and attachments for elements required to corrosion resistant.			
1403.5.4	**Adhered Veneer Mortar:** Type S.			
	Adhered Veneer Setting Bed Mortars: Use proportions per UBC Table 14-A.			
	Setting Bed Thickness: Minimum 3/8" (9.5 mm), maximum 3/4" (19.1 mm).			
1403.6.4.2	**Anchored Masonry and Stone Veneer Wall Ties:** Corrosion resistant of size, configuration, and spacing indicated on the Drawings.			
1403.6.4.2	**Masonry and Stone Wall Ties in Seismic Zones 3 and 4:** Provide lip or hook on extended leg to engage horizontal joint reinforcement wire.			
	Horizontal Joint Reinforcement: Minimum diameter 9 gage (0.148") (3.76 mm) wire; continuous with butt splices between ties.			

Structural Steel

CSI Section 05120

Code Ref.	Code Compliance Item	OK	NA	ID
2202.1 2202.2 2202.3	**Standards of Quality:** UBC Standard 22-1, Material Specification for Structural Steel. ANSI/ASCE 8, Specification for the Design of Cold-formed Stainless Steel Structural Members, American Society of Civil Engineers. ASTM A502, Structural Rivet Steel.			
2203.2	**Identification:** Identify structural steel in mill in accordance with nationally recognized standards, UBC Standards, and UBC requirements. Maintain identity of material and provide procedures and reports attesting that material meets the specified standard. Establish fabricator's identification mark prior to fabrication.			
	Identification - Material Greater Than 36,000 psi (248 Mpa) Yield Point: Include ASTM designation near erection mark or each shipping assembly or construction component over any shop paint prior to shipment. When such pieces are cut to smaller sizes, mark fabricator's mark on each smaller piece. Provide steel die stamp or firmly attached tag on pieces subject to blast cleaning, galvanizing, or heating for forming.			
	Identification - Bundled Pieces: When only the top piece in a bundle received by the fabricator is mill marked or bundle is tagged, mark each piece with fabricator's mark prior to fabrication.			
2203.3	**Cold-Formed Carbon and Low Alloy Steel Identification:** Identify structural steel in mill in accordance with nationally recognized standards. When such material is greater than 33,000 psi (228 Mpa) yield point, provide ASTM designation on each lift or bundle of fabricated items.			
	When such material is greater than 33,000 psi (228 Mpa) yield point which was obtained through additional treatment, provide yield point designation in addition to ASTM designation.			

Code Ref.	Code Compliance Item	OK	NA	ID
2203.4	**Cold-Formed Stainless Steel Identification:** Identify grade through mill test reports and furnish certification that chemical and mechanical properties of the material supplied meets or exceeds the specified requirements. Identify each bundle or lift of fabricated items.			
2205.11	**Anchor Bolt Installation:** Set anchor bolts accurately to pattern and dimensions indicated on the Drawings.			
	Threaded ends shall protrude through connected material sufficiently to engage threads of nuts, but not greater than length of threads on bolts.			
2206 2208 2210	**Design and Construction Standards:** AISC Load and Resistance Factor Design Specification for Structural Steel Buildings (AISC LRFD).			
	AISC Specification for Structural Steel Buildings - Allowable Stress Design and Plastic Design (AISC ASD).			
	AISC Seismic Provisions for Structural Steel Buildings.			
2221	**Steel Joists and Girders - Standards:** Standard Specification for Steel Joists, K-Series, LH-Series, DLH-Series and Joist Girders published by Steel Joist Institute.			

Structural Aluminum

CSI Section 05140

Code Ref.	Code Compliance Item	OK	NA	ID
2001.4	**Identification:** At the fabricator's plant, mark fabricated pieces to identify alloy and temper. Mark members, assemblies, or boxed or bundled shipments of multiple units.			
2004.1	**Cutting:** Do not use oxygen cutting.			
2004.2	**Fasteners:** Use only aluminum, stainless steel, or aluminized, hot-dip galvanized, or electro-galvanized steel. Do not use steel rivets except where aluminum is joined to steel or where corrosion resistance of structure is not a requirement, or where structure is protected against corrosion.			
2004.3	**Dissimilar Materials:** Separate faying surfaces by paint.			
2004.5	**Welding:** Use inert gas shielded arc or resistance welding process. Do not use process requiring welding flux.			
2004.7	**Erection:** Brace and fasten to resist dead, wind, and erection loads.			
2011	**Fabrication:** **Layout:** Do not use center punching or scribing where marks remain after fabrication.			
	Cutting: Shear, saw, or cut with router or arc cut. Plane arc cut edges to remove edge cracks.			
	Cut edges shall be true, smooth, and free from excessive burrs or ragged breaks.			
	Avoid re-entrant cuts, fillet by drilling prior to cutting where used.			
	Heating: Do not heat structural material.			
	Punching, Drilling, and Reaming: Rivet holes may be either punched or drilled. Do not punch if metal thickness is greater than diameter of hole.			
	Riveting: Fill holes completely. Set rivet heads concentric with rivet holes and in proper contact with metal surface. Remove defective rivets by drilling.			
2011.6	**Painting:** Clean, paint, and protect aluminum surfaces in contact with, or fastened to, steel members or other dissimilar materials.			

Code Ref.	Code Compliance Item	OK	NA	ID
	Contact with Dissimilar Metals: **Contact with Steel:** Paint with zinc chromate primer, FS TT-P-645, or 1 coat of nonhardening joint compound. Apply joint compound over primer where severe corrosion conditions are expected.			
	Painting not required at contact with stainless steel, aluminized, hot-dip galvanized, or electrogalvanized steel in contact with aluminum.			
	Contact with Wood, Fiberboard, or Porous Material: Place insulating barrier between aluminum and porous material. Apply heavy coat of alkali-resistant bituminous paint.			
	Contact with Concrete or Masonry: Apply heavy coat of alkali-resistant bituminous paint.			
	Embedment in Concrete: Protection not required.			
	Provide zinc chromate primer, FS TT-P-645, or plastic tape where corrosive components are added to concrete or concrete is exposed to corrosive conditions.			

Steel Wire Rope Assemblies

CSI Section 05150

Code Ref.	Code Compliance Item	OK	NA	ID
2230	**Design, Fabrication, and Installation - Standard:** ASCE Standard 17-95, Structural Applications of Steel Cables for Buildings.			

Steel Joists

CSI Section 05210

Code Ref.	Code Compliance Item	OK	NA	ID
2203.5	**Open-Web Steel Joist Identification:** Identify as to type, size, and manufacturer by tagging or other suitable means. Maintain such identification to the point of installation.			
2221	**Standards:** Standard Specification for Steel Joists, K-Series, LH-Series, DLH-Series and Joist Girders published by Steel Joist Institute.			

Wood Treatment

CSI Section 06070

Code Ref.	Code Compliance Item	OK	NA	ID
207	**Fire-Retardant-Treated Wood:** Wood products impregnated with chemicals by a pressure process or other means during manufacture.			
	Flame Spread: 25 or less; no evidence of progressive combustion when tested for 30 minutes in accordance with UBC Standard 8-1. Flame front shall not progress more than 10'-6" (3200 mm) beyond centerline of burner at any time during test.			
	Materials Exposed to Weather: Identify materials as exterior type; pass accelerated weathering test; UBC Standard 23-4.			
	Materials not Exposed to Weather, Exposed to High Humidity: Identify materials as Interior Type A; pass hygroscopic test; UBC Standard 23-4.			
2303	**Standards of Quality** **Preservative Treatment by Pressure Process and Quality Control:** Standard Specifications C1, C2, C3, C4, C9, C14, C15, C16, C22, C23, C24, C28, and M4, AWPA.			
	Fire Retardancy: UBC Standard 23-5, Fire-retardant-treated Wood Tests on Durability and Hygroscopic Properties. UBC Standard 23-6, Fire-retardant-treated Wood.			
2304.1	**Identification:** Identify all preservative-treated wood by the quality mark of an approved inspection agency.			
2304.5	**Maximum Moisture Content of Fire-Retardant-Treated Wood:** **Solid Sawn Lumber 2" (51 mm) Thick or Less:** 19% after treatment.			
	Plywood: 15% after treatment.			

Rough Carpentry

CSI Section 06100

Code Ref.	Code Compliance Item	OK	NA	ID
708.2.1	**Fire Blocks Required:** In concealed spaces of stud walls and furred spaces, at floor and ceiling levels, and at 10'-0" (3048 mm) intervals, vertical and horizontal.			
	At interconnections between concealed vertical and horizontal spaces which occur at soffits, drop ceilings, and cove ceilings.			
	In concealed spaces between stair stringers at top and bottom of run and between studs along and in line with run of stairs if walls under stairs are unfinished.			
	Around vents, pipes, ducts, chimneys, fireplaces, and similar openings providing passage for fire at ceiling and floor levels; use noncombustible materials.			
	At openings between attics and chimney chases for factory-built chimneys.			
	Wood Flooring on Rated Masonry or Concrete Floors: Divide open spaces between sleepers into spaces not more than 100 sf (9.3 m^2) and fill space under partitions with noncombustible materials or fire blocking.			
	Not required in gym floors at or below grade.			
	In bowling lanes, fire blocks only required at juncture of alternate lanes and at lane ends.			
708.3	**Fire Blocking Materials:** 2" (51 mm) nominal lumber or 2 thickness of 1" (25 mm) nominal lumber with broken lap joints, 1 thickness of 23/32" (18.3 mm) plywood with joints backed by 23/32" (18.3 mm) plywood, 1 thickness of 3/4" (19.1 mm) Type 2-M particle board with joints backed by 3/4" (19.1 mm) Type 2-M particle board.			
	Gypsum board, cement board, mineral fiber, glass fiber or other approved noncombustible materials, securely fastened in place.			
708.3.1.3	**Draft Stop Openings:** Provide self-closing doors with automatic latches.			

Code Ref.	Code Compliance Item	OK	NA	ID
2303.1	**Standards of Quality - Grading Rules:** UBC Standard 23-1, Classification, Definition, and Methods of Grading for All Species of Lumber. Standard Grading Rules for Canadian Lumber, United States Edition, NLGA. Standard Grading Rules No. 17, WCLIB. Standard Grading Rules, WWPA. Grading Rules, NHPMA. Standard Specifications for Grades of California Redwood Lumber, RIS. Standard Grading Rules, NELMA.			
	Standards of Quality - Product Standards: UBC Standard 23-2, Construction and Industrial Plywood. UBC Standard 23-3, Performance Standard for Wood-based Structural-use Panels. UBC Standard 23-4, Mat-formed Wood Particleboard. ANSI 05.1, Wood Poles - Specifications and Dimensions. ANSI/AHA A194.1, Cellulosic Fiber Insulating Board (fiberboard). ANSI/AHA 135.6, Hardboard Siding.			
2303.1	**Standards of Quality - Adhesives and Glues:** ASTM D3024, Dry Use Adhesives with Protein Base, Casein Type. ASTM D2559, Wet Use Adhesives. APA Specification AFG-01, Adhesives for Field Gluing Plywood to Wood Framing.			
2304.1	**Identification:** Identify lumber, wood structural panels, particleboard, endjointed lumber, fiberboard sheathing (when used structurally), hardboard siding (when used structurally), piles, and poles by the grade mark or certificate of inspection issued by an approved agency.			
	Fabrication: Prepare, fabricate, and install wood members and fastenings according to accepted engineering principals and building code requirements.			
	Workmanship: Frame, anchor, tie, and brace all members to develop strength and rigidity necessary for the designed use.			

Code Ref.	Code Compliance Item	OK	NA	ID
2304.3	**Timber Connectors and Fasteners:** Use hot-dipped zinc-coated galvanized, stainless steel, silicon bronze or copper fasteners for pressure-preservative-treated and fire-retardant-treated wood.			
	Nails: Provide number and size of nails connecting wood members per UBC Tables 23-II-B-1 and 23-II-B-2. Zinc-coated, aluminum alloy wire, or stainless steel.			
	Corrosion-Resistant Nails: Provide for treated woods; hot-dipped zinc coated galvanized, stainless steel, or aluminum alloy wire.			
2304.8	**Rejection:** Wood members with permissible grade characteristics or defects in a combination that affects the serviceability of the member are subject to rejection.			
2306.4	**Plates, Sills, and Sleepers:** Provide treated wood or decay-resistant wood for foundation plates or sills and sleepers on concrete or masonry slabs on grade.			
2306.10	**Moisture Content of Water-borne Preservative Treated Wood:** 19% maximum prior to covering where in-service drying will not readily occur.			
2312.2	**Wood Structural Panel Roof Sheathing:** Bonded by intermediate or exterior glue; bonded by exterior glue where exposed on underside.			
2315.1	**Diaphragm Nailing:** Drive nails or connectors flush but do not fracture surface of sheathing.			
2315.3	**Wood Structural Panel Installation:** Bear panel edges on framing members and butt along center lines.			
2315.5.3	**Wood Structural Panel Diaphragms in Seismic Zones 3 and 4:** Provide panels manufactured with exterior glue.			
2314.5.5	**Particleboard Diaphragms in Seismic Zones 3 and 4:** At a minimum, provide Type M "exterior glue."			
2320.9.4	**Particleboard Subfloor:** Comply with UBC Table 23-II-F-2.			
2320.10	**Particleboard Underlayment:** Type PBU, 1/4" (6.4 mm) minimum thickness.			
	Identify by grade mark of approved inspection agency.			
	Install as recommended by the manufacturer.			

Treated Wood Foundations

CSI Section 06140

Code Ref.	Code Compliance Item	OK	NA	ID
2301.1	**Standards of Quality:** UBC Standard 23-2, Construction and Industrial Plywood. UBC Standard 23-3, Performance Standard for Wood-based Structural-use Panels.			
1811.1	**Lumber:** Provide treated materials bearing grade mark of lumber grading agency or inspection bureau. Where treated, provide FDN grade mark.			
1811.2	**Plywood Materials:** Bonded with exterior glue, grade marked indicating compliance with UBC Standard 23-2, and bearing grade mark of plywood inspection agency. Where treated, provide FDN grade mark.			
1811.3	**Fasteners:** **Full Ground Contact:** Silicon bronze, copper, or stainless steel.			
	Protected Construction: Hot-dipped zinc-coated steel, coated after manufacture, where protected by polyethylene sheeting. Electro-galvanized nails or staples and hot-dipped zinc-coated staples are not acceptable.			
	Framing Anchors: Hot-dipped zinc-coated sheet steel, ASTM A446 Grade A, UBC Standard 22-1.			
1811.4	**Footings Fill:** **Gravel:** Washed and well graded, maximum stone size of 3/4" (19.1 mm), free from organic, clayey, or silty soils.			
	Sand: Coarse, minimum 1/16" (1.6 mm) grains, free from organic, clayey, or silty soils.			
	Crushed Stone: Maximum size of 1/2" (13 mm).			
1811.5	**Polyethylene Sheeting:** Comply with requirements of governing jurisdiction.			

Code Ref.	Code Compliance Item	OK	NA	ID
1811.6	**Sealants:** Provide materials compatible with plywood and polyethylene sheeting and capable of forming continuous seal.			
	Plywood Joint Sealant: Provide materials compatible with treated plywood and recommended for conditions of use.			
1811.7	**Preservative Treatment:** Pressure treatment conforming to FDN requirements.			
	Moisture Content of Lumber and Plywood: 19% maximum after treatment.			
	Treatment Quality or Inspection Marks: Provide on each piece of lumber or plywood.			
	Field Fabricated Lumber or Plywood: Where material is field cut or drilled after treatment, field treat material by repeated brushing, dipping, or soaking until wood will no longer absorb preservative using same chemical used for treatment or as permitted by UBC Section 1811.7.			
1811.7	**Materials Required to be Treated:** Plywood and lumber used in exterior foundation walls (except upper top plate); interior bearing wall framing and sheathing, posts, and wood supports in crawl spaces; sleepers, joists, blocking, and plywood subfloor in basement floors; plates framing, and sheathing in the ground or in direct contact with concrete.			
	Minimum Requirements: All exterior wall framing materials less than 6" (152 mm) above finish grade.			
1812.4	**Basement Floor Sheeting:** Provide 6 mil polyethylene sheeting over gravel layer and under concrete slabs or wood floor systems.			
	Place sheeting over wood sleepers supporting joists; do not extend beneath wood footing plate.			
	Basement Wall Caulking: Caulk plywood panel joints full length.			
	Basement Wall Sheeting: Provide 6 mil polyethylene sheeting over below-grade portion of walls.			
	Set top of sheeting in sealant and cover with treated lumber or plywood strip extending minimum 2" (51 mm) above grade and minimum 5" (127 mm) below grade; set strip in sealant along edge.			
	Extend sheeting to bottom of wood plate but do not overlap or extend into gravel footing.			

Wood Trusses

CSI Section 06170

Code Ref.	Code Compliance Item	OK	NA	ID
2321.1	**Design and Fabrication Standards:** ANSI/TPI 1-1995.			
2321.3 2304.4	**In-plant Inspection:** Truss manufacturer shall retain approved independent inspection agency to provide nonscheduled inspections of truss fabrication, delivery, and operations, including all phases of truss construction and plant operation.			
2321.4	**Markings:** Provide legible mark on bottom chord within 24" (610 mm) of center of span identifying truss manufacturer, design load, and truss spacing.			

Wood I Joists

CSI Section 06175

Code Ref.	Code Compliance Item	OK	NA	ID
2303	**Standards of Quality:** ASTM D5055, Structural Capacities of Prefabricated Wood I-Joists.			

Glued-Laminated Construction

CSI Section 06180

Code Ref.	Code Compliance Item	OK	NA	ID
2303	**Standards of Quality:** ANSI/AITC Standard A190.1 and ASTM D3737, Design and Manufacture of Structural Glued-Laminated Timber. Standard Specifications for Structural Glued -laminated Timber of Softwood Species, AITC 117; Manufacturing, AITC 117; Design and Standard Specifications for Hardwood Glued-laminated Timber, AITC 119. Inspection Manual AITC 200 of the American Institute of Timber Construction, Tests for Structural Glued-laminated Timber. AITC 500, Determination of Design Values for Structural Glued-laminated Timber in accordance with ASTM D3737, American Institute of Timber Construction. ASTM D1101 and AITC 200 in Testing of Glue Joints in Laminated Wood Product. ASTM D3024, Dry Use Adhesives with Protein Base, Casein Type. ASTM D2559, Wet Use Adhesives.			
2304.4.3	**Fabrication:** Provide qualified supervisory personnel.			
2306.12	**Weather Exposure:** Use decay-resistant or preservative treated wood where timbers are exposed to weather or not protected by roof or eave overhangs.			

Dampproofing

CSI Section 07110

Code Ref.	Code Compliance Item	OK	NA	ID
1822.2	**Floor Dampproofing Materials:** 6 mil (0.152 mm) polyethylene.			
	4 mil (0.1 mm) polyethylene or mopped-on bitumen when installed on top of slab.			
1823	**Wall Dampproofing:** Provide on exterior surface of walls, extending from 6" (152 mm) above grade down to top of footing.			
	Wall Dampproofing Materials: Bituminous material, acrylic modified cement base coating, or other approved material.			
	Where materials are not approved for direct application to masonry, parge exterior below-grade masonry surfaces with 3/8" (9.5 mm) minimum thickness portland cement mortar.			
1824.3	**Foundation Drain Materials:** Gravel and crushed stone, not more than 10% material passing a No. 4 (4.75 mm) sieve.			
	Cover top of gravel or crushed stone with filter fabric.			
	Drain Tile Installation: Place on 2" (51 mm) minimum of gravel or crushed stone and cover with 6" (152 mm) minimum of gravel or crushed stone.			
	Cover top of joints in drain tile or top of perforated pipe with filter fabric.			
1827.2	**Wall Preparation:** Remove fins or sharp projections that may pierce membrane and seal all holes and recesses resulting from removal of form ties with dry-pack mortar or bituminous material prior to application of waterproofing materials.			

Waterproofing

CSI Section 07120

Code Ref.	Code Compliance Item	OK	NA	ID
1826.2 1827.4	**Waterproofing Materials:** Rubberized asphalt, polymer-modified asphalt, butyl rubber, neoprene, or 6 mil (0.15 mm) minimum thickness polyvinyl chloride or polyethylene capable of bridging nonstructural cracks.			
	Joints: Lap 6" (152 mm) minimum and seal.			
1827.2	**Wall Preparation:** Remove fins or sharp projections that may pierce membrane and seal all holes and recesses resulting from removal of form ties with dry-pack mortar or bituminous material prior to application of waterproofing materials.			
1827.5	**Wall and Floor Joints:** Seal joints between wall and floor, and penetrations of wall and floor watertight.			

Building Insulation

CSI Section 07210

Code Ref.	Code Compliance Item	OK	NA	ID
601.3 703.4	**Standards of Quality:** UBC Standard 7-1, Fire Test of Building Construction Materials. UBC Standard 8-1, Test Method for Surface Burning Characteristics of Building Materials. UBC Standard 26-3, Room Fire Test Standard for Interior Foam Plastic Systems, ICBO Standard. UBC Standard 26-4, Method of Test for Evaluation of Flammability Characteristics of Exterior, Nonload Bearing Wall Panel Assemblies Using Foam Plastic Insulation, ICBO Standard. ASTM C516, Vermiculite Loose Fill Insulation. ASTM C549, Perlite Loose Fill Insulation. ASTM D1929, Ignition Properties of Plastics. CPSC 16 CFR, Parts 1209 and 1404 Test Standard for Cellulose Insulation.			
707.3	**Insulation Materials:** Provide insulation and facings as follows: Flame Spread Rating: 25 maximum. Smoke Density Rating: 450 maximum.			
	In Types III, IV, and V construction, flame spread and smoke density limitations do not apply when facing is installed in contact with unexposed face of ceiling, floor, or wall.			
2602.3	**Foam Plastic Insulation - Surface Burning Characteristics:** Flame Spread Rating: 75 maximum. Smoke Developed Rating: 450 maximum.			

Roof and Deck Insulation

CSI Section 07220

Code Ref.	Code Compliance Item	OK	NA	ID
601.3	**Standards of Quality:** UBC Standard 7-1, Fire Test of Building Construction Materials. UBC Standard 8-1, Test Method for Surface Burning Characteristics of Building Materials. UBC Standard 26-2, Test Method for the Evaluation of Thermal Barriers, ICBO Standard. UBC Standard 26-3, Room Fire Test Standard for Interior Foam Plastic Systems, ICBO Standard. ASTM D1929, Ignition Properties of Plastics. FM Standard Fire Test Standard for Insulated Roof Deck Construction. UL 1256, Fire Test Standard for Insulated Roof Deck Construction.			
1510	**Roof Insulation - Built-up Roofs:** Apply in accordance with Table 15-E.			
	Roof Insulation - Modified Bitumen, Thermoplastic, Thermoset Membrane Roofs: Apply in accordance with manufacturer's instructions.			
	Fire Retardancy Requirements: Specify minimum roof cover class required by Table 15-A.			
2602.3	**Foam Plastic Insulation - Surface Burning Characteristics:** **Flame Spread Rating:** 75 maximum. **Smoke Developed Rating:** 450 maximum.			

Shingles

CSI Section 07310

Code Ref.	Code Compliance Item	OK	NA	ID
1501.1	**Standards of Quality:** UBC Standard 15-2, Fire Retardancy of Roof-covering Materials. UBC Standard 15-3, Wood Shakes. UBC Standard 15-4, Wood Shingles. ASTM C406, Slate Shingles. ASTM D1970, Self-adhering Polymer Modified Bituminous Sheet Materials Used as Steep Roofing Underlayment for Ice Dam Protection.			
1503	**Roof Covering Requirements:** Specify minimum roof covering classification as required by UBC Table 15-A.			
1507.2	**Wood Shake or Shingle Identification:** Provide bundles bearing label or identification mark of approved inspection agency showing grade.			
	Asphalt Shingle Identification: Deliver in packages bearing manufacturer's label or identifying mark and the label of an approved inspection agency.			
1507.5	**Asphalt Shingle Installation:** Comply with manufacturer's instructions and UBC Table 15-B-1.			
1507.9	**Nonferrous Metal Shingles:** Minimum 28 B&S gage, (0.159") (0.40 mm).			
1507.12	**Wood Shakes:** UBC Table 15-B-2 and UBC Standard 15-3.			
1507.13	**Wood Shingles:** UBC Table 15-B-2 and UBC Standard 15-4.			

Roof Tiles

CSI Section 07320

Code Ref.	Code Compliance Item	OK	NA	ID
1501.1	**Standards of Quality:** UBC Standard 15-5, Roofing Tile. ASTM B134, B211, and B250, Wire. UBC Standard 15-2, Fire Retardancy of Roof-covering Materials.			
1507.7	**Clay or Concrete Tile:** UBC Standard 15-5.			
	Install in accordance with manufacturer's instructions and UBC Tables 15-D-1 and 15-D-2.			

Siding

CSI Section 07460

Code Ref.	Code Compliance Item	OK	NA	ID
1401.2 2302.1	**Standards of Quality:** UBC Standard 14-1, Kraft Waterproof Building Paper. UBC Standard 14-2, Vinyl Siding. UBC Standard 23-2, Construction and Industrial Plywood. UBC Standard 23-3, Performance Standard for Wood-based Structural-use Panels. ANSI/AHA 135.6, Hardboard Siding.			
1402.1	**Weather-Resistive Barrier:** Asphalt-saturated rag felt or kraft waterproof building paper complying with UBC Standard 14-1.			
	Building Paper and Felt Installation: Apply horizontally over studs or sheathing of all exterior walls, upper layers lapped over lower not less than 2" (51 mm); end joints lapped not less than 6" (152 mm); free from tears and holes other than from fasteners.			
1404.1	**Vinyl Siding:** UBC Standard 14-2.			
	Apply over sheathing or other approved materials. Install in accordance with the manufacturer's written instructions to provide weather-resistive barrier required by UBC Section 1402.1.			
	Vinyl Siding Fasteners: Nails, minimum head diameter of 3/8" (9.5 mm), minimum shank diameter of 0.120" (3.05 mm), corrosion resistant. Provide 3/4" (19.1 mm) minimum penetration of stud or nailing strip.			
	Nail Spacing - Horizontal Siding Applications: 16" (406 mm) horizontal, 12" (305 mm) vertical.			
	Nail Spacing - Vertical Siding Applications: 12" (305 mm) horizontal, 12" (305 mm) vertical.			

Code Ref.	Code Compliance Item	OK	NA	ID
2310.2	**Solid Wood Siding - Materials:** **Rustic, drop, or shiplap:** 19/32" (15 mm) average thickness, 3/8" (9.5 mm) minimum thickness.			
	Bevel: 7/16" (11 mm) minimum butt thickness, 3/16" (4.8 mm) tip thickness.			
	Lesser dimensions may be used if siding is placed over sheathing.			
	Installation: Nail to each stud with at least 1 nail or to sheathing with 1 line of nails spaced at 24" (305 mm) on center maximum.			
	1-1/2" (38 mm) minimum penetration into studs or studs and sheathing.			
	Install over weather-resistive barrier.			
2310.3	**Plywood Siding - Materials:** 3/8" (9.5 mm) minimum thickness, exterior type.			
	Installation: Install in accordance with UBC Table 23-II-A-1. Unless installed over sheathing, locate joints over framing members.			
	Protect joints with continuous wood batten, flashing, sealant, or vertical or horizontal shiplaps.			
	Install over weather-resistive barrier.			
2310.4	**Shingles or Shakes:** Install over weather-resistive barrier. Secure to sheathing or nailing strips.			
	Weather Exposure: UBC Table 23-II-K.			
2310.5	**Particleboard Siding - Materials:** Exterior Type 2-M grades conforming to UBC Standard 23-4. Seal and protect with exterior finishes.			
	Installation: UBC Tables 23-II-A-2 and 23-I-B-2. Gap panels 1/8" (3.2 mm), locate nails 3/8" (9.5 mm) minimum from panel edges. Locate joints over framing members unless installed over sheathing.			
	Cover joints with continuous wood batten, lap horizontally, or otherwise make joints waterproof.			
	Install over weather-resistive barrier.			
2310.6	**Hardboard Siding:** UBC Table 23-II-C; locate joints over framing members; provide 1/8" gap around all openings.			
	Install over weather-resistive barrier.			
2310.7	**Nails:** Provide corrosion-resistant type.			

Membrane Roofing

CSI Section 07500

Code Ref.	Code Compliance Item	OK	NA	ID
601.3 1501.1	**Standards of Quality:** UBC Standard 7-1, Fire Test of Building Construction Materials. UBC Standard 8-1, Test Method for Surface Burning Characteristics of Building Materials. UBC Standard 14-1, Kraft Waterproof Building Paper. UBC Standard 15-1, Roofing Aggregates. UBC Standard 15-2, Test Method for Determining the Fire Retardancy of Roof Assemblies. UBC Standard 15-6, Modified Bitumen, Thermoplastic, and Thermoset Membranes. ASTM D312 and D450, Roofing Asphalt and Coal Tar Bitumen. UL Standard Specification 55A, Materials for Construction of Built-up Roofing.			
1503	**Roof Covering Requirements:** Specify minimum roof covering classification per UBC Table 15-A.			
1507.2	**Identification:** Deliver materials in packages bearing manufacturer's label or identifying mark and the label of an approved inspection agency.			
	Asphalt: Deliver in cartons bearing name of manufacturer, equiviscous temperature, flash point, and type of product.			
	Coal Tar Pitch: Deliver in cartons bearing name of manufacturer, equiviscous temperature, and type of product.			
1507.5	**Built-up Roofing Installation:** Comply with manufacturer's instructions and UBC Tables 15-E through 15-G.			
1507.14	**Modified Bitumen, Thermoplastic, and Thermoset Membrane Installation:** Comply with manufacturer's instructions.			

Sheet Metal Roofing

CSI Section 07610

Code Ref.	Code Compliance Item	OK	NA	ID
1501.1	**Standards of Quality:** UBC Standard 15-2, Fire Retardancy of Roof-covering Materials. ASTM A570 and A611, Sheet Metals. ASTM A219 and A239, Corrosion-resistant Metals.			
1503	**Roof Covering Requirements:** Specify minimum roof covering classification as required by Table 15-A.			
1507.8	**Metal Roofing:** Minimum 30 galvanized gage (0.013") (0.33 mm).			
	Flat Steel Sheets: Minimum 30 galvanized gage (0.013") (0.33 mm), other ferrous sections or shapes minimum 26 gage.			
	Flat Nonferrous Sheets: Minimum 28 B&S gage (0.0159") (0.40 mm), other nonferrous sections or shapes minimum 25 B&S gage (0.179") (0.45 mm).			
	Load Bearing Panels: Design to support live loads between supports.			

Sheet Metal Flashing and Trim

CSI Section 07620

Code Ref.	Code Compliance Item	OK	NA	ID
1501.1	**Standards of Quality:** ASTM A570 and A611, Sheet Metals. ASTM A219 and A239, Corrosion-resistant Metals.			
1402.2	**Flashing and Counterflashing - Minimum Thickness:** 26 galvanized gage (0.019") (0.48 mm), corrosion-resistant metal.			
1508.2	**Valley Flashing - Asphalt Shingles:** Minimum 28 galvanized gage (0.016") (0.41 mm), corrosion-resistant metal.			
	Extend metal valleys minimum 8" (203 mm) each way from center line; end lap sections minimum 4" (102 mm) in direction of water flow.			
	Valley Underlayment: 36" (914 mm) wide Type 15 felt, centered on valley and running full length; apply over roof underlayment.			
	Valley Underlayment - Severe Climates: 36" (914 mm) wide Type 15 felt, centered on valley and running full length; solidly cemented to roof underlayment on roof slopes under 7:12 (58.3%).			
1508.3	**Valley Flashing - Metal Shingles:** Minimum 28 galvanized gage (0.016") (0.41 mm), corrosion-resistant metal with splash diverter rib, 3/4" (19.1 mm) high minimum, at flow line.			
	Extend valley minimum 8" (203 mm) each way from center line; end lap sections minimum 4" (102 mm) in direction of water flow.			
	Valley Underlayment: 36" (914 mm) wide Type 15 felt, centered on valley and running full length; apply over roof underlayment.			
	Valley Underlayment - Severe Climates: 36" (914 mm) wide Type 15 felt, centered on valley and running full length; solidly cemented to roof underlayment on roof slopes under 7:12 (58.3%).			

Code Ref.	Code Compliance Item	OK	NA	ID
1508.4	**Valley Flashing - Slate Shingles, Clay and Concrete Tile:** Minimum 28 galvanized gage (0.016") (0.41 mm), corrosion-resistant metal with splash diverter rib, 1" (25 mm) high minimum, at flow line.			
	Extend valley minimum 11" (279 mm) each way from center line; end lap sections minimum 4" (102 mm) in direction of water flow.			
	Valley Underlayment - Roof Slopes 3:12 (25%) and Greater: 36" (914 mm) wide Type 15 felt, centered on valley and running full length; apply over roof underlayment.			
	Valley Underlayment - Severe Climates: 36" (914 mm) wide Type 15 felt, centered on valley and running full length; solidly cemented to roof underlayment on roof slopes under 7:12 (58.3%).			
1508.5	**Valley Flashing - Wood Shingles and Shakes:** Minimum 28 galvanized gage (0.016") (0.41 mm), corrosion-resistant metal.			
	Extend valley minimum 8" (203 mm) each way from center line; end lap sections minimum 4" (102 mm) in direction of water flow.			
	Valley Underlayment: 36" (914 mm) wide Type 15 felt, centered on valley and running full length; apply over roof underlayment.			
	Valley Underlayment - Severe Climates: 36" (914 mm) wide Type 15 felt, centered on valley and running full length; solidly cemented to roof under-layment on roof slopes under 7:12 (58.3%).			

Roof Accessories

CSI Section 07720

Code Ref.	Code Compliance Item	OK	NA	ID
902	**Standards of Quality - Smoke and Heat Vents:** UBC Standard 15-7, Automatic Smoke and Heat Vents.			
217	**Plastics Permitted In Skylights:** **Self-ignition Temperature:** 650°F (343° C) or greater. **Smoke Density Rating:** 450 maximum, UBC Standard 8-1; or 75 maximum, UBC Standard 26-5. **Classification:** CC1 or CC2 in accordance with UBC Standard 26-7.			

Fireproofing

CSI Section 07805

Code Ref.	Code Compliance Item	OK	NA	ID
703.4	**Standards of Quality:** UBC Standard 7-1, Fire Tests of Building Construction and Materials. UBC Standard 7-6, Thickness and Density Determination for Spray-applied Fireproofing.			
704.6 1701.5.10	**Field Quality Control:** The Owner's special inspector or testing agency shall test installed fireproofing for thickness and density verification in accordance with UBC Standard 7-6.			

Firestopping

CSI Section 07840

Code Ref.	Code Compliance Item	OK	NA	ID
703.4	**Standards of Quality:** UBC Standard 7-1, Fire Tests of Building Construction and Materials. UBC Standard 7-5, Fire Tests of Through-penetration Fire Stops.			
706	**Construction Joints in Rated Construction:** Securely install firestopping material in or on joint for its entire length in such a manner to accommodate the expected building movements and resist spread of fire and hot gases.			
709.3.2.2	**Vertical Fire Spread - Exterior Walls:** At rated floor and floor-ceiling assemblies, firestop voids created at intersection of exterior wall and floor assemblies; securely fasten firestop materials to prevent passage of flame and hot gases.			
	Firestop Materials: UBC Standard 7-1, prevent ignition of cotton waste under minimum positive pressure differential of 0.01" (25 mm) water column for time period equal to rating of floor assembly.			
709.6 710.2	**Through-penetrations:** Firestop around items penetrating both membranes of rated bearing walls, walls requiring opening protection, and rated floor or floor/ceiling assemblies; F-rating to match rating of assembly.			
	Provide T-rating to match rating of assembly at through-penetrations above ceilings not a part of rated assembly, and at through-penetrations below ceilings.			
	Provide T-rating to match rating of assembly at floor/ceiling assembly penetrations not contained within a wall at the point of penetration of the floor, and at penetrations larger than 4" (100 mm) nominal pipe or 16 si (10320 mm^2).			
709.7 710.3	**Membrane Penetrations:** Firestop around items penetrating 1 membrane of rated construction; F-rating to match rating of assembly.			
714	**Sleeves:** Where used, securely fasten to assembly penetrated.			
	Protect space between sleeve and penetrating item and sleeve and assembly.			
	Insulation and coverings on penetrating items shall not penetrate assembly unless specific materials used have been tested as part of assembly.			

Metal Doors and Frames

CSI Section 08100

Code Ref.	Code Compliance Item	OK	NA	ID
703.4	**Standards of Quality:** UBC Standard 7-1, Fire Test of Building Construction Materials. UBC Standard 7-2, Fire Tests of Door Assemblies. UBC Standard 7-3, Tinclad Fire Doors. ASTM/NFPA 80, Standard for Fire Doors and Fire Windows.			
713.3	**Identification of Fire Doors:** Provide label or listing mark indicating rating, name of manufacturer, and name of inspection service, permanently affixed at factory.			
	Temperature Rise Fire Doors: Indicate on label that temperature rise on unexposed surface does not exceed 450°F (232°C) above ambient after 30 minutes of fire exposure complying with UBC Standard 7-2.			
	Oversize Doors: Provide label or certificate of inspection from approved agency.			
713.4	**Installation of Fire Doors and Frames:** Anchor and install in accordance with listing.			
713.5	**Fire-Resistive Tests:** Determine rating of fire assemblies in accordance with UBC Standard 7-2 and 7-3.			
1004.3.4.3.2.1	**20-Minute Rated Corridor Doors:** Test in accordance with UBC Standard 7-2.			
	Provide label or other identification on door and frame showing rating, the letter "S," name of manufacturer, and identification of inspection service at factory.			

Wood and Plastic Doors

CSI Section 08200

Code Ref.	Code Compliance Item	OK	NA	ID
703.4	**Standards of Quality:** UBC Standard 7-1, Fire Test of Building Construction Materials. UBC Standard 7-2, Fire Tests of Door Assemblies. ASTM/NFPA 80, Standard for Fire Doors and Fire Windows.			
713.3	**Identification of Fire Doors:** Provide label or listing mark indicating rating, name of manufacturer, and name of inspection service, permanently affixed at factory.			
	Temperature Rise Fire Doors: Indicate on label that temperature rise on unexposed surface does not exceed 450°F (232°C) above ambient after 30 minutes of fire exposure complying with UBC Standard 7-2.			
	Oversize Doors: Provide label or certificate of inspection from approved agency.			
713.4	**Installation of Fire Doors and Frames:** Anchor and install in accordance with listing.			
713.5	**Fire-Resistive Tests:** Determine rating of fire assemblies in accordance with UBC Standard 7-2 and 7-3.			
1004.3.4.3.2.1	**20-Minute Rated Corridor Doors:** Test in accordance with UBC Standard 7-2.			
	Provide label or other identification on door and frame showing rating, the letter "S," name of manufacturer, and identification of inspection service at factory.			

Specialty Doors

CSI Section 08300

Code Ref.	Code Compliance Item	OK	NA	ID
703.4	**Standards of Quality:** UBC Standard 7-1, Fire Test of Building Construction Materials. UBC Standard 7-2, Fire Tests of Door Assemblies. UBC Standard 7-3, Tinclad Fire Doors. UBC Standard 26-8, Room Fire Test Standard for Garage Doors Using Foam Plastic Insulation. ASTM/NFPA 80, Standard for Fire Doors and Windows.			
713.3	**Identification of Fire Doors:** Provide label or listing mark indicating rating, permanently affixed at factory.			
713.4	**Installation of Fire Doors:** Anchor and install in accordance with listing.			
713.5	**Fire-Resistive Tests:** Determine rating of fire assemblies in accordance with UBC Standard 7-2.			

Automatic Entrance Doors

CSI Section 08460

Code Ref.	Code Compliance Item	OK	NA	ID
1001.1	**Standards of Quality:** UBC Standard 10-1, Power-operated Exit Doors. UBC Standard 7-8, Horizontal Sliding Fire Doors Used in an Exit.			

Windows

CSI Section 08500

Code Ref.	Code Compliance Item	OK	NA	ID
703.4	**Standards of Quality:** UBC Standard 7-1, Fire Test of Building Construction Materials. UBC Standard 7-4, Fire Tests of Window Assemblies. ASTM/NFPA 80, Standard for Fire Doors and Windows.			
713.3	**Identification of Fire Windows:** Provide label or listing mark indicating rating, permanently affixed at factory.			
713.4	**Installation of Fire Windows:** Anchor and install in accordance with listing.			
713.5	**Fire-Resistive Tests:** Determine rating of fire assemblies in accordance with UBC Standard 7-4.			

Hardware

CSI Section 08700

Code Ref.	Code Compliance Item	OK	NA	ID
703.4	**Standards of Quality:** UBC Standard 7-2, Fire Tests of Door Assemblies. UBC Standard 10-4, Panic Hardware. ASTM/NFPA 80, Standard for Fire Doors and Windows.			
713.3	**Identification of Fire Door Hardware:** Provide label or listing mark indicating rating, permanently affixed at factory.			
713.4	**Installation of Fire Door Hardware:** Anchor and install in accordance with listing.			
713.6.2	**Hinges:** Provide ball-bearing or anti-friction type.			
	Fire Doors: Provide at least 2 hinges up to 60" (1524 mm) in height, and 1 additional hinge for each additional 30" (762 mm).			
1003.3.1.9	**Panic Hardware:** UBC Standard 10-4.			
	Mount at 30" (762 mm) to 44" (1118 mm) above floor.			
	Unlatching Force: 15 pounds (66.72 N) maximum in direction of exit travel.			

Glazing

CSI Section 08800

Code Ref.	Code Compliance Item	OK	NA	ID
713.9	**Glazing in Rated Assemblies:** Meet or exceed UBC Standards 7-2 or 7-4 as applicable; label for the required rating; install in accordance with listing.			
2401.4	**Standards of Quality - Glass:** UBC Standard 24-1, Glass Standard Specification. UBC Standard 24-2, Safety Glazing.			
2402	**Glass Identification:** Provide manufacturer's label on each light designating type and thickness of glass.			
2406.2	**Safety Glass Identification:** Provide permanent manufacturer's label on each light designating the labeler, and stating that safety glazing material has been used in such installation.			
	Tempered Glass Identification: Provide permanent identification on each light, etched or ceramic fired, visible when unit is glazed. Provide removable paper label at tempered spandrel glass.			
2406.3	**Plastic Safety Glazing in Exterior Applications:** Comply with weathering requirements of UBC Standard 24-2, Part II.			
2406.5	**Wardrobe Door Glazing:** Comply with impact test requirements of UBC Standard 24-2, Part II.			
	Laminated Glass: Comply with boil test requirements of UBC Standard 24-2, Part II.			
2408.1	**Racquetball and Squash Courts - Glazing Test Method:** Impactor and procedure in accordance with UBC Standard 24-2, Part I, Category II. Impact point at 59" (1499 mm) above playing surface, drop height of 48" (1219 mm).			

Code Ref.	Code Compliance Item	OK	NA	ID
2408.2	**Racquetball and Squash Courts - Glazing Test Minimum Requirements:** Glass shall not break, deflection at point of impact shall not exceed 1-1/2" (38 mm), door hardware shall remain intact and operable, deflection of door edges shall be no greater than limits set forth in Section 2408.2.			
2603.1.3	**Light-Transmitting Plastics - Identification:** Identify each unit or package with mark identifying material classification.			
2603.1.6	**Standards of Quality - Light-Transmitting Plastics:** UBC Standard 26-5, Chamber Method of Test for Measuring Density of Smoke from Burning or Decomposition of Plastic Materials. UBC Standard 26-6, Test Method for Ignition Properties of Plastics. UBC Standard 26-7, Method of Test Determining Classification of Approved Light Transmitting Plastics.			
217	**Plastics - Materials:** **Self-ignition Temperature:** 650°F (343° C) or greater. **Smoke Density Rating:** 450 maximum, UBC Standard 8-1; or 75 maximum, UBC Standard 26-5. **Classification:** CC1 or CC2 in accordance with UBC Standard 26-7.			

Lath and Plaster

CSI Section 09200

Code Ref.	Code Compliance Item	OK	NA	ID
703.4 1401.2 2502	**Standards of Quality:** UBC Standard 7-1, Fire Tests of Building Construction and Materials. UBC Standard 14-1, Kraft Waterproof Building Paper. UBC Standard 21-11, Masonry Cement. ASTM C150, Portland Cement. UBC Standard 25-1, Plastic Cement. United States Government Military Specification MIL-B-19235 (Docks), Plaster Bonding Agents. ASTM C35, Perlite, Vermiculite, and Sand Aggregates for Gypsum Plaster. ASTM C37, Gypsum Lath. ASTM C28, Gypsum Plasters. ASTM C61, Keene's Cement. ASTM C587 and C588, Gypsum Base for Veneer Plaster and Gypsum Veneer Plaster. ASTM C6 and C206, Lime. ASTM C144 and C897, Aggregate for Masonry Mortar and Aggregate for Job-mixed Portland Cement-based Plaster.			

Code Ref.	Code Compliance Item	OK	NA	ID
2502	**Standards of Quality, Continued:** ASTM C843 and 844, Application of Gypsum Base for Veneer Plaster and Gypsum Veneer Plaster.			
	ASTM C514, Nails for the Application of Gypsum Wallboard, Gypsum Backing Board, and Gypsum Veneer Plaster.			
	ANSI A42.2-1995 and Specification 2.6.73 of the California Lathing and Plastering Contractors Association, Metal Lath, Wire Lath, Fabric Lath, and Metal Accessories.			
2505.2	**Interior Gypsum Lath Installation:** Provide thickness, support spacing, and attachment complying with UBC Tables 25-B and 25-C.			
	Install with long dimension perpendicular to supports, end joints staggered in successive courses. Where end joints occur on 1 support, provide stripping full length of joints.			
	Cover gaps in joints greater than 3/8" (9.5 mm) with stripping or cornerite except when entire surface is reinforced with minimum 1" (25 mm), 20 B.W. gage (0.89 mm) woven wire.			
	When applied to horizontal or vertical supports which are not structural diaphragms, end joints may occur between supports if secured together.			
	Install cornerite to retain position during plastering at interior corners.			
2505.3 2506.5	**Interior and Exterior Metal Plaster Base Installation - Wood Supports:** Provide type and weight of metal lath, or gage and spacing of wire in wire lath, support spacing, and attachment complying with UBC Tables 25-B and 25-C.			
	Metal Supports: Attach with minimum 18 B.W. gage (0.049") (1.2 mm) tie wires spaced at 6" (152 mm) maximum.			
	Install with long dimension perpendicular to supports.			
	Lap metal lath 1/2" (13 mm) minimum at sides, 1" (25 mm) minimum at ends.			
	Lap wire fabric lath at least 1 mesh, or minimum 1" (25 mm).			
	Lap rib lath 1/2" (13 mm) at sides or nest outside ribs. Where end laps do not occur over supports, tie end laps securely with minimum 18 B.W. gage (0.049") (1.2 mm) wire.			
	Install cornerite at internal corners to retain position during plastering.			
	Furr metal plaster bases out 1/4" (6.4 mm) from vertical supports and backing or provide self-furring plaster bases.			
	Furr out and carry lath around corners or provide external corner reinforcement.			
2506.2	**Exterior Lath:** Provide corrosion-resistant materials.			
	Provide supports and solid backing to support lath and attachments.			

Code Ref.	Code Compliance Item	OK	NA	ID
1402.1 2506.4	**Weather-Resistive Barrier:** Asphalt saturated rag felt or kraft waterproof building paper complying with UBC Standard 14-1.			
	Building Paper and Felt Installation: Apply horizontally over studs or sheathing of all exterior walls, upper layers lapped over lower not less than 2" (51 mm); end joints lapped not less than 6" (152 mm); free from tears and holes other than from fasteners.			
2506.5	**Weep Screeds:** Minimum 26 galvanized gage (0.019") (0.48 mm), corrosion resistant, minimum vertical attachment flange of 3-1/2" (89 mm).			
2507.1 2508.1	**Interior and Exterior Plaster:** Provide 3 coats over metal lath or wire fabric, 2 coats over masonry, concrete, or gypsum backing.			
2507.2 2508.2	**Base Coat Proportions - Interior and Exterior Gypsum Plaster:** UBC Table 25-E.			
	Interior and Exterior Cement Plaster: UBC Table 25-F.			
2507.3.1 2508.3	**Base Coat Application:** Apply with sufficient material and pressure to provide complete key or bond.			
2507.3.2	**Gypsum Plaster - Base Coat Application:** **2-Coat Work:** Bring first coat out to grounds, straighten to true surface, leave rough to receive finish coat.			
	3-Coat Work: Score first coat to provide adequate bond, allow to harden and set. Bring second coat out to grounds and straighten to true surface, leave rough to receive finish coat.			
2507.3.3 2508.3	**Cement Plaster - Base Coat Application:** Score first coat horizontally to provide adequate bond to receive second coat. Bring second coat out to proper thickness, rod and float rough to receive finish coat.			
	Second Coat Tolerance: No variation greater than 1/4" (6.4 mm) in any direction with a 5'-0" (1524 mm) straight edge.			
	Moist Cure Time: Not less than 24 hours between first and second coats. Moist cure not required under weather conditions favorable to retention of moisture.			
	Thickness: UBC Table 25-D.			
2507.4	**Interior Finish Coat Application:** Apply with sufficient material and pressure to provide complete bond.			
	Provide finish coats proportioned and mixed in an approved manner.			
	Apply gypsum and lime or other interior finishes after gypsum base coats have hardened and set.			
	Finish Coat Thickness: 1/16" (1.6 mm) minimum.			
	Cement plaster finish coat may be applied to base coat after 24-hour minimum.			

Code Ref.	Code Compliance Item	OK	NA	ID
2507.5 2508.8	**Preparation of Masonry or Concrete:** Clean surfaces, remove efflorescence, roughen and dampen to provide bond.			
	On smooth surfaces, provide bonding agent or portland cement dash coat, proportions of 1-1/2 part sand to 1 part portland cement or plastic cement by volume. Moist cure and leave dash coat undisturbed for 24 hours minimum.			
	Moist cure and leave dash coat undisturbed for 24 hours minimum.			
2508.1	**Plasticity Agents:** Only approved materials may be added to portland cement. When added, do not add lime or plasticizers.			
	Hydrated Lime or Lime Putty: Comply with UBC Table 25-F for use as plasticizer.			
2508.4	**Environmental Conditions - Exterior Portland Cement:** Do not apply to frozen bases or bases containing frost. Do not use frozen materials in plaster mix. Protect plaster coats from freezing for a minimum of 24 hours after set.			
2508.5	**Curing and Interval - Exterior Portland Cement Plaster:** Apply and moist cure first and second coat in compliance with UBC Table 25-F.			
	Plaster Applied to Gypsum Backing, Masonry, or Concrete: Second coat may be applied as soon as first coat has set.			
2508.6	**Alternate Application Methods:** Second coat may be applied as soon as first coat has sufficient rigidity to receive second coat. Calcium aluminate cement up to 15% of portland cement weight may be added to mix. First coat curing may be omitted and second coat cured in compliance with UBC Table 25-F.			
2508.7	**Exterior Finish Coats:** Proportion and mix in compliance with UBC Table 25-F.			
	Apply over base coats in place for time periods set forth in UBC Table 25-F.			
	Apply with sufficient material and pressure to provide bond and conceal brown coat.			
2509.2	**Exposed Aggregate Plaster - Aggregate Materials:** Marble chips, pebbles, or similar materials; nonreactive and moderately hard (3 or more on Measure of Hardness scale).			
2509.3	**Exposed Aggregate Plaster - Bedding Coat Proportions:** **Exterior Bedding Coat:** 1 part portland cement, 1 part Type S lime, and maximum of 3 parts graded white or natural sand by volume, or factory-prepared bedding coat; 1,000 psi (6894.8 kPa) minimum compressive strength.			
	Interior Bedding Coat: 100 lbs (45.4 kg) neat gypsum plaster and a maximum of 200 lbs (90.7 kg) of graded white sand, or factory prepared-bedding coat.			
2509.4	**Exposed Aggregate Plaster - Application over Lath:** Bedding coat may be applied directly over plaster scratch coat if ultimate thickness is 7/8" (22 mm) minimum, including lath.			
	Application over Concrete or Masonry: Apply bedding coat over scratch coat to thickness of minimum 1/2" (13 mm).			

Code Ref.	Code Compliance Item	OK	NA	ID
2509.6	**Exposed Aggregate Plaster - Concrete and Masonry Preparation:** Clean surfaces, remove efflorescence, roughen and dampen to provide bond.			
	On smooth surfaces, provide bonding agent or portland cement dash coat, proportions of 1-1/2 part sand to 1 part portland cement or plastic cement by volume. Moist cure and leave dash coat undisturbed for 24 hours minimum.			
2509.7	**Exposed Aggregate Plaster - Curing:** UBC Table 25-F. Moist cure for 24 hours unless bedding coat retains sufficient water for hydration.			
2510	**Pneumatically Placed Plaster (Gunite):** **Materials and Placement:** Mixture of portland cement and sand, mixed dry, conveyed through pipe or flexible tube, hydrated at nozzle end of tube, and deposited by air pressure in its final position.			
	Rebound Material: May be screened and reused as sand, but not more than 25% of total sand in any batch.			
	Mix: 1 part portland cement to not more than 5 parts sand.			
	Plasticity Agents: Only approved materials may be added to portland cement. When added, do not add lime or plasticizers.			
	Hydrated Lime or Lime Putty: When used as a plasticizer, comply with UBC Table 25-F.			
	Minimum Thickness: Apply in 2 coats to 7/8" (22 mm) total. Rod and float first coat to provide bond for second coat.			
	Curing: UBC Table 25-F.			

Gypsum Board

CSI Section 09250

Code Ref.	Code Compliance Item	OK	NA	ID
703.4 2502	**Standards of Quality:** UBC Standard 7-1, Fire Tests of Building Construction and Materials. ASTM C557, Adhesives for Fastening Gypsum Wallboard to Wood Framing. ASTM C1002, Drill Screws. ASTM C475 and C474, Gypsum Wallboard Tape and Joint Compound. ASTM C442, Gypsum Backing Board. ASTM C79, Gypsum Sheathing. ASTM C36, Gypsum Wallboard. ASTM C630, Water-resistant Gypsum Backing Board. ASTM C22, C472, and C473, Testing Gypsum and Gypsum Products. ASTM C514, Nails for Application of Gypsum Wallboard, Gypsum Backing Board, and Gypsum Veneer Base. ASTM C931, Exterior Gypsum Soffit Board.			
2511.1	**Installation - General:** Do not install until protected from weather.			
2511.2	**Panel Thickness:** UBC Table 25-G.			
2511.3	**Fastener Size and Spacing:** Follow UBC Table 25-G except where modified by rated construction requirements.			
	Space fasteners minimum of 3/8" (10 mm) from edges and ends of panels.			
	Do not fracture face paper with fastener head.			

Code Ref.	Code Compliance Item	OK	NA	ID
2511.3	**Adhesive Application to Wood Framing:** Provide continuous bead of adhesive to face of framing members, except top and bottom plates, sufficient to spread to average width of 1" (25 mm) and thickness of 1/16" (1.6 mm) after gypsum panel installation.			
	Provide 2 parallel beads of adhesive where edges or ends of 2 pieces occur on the same member.			
	Provide fasteners complying with UBC Table 25-G.			
2511.4	**2-Ply Application - Base Layer:** Apply following fastener size and spacing in UBC Table 25-H except where modified by rated construction requirements.			
	2-Ply Application - Face Layer: Apply with joint compound, adhesive providing full coverage between layers, or with fasteners complying with UBC Table 25-H.			
	When adhesively applied, provide temporary nails or shoring to hold face layer in position until adhesive develops adequate bond.			
2512	**Water-Resistant Gypsum Board:** Provide on wall behind tile or wall panels around showers, tubs, or water closets.			

Tile

CSI Section 09300

Code Ref.	Code Compliance Item	OK	NA	ID
1403.5.5	**Ceramic Tile Setting Mortars:** UBC Table 14-A.			

Acoustical Ceilings

CSI Section 09510

Code Ref.	Code Compliance Item	OK	NA	ID
801.2 2502	**Standards of Quality:** UBC Standard 8-1, Test Method for Surface-burning Characteristics of Building Materials (ASTM E84-91a). UBC Standard 25-2, Metal Suspension Systems for Acoustical Tile and for Lay-in Panel Ceilings.			
710.1	**Fire Rated Ceilings:** Provide holddowns to prevent vertical displacement of lay-in panels where weight of panel is not sufficient to resist upward force of 1 psf (0.048 kN/m^2).			

Flooring

CSI Section 09600

Code Ref.	Code Compliance Item	OK	NA	ID
801.2	**Standards of Quality:** UBC Standard 8-1, Test Method for Surface-burning Characteristics of Building Materials (ASTM E84-91a).			

Wall Covering

CSI Section 09720

Code Ref.	Code Compliance Item	OK	NA	ID
801.2	**Standards of Quality:** UBC Standard 8-1, Test Method for Surface-burning Characteristics of Building Materials (ASTM E84-91a). UBC Standard 8-2, Standard Test Method for Evaluating Room Fire Growth Contribution of Textile Wall Covering.			

Smoke Detectors

CSI Section 13855

Code Ref.	Code Compliance Item	OK	NA	ID
905.9.5	**Smoke Detectors:** Provide listed detectors.			
310.9.1.3	**Smoke Detectors - Power Source:** Hardwire to building power system without disconnect switch and provide battery back-up when commercial power is provided.			
	Detector shall emit signal when battery is low.			

Fire Suppression Systems

CSI Section 13900

Code Ref.	Code Compliance Item	OK	NA	ID
902	**Standards of Quality:** UBC Standard 9-1, Installation of Sprinkler Systems. UBC Standard 9-2, Standpipe Systems. UBC Standard 9-3, Installation of Sprinkler Systems in Group R Occupancies Four Stories or Less.			
903	**Definitions:** **Class I Standpipe System:** System equipped with 2-1/2" (63.5 mm) outlets.			
	Class II Standpipe System: System directly connected to water supply and equipped with 1-1/2" (38 mm) outlets and hose.			
	Class III Standpipe System: System directly connected to water supply and equipped with 2-1/2" (63.5 mm) outlets or 2-1/2" (63.5 mm) and 1-1/2" (38 mm) outlets when a 1-1/2" (38 mm) hose is required.			
	Hose connections may be 2-1/2" (63.5 mm) hose valves with easily removable 2-1/2" by 1-1/2" (63.5 mm by 38 mm) reducers.			
904.1.1	**Fire Hose Threads:** Provide national standard hose thread approved by Fire Department when used with fire extinguishing systems.			
904.6.1	**Fire Protection in Buildings Under Construction:** Provide at least 1 standpipe in buildings with sprinkler systems 4 or more stories in height for use during construction until permanent systems are installed and in service.			
	Install standpipes when construction is not more than 35'-0" (10 668 mm) above lowest level of fire department access.			
	Provide hose connections at accessible locations adjacent to usable stairs and locate outlets adjacent to such usable stairs.			

Code Ref.	Code Compliance Item	OK	NA	ID
904.6.1	**Fire Protection in Buildings Under Construction, Continued:** Extend system as construction progresses to within 1 floor of highest point having secured decking or flooring.			
	Provide 2-1/2" (63.5 mm) valve outlet on each floor.			
	When construction height requires Class III standpipe, provide fire pumps and water main connections to serve standpipe.			
904.6.3	**Temporary Standpipes in Buildings Under Construction:** May be provided in place of permanent systems if designed to furnish minimum of 500 gallons (1893 L) per minute at 50 psi (345 kPa); standpipe size 4" (102 mm) minimum.			
	When Class III standpipe system is required, provide pump equipment to provide such pressure and volume at all times.			
	Fire Protection in Buildings Under Construction: Install temporary standpipe system as required for permanent systems.			

Elevators

CSI Section 14200

Code Ref.	Code Compliance Item	OK	NA	ID
3003.2	**Smoke-Detection Recall System:** Provide smoke-detection recall system in elevators with vertical travel of 25'-0" (7620 mm) or more.			
	Upon activation of lobby or entrance area smoke detector or machine room smoke detector, elevator doors shall be prevented from opening and all cars serving such lobby or entrance area or controlled by such machine room shall return to main floor and revert to manual control only.			
	If main floor or transfer floor lobby or entrance area smoke detector is activated, all cars serving main floor shall return to a designated secondary floor and revert to manual control only.			
3003.4.2	**Cab Operation and Leveling:** Provide automatic operation and self-leveling features to automatically bring car to floor landings within tolerance of plus or minus 1/2" (13 mm) under normal loading and unloading conditions.			
	Self-leveling device shall be entirely independent of operating device and shall correct overtravel and undertravel.			
	Device shall maintain car approximately level with landing irrespective of load.			
3003.4.3	**Door Operation:** Power-operated horizontal sliding, automatic operation.			
3303.4.4	**Minimum Door Width:** 36" (914 mm) clear.			
3003.4.5	**Door Protective and Reopening Device:** Provide device to stop and reopen car and hoistway doors when doors are obstructed when closing. Device shall be capable of sensing object or person in path of closing door without requiring contact for activation at 5" (127 mm) and 29" (737 mm) above floor.			
3003.4.6.1	**Door Delay - Hall Call:** Comply with UBC Section 3003.4.6.1.			
3003.4.6.2	**Door Delay - Car Call:** Doors shall remain fully open at least 3 seconds.			
3003.4.7	**Car Inside - Minimum Dimensions:** Allow for turning of wheelchair.			
	68" by 54" (1727 mm by 1372 mm) minimum between wall and wall, or wall and door, excluding return panels.			
	51" (1295 mm) minimum between wall and return panel.			

Code Ref.	Code Compliance Item	OK	NA	ID
3003.4.8	**Car Controls:** Readily accessible from a wheelchair upon entering elevator.			
	Alarm Button and Emergency Stop Switch Height: 35" (889 mm) from floor to center line.			
	Highest Floor Button Height: 54" (1372 mm) maximum from floor to center line.			
	Floor Registration Buttons: Minimum 3/4" (19.1 mm) size exclusive of border, raised, flush, or recessed; 3/8" (10 mm) depth of flush or recessed buttons when operated.			
	Provide visual indication of calls registered and extinguish indication when answered.			
	Controls Markings: Provide adjacent to controls on left side on contrasting background.			
	5/8" (16 mm) high raised or recessed 0.030" (0.8 mm) minimum height of letters or numbers.			
	Permanently attached plates are acceptable.			
	Group emergency controls together at bottom of panel.			
3003.4.9	**Car Position Indicator:** Locate above car operating panel or over opening to show position of car in hoistway by illumination of the indication corresponding to landing at which car is stopped or passing.			
	Size and Color: 1/2" (13 mm) high, on contrasting color.			
	Signal: Provide audible signal to indicate that car is stopping or passing a floor served by elevator.			
3003.4.10	**Telephone or Intercommunication System:** Provide 2-way communication between elevator and point outside hoistway.			
	Locate telephones 54" (1372 mm) maximum height with 29" (737 mm) cord length.			
	Provide markings or international symbol for telephone adjacent to control on a contrasting color background.			
	5/8" (16 mm) minimum letter or number height, raised or recessed 0.030" (0.8 mm).			
	Permanently attached plates are acceptable.			
3003.4.11	**Floor Covering:** Nonslip hard surface permitting easy wheelchair movement.			
	Carpeting: Heavy-duty with a tight weave and low pile, installed without padding and securely attached.			
3003.4.12	**Handrails:** Provide on 1 wall of car, preferably on rear wall, 32" (813 mm) above floor.			
	Provide smooth surface, inside surface 1-1/2" (38 mm) clear of walls.			
3003.4.13	**Minimum Illumination of Car Controls and Landing:** 5 footcandles (54 lx) when doors are open.			

Code Ref.	Code Compliance Item	OK	NA	ID
3003.4.14	**Hall Button:** Provide visual indication of each call registered and extinguish indication when call is answered.			
	Height: 42" (1067 mm) above floor to centerline.			
	Hall Button Size: 3/4" (19 mm) minimum exclusive of border; raised, flush, or recessed.			
	Flush or Recessed Button Depth: 3/8" (10 mm) maximum when operated.			
3003.4.15	**Hall Lantern:** Provide visual and audible signal at each hoistway entrance indicating cars answering call and direction of travel.			
	Visual Signal Size: 2-1/2" (64 mm) minimum, visible from proximity of hall call button.			
	Audible Signal: Sound once for up direction and twice for down direction.			
	Hall Lantern Height: 6'-0" (1829 mm) minimum above floor to centerline.			
3003.4.16	**Door Jamb Markings:** Provide floor designation indicators at each hoistway entrance on both sides of jamb.			
	Make markings visible from inside car and from elevator lobby at height of 60" (1524 mm) above floor.			
	Provide contrasting background 2" (51 mm) high and raised 0.030" (0.8 mm).			
	Permanently attached plates are acceptable.			

Mechanical Insulation

CSI Section 15080

Code Ref.	Code Compliance Item	OK	NA	ID
707.2	**Insulation and Covering on Pipe and Tubing:** UBC Standard 8-1. **Maximum flame spread rating:** 25. **Maximum smoke density rating:** 450.			
2602	**Foam Plastic Insulation:** **Maximum flame spread rating:** 75. **Maximum smoke density rating:** 450.			

Process Piping

CSI Section 15200

Code Ref.	Code Compliance Item	OK	NA	ID
307.11.6.1	**Piping System Materials:** Metallic unless material being transported is incompatible with such metallic materials.			
	Piping System Materials - Health Hazard Ranking of 3 or 4: Welded throughout, except for connections, valves, and fittings to systems in ventilated enclosures.			
307.11.6.3	**Group H-6 - Piping Identification:** Identify piping and tubing and HPM waste lines to indicate material being transported in accordance with nationally recognized standards.			

Smoke Control Ducts

CSI Section 15815

Code Ref.	Code Compliance Item	OK	NA	ID
905.7.3	**Smoke Control Ducts:** Provide materials and joints capable of withstanding probable temperatures and pressures.			
	Construct and support in compliance with Mechanical Code.			
	Leak test ducts to 1.5 times maximum design pressure in accordance with nationally accepted practices; maximum measured leakage of 5% of design flow.			
	Support ducts directly from rated structural elements by substantial, noncombustible supports.			
	Flexible isolation connections may be used if constructed of fire-resistive materials.			

Ductwork Accessories

CSI Section 15820

Code Ref.	Code Compliance Item	OK	NA	ID

601.3
703.4
	Standards of Quality - Fire Dampers:
	    UL 555, Fire Dampers.
	
	    UL 555C, Ceiling Dampers.
	
	    UL 555S, Leakage Rated Dampers for Use in Smoke Control Systems.			

713.3	**Identification of Fire Dampers:** Provide label or listing mark indicating rating, permanently affixed at factory.			
713.4	**Installation of Fire Dampers:** Fabricate and install in accordance with listing.			
713.5	**Fire-Resistive Tests:** Determine rating of fire assemblies in accordance with approved recognized standards.			
713.10	**Smoke Dampers:** Minimum Class II, 250°F (121°C) complying with recognized standards.			
713.11	**Fire Dampers:** Comply with nationally recognized standards.			
713.11	**Fire Damper Actuating Device Operating Temperature:** Set at approximately 50°F (10°C) above normal temperature in duct system, 160°F (71°C) minimum. When located in smoke-control system, operating temperature may be increased to 286°F (141°C) maximum.			
713.12	**Fire Damper Installation:** When installed in HVAC systems intended to operate with fans on during fire, provide dampers labeled for use in dynamic systems.			
905.7.5	**Smoke-Control System - Automatic Dampers:** Provide listed dampers complying with nationally recognized standards.			

Smoke-Control Fans

CSI Section 15835

Code Ref.	Code Compliance Item	OK	NA	ID
905.7.1	**Smoke-Control Equipment:** Provide equipment suitable for intended use, and suitable for probable temperatures to which they may be exposed.			
905.7.2	**Smoke System Exhaust Fans:** Rate and certify components for probable temperature rise to which they may be exposed.			
905.7.6	**Smoke System - Belt Driven Fans:** Provide 1.5 times number of belts required for design duty, with minimum of 2 belts.			
	Selection: Select fans for stable performance based on normal temperature and elevated temperature where applicable. Provide calculations and fan curves.			
	Support: Support and restrain with noncombustible devices.			
	Motors: Do not operate beyond nameplate horsepower (kilowatts) determined by actual draw.			
	Provide minimum service factor of 1.15.			

Smoke-Control System Controls

CSI Section 15938

Code Ref.	Code Compliance Item	OK	NA	ID
905.9.2	**Smoke-Control System Wiring:** Enclose all wiring in continuous raceways, regardless of voltage.			
905.10.1	**Smoke System Control Air Tubing:** Provide size sufficient to meet required response times.			
	Flush clean and dry prior to final connections.			
	Provide adequate support and protection from damage.			
	Where passing through concrete or masonry, sleeve and protect from abrasion and electrolysis.			
905.10.2	**Smoke System Control Air Tubing Materials:** Hard drawn copper, Type L, ACR; ASTM B42-92, B43-91, B88-92, B251-88, and B280-92.			
	Fittings: Wrought copper or brass (solder type); ANSI B16.22-89 and B16.18-84.			
	Changes in Direction: Tool bends.			
	Connections: May be brass compression-type fittings at device connections; braze other joints using $BcuP_5$ brazing alloy with solidus above $1,100°F$ ($593°C$) and liquidus below $1,500°F$ ($816°C$). Use brazing flux on copper to brass joints.			
	Nonmetallic Tubing: Where listed for flame and smoke characteristics, may be used in control panels and at final connections to devices.			
	Completely enclose tubing and connected devices in galvanized or paint grade steel enclosure not less than 22 gage (0.30") (0.76 mm) thick with tubing entry into enclosure of copper tubing with protective grommet of neoprene or teflon or by suitable brass compression to male barbed adapter.			
	Neatly tie and support tubing in enclosure and protect against abrasion.			
	Identify tubing by documented coding.			
	Provide sufficient length of tubing to bridge cabinet door or moveable device to avoid tension and stress. Fasten tubing serving devices on doors along hinges.			

Code Ref.	Code Compliance Item	OK	NA	ID
905.10.3	**Smoke System Control Air Tubing:** **Isolation from other Functions:** Provide automatic isolation valves where control tubing serves other than smoke-control functions.			
905.10.4	**Testing:** Prior to final connection to devices, test tubing at 3 times operating pressure for at least 30 minutes without noticeable loss in gage pressure.			
905.11	**Smoke System - Identification:** Clearly mark detection and control systems at junctions, accesses, and terminations.			
905.12	**Smoke System - Control Diagrams:** Provide diagrams to building official, fire department, and with fire fighter's control panel; show all devices and identify location and function.			
905.13	**Fire-fighter's Control Panel:** Verify that panel control capabilities, annunciation, control action and priorities are per Section 905.13.			
905.14	**Smoke-Control System Response Time:** Verify that system activation and response times are per Section 905.14.			
905.15	**Smoke-Control System Acceptance Testing:** Individually test devices, equipment, components, and sequences. Determine function, sequence, and capacity of installed conditions.			
	Detection Devices: Test in installed condition in accordance with Fire Code; include verification of airflow in minimum and maximum conditions where applicable.			
	Ducts: Traverse using generally accepted practices to determine actual air quantities.			
905.15	**Dampers:** Test for function in installed condition.			
	Inlets and Outlets: Determine air quantities using accepted practices.			
	Fans: Examine for correct rotation; measure voltage, amperage, revolutions per minute, and belt tension.			
	Smoke Barriers: Measure pressure differences for each possible condition using inclined manometers.			
	Controls: In each smoke zone equipped with automatic initiating devices, initiate operation by actuation of 1 such device. Verify each additional device in the zone to cause same sequence but operation of fan motors may be bypassed. Verify controls throughout system, including override from fire-fighter's control panel and simulation of standby power condition.			
905.15.9	**Acceptance Testing Reports:** Submit test report prepared by special inspector or special inspection agency.			
	Identify all devices by manufacturer, nameplate data, design values, measured values, and identification tag or mark.			
	Submit test report to responsible designer; adjust system and submit revised test data until responsible designer is satisfied that design intent is achieved.			

Code Ref.	Code Compliance Item	OK	NA	ID
905.15.10	**Smoke Control System Identification:** Submit charts, drawings, and other documents identifying and locating each component of system and describe function and maintenance requirements of each.			
	Identify each device by tag or mark consistent with submitted documentation and provide date indicating the last successful test and identity of tester.			

Lighting

CSI Section 16500

Code Ref.	Code Compliance Item	OK	NA	ID
2603.8.1	**Light-Diffusing Plastics:** Materials shall fall from their mountings at ambient temperature of at least 200°F (93°C) below ignition temperature.			
	Material shall remain in place at ambient room temperature of 175°F (79°C) for not less than 15 minutes.			

ABOUT THE AUTHOR

Scott Parish, AIA, CSI, is a licensed architect currently employed at Mangini Associates in Visalia, California. The author of the *National Building Code Compliance Manual*, also published by McGraw-Hill, he has extensive experience with construction documents, specification writing, quality control, and construction administration on many different types of projects, including medical, commercial high-rise, municipal, educational, manufacturing, airport, and office projects.

This book provides checklists of code requirements aimed at five different aspects of the design professional's services: *Code Information, Design Requirements, Detailed Construction Requirements, Structural Documentation Requirements, and Specifications Requirements*. These five groupings of information allow the reviewer to concentrate on the specific needs of the review process and on the information needed at that particular point in the pase of the design services that the review occurs.

Using the 1996 National Building Code as its basis, *Uniform Building Code Compliance Manual* provides the following unique features:

- It places the condensed code requirements into a checklist format, allowing easy scanning for code review and document checking.

- It reformats the code requirements to align with the normal progression services and allows the design professional to focus on those requirements that apply to the project at the particular time.

- It provides the checklists in electronic format allowing viewing of the lists on a PC and reproduction of selected files for use in code compliance reviews.

- As part of the project file, it provides tangible evidence that a code compliance review was performed.

Uniform Building Code Compliance Manual is designed to be used in conjunction with the 1996 edition of the BOCA National Building Code. The user will need to refer to the NBC for information found in tables and figures, for word definitions, for detailed descriptions of equipment functions and construction assemblies, and for the actual code wording for legal purposes.

This CD-ROM has been provided with the book as the means of reproducing the checklists necessary for each project. Use the table of contents to determine the checklists required. The chapter number in the Table of Contents corresponds to the file number of each chapter. The chapter number/file number is also found on each page in the bottom right hand corner in conjunction with the page number. The text is in PDF format, readable by Adobe Acrobat. If you do not have a reader on your computer, it can be downloaded free of charge from the Adobe website.

It's Not Just the Latest Code, It's the Best Code

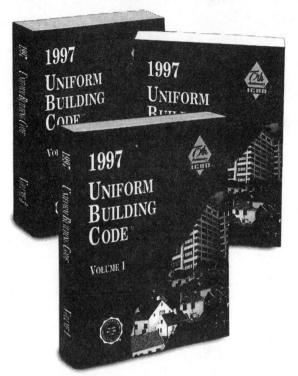

The 1997 *Uniform Building Code*™ (UBC) is the one code book that no building official or design professional should be without. In addition to being the predecessor of the 2000 *International Building Code*™, the UBC reflects the latest technological advances in building design. New or revised provisions in the 1997 UBC cover topics such as means of egress, concrete, seismic isolation, accessibility, structural forces, roofing and much more.

Volume One contains administrative, fire- and life-safety, and field-inspection provisions, including all nonstructural provisions and those structural provisions necessary for field inspections.

Volume Two contains provisions for structural engineering design, including those design standards formerly published as UBC standards.

Volume Three contains the remaining material, testing and installation standards.

The 1997 UBC is also available on CD-ROM for Windows. Fast, accurate and comprehensive, this convenient format will help you to:

◆ Search for any section that contains a certain provision.

◆ Cut and paste code provisions into correspondence, reports, etc.

◆ Obtain printouts of sections of the code.

◆ Obtain a list of pages on which a provision appears.

	Item No.	ICBO Members	Nonmembers
UBC Volumes 1, 2 and 3 soft cover	099S97	$139.00	$173.75
loose leaf	099L97	159.85	199.80
UBC on CD-ROM (contains Volumes 1, 2, and 3)*	001C97	139.00	173.75
UBC soft cover and UBC on CD-ROM	099CSC	214.00	267.50
UBC loose leaf and UBC on CD-ROM	099CLL	234.85	293.55

*Does not include NFPA standards.
Please call ICBO for individual book prices or quantity discounts.
Prices subject to change.

To order, please call ICBO toll-free at

(800) 284-4406

International Conference of Building Officials

www.icbo.org

Publications • Seminars • Certification • Software • Evaluation Service • Videos • Membership

SOFTWARE AND INFORMATION LICENSE

The software and information on this diskette (collectively referred to as the "Product") are the property of The McGraw-Hill Companies, Inc. ("McGraw-Hill") and are protected by both United States copyright law and international copyright treaty provision. You must treat this Product just like a book, except that you may copy it into a computer to be used and you may make archival copies of the Products for the sole purpose of backing up our software and protecting your investment from loss.

By saying "just like a book," McGraw-Hill means, for example, that the Product may be used by any number of people and may be freely moved from one computer location to another, so long as there is no possibility of the Product (or any part of the Product) being used at one location or on one computer while it is being used at another. Just as a book cannot be read by two different people in two different places at the same time, neither can the Product be used by two different people in two different places at the same time (unless, of course, McGraw-Hill's rights are being violated).

McGraw-Hill reserves the right to alter or modify the contents of the Product at any time.

This agreement is effective until terminated. The Agreement will terminate automatically without notice if you fail to comply with any provisions of this Agreement. In the event of termination by reason of your breach, you will destroy or erase all copies of the Product installed on any computer system or made for backup purposes and shall expunge the Product from your data storage facilities.

LIMITED WARRANTY

McGraw-Hill warrants the physical diskette(s) enclosed herein to be free of defects in materials and workmanship for a period of sixty days from the purchase date. If McGraw-Hill receives written notification within the warranty period of defects in materials or workmanship, and such notification is determined by McGraw-Hill to be correct, McGraw-Hill will replace the defective diskette(s). Send request to:

Customer Service
McGraw-Hill
Gahanna Industrial Park
860 Taylor Station Road
Blacklick, OH 43004-9615

The entire and exclusive liability and remedy for breach of this Limited Warranty shall be limited to replacement of defective diskette(s) and shall not include or extend to any claim for or right to cover any other damages, including but not limited to, loss of profit, data, or use of the software, or special, incidental, or consequential damages or other similar claims, even if McGraw-Hill has been specifically advised as to the possibility of such damages. In no event will McGraw-Hill's liability for any damages to you or any other person ever exceed the lower of suggested list price or actual price paid for the license to use the Product, regardless of any form of the claim.

THE McGRAW-HILL COMPANIES, INC. SPECIFICALLY DISCLAIMS ALL OTHER WARRANTIES, EXPRESS OR IMPLIED, INCLUDING BUT NOT LIMITED TO, ANY IMPLIED WARRANTY OF MER-CHANTABILITY OR FITNESS FOR A PARTICULAR PURPOSE. Specifically, McGraw-Hill makes no representation or warranty that the Product is fit for any particular purpose and any implied warranty of merchantability is limited to the sixty day duration of the Limited Warranty covering the physical diskette(s) only (and not the software or in-formation) and is otherwise expressly and specifically disclaimed.

This Limited Warranty gives you specific legal rights; you may have others which may vary from state to state. Some states do not allow the exclusion of incidental or consequential damages, or the limitation on how long an implied warranty lasts, so some of the above may not apply to you.

This Agreement constitutes the entire agreement between the parties relating to use of the Product. The terms of any purchase order shall have no effect on the terms of this Agreement. Failure of McGraw-Hill to insist at any time on strict compliance with this Agreement shall not constitute a waiver of any rights under this Agreement. This Agreement shall be construed and governed in accordance with the laws of New York. If any provision of this Agreement is held to be contrary to law, that provision will be enforced to the maximum extent permissible and the remaining provisions will remain in force and effect.